West Germany and Namibia's Path to Independence, 1969–1990

THORSTEN KERN

West Germany and Namibia's Path to Independence, 1969–1990
Foreign Policy and Rivalry with East Germany

Basel Namibia Studies Series 21

Basler Afrika Bibliographien 2020

©2020 The authors
©2020 Basler Afrika Bibliographien

Basler Afrika Bibliographien
Namibia Resource Centre & Southern Africa Library
Klosterberg 23
PO Box
4001 Basel
Switzerland
www.baslerafrika.ch

The Basler Afrika Bibliographien is part of the Carl Schlettwein Foundation

All rights reserved.

2nd, revised edition.

Cover image: Federal Foreign Minister Hans-Dietrich Genscher and the President of the South-West Africa People's Organisation (SWAPO), Sam Nujoma, during talks on the future of Namibia, the former German colony of German South-West Africa, 23. Photo taken by Peter Popp in Bonn on 23 October 1980. © Keystone

ISBN 978-3-906927-23-7
ISSN 2234-9561

Basel Namibia Studies Series

In 1997, *P. Schlettwein Publishing* (PSP) launched the *Basel Namibia Studies Series*. Its primary aim was to lend support to a new generation of research, scholars and readers emerging with the independence of Namibia in 1990.

Initially, the book series published crucially important doctoral theses on Namibian history. It soon expanded to include more recent political, anthropological, media and cultural history studies by Namibian scholars.

P. Schlettwein Publishing, as an independent publishing house, maintained the series in collaboration with the *Basler Afrika Bibliographien* (BAB), Namibia Resource Centre and Southern Africa Library in Switzerland. All share a commitment to encourage research on Africa in general and southern Africa in particular. Through the incorporation of PSP into the *Carl Schlettwein Stiftung*, the series, by then a consolidated platform for Namibian Studies and beyond, was integrated into the publishing activities of the BAB.

Academic publishing, whether from or about Namibia, remains limited. The *Basel Namibia Studies Series* continues to provide a forum for exciting scholarly work in the human and social sciences.

The editors welcome contributions. For further information, or submission of manuscripts, please contact the *Basler Afrika Bibliographien* at www.baslerafrika.ch.

Für meine Eltern

Contents

Foreword *by Chris Saunders*	ix
Preface	xiii
Introduction	1
1 The origins of rivalry over Namibia	**11**
East Germany's solidarity with African liberation movements	11
Ostpolitik: The two German states' rivalry in Namibia	26
Instruments of Foreign Policy	31
2 Political Parties and SWAPO	**38**
West Germany	38
Social Democratic Party of Germany (SPD)	38
Free Democratic Party (FDP)	48
Christian Democratic Union (CDU) and Christian Social Union (CSU)	56
The Green Party	62
East Germany	66
The Socialist Unity Party of Germany (SED)	66
3 SWAPO: the *Bundestag* and the Foreign Office	**81**
The *Bundestag*	81
The Kohl government in the *Bundestag* in the early 1980s	99
The Foreign Office	102
4 The decision-making process regarding Namibia	**108**
The Germans of Namibia	130
5 East and West German rivalry: the mid-to-late 1970s	**137**
The controversy over West Germany's consulate in Windhoek	137
West Germany's cultural programme with South Africa and Namibia	143
West Germany's relations with South Africa in the late 1970s	149
East and West Germany's Intensification of Relations with SWAPO in the late 1970s	165
6 East and West German rivalry: the early to mid-1980s	**174**
The mid-1980s: the Kohl government and the Namibia question	187

7 The mid-to-late 1980s	**207**
Non-governmental organisations and West Germany's policy towards Namibia	207
The late 1980s: The two Germanys and Namibia	222
The two German states' involvement in the UNTAG mission in Namibia between 1989 and 1990	237
8 Conclusion	**246**
List of Abbreviations	**252**
Bibliography	**254**
Index	**269**

Foreword

Namibia was colonized and occupied in the late 19th century by the German empire, which in the early 20th century carried out a policy of genocide there against the Herero and Nama people. After German rule of Namibia came to an end in 1915, a German-speaking white community with considerable economic and strategic influence remained in the territory. Not surprisingly, when after the Second World War there existed two Germanys, on different sides of the Cold War, both played influential roles in the long struggle to achieve Namibia's independence. These roles were very different. The Federal Republic of Germany (FRG) was part of the West, while its counterpart in the East was a member of the Warsaw Pact and belonged to the Soviet bloc of countries. It is the Cold War rivalry between the two Germanys in relation to Namibia that Thorsten Kern chose as the topic for his doctorate at the University of Cape Town. He has now revised his thesis for this publication. Drawing on extensive and careful research, he tells the story, in rich detail, of rivalry between the two Germanys in relation to Namibia in the 1970s and 1980s, which he sets in both a European and Southern African context, weaving political developments in West Germany into changing policy on such matters as the closure of the West German consulate in Windhoek and cultural ties with the German community in South West Africa/Namibia. Kern writes with admirable clarity on what is a highly complex topic, involving, on the one hand, relations between the two Germanys that changed over time, and, on the other, relations between each Germany and those involved with the Namibian issue, ranging from South African lobby groups to the main Namibian liberation movement, the South West Africa People's Organisation (SWAPO).

Though, as Kern fully acknowledges, previous studies have been undertaken on aspects of this story, what sets his book apart and gives it its main importance, is that it is based on a wealth of archival material not previously used by scholars. This is primarily because a thirty-year rule (*Sperrfristen*) had blocked access to the main German archives before Kern undertook his research. He trawled through various German archives, including the Political Archive of the West German Foreign Office (PAAA), the Foundation for the Archives of the Parties and Mass Organizations of the GDR (SAPMO) at the *Bundesarchiv*, and the GDR Ministry of State Security Archive (BStU) in Berlin, as well as the archives of West German political parties. He used the National Archives of Namibia in Windhoek and conducted interviews with key individuals. Especially useful for those who do not easily read German, he draws upon a wide range of relevant secondary sources, many of which are in German.

His main focus is on FRG policy on the Namibian issue in the 1970s and 1980s. In West Germany the different political parties that formed coalition governments in these decades –the Social Democrats (SPD) and the Liberals (FDP) under Willy Brandt and Helmut Schmidt; the Christian Democratic Union (CDU) and the FDP under Helmut Kohl – disagreed on what strategies West Germany should pursue on the question of Namibia. Some had conservative sympathies for the apartheid state that occupied Namibia, while others wanted no dealings with it. Economic considerations, however, meant that the FRG was reluctant to challenge South Africa over Namibia. Kern shows how, as a non-permanent Western member of the United Nations (UN) Security Council, the FRG played an active part in the Western Contact Group (WCG), which was established to get both South Africa and SWAPO to agree to a plan for a transition to Namibian independence. At the same time, successive FRG's coalition governments sought to protect the interests of the Germans in the former colony and at different stages of the negotiations the 'South Westers' there were able to influence FRG policy. Kern also analyses in detail the power struggles in the West German bureaucracy, between say the West German Ministry for Economic Cooperation and Development (BMZ) and the Foreign Office. The BMZ used its financial muscle to support social and cultural initiatives in Namibia in ways that sought to push SWAPO into the background. In the mid-1980s its financial support for the interim government in Namibia was seen by SWAPO as tacit collaboration with the apartheid regime.

Hans-Dietrich Genscher, who passed away just before Kern could interview him, remained the FRG's foreign minister from 1974 to 1992, providing important continuity and enabling the FRG to gain a measure of trust from SWAPO and the Southern African frontline states. Genscher believed in engaging SWAPO, fearing that the policies of Western governments were driving African liberation movements into the arms of the communist East. He realised that SWAPO was an essentially nationalist organisation, aiming at achieving independence and not committed to Marxism. The hardliners in the CDU and the Christian Social Union (CSU), on the other hand, saw SWAPO as a communist organisation involved in terrorist activities and one that claimed, falsely, to be the sole representative of the Namibian people. They did not want to see SWAPO come to power in Namibia and, they anticipated, serve GDR's interests in southern Africa.

With great sophistication, Kern traces how relations between the two Germanys changed over time. Whereas under both Brandt, architect of *Ostpolitik,* and the succeeding Schmidt government there was a focus on rapprochement with the GDR, the CDU/CSU hardliners sought to be more confrontational. In the 1980s the SPD strategy was aided by the decline of Soviet military power and the way a number of Southern African states turned towards the West. As Kern shows, SWAPO had, not surprisingly, much closer relations with the GDR than with the FRG, which lacked the anti-imperialist convictions that the GDR proclaimed as its official policy. He suggests that GDR support for SWAPO was in part a domestic policy tool, a way to shame the FRG for its 'imperialist' collaboration in the oppression of the Namibian people. Especially from the late 1970s on, the GDR tried to pursue initiatives in southern Africa that were separate from those of the Soviet Union. By the early 1980s GDR strategic thinking focused less on purely ideological motivations and more on pragmatic ways to achieve Namibian independence. Worried about West Germany's influence with SWAPO, the GDR hoped to gain privileged access to Namibia's natural resources when SWAPO came to power. At the same time, the one-party East German state did not have to deal with the internal feuds that characterised West German democracy. Whereas the FRG was influenced by South African lobby groups and ties to the German community in Namibia, the SED government in the GDR could maintain a principled policy uninfluenced by disagreements between rival factions. While SWAPO gratefully recognized the aid that the GDR gave, SWAPO's goal remained self-determination under a SWAPO-led government, and most of its members and leaders never held strong anti-imperialist ideological convictions.

Kern recognises that the rivalry between West and East Germany, on which he focuses, was only one motive driving policy towards Namibia, and that at times other interests were also important, such as relations with others in the West. He shies away, however, from weighing the importance of the two Germanys in the achievement of Namibian independence. While the GDR supplied SWAPO with large quantities of military equipment and training, the FRG played a key role as a member of the WCG, and Kern is interesting on attempts that were made to revive the WCG after its effective dissolution in 1983. He leaves others to provide a full study of GDR solidarity with SWAPO, and to set more fully the two Germanys' policies to Namibia in the context of their general Southern African policies.[1] With the exception of some limited church related activities, there was no civil society solidarity movement in the GDR, whereas in the FRG such a movement, which included church and trade union groups, had a role to play, at times even managing to influence political discourse. Kern uses critical literature published by the Anti-Apartheid Movement, the Information Centre for Southern Africa and others, but does not assess the significance of the lobbying by such groups. He leaves others to say more about, say, the connections between

---

[1] See, e.g., Chris Saunders, 'Swapo's Eastern Connections' in Lena Dallywater et al. ,*Southern African Liberation Movements and the Global Cold War `East': Transnational Activism 1960–1990*(Berlin: De Gruyter, 2019). Kern does not show, say, how in the GDR popular fiction played a relatively strong role in mobilizing support for the anti-imperialist struggle, along with such academic studies as Horst Drechsler's seminal study of the German war against the Herero and Nama, published in English as *Let Us Die Fighting* (London: Zed Press, 1981).

pro-South African elements in the FRG and those in Namibia, such as the Interessengemeinschaft (IG) Deutschsprachiger Südwester. It is to be hoped that the publication of *West Germany and Namibia's Path to Independence, 1969–1990* will stimulate further research on such topics.

Namibia's first democratic election was held as the Berlin Wall fell. Some of the journalists in Windhoek covering Namibia's move to independence were quick to return to Germany when news of the fall of the Wall broke in November 1989.[2] Though the GDR appointed an ambassador to independent Namibia, the embassy was closed within weeks, and the new Namibian government had instead to establish bilateral relations with a unified German state. Relations with the former GDR became only a topic for nostalgic reminiscence. While the UN mission to Namibia in 1989 included members from both Germanys and successfully monitored the country's first democratic election, the GDR's collapse and disappearance meant that the new Namibia now had to deal with a re-united Germany, which has, since 1990, given Namibia more development aid than any other country. Namibia-German relations since Namibia's independence, discussed elsewhere,[3] cannot be understood without knowing what happened during the last two crucial decades of the Cold War, in which Namibia moved towards independence. We are fortunate indeed now to have Kern's scholarly study, which is likely to remain the definitive account of the relations between a divided Germany and Namibia during those decades.

Chris Saunders

---

[2] David Lush, *Last Steps to Uhuru: An Eye-witness Account of Namibia's Transition to Independence* (Windhoek: New Namibia Books, 1993).

[3] See Peter H. Katajavivi, 'Namibia's Bilateral Relations with Germany: A Crucial Relationship', in Anton Bosl et al, *Namibia's Foreign Relations. Historic Contexts, Current Dimensions, and Perspectives for the 21st Century* (Windhoek: Macmillan Education, 2014); Reinhart Kössler, *Namibia and Germany: Negotiating the past* (Windhoek, Namibia: University of Namibia Press, 2015; Henning Melber, *Understanding Namibia* (Auckland Park: Jacana Media, 2014).

Preface

This book is a slightly revised and updated version of my Ph.D. thesis, submitted to the University of Cape Town, South Africa, in 2016. It seeks to establish the grounds for a better comprehension of, and hopefully new insights into, West Germany's relationship with Namibia during the Cold War. Hence, this is by no means an exhaustive study of Namibia's path to independence, but an in-depth examination of West Germany's relationship with Namibia during the liberation struggle, from the perspective of Cold War rivalry. Yet, despite its strong focus on Cold War dynamics, the book provides wide-ranging insights into Namibia's difficult path to national independence. Still, I am deeply conscious of all that is left out. The book is based on many years of extensive and far-reaching research; yet more often than not the outcomes of my research generated additional questions that require further in-depth study and research. Clearly, our knowledge of Namibia's long struggle for the realization of the right of national self-determination is still incomplete. It is thus my hope that this book will inspire further thought and research, ultimately generating further publications from new angles.

It is only appropriate to acknowledge here that Professor Chris Saunders' advice was instrumental in my decision to approach West Germany's role in Namibia's path to independence from the perspective of East and West German rivalry.

A very large number of people have provided invaluable support and assistance to my dissertation and thus ultimately also to this book. I would like to express my deepest gratitude to everyone who has contributed in one way or another to the completion of this project. The support of friends was invaluable throughout. I also wish to express special heartfelt thanks to my sister Tatjana. You have always been outstandingly supportive and such a special friend. Letizia and Giulia, you guys mean the world to me.

Special thanks go to Pauline and Manfred Mittelbach, and Nicole and Nawaf Bayoumi, without whom this book would have never seen the light of day. I also need to express a special word of thanks to Simon Evans, Vanessa Finaughty, David Weidong Kong and Dr. Michael Schmidt.

I am also very grateful to Hein Möllers, the general manager of ISSA, for many interesting discussions and most valuable support. Special thanks go also to Professor Ulrich van der Heyden at the Humboldt University for giving me valuable advice during the early stages of this project. In the Stasi-Archive, my sincere gratitude goes to Kerstin Schädler, who has been outstandingly supportive and repeatedly unearthed valuable documents for this project. I would also like to thank the entire team of the newspaper archive of the former GDR, the *Zeitgeschichtliches Archiv* in Berlin. In the archive of the Foreign Office, I am sincerely grateful to Ulrich Geyer for motivating me to apply for the removal of the thirty-year blocking period. Birgit Kmezik and Thomas Hermeling have also been of great help. In the National Archives of Namibia, my thanks go to Werner Hillebrecht, the former head of the archive, who was extremely helpful in unravelling relevant files and a source of interesting conversations.

I would also like to thank the many contemporary witnesses I have interviewed and corresponded with. Special thanks go to Dr. Hans-Georg Schleicher, the former GDR Ambassador to Zimbabwe, who was very welcoming and generous with his time. I would also like to thank Uwe Zeise, who followed Dr. Schleicher as GDR Ambassador to Zimbabwe. Dr. Klaus Freiherr von der Ropp, a contemporary observer, has also been outstandingly helpful. I am also very grateful to Dr. Chester Crocker, the Assistant Secretary of State for African Affairs in the Reagan administration, for his help. My thanks also go to Professor Hans-Joachim Vergau, the former head of the southern Africa desk in the Foreign office and close aide to Genscher. Special thanks also to Dieter Petzsch, the former South African Permanent Representative at the UN in Geneva and to the former 'GDR Kids of Namibia': Winnie Ya-Otto and Selma Kamati.

My deepest gratitude goes to the former German Foreign Minister, the late Hans-Dietrich Genscher, for inviting me to meet him when he had recovered from being unwell. Sadly, Bundesminister Genscher did not recover from what turned out to be his final illness.

I would also like to use this opportunity to express my gratitude to former lecturers who inspired me: Dr Katharine Lerman and Paul McGilchrist at London Metropolitan University, and Professor Nigel Penn at the University of Cape Town.

With great respect for their outstanding work, I would also like to thank the entire team at the inter-library loan section at the University of Cape Town.

Most of all, however, I want to express my deepest gratitude to my supervisors, Associate Professor Mohamed Adhikari and Professor Chris Saunders. I could not have completed this project without their unwavering confidence, their tremendous support and enthusiasm for this assignment, and, ultimately, their knowledge and insights. I could not have asked for better supervisors. *Thank you.* A special note of thanks also goes to Sarah Schwarz, Dr. Dag Henrichsen and Petra Kerckhoff at the Basler Afrika Bibliographien.

Introduction

The dynamics of inter-German competition can only be understood within the framework of the division of Germany after the Second World War into two separate, ideologically opposed states. After defeating Nazi-Germany, the allied forces divided Germany into spheres of influence. The Soviet Union's war efforts led to the occupation of the eastern part of Germany, including the eastern part of Berlin, while the western part, including the western part of Berlin, was occupied by the United States (US), France and Great Britain. Hence, the eastern part of Germany fell under the influence of communism and became known as the German Democratic Republic (GDR), with East Berlin its capital. West Germany moved its capital to Bonn after the division of Berlin between the East and the West. Consequently, Germany's division led to the establishment of two German states that existed as separate, independent political and ideological entities.

There has been no in-depth study of East and West German rivalry in southern Africa during the Cold War. The only comparative study on their rivalry on the African continent approaches the issue from a general perspective. Ulf Engel, a leading German scholar on West German policy towards Africa, and Hans-Georg Schleicher, a former GDR diplomat and expert on GDR relations with Africa, have produced the most comprehensive and authoritative work to appear on the two German states' relationship with Africa so far.[1] Their work includes important case studies on Tanzania, Ghana and Namibia.[2] The aim of this book is therefore to explore West Germany's rivalry with the GDR in Namibia in greater depth. To achieve this objective, this book concentrates on areas that have received only marginal attention or none at all. For further insights into the GDR's solidarity with liberation movements and its policies towards Africa, this study can fall back on a wide range of secondary sources.

The numerous publications of Hans-Georg Schleicher and Ilona Schleicher are particularly valuable and far-reaching, not least because their work is largely based on archival research.[3] Equally important are the publications of Ulrich van der Heyden, an expert on GDR

---

[1] U. Engel und H.-G. Schleicher, *Die beiden deutschen Staaten in Afrika, Zwischen Konkurrenzkampf und Koexistenz 1949–1990*, Hamburg, Institut für Afrika-Kunde, 1998.

[2] Winrich Kühne and Bernard von Plate published a short analysis: W. Kühne and B. von Plate, 'The two Germanys in Africa', *Africa Report*, July/August, Vol. 25, No. 4, New York, 1980, 11–15.

[3] H.-G. Schleicher, 'Interessenlage der Afrikapolitik der DDR', in S. Bock, I. Muth and H. Schweisau (eds.), *DDR – Außenpolitik im Rückspiegel, Diplomaten im Gespräch*, Münster, LIT, 2004; H. Bley und H.-G. Schleicher, 'Deutsch-Deutsch-Namibische Beziehungen 1960–1990', in L. Förster, D. Henrichsen and M. Bollig (eds.), *Namibia-Deutschland. Eine geteilte Geschichte. Widerstand-Ge-*

policy towards Africa. Particularly important, Van der Heyden's research has, among other things, illuminated the economic side of the GDR's involvement in southern Africa.[4] With respect to East German military cooperation with the Third World, Klaus Storkmann has published, based on his doctoral thesis, an exceptionally well-researched and far-reaching study.[5]

Moreover, numerous studies that were conducted before the collapse of the Soviet Union lacked access to primary source materials.[6] This was an unavoidable problem for scholars dealing with the GDR's involvement in Africa during the Cold War, often leading to speculation rather than fact-based conclusions.[7] Nonetheless, one earlier study needs to be mentioned here, although it also suffers from a lack of access to relevant archives: Gareth M. Winrow's well-rounded and important overview of the GDR's involvement in Africa.[8]

Furthermore, for scholars in the GDR, any objective analysis of the GDR's involvement in Africa was out of the question, for East Berlin demanded that authors, particularly of

---

walt-Erinnerung, Köln, Ethnologica, 2004; See also H.-G., Schleicher, 'GDR Solidarity: The German Democratic Republic and the South African Liberation Struggle', in *The Road to Democracy in South Africa: International Solidarity*, Volume 3, Pretoria, Education Trust; H.-G. Schleicher and I. Schleicher, *Die DDR im südlichen Afrika: Solidarität und Kalter Krieg*, Hamburg, Institut für Afrika-Kunde, 1997; H.-G. Schleicher and I. Schleicher, *Special Flights: The GDR and liberation movements in southern Africa*, Harare, Southern Africa specialised Studies Series, 1998; I. Schleicher, *DDR-Solidarität im südlichen Afrika. Auseinandersetzung mit einem ambivalenten Erbe*, Berlin, Solidaritätsdienst-international e.V., 1999.

[4] U. van der Heyden, *GDR International Development Policy Involvement, Doctrine and Strategies between Illusions and Reality 1960–1990. The example (South) Africa*, Berlin, LIT, 2013; U. van der Heyden, *Zwischen Solidarität und Wirtschaftsinteressen: Die 'geheimen' Beziehungen der DDR zum südafrikanischen Apartheidregime*, Münster, LIT, 2005; U. van der Heyden, I. Schleicher and H.-G. Schleicher (eds.), *Engagiert für Afrika, die DDR und Afrika II*, Münster, LIT, 1994; U. van der Heyden, I. Schleicher and H.-G. Schleicher (eds.), *Die DDR und Afrika: Zwischen Klassenkampf und neuem Denken*, Münster, LIT, 1993.

[5] K. Storkmann, *Geheime Solidarität, Militärbeziehungen und Militärhilfen der DDR in die "Dritte Welt"*, Berlin, Christoph Links Verlag GmbH, 2012. For an analysis on the GDR's monitoring role in Namibia's first free elections in 1989/90, see D. Lange, *Auf deutsch-deutscher UN-Patrouille. Die polizeiliche Beobachtereinheit der DDR in Namibia (1989/90)*, Schkeuditz, Schkeuditzer Buchverlag, 2011. Lange's study is based on his Magister thesis and provides a well-researched account of the GDR's first and only involvement in an international peace-keeping mission.

[6] Although early publications are valuable in terms of gaining insight into contemporary perceptions of the GDR's policies towards Africa, and sometimes even convince through a wide array of primary sources, early studies need to be treated with some scepticism. With this in mind, one earlier publication needs to be mentioned here, not least because it is the only work that provides an overview of the East-West conflict in Namibia: H. Löwis von Menar, *Namibia im Ost-West-Konflikt*, Köln, Verlag Wissenschaft und Politik, 1983.

[7] See also U. van der Heyden, 'GDR Development Policy with special reference to Africa, c. 1960–1990', PhD Thesis, Rhodes University, 2012, 12–13.

[8] G. M. Winrow, *The Foreign Policy of the GDR in Africa*, Cambridge, Cambridge University Press, 1990.

academic publications, conformed with the ideological orientation and political system of the GDR.⁹ GDR scholars had to follow the party line, which, in the case of Africa, was deeply embedded in the ideology of international solidarity among the working classes against capitalism, imperialism and neo-colonialism. Thus, state censorship and surveillance strongly affected these scholars' ability to examine the GDR's involvement in Africa objectively.

With regard to West Germany's policy towards Africa, the publications of Ulf Engel are particularly insightful and provide valuable analyses on West Germany's intentions, motives and expectations in Africa.¹⁰ Thus far, however, only one study exists which examines West Germany's relationship with Namibia during the liberation struggle. Gabriele Brenke's groundbreaking study is based on her doctoral dissertation and thus largely constructed around original research. Although an excellent and painstakingly researched study, Brenke considers only marginally West Germany's relationship with Namibia from the perspective of Cold War rivalry and thus also offers little insight into the two German states' competition over influence in Namibia.¹¹ Consequently, there is no need to repeat or correct Brenke's outstanding work unless appropriate and in relation to this study. Rather, this book seeks to provide a different angle on West Germany's relationship with Namibia at the height of the national liberation struggle.

With regard to West Germany's relationship with South Africa, a number of studies have been particularly valuable to this research project. Here, three different publications cover the most crucial periods in the relationship between West Germany and South Africa.¹² In this respect, Reinhard Rode examines West Germany's policy towards South Africa between 1968 and 1972,¹³ while Werner Stier offers valuable insight into West German perception on developments in southern Africa between 1960 and 1979,¹⁴ and Claudius Wenzel

---

9   See also Van der Heyden, 'GDR Development', 15–16.
10 U. Engel, *Die Afrikapolitik der Bundesrepublik Deutschland 1949–1999: Rollen und Identitäten*, Hamburg, LIT, 2000; U. Engel and R. Kappel (eds.), *Germany's Africa Policy Revisited: Interests, Images and Incrementalism*, Münster, LIT, 2002.
11 G. Brenke, *Die Bundesrepublik Deutschland und der Namibia-Konflikt*, München, R. Oldenbourg Verlag, 1989.
12 A fourth publication should be mentioned here as well. The work of Günther Verheugen, who left Genscher's Free Democratic Party (FDP) and joined the Social Democratic Party of Germany (SPD) after Genscher made a coalition pact with Kohl's Christian Democratic Party (CDU) in 1982. The book offers a valuable overview, including some first-hand insights, into West Germany's wider interests in South Africa. Importantly, however, Verheugen's work needs to be treated critically, for he does not provide any references: G. Verheugen, *Apartheid: Südafrika und die deutschen Interessen am Kap*, Köln, Verlag Kiepenheuer und Witsch, 1986. For a more general study of West Germany's Foreign policy towards Africa, see B. M. Eyinla, *The Foreign Policy of West Germany towards Africa*, Ibadan, Ibadan University Press, 1996.
13 R. Rode, *Die Südafrikapolitik der Bundesrepublik Deutschland 1968–1972*, München, Chr. Kaiser Verlag, 1975.
14 W. Stiers, *Perzeptionen der Entwicklung im südlichen Afrika in der Bundesrepublik Deutschland:*

focuses on the period between 1982 and 1992.[15] Importantly, however, none of these studies had access to the East and West German files held in the Foreign Office, for the primary source materials in the archive of the Foreign Office fall under the protection of a 30-year *Sperrfrist*, or blocking period. A further study, consisting of a collection of analyses edited by Helmut Bley and Rainer Tetzlaff, needs to be considered here as well. This book provides valuable analyses of Bonn's policy towards Africa and is one of the most authoritative studies on Bonn's relationship with southern Africa.[16]

Additionally, Hans-Joachim Vergau, the former deputy permanent representative of Germany to the United Nations (UN), has published an outstandingly important account of the efforts of the Western Contact Group (WCG), the five Western members of the Security Council, namely, Canada, France, West Germany, the United Kingdom and the US. The book provides an in-depth account of the WCG's endeavour to resolve the deadlock between Pretoria and SWAPO.[17] The value of the book lies also in Vergau's personal involvement in the WCG and therefore his ability to give first-hand insight into Genscher's efforts to achieve a solution to the Namibia problem.

Apart from the main studies mentioned above, a number of smaller studies, largely based on postgraduate degrees, have been published over the last fifteen years. This book will refer to these studies whenever appropriate. Also, it is important to note that a number of important studies have not been listed here because of space limitations and partial relevance. However, appropriate references to these studies can be found throughout the book. Finally, the bibliography at the end of this book will provide evidence of the extensive scholarly interest in southern African conflicts during the Cold War.

It is apparent, then, that although the two German states' relations with Namibia and South Africa have been analysed to some extent, little groundwork has been done on West Germany's policy towards Namibia against the backdrop of inter-German rivalry. The aim of this book is to fill this gap. Furthermore, the two German states' rivalry in Africa has received little scholarly attention in the form of in-depth comparative analysis. Hence, this book is the first to provide far-reaching insight into East and West Germany's competition for influence in Namibia, from the early contacts between the two German states and SWAPO until the unification of East and West Germany and Namibia's independence.

1960–1979, Frankfurt/M., Peter Lang GmbH, 1983.

[15] C. Wenzel, *Südafrika-Politik der Bundesrepublik Deutschland 1982–1992: Politik gegen Apartheid?*, Wiesbaden, Deutscher Universitäts-Verlag GmbH, 1994.

[16] H. Bley and R. Tetzlaff (eds.), *Afrika und Bonn. Versäumnisse und Zwänge deutscher Afrika-Politik*, Hamburg, Rowohlt, 1978.

[17] H. J., Vergau, *Negotiating the Freedom of Namibia, The diplomatic achievement of the Western Contact Group*, Basel, Basler Afrika Bibliographien, 2010.

Given that the studies mentioned above are based on extensive archival research, it was reasonable to expect that the relevant archives would provide a great volume of primary sources material. However, there is one major obstacle that all of the above mentioned studies encountered: the thirty-year archival blocking period.

Although most of the relevant German archives grant researchers fairly unrestricted access, the files of the Political Archive of the Office for Foreign Affairs (PAAA) in Berlin are subject to the thirty-year rule.[18] Importantly, the PAAA contains both the files of the GDR's Ministry of Foreign Affairs (MfAA) and the files relating to West German foreign policy. Thus, the studies above had, depending on the year of publication, either extremely limited or no access to the PAAA. In most cases, scholars fill such gaps in their research largely by studying contemporary newspapers, which, however, do not necessarily offer deep or revealing insights. This research project was in the fortunate position of having nearly unrestricted access to all the relevant files held at the PAAA. Thus, this study had access to both the relevant East and West German files covering the period between 1969 and 1990. With the consideration that the scholars mentioned above had to conduct their research around the blocking period, future researchers may observe with interest that the Foreign Office lifted the thirty-year rule for this study. Thus, future researchers should feel encouraged to apply for the removal of the blocking period, although the outcome remains still uncertain.

The Federal Commissioner for the Stasi Records (BStU) holds the files of the former Ministry of States Security (MfS), the *Stasi*. One of the main tasks of the *Stasi* was foreign espionage, which included, among other things, monitoring West Germany's involvement in Namibia. Thus, the *Stasi's* analyses of West Germany's changing policies towards Namibia have been particularly valuable. Although the files of the BStU are not subject to the 30-year rule, the archive regulates which files are available for scholarly research. Files containing potentially sensitive material that may violate the privacy of the individual or compromise state security are filtered out by archivists, as outlined in the Stasi Records Act (December 1991).[19] Thus, for example, files containing information about the military training of SWAPO cadres in the GDR are not accessible for research.[20]

---

[18] The Foreign Office publishes each year new archival documents that fall within the 30-year rule: 'Akten zur Auswärtigen Politik der Bundesrepublik Deutschland (AAPD)' in the archive of the Foreign Office in Berlin.

[19] For further information on the Stasi Records Act, see E. S., Danielson, 'Privacy Rights and the Rights of Political Victims: Implications of the German Experience', *The American Archivist*, Vol. 67, 2004. Accessed November 2015, available from: www.americanarchivist.org/doi/abs/10.17723/aarc.67.2.1w06730777226771. The Stasi Records Act can be accessed in English at the BStU homepage under: www.bstu.bund.de/EN/Agency/LegalBasis/StasiRecordsAct/_node.html

[20] See also Van der Heyden, 'GDR Development', 23.

It is important to note, however, that documents regarding the GDR's military cooperation with liberation movements and independent African states are held at the military archives of the Federal Republic in Freiburg and Potsdam. However, the GDR's solidarity with the African liberation struggle, including military support, has been examined extensively in a number of studies, as outlined in the above examples. Thus, for the sake of avoiding repetition, this book will not examine the full extent of the GDR's solidarity with SWAPO. The same also applies to West Germany's relationship with Namibia. However, the book will briefly touch upon most issues and include references to previous studies. Consequently, a full picture will emerge of both German states' role in the Namibian liberation struggle.

A more comprehensive understanding of the GDR's relationship with liberation movements also requires research visits to the German Federal Archive, the *Bundesarchiv* Berlin-Lichterfelde (BArch). In its GDR section (Abteilung GDR), this archive holds files on all central civilian administrative bodies of the GDR, providing extensive insight into the system established by the GDR's leading political organ, the Socialist Unity Party (SED). In regard to the GDR's solidarity with African liberation movements, the Foundation for the Archives of the Parties and Mass Organizations of the GDR (SAPMO) at the *Bundesarchiv* is of particularly interest. SAPMO holds all records of the SED and its organizational structure. Thus the SED collection in SAPMO is particularly valuable, considering that the SED was, among other things, also responsible for cultivating the GDR's relationship with liberation movements and independent African countries.

It is important to note, however, that access to the archives of West German political parties and their foundations is limited. Files with material that were once published are available for scholarly research. This includes political statements, policy reports, minutes of political party meetings and debates held in the German parliament, the *Bundestag*. However, confidential and internal documents are not accessible. Thus, party secrecy makes it impossible to gain insight into internal party debates and decision making processes. Nonetheless, the records available for scholarly research provide valuable information. With regard to party positions, *Bundestag* debates provided the most extensive overview.[21]

In the course of researching this book, the following party archives have been visited: the archive of the Christian Democratic Party (CDU), *Archiv für Christlich-Demokratische Politik* (ACDP), at the Konrad Adenauer Foundation in St. Augustin; the archive of the Free Democratic Party (FDP), *Archiv des Deutschen Liberalismus* (ADL), at the Friedrich Naumann Foundation (FNS) in Gummersbach; and the archive of the Green Party, *Archiv Grünes*

---

[21] *Bundestag* debates are available online at www.bundestag.de/documente/

Gedächtnis (AGG), at the Heinrich Böll Foundation in Berlin. The records held in the archive of the Green Party were particularly valuable, for the Green Party's position on the Namibian liberation struggles has received little scholarly attention so far. This is partly because the Green party is relatively young and thus first entered the Bundestag in 1983. Furthermore, although certain research restrictions, as mentioned above, also apply to the archive of the Green Party, in stark contrast to other party archives, it does not enforce the 30-year rule.[22]

Furthermore, the archive of the *Informationsstelle Südliches Afrika* (ISSA) in Bonn holds a large collection of West German newspaper articles, party statements and press releases, which are placed in regional chronological context. The archive also holds a wide array of grey literature and journals. The *Zeitgeschichtliches Archiv* (ZGA) in Berlin has been beneficial with regard to gaining insight into the GDR press coverage of the Namibian independence struggle.

Finally, the National Archives of Namibia in Windhoek have records concerning visits of West German politicians to Namibia during the liberation struggle. Also, the archive provides some insight into the position of the German-speaking minority towards West Germany and SWAPO, particularly from the perspective of the Interest Group of German-speaking Southwesterners (IG). The archive, however, holds only a small number of files relevant to this study. With regard to contemporary newspapers, the National Library of Namibia holds copies of the main Namibian newspapers.

The SWAPO Party Archive and Research Centre (SPARC) in Windhoek is not open for academic research, and little work has been done to examine the Namibian liberation struggle from the perspective of SWAPO.[23] However, German archives have proved important in providing primary source insights into SWAPO's position towards the two German states and issues surrounding Namibia's independence. The numerous visits of SWAPO delegates to both East and West Germany have been particularly insightful. Accounts of such visits can be found in the archives of the Foreign Office (PAAA), the Secret Service (BStU) and the Federal Archives (BArch). Furthermore, the PAAA provides substantial access to SWAPO statements, minutes of meetings with West German diplomats both in West Germany and

---

[22] For a good descriptive overview of German archives, with an emphasis on GDR sources, see B. Schäfer, H. Hoff and U. Mählert (eds.), 'The GDR in German Archives, A Guide to Primary Sources and Research Institutions on the History of the Soviet Zone of Occupation and the German Democratic Republic, 1945–19190', *German Historical Institute (Washington, DC)*, Reference Guide No. 14, 'The GDR in German Archives, A Guide to Primary Sources and Research Institutions on the History of the Soviet Zone of Occupation and the German Democratic Republic, 1945–19190'. Accessed November 2015, available from: http://www.bundesstiftung-aufarbeitung.de/uploads/pdf/ghiguide.pdf

[23] Recently the archives of the Department of International Relations and Cooperation in Tshwane, South Africa, have also become difficult to access for research.

Africa, as well as talks and meetings at the side-lines of the UN. As my research was not restricted by the blocking period, I was able to gain a meaningful understanding of SWAPO's changing attitudes between 1969 and 1990.

The most important primary sources on the history of the two German states' position during the Namibian liberation struggle are held at the archives of the Foreign Office (PAAA) and the Secret Service (BStU). Both archives have provided a substantial amount of hitherto unused primary sources. The Federal Archives (BArch) were less exhaustive in providing unused primary source materials. For the investigation of West Germany's position towards Namibia, the archive of the Foreign Office was particularly valuable. Although previous studies had either no access or extremely limited access to the vast array of primary source materials housed in the archive of the Foreign Office, the research for this book has not been restricted by the 30-year rule. Consequently, the large numbers of foreign affairs files examined for this book have not been used in previous studies. Similarly, the relevant Ministry of Foreign Affairs files held at the archive of the Foreign Office have also been examined for this book without the usual restrictions imposed by the blocking period.

The BStU and BArch archives have been a central pillar of research for scholarly studies on the GDR. Although the GDR's involvement in Africa has received substantial scholarly attention, there still remains ample room for original research. Though some primary sources were analysed in the studies mentioned above, this book approaches West Germany's relationship with Namibia from a hitherto under-researched angle. Consequently, it is not necessary to highlight whether the primary materials have been used by the works mentioned above, for this study approaches primary documents from a different perspective.

This study demonstrates that the wider realities of German division need to be considered carefully when examining West Germany's position towards Namibia. Therefore, this work investigates whether the division of Germany promoted conflict between the two German states over Namibian issues. West Germany's relations with Namibia during the liberation struggle can only be comprehended in its full complexity by investigating the political dynamics that determined Bonn's position towards Namibia. Particularly, factors that promoted or hindered interactions between political parties and liberation movements can only be vaguely understood in generalised terms. Thus, for the purpose of this enquiry, it is necessary to look at West Germany's political landscape in all its complexity. At the centre of this enquiry are inner-political issues that promoted different political positions towards both SWAPO and the question of Namibian independence. It is, therefore, necessary to analyse what motivated the political parties' varied approaches to the question of Namibian independence. This analysis asks (i) what political dynamics shaped party positions towards the Namibia question? (ii) what factors made the case for or against solidarity with SWAPO?

and (iii) was foreign policy towards Namibia marked by continuity or change? Any in-depth examination of each of these questions will lead, inter alia, to intra-German issues.

It is the aim of this book to show that West Germany's policy towards Namibia was strongly influenced by the wider implication of Germany's division into two separate and competing states. However, even without a particular focus on intra-German issues, questions about West Germany's position towards Namibia lead inevitably also to questions about East Germany's role in the Namibian liberation struggle. Thus, in the case of the present study, the questions above can also be applied to East Germany, although the GDR's centralized political system did not produce a political landscape influenced by positional variations. Yet, it is important to investigate what motivated the GDR leadership to make Namibia's independence a central foreign policy issue. And was East Berlin's foreign policy towards Namibia marked by continuity? However, the more important question in this research project is the extent to which inter-German competition and conflict influenced the two states' approach towards Namibia.

Furthermore, given that both Germanys had been deeply involved in the Namibian question for over two decades, the aim of this book is also to examine the strategic approaches implemented by the two states between 1969 and 1990. Here, it is important to ask whether the two Germanys tried to influence SWAPO ideologically. This leads to the further issue of whether exerting ideological influence was part of the two German states' policy towards Namibia, and, if so, did this lead to competition for ideological influence between them. It is also important to investigate how the two Germanys interpreted SWAPO's ideological orientation and whether it shaped attitudes and policies towards the liberation movement. This raises also the question whether there was common ground between the GDR and West Germany, or even efforts to overcome differences that impeded co-operation in Namibia. Here, the role of ideology is central to the analysis of the underlying causes of Cold War rivalry between East and West Germany in relation to the former German colony. Finally, it is important to investigate whether the two German states' policies towards Namibia ultimately influenced the wider dynamics that led to Namibia's independence. How significant were the two German states in the processes that led to independence?

This book is organized as follows. The first four chapters explore the underlying political, ideological and economic factors that played an instrumental role in West Germany's relationship with Namibia as a whole, and SWAPO in particular. Here, the book considers GDR's solidarity with the Namibian liberation struggle and its wider effects on intra German relations. Chapters five to seven examine, in a chronological review of main events, West Germany's approach to the Namibia question against the backdrop of East and West German rivalry.

Following the introduction, Chapter One outlines the origins of East and West German rivalry in southern Africa as a whole and Namibia in particular. Chapter Two examines West German political parties' attitude towards SWAPO and the question of Namibian independence. This includes examining the relationship of the GDR's ruling party, the SED, with SWAPO. Chapter Three is devoted to debates in the *Bundestag*, the West German parliament, between the late 1970s and early 1980s. At the centre of this investigation stands the attitude of political parties towards the growing Soviet influence in southern Africa and SWAPO's close relations with the Soviet bloc. This chapter also explores the Foreign Office's assessment of SWAPO's ideological orientation in the mid-to-late 1970s. West Germany's economic relations with South Africa are examined in Chapter Four. The aim is to investigate whether Bonn used West Germany's extensive economic relations with South Africa as an instrument of foreign policy. Here, the book also examines the two German states' economic interests in Namibia, followed by an analysis of the two Germanys' relationship with Namibian Germans.

In Chapter Five, West Germany's changing relationship with both South Africa and SWAPO is investigated against the backdrop of intra-German rivalry in the mid-to-late 1970s. Chapter Six takes a closer look at West Germany's policy towards Namibia after the 1983 general election. Overall, Chapter Five and Six shed further light on the two German states' rivalry for influence over SWAPO. Chapter Seven analyses to what extent factions within the governing parties tried to use foundations and non-governmental organisations to pursue a policy towards Namibia that was independent of the government. The chapter then concludes with an examination of the role of the two German states in Namibia's first free elections and the final political efforts that led to the country's independence. Chapter Eight draws conclusions and answers key questions. In sum, this book presents a comparative analysis of the two German states' relationship with Namibia during the national liberation struggle. Analysing Namibia's path to independence from the perspective of both German states offers new insights into Cold War rivalry and its wider effects on both the African liberation struggles in general and Namibia's independence struggle in particular.

1 The origins of rivalry over Namibia

This Chapter introduces the intense political context that shaped rivalry between the two Germanys in southern Africa as a whole and Namibia in particular. In this respect, the dynamics of inter-German competition for influence in Namibia can only be understood within the wider framework of the Cold War. Chapter One focuses on the underlying causes behind the rivalry between the two Germanys in southern Africa, against the backdrop of Cold War realities. As Germany was divided into two separate, independent political entities, it is useful to examine the causes behind the two states' competition in southern Africa separately.

East Germany's solidarity with African liberation movements

In an attempt to isolate communist Germany within the perimeters of the Iron Curtain, the first government of the Federal Republic, under the Chancellorship of Konrad Adenauer (CDU), threatened, in 1955, diplomatic and economic sanctions against countries that recognized the GDR as a sovereign state. West Germany saw itself as the sole representative of the German people – including the approximately 17 million Germans who were under the control of the Soviet Union. In what became known as the Hallstein Doctrine, West Germany developed a strategic plan, designed to force East Germany, through isolation, into unification.[1] By the late 1960s, however, it had become apparent that the GDR under Walter Ulbricht could not be isolated behind the infamous Iron Curtain. For the GDR's policy-makers, solidarity with African liberation movements was more than a concept that embodied the principles of Marxism-Leninism. It was the GDR's own Trojan-Horse, a vehicle employed to break through the isolation imposed by West Germany's Hallstein Doctrine. Solidarity with liberation movements and newly independent Third World countries proved effective in opening up opportunities for establishing close ties with countries beyond the Soviet bloc.[2]

The GDR had no difficulty in establishing a link between its own struggle and the struggle of indigenous southern African peoples for national independence. Erich Correns, chair-

---

[1] For a detailed analysis of the Hallstein Doctrine, see, e.g., W.G. Gray, *Germany's Cold War: The Global Campaign to Isolate East Germany, 1949–1969*, Chapel Hill, NC, University of North Carolina Press, 2003; W. Kilian, *Die Hallstein-Doktrin. Der diplomatische Krieg zwischen der BRD und der DDR 1955–1973*, Berlin, Duncker & Humblot, 2001.

[2] At present, the politically correct term is underdeveloped countries or developing countries; during the Cold War, however, the world was divided into three Worlds: the First, the Second and the Third World.

man of the National Front of the GDR had the following exchange with Joshua Nkomo, founder of the National Democratic Party of Rhodesia:

> [West Germany] openly demand the assimilation of the GDR into the FRG, only to have a free hand for annexing big areas of neighbouring states such as the CSSR, Poland and the Soviet Union ... through our vital interests, we are allies [the GDR and Zimbabwe] in the fight for freedom and self-determination of all nations... This is clearly not an internal German dispute, but the removal of the grave danger that West German imperialism is for the German people, the peoples of Europe and Africa, indeed the peoples of the entire world.[3]

Unmistakably, the proverb 'the enemy of my enemy is my friend' mirrors the GDR's state of mind here. Even more significant, perhaps, Horst Brasch, the first chairman of the GDR's Solidarity Committee (1960–1964), underlined, in a letter to the leaders of various African liberation movements and political parties, the GDR's common struggle with African nations: 'West Germany has become the most aggressive exponent of NATO and is actively preparing for a third world war with atomic weapons. Our common interest is our united struggle against imperialism and colonialism, our united fight for peace, independence and increasing prosperity for all nations...'[4]

Here, it is important to note that the National Front and the Solidarity Committee were subordinated to, and controlled by, the Socialist Unity Party of Germany (SED), the GDR's ruling party.[5] Furthermore, the mission statement of the Solidarity Committee, which consisted of representatives from state ministries, mass organizations and party members, mirrored the world view held by the GDR leadership and therefore was deeply embedded in the ideology of international solidarity among the working classes against capitalism, imperialism and neo-colonialism.[6] Thus, statements made on national and international platforms, or within an international context, were state-dictated and a reflection of the wider political orientation of the GDR. Within this context, it is useful to note that both statements

---

[3] BArch, DZ 8/52, Letter Erich Correns, president of the National Front of the German Democratic Republic, to Joshua Nkomo, president of the National Democratic Party of Rhodesia, 01.09.1961 Quotations from German sources have been translated by the author.

[4] BArch, DZ 8/52, Letter Horst Brasch, Chairman of the Solidarity Committee, to the President of the Zanzibar Nationalist Party; and the President of Le Movement populaire de libération de l'Angola, the Secretary General of the Malawi Congress Party and the President of Uganda People's Congress, 1961.

[5] The 'GDR Solidarity Committee' was initially called 'Committee of Solidarity with the Peoples of Africa', founded in mid-1960. The committee was established in solidarity with the 17 African nations that achieved independence in 1960, during the so-called 'Year of Africa'. For more information, see Van der Heyden, 'GDR Development', 72–78.

[6] G. Witkowski, 'Between Fighters and Beggars, Socialist Philanthropy and the Imagery of Solidarity in East Germany', in Q. Slobodian (ed.), *Comrades of Color: East Germany in the Cold War*, New York, Berghahn Books, 2015, 73–75.

emerged in late 1961, only weeks before the Berlin Wall was erected, at a time when the SED's main thinkers mapped out the future of East Germany. The apocalyptic perception of West Germany and the ensuing solidarity with the African liberation struggle was not only a manifestation of the inter-German confrontation; it was also a reflection of the principles that determined the GDR's foreign policy right through until the mid-1980s.

Although the GDR was, as most states with totalitarian structures, far less concerned about public opinion than democratic countries, international opinion and support carried great importance for East Berlin's ruling elite.[7] This was largely because the GDR needed the support of countries outside of the Iron Curtain for its continuing efforts to break through the Hallstein Doctrine.[8] Yet, the GDR's forays into international politics were not particularly promising as long as West Germany asserted its opposition to East Germany's quest for recognition. The Hallstein Doctrine made it impossible for the GDR to establish meaningful relations with sovereign countries that enjoyed good bilateral relations with West Germany.

Only in late 1969 did the tide finally begin to turn in the GDR's favour. The newly elected social-liberal coalition of the Social Democratic Party (SPD) and the Liberal Democratic Party (FDP), with Willy Brandt as chancellor, radically broke with the Hallstein Doctrine, allowing communist East Germany to establish normal bilateral relations with countries on the other side of the Iron Curtain. Under Brandt's so-called *Ostpolitik*, the Federal Republic pursued a policy of rapprochement with the Eastern bloc and especially the GDR.[9] *Ostpolitik* led to the normalisation of relations between the two Germanys and paved the way for a radical improvement of the GDR's international standing in the 1970s.[10] Hence, solidarity

---

[7] Elections in the GDR had only symbolic value and were designed to show unity and public consent for the ruling party, the Socialist Unity Party of Germany (SED). Although other political parties existed in the GDR, they were united under the National Front of Democratic Germany (NFDG) and the SED was in de facto control of the NFDG. Thus, the SED also controlled all aspects of the election process. For an in-depth analysis with regard to the question of whether or not the GDR was a totalitarian state, see A. I. Port, 'The Banalities of East German Historiography', in M. Fulbrook and A. I. Port (eds.), *Becoming East Germany: Socialist Structures and Sensibilities after Hitler*, New York, Berghahn Books, 2013, 1–31. Overall, it is debatable to what extent the GDR was in effect a de facto totalitarian state: M. Fulbrook, 'Jenseits der Totalitarismustheorie? Vorläufige Bemerkungen aus sozialgeschichtlicher Perspektive', in P. Barker (ed.), *The GDR and Its History: Rückblick und Revision*, Amsterdam and Atlanta, Rodobi, 2000, 21–35.

[8] It is important to note, however, that the GDR's totalitarian structures, that is, East Berlin's attempt to control all aspects of public and private life was not necessarily an hindrance to the recognition of the GDR as a sovereign state, for the international community recognized under 'favourable conditions' regimes that were more repugnant than the GDR.

[9] M. E. Sarotte, *Dealing with the Devil: East Germany, Détente, and Ostpolitik, 1969–1973*, Chapel Hill, University of North Carolina Press, 2001.

[10] For an insightful analysis of the effects of *Ostpolitik* on West German-South African relations, see T. Dedering, 'Ostpolitik and the relations between West Germany and South Africa', *academia.edu*. Accessed online February 2015, available from: www.academia.edu/3843165/Ostpolitik_

with liberation movements was no longer a strategic undertaking, designed to undermine Bonn's isolation policy towards the GDR, but a vehicle to establish the GDR's credentials as an internationally recognized sovereign German state. In the 1970s, solidarity with liberation movements developed into East Berlin's anti-imperialist foreign policy, which was in line with the Soviet Union's wider strategic interests in Africa.

Yet, even after Bonn removed the barriers that had hindered the GDR from achieving international recognition, East Berlin continued to struggle to gain West German approval of the GDR's sovereignty.[11] On 18 September 1973, East Germany was finally admitted as a full member of the UN, which further improved the GDR's international position. Only eight months later, the GDR proudly hosted a meeting of the UN Anti-Apartheid Committee.[12] The meeting took place under the umbrella of the Decade to Combat Racism and Racial Discrimination, launched by the UN in 1972. Oscar Fischer, the Foreign Minister of the GDR, used this opportunity to emphasise the GDR's track record of championing southern Africa's struggle against racism.[13] After all, the GDR was able to point to over a decade of support for liberation movements in southern Africa, dating back to the early 1960s.[14] Under the passionate socialist and internationalist Erich Honecker, who came to power in 1971, the GDR's focus on Africa continued to grow steadily, reaching a peak in the late 1970s.[15]

Solidarity with African liberation movements was largely based on material, educational and financial support, but included also military training and military aid, as well as weapons, ammunition, tanks and other military hardware. The GDR also made a commitment to providing humanitarian aid such as medical supplies, medicines, bandages and lorries.[16] Great effort was made to enable wounded liberation fighters to receive medical treatment in the GDR.[17] In the late 1970s and early 1980s, at the height of East-West tensions in southern

---

and_the_Relations_between_West_Germany_and_South_Africa

[11] Gray, *Germany's Cold War*, 212.

[12] See also B. H. Schulz,'The politics of East-South relations: The GDR and Southern Africa', in T. A. Baylis, D. Childs, E. L. Collier and M. Rueschemeyer (eds.), *East Germany in Comparative Perspective*, London, Routledge, 1989, 161.

[13] BArch, DZ 8/37, UNO Sonderausschuss gegen Apartheid, Berlin, 24.–29.05.1974.

[14] See A. Babing, *Gegen Rassismus*, 1949–1977, Interview mit dem Generalsekretär des Solidaritätskomitees der DDR, Kurt Krüger, anlässlich des 15. Jahrestages der Gründung des Solidaritätskomitees, 21.07.1975, 474–476. (GDR established the African People's Committee for Solidarity on 22.07.1960).

[15] See Ibid., 1977–1982, Aus der Rede von Kurt Seibt, Vorsitzender der Zentralen Revisionskommission der Sozialistischen Einheitspartei Deutschlands und Präsident des Solidaritätskomitees der DDR in Berlin, 02.05.1977, 62–63.

[16] See Van der Heyden, 'GDR Development', 111.

[17] For further information on the GDR's considerable support programme for the liberation movements in southern Africa, see, e.g., Schleicher/Schleicher, *Special Flights*; Schleicher/Schleicher, *Die DDR im südlichen Afrika*. For a primary source account of East German support to liberation struggles in southern Africa, see Babing, *Gegen Rassismus*, 1977–1982, Aus der Rede von

Africa, particular attention was directed towards 'political and diplomatic support, extensive material support, the education of cadres and growing political cooperation'.[18]

The GDR's support of nations struggling for national independence placed East Germany in an authoritative position to champion the plight of southern African nations on the international stage.[19] Solidarity with liberation movements allowed East Berlin to speak with authority on the behalf of people who still suffered the ill effects of European colonialism. International conferences provided opportunities to voice the GDR's commitment to the struggle against neo-colonialism, imperialism, and racism and represented a first step towards an active role in international politics. In other words, the GDR's ambition to bolster its standing as an internationally recognised sovereign state promoted its participation in international conferences.[20] The aim was to become an active participant in international politics and ultimately to move towards a bigger role on the world stage.

Despite East Germany's growing role in international politics after admission into the UN, the GDR's ruling elite remained locked in the perception that the GDR had to step out from under the shadow of West Germany to become a global power in its own right. Even four years after the GDR's acceptance into the inner circle of the United Nations, the GDR's leader, Honecker, who presided over the GDR's outward-looking foreign policy, rarely missed an opportunity to emphasise the international relevance and global importance of conferences in which the GDR participated.[21] Perhaps more than ever before, the SED was

---

Kurt Seibt, Vorsitzender der Zentralen Revisionskommission der Sozialistischen Einheitspartei Deutschlands und Präsident des Solidaritätskomitees der DDR in Berlin, 02.05.1977, 62–63.

[18] BStU, JHS Potsdam, Mikrofilmstelle, VVS JHS o001-110/82, Lehrkonzeption für Grundlehrgänge auf dem Gebiet der politisch-operativen Sicherung von Befreiungsorganisationen des südlichen Afrika, 01.09.1982, 4.

[19] See Babing, *Gegen Rassismus*, 1977–1982, Rede des Leiters der DDR-Delegation, Hans-Jürgen Weitz, auf der UN-Konferenz für die Unterstützung der Völker Simbabwes und Namibias vom 16.05. bis 21.05.1977 in Maputo, 16.05.1977, 71–73.

[20] East Berlin was eager to participate in conferences with an international setting. It was not particularly important whether the conference was held, for example, in Ethiopia, Egypt or Azerbaijan. See, e.g., BArch, DZ 8/3a, Baku-Azerbaijan, IV Soviet Afro-Asian Solidarity Conference, 12.06.–14.06.1976; BArch, DZ 8/535, Politische Zielsetzung für Woche der Solidarität, 23.05.1989. In fact, East Berlin scarcely ever missed an opportunity to express the GDR's commitment in the fight against neo-colonialism, imperialism and racism. See, e.g., Babing, *Gegen Rassismus*, 1949–1977, Rede des Abgeordneten der Volkskammer der DDR, Frau Prof. Dr. Anneliese Sälzler, im Dritten Komitee der XXIX. Tagung der UN-Vollversammlung zur Beseitigung aller Formen der Rassendiskriminierung, 01.10.1974, 384; Ibid., 1977–1982, Information der DDR über die Unterstützung des unterdrückten Volkes von Südafrika sowie über die Einhaltung der Resolutionen der UN, 12.05.1977, 69–71.

[21] See, e.g., 'Gegen Apartheid, Rassismus und Kolonialismus', *Horizont*, Nr 28/1977; Babing, *Gegen Rassismus*, 1977–1982, Grußadresse des Generalsekretärs des Zentralkomitees der Sozialistischen Einheitspartei und Vorsitzenden des Staatsrates der DDR, Erich Honecker, an die Weltkonferenz zum Kampf gegen Rassismus und Rassendiskriminierung in Genf, 11.08.1978.

fixated on improving East Germany's international standing and image. This also became apparent in the SED's growing contact with liberation movements in the early 1970s.[22]

Indisputably, solidarity with southern African liberation struggles supported the GDR's aim to gain greater international exposure. What remains open to debate is whether such exposure helped to increase the GDR's standing in the eyes of the world. What is unquestionable, however, is that East Berlin believed that solidarity with liberation struggles was potentially beneficial to the GDR's image and international standing. There were sound reasons for such optimism. Particularly in southern Africa, the GDR's reputation as a reliable partner grew steadily through the 1970s.

Appropriately enough, the GDR published the first of the two volumes, *Against Racism, Apartheid and Colonialism; Documents of the GDR, 1949–1977*,[23] a collection of speeches documenting over two decades the GDR's international participation in the fight against racism, apartheid and colonialism, during the International Anti-Apartheid Year in 1978. The fact that the book was published both in German and English reflects the GDR's continuing strive for international recognition in the late 1970s.

In the 1970s, the GDR found itself increasingly in a position of strength in southern Africa. Its relationship with liberation movements and newly independent states enhanced the GDR's influence in the region. From a position of strength, the GDR's propaganda campaign against West Germany in Africa increased in the latter part of the 1970s. It was not particularly difficult for the GDR to discredit the other Germany, not least because West Germany strongly opposed sanctions against South Africa while at the same time maintaining extensive economic relations with the apartheid state. There could be no question that the conditions imposed by apartheid on the black majority in Namibia and South Africa promoted exploitive and 'slave-like working conditions', which only helped to increase the profits of Western monopolies, particularly West German firms.[24] East Berlin had little doubt that West Germany's extensive economic relations with South Africa not only strengthened apartheid, but also perpetuated white minority rule in both Namibia and South Africa. Hence, the GDR's propaganda machine in southern Africa emphasised that it was the mor-

---

[22] Schleicher/Schleicher, *Special Flights*, 119.
[23] A. Babing, *Gegen Rassismus, Apartheid und Kolonialismus, Dokumente der DDR, 1949–1977*, Berlin, Staatsverlag der Deutschen Demokratischen Republik, 1978. The second volume was published in 1983: A. Babing, *Gegen Rassismus, Apartheid und Kolonialismus, Dokumente der DDR, 1977–1982*, Berlin, Staatsverlag der Deutschen Demokratischen Republik, 1983.
[24] Babing, *Gegen Rassismus*, 1949–1977, Erklärung des Solidaritätskomitees der DDR, des Friedensrates der DDR, des DDR-Komitees für Menschenrechte und des DDR-Komitees für die Kampfdekade gegen Rassismus und Rassendiskriminierung an das Volk von Namibia und seine Befreiungsbewegung, die Südwestafrikanische Volksorganisation (SWAPO), 25.08.1975. See also Schulz, 'The politics of East-South relations', 160.

ally superior of the two Germanys; that the GDR pursued policies that were fundamentally distinct from those of West Germany.

There were, however, also domestic considerations behind East Germany's considerable involvement in southern Africa. The GDR's solidarity with liberation struggles can also partly be understood as an attempt to wipe out the stain of humiliation felt in 1961, when only an elaborate system of walls, watchtowers, electrified fences, and the infamous death strip that separated East and West Germany, could stop a mass exodus of East German citizens to West Germany.[25] The SED's close relations with liberation movements also contained an element of self-righteousness, for solidarity with Third World nations in their struggle against oppression, racism and neo-colonialism assisted the ruling party in its effort to instil a positive image of the GDR in the hearts and minds of its wider population. The SED viewed anti-colonial liberation wars as just wars.[26] Hence, solidarity with liberation struggles supported East Berlin's presentation of the GDR as a just state, which was an important aspect of SED's domestic propaganda.[27] The SED's emphasis on the GDR's efforts to quell injustice in Third World countries was in line with the party's projected image of the GDR as a state of 'peace and anti-imperialist solidarity'.[28] Thus, solidarity with southern African liberation movements gave East Berlin the satisfaction of 'being on the right side of history'. Presenting this image to the wider population was viable for the inner consolidation of the GDR.[29]

Consequently, solidarity with the people of the Third World in their fight against neocolonialism, imperialism and racism gave East Berlin, in some subliminal sense, purpose, perspective, and the confirmation that the GDR was a morally good state. In some respect, the GDR's leadership hid behind a dense screen of humanitarianism, attempting to distract from the state's authoritarian grip on its own citizen with a compassionate foreign policy. Overall, it seems plausible to suggest that the GDR's controversial state structure, and an underlying sense of inferiority vis-à-vis West Germany, motivated the ruling elite to strive,

---

[25] The exodus from East Berlin to West Berlin and through the East-West border was substantial before the erection of the Berlin Wall. About 144,000 people fled in 1959, which rose to 199,000 in 1960 and about 207,000 in 1961.

[26] Schleicher, 'Waffen für den Süden', 8.

[27] T. Weis, 'Shaping the Discourse on Africa. The Concept of 'Solidarity' in East German Relations with SWAPO' Master's Thesis: University of Oxford, 2008, 36–40.

[28] E. Honecker, 'Party and Revolutionary Young Guard Firmly Allied', Honecker speech to the Free German Youth in 1984 and 1989, German Propaganda Archive, Calvin College. Accessed online November 2014, available from: http://research.calvin.edu/german-propaganda-archive/fdj.htm

[29] H. Bley und H.-G. Schleicher, 'Deutsch-Deutsch-Namibische Beziehungen 1960–1990', in L. Förster, D. Henrichsen and M. Bollig (eds.), *Namibia-Deutschland. Eine geteilte Geschichte. Widerstand-Gewalt-Erinnerung*, Köln, Ethnologica, 2004. Accessed online April 2015, available from: www.vip-ev.de/text85.htm

inter alia, for international approval. East Berlin felt an underlying need to prove the GDR's value to both its own population and the international community. Ultimately, East Berlin and not Bonn needed to justify the division of Germany and the GDR's communist state system, particularly to its own citizens.[30]

The GDR's propaganda machine rarely missed an opportunity to portray West Germany as an exploitative neo-imperialistic power that threatened world peace and the GDR as a power striving to create a better world, a truly anti-fascist state that had eradicated the remnants of Nazi Germany within its own rank and file while Bonn was still held hostage by the shadows of the past.[31] Ultimately, the image propagated by East Berlin that the GDR was as a truly anti-fascist state served as the basic legitimation of the state's very existence.[32]

Understandably enough, in order to mature into an independent and internationally recognized, fully sovereign state, the GDR attempted to develop a positive national identity that would make it difficult, if not impossible, for the West to disregard it as 'the other Germany'. Solidarity with oppressed nations struggling against neo-colonialism, imperialism and racism was central in East Berlin's endeavour to show that the GDR was the morally superior Germany. In the West, however, the erection of the Berlin Wall had created an irreversible image of the GDR as an oppressive state. The Federal Republic was the 'real' Germany, while the GDR was viewed as a satellite of the Soviet Union.[33]

The GDR's close relations with liberation movements were not, however, solely based on strategic calculations, nor simply based on a calculated effort to improve the GDR's national and international image. To sympathise with the liberation struggle in Third World countries was – at least for the GDR's ruling class – a natural consequence born out of the GDR's history. The GDR's experience of having to rely on other nations, most of all the Soviet Union, had defining repercussions on the GDR's progression into statehood. This was particularly true of the early 1960s, when only the continued solidarity of the Soviet bloc could guarantee the very existence of Ulbricht's state. Moscow's approval of the erection of the Berlin Wall in 1961, and the extension of Soviet defence guarantees to the GDR in 1964, gave the GDR's ruling party the scope and security it needed for state development. Hence, the solidarity of another nation, experienced during the GDR's most taxing periods, left a

---

[30] D. Smith, *Walls and Mirrors: Western Representation of Really Existing German Socialism*, Lanham, University Press of America, 1988, 126.
[31] See Babing, *Gegen Rassismus*, 1949–1977, Aus dem Aufruf des Zentralkomitees der sozialistischen Einheitspartei Deutschlands, des Staatsrates, des Ministerrates und des Nationalrates der Nationalen Front der DDR zum 30. Jahrestag der Befreiung vom Hitlerfaschismus, 21.01.1975, 443.
[32] M. Fulbrook, *Anatomy of a Dictatorship: Inside the GDR, 1949–1989*, Oxford, Oxford University Press, 1995, 24.
[33] Smith, *Walls and Mirrors*, 123.

deep impression on the young state, as an unnamed GDR delegate explained in 1976, at the 4th Soviet Afro-Asian Solidarity Conference in Azerbaijan:

> ...solidarity is in the GDR indeed state policy and for its citizens a matter of the heart. We ourselves have received solidarity from the Soviet Union, the other brotherly states, and the progressive and democratic powers of this world. Hence, we ourselves have experienced that solidarity helps winning, and out of this experience derives the enormous support the GDR gives to nations who fight exploitation and imperialistic oppression...[34]

Although it would have been difficult, if not impossible, to compare the GDR's rocky path to statehood with the liberation movements' struggle for independence from European colonialism, East Berlin had evidently no trouble highlighting apparent similarities.

The mutual inability to achieve the objective of independent statehood under their own steam and the subsequent dependence on solidarity from stronger powers was most conspicuous. Furthermore, African nations and the GDR were to varying degrees concerned with the possibility of annexation, regardless of whether the threat was real or imagined. In this context, the GDR's ruling elite found it difficult to trust the other Germany, and felt threatened by the perceived expansionist aims of their capitalist neighbour, suspicions that were not entirely unjustified. In fact, already in 1951, the Bundestag declared that 'in a free Europe, the unification of Germany was the highest goal of German politics'.[35] New research has even revealed that Ludwig Erhard, West Germany's chancellor from 1963 to 1966, considered offering the financially weak Soviet Union 100 billion deutsche marks for the reunification of Germany.[36] West Germany never ceased to put pressure on East Germany, as support for reunification was strong on both sides of the Wall. There were periods when even Moscow and East Berlin were flirting with the practicality of a united Germany. And yet, even though the GDR had reason to question its future as a fully independent state, it is also important to consider that authoritarian states are commonly prone to paranoia and paternalism.

In the 1970s and 1980s, Third World countries had reason to be concerned about foreign occupation and possible annexation, not least because of South Africa's occupation of Namibia and the Soviet's invasion of Afghanistan. The GDR, on the other hand, knew what life was like under foreign occupation, for the Soviet Union occupied and administered

---

[34] BArch, DZ 8/3a, Baku-Azerbaijan, IV Soviet Afro-Asian Solidarity Conference, 12.06.1976 – 14.06.1976. See also BArch, DZ 8/535, Politische Zielsetzung für Woche der Solidarität, 23.05.1989.
[35] Deutscher Bundestag, 1. Wahlperiode, Drucksache Nr. 2621, Antrag der Fraktion des Zentrums, 26.09.1951. See also Gray, *Germany's Cold War*, 198.
[36] J. Friedmann and A. Frohn, 'Preis der Freiheit', *Der Spiegel*, 40/2011, 01.10.2011.

the Eastern part of Germany after the Second World War.[37] Though East Germany gained relative independence from Soviet domination after the GDR was established in 1949, East Berlin continued to long for greater national self-determination, and ultimately recognition as an independent and sovereign state, as did liberation movements in Africa. It is important to note, however, that the GDR largely denied its citizens the right to internal self-determination. Although the rights of the black majority in Namibia and South Africa were much more severely restricted than the rights of ordinary GDR citizens, the desire for internal self-determination seemed equally strong. Thus, the GDR's solidarity with liberation struggles was, although in many respects genuine and based on shared desires, to some degree hypocritical. Nonetheless, all of these factors fostered the idea in the GDR of the need to fight for a common cause with liberation movements and newly independent states around the world.

The GDR's sympathy for nations fighting for self-determination was rooted in the understanding that their struggle was fought against the GDR's class enemy, the capitalist West, on the principle of anti-imperialism and anti-colonialism.[38] The GDR's fight against imperialism, neo-colonialism and racism became an increasingly central aspect of East Berlin's foreign policy and therefore was incorporated in the GDR constitution in 1974.[39] East Berlin rarely missed an opportunity to express the GDR's commitment to the cause of liberation movements, as for example emphasised by the Solidarity Committee at the UN World Conference in 1977:

> In accordance with the principles of proletarian internationalism, which guides the foreign policy of the German Democratic Republic, the Solidarity Committee of the GDR has stood and is standing firmly on the side of those forces fighting for the final liquidation of all forms of colonialism, racial discrimination and the abhorring policy of apartheid.[40]

---

[37] For a far-reaching account of the Soviet Union's occupation of Germany, see F. Slaveski, *The Soviet Occupation of Germany: Hunger, Mass Violence and the Struggle for Peace, 1945 1947*, Cambridge, Cambridge University Press, 2013.

[38] See, e.g., BArch, DZ 8/37, Bericht des UNO-Sonderausschusses gegen Apartheid in Berlin, Alfred Babing, 24. 19.05. 1974; Babing, *Gegen Rassismus*, 1949 1977, Aus der Rede von Kurt Seibt, Vorsitzender der Zentralen Revisionskommission der Sozialistischen Einheitspartei Deutschlands und Präsident des Solidaritätskomitees der DDR, vor der Tagung des Präsidiums des Solidaritätskomitees der DDR, 02.05.1977, 684 699; Ibid., 1977 1982, Rede des DDR-Vertreters Gerhard Schröter im Vierten Komitee der XXXVI. Tagung der UN-Vollversammlung zu den Aktivitäten ausländischer ökonomischer und anderer Kreise, die die Verwirklichung der UN-Deklaration über die Gewährung der Unabhängigkeit an die kolonialen Länder und Voelker behindern, 01.10.1981, 519.

[39] Babing, *Gegen Rassismus*, 1977 1982, Zweiter periodischer Bericht der DDR über die Erfüllung der Konvention über die Beseitigung aller Formen der Rassendiskriminierung, 14.11.1975, 44– 45.

[40] BArch, DZ 8/40, Solidarity Committee of the GDR at the UNO-World conference, 1977.

The ideological principles of proletarian internationalism envisioned the unification of the oppressed masses, the international working class, in a socialist revolution against capitalist exploitation and imperial domination.[41]

Thus, the aim was to create in Third World countries conditions favourable for the emancipation from foreign domination. Hence, for the SED and the Solidarity Committee, the African liberation struggle was linked with the proletarian struggle against capitalist exploitation.[42] Obviously, the SED had great faith in the revolutionary potential of the African population, which was thought to resemble, in the broadest sense, the revolutionary character of the European working class.[43] GDR solidarity with liberation movements was strongly influenced by Vladimir Lenin's economic theory that imperial colonialism is the final stage of capitalist development.[44] Logically enough, the October Revolution in Russia in late 1917 played for the SED an instrumental role in awakening the rise of national liberation movements against Western colonial rule.[45] Hence, solidarity with liberation movements was a vital aspect of supporting the world revolutionary process. Liberation movements were fighting capitalism at its highest stage and thus played a pivotal role in the international fight against Western imperialism.[46]

Furthermore, from a Marxist-Leninist perspective, the revolutionary developments in Africa were inseparable from the emancipation of the European working class, for colonial exploitation gave the European bourgeoisie the material and economic power to corrupt the working class. In other words, the European bourgeoisie pulled the working class away

---

[41] See Babing, *Gegen Rassismus*, 1977 1982, Aus der Rede von Kurt Seibt, Vorsitzender der Zentralen Revisionskommission der Sozialistischen Einheitspartei Deutschlands und Präsident des Solidaritätskomitees der DDR, auf der Präsidiumstagung des Solidaritätskomitees der DDR in Berlin, 02.05.1977, 60–61.

[42] For a detailed assessment of the GDR's perspective of proletarian internationalism, see Schulz, 'The politics of East-South relations', 158–160.

[43] Hence, imperialism was understood as the highest stage of capitalist development, as proposed by Lenin in 1917: V. I. Lenin, *Imperialism, the Highest Stage of Capitalism*, London, Penguin Books, 2011.

[44] See also BStU, JHS Potsdam, Mikrofilmstelle, VVS JHS o001–110/82, Lehrkonzeption für Grundlehrgänge auf dem Gebiet der politisch-operativen Sicherung von Befreiungsorganisationen des südlichen Afrika, 01.09.1982, 11.

[45] See, e.g., Babing, *Gegen Rassismus*, 1977–1982, Rede des Leiters der DDR-Delegation, Hans Jürgen Weitz, auf der UN-Konferenz für die Unterstützung der Völker Simbabwes und Namibias vom 16.05. bis 21.05.1977 in Maputo, 16.05.1977, 72; Ibid., Gemeinsames Kommuniqué über den Besuch einer Delegation der Südwestafrikanischen Volksorganisation (SWAPO) von Namibia in der DDR, 20.12.1977, 111.

[46] See also ibid., Rede des Generalsekretärs des Zentralkomitees der Sozialistischen Einheitspartei und Vorsitzenden des Staatsrates der DDR, Erich Honecker, auf der Internationalen Wissenschaftlichen Konferenz 'Der gemeinsame Kampf der Arbeiterbewegung und der nationalen Befreiungsbewegungen gegen Imperialismus, für sozialen Fortschritt', 20.10.1980.

from revolutionary tendencies and toward reform by redistributing part of the profits made through colonial exploitation to the working-class. In the Third World, however, the oppressive systems of colonial rule promoted revolutionary and anti-imperialist tendencies. Hence, the support of African nations in the struggle for independence from colonial rule had a further purpose, namely to promote the emancipation of the working class in Europe from the capitalist ruling elite.[47] Independent African countries no longer supplied the European bourgeoisie with the economic and material profits necessary to fend off proletarian revolution in Europe.

The combined importance of the proletarian revolution in the advanced countries and the liberation struggles in Third World countries becomes even more apparent in Lenin's theory of proletarian revolution:

> While the proletariat of the advanced countries is overthrowing the bourgeoisie and repelling its attempts at counter-revolution, the undeveloped and oppressed nations do not just wait, do not cease to exist, do not disappear ... The social revolution can come only in the form of an epoch in which are combined civil war by the proletariat against the bourgeoisie in the advanced countries and a whole series of democratic and revolutionary movements, including the national liberation movement, in the undeveloped, backward and oppressed nations.[48]

The concept of solidarity was, however, not simply a political tool to achieve a strategic aim. Solidarity was tightly interwoven into the civil and political fabric of communist Germany, as explained in *Against Racism, Apartheid and Colonialism; Documents of the GDR, 1949–1977*:

> The leading political power in the GDR, the Socialist Unity Party, follows the working class traditional principal of action, which sees solidarity in the fight against exploitation and oppression as an important experience of the class struggle of all classes and layers in the GDR. Hence, the awareness that anti-imperialistic solidarity is characteristic and at the same time guiding principle of the state's policy.[49]

State-solidarity was crucial for improving the GDR's image in countries west of the Iron Curtain. Notably though, the utilization of mass solidarity for political ends by its leadership was, despite its ulterior motives, based on a sincere effort to implement the internationalist principles of socialist ideology into the GDR's political and civil base. The Marxist-Leninist ideology stood at the centre of the GDR's political foundation. Solidarity with the plight of

---

[47] See R. v. Albertini, *Dekolonisation: Die Diskussion über Verwaltung und Zukunft der Kolonien 1919–1960*, Köln, Opladen, 1966, 18–19.
[48] V.I. Lenin, *Collected Works*, Vol. 23, London, Lawrence & Wishart, 1964, 60.
[49] Babing, *Against Racism, 1949–1977*, Introduction, 25.

the world's proletariat was, in principle, the cornerstone of GDR socialism, and world revolution its final goal.[50]

Although East Berlin worked hard to propagate a whitewashed image of its authoritarian state, there is no denying that the GDR's wider population showed, at times, genuine enthusiasm for humanitarian causes in Third World countries. There existed a noteworthy sensitivity to world inequality, that is, the widening gap between rich and poor nations, across all layers of society. Atrocities such as the Sharpeville Massacre awakened the empathy of an otherwise rather passive GDR population. Needless to say, the GDR's propaganda machine was skilled at milking the population's willingness to embrace humanitarian causes mainly for creating an atmosphere of unity within the GDR and improving the GDR's international image. It is not surprising therefore that the GDR's solidarity campaigns were, in the overwhelming majority of cases, state dictated. On rare occasions, members of the wider GDR population organised events which served fund-raising purposes. More commonly, personal contacts between GDR-citizens and people from Third World countries living in the GDR stimulated gestures of genuine solidarity and generosity.

Furthermore, GDR-citizens and especially the GDR's working population made a monthly donation to the Solidarity fund. The 'soli-contribution' was automatically deducted from a workers' salary and administered by the Free German Trade Unions Federation (FDGB). There was also the possibility to buy Solidarity stamps, which then could be collected in the FDGB membership booklet.[51] There was no compulsion for anybody to donate, yet people felt pressure to contribute to the tradition of working-class solidarity, particularly in the workplace. Clearly, on a subliminal level, people felt pressure to publicly show their generosity, for the GDR leadership demanded conformity and at least outwardly expressed loyalty to the state and its ideological foundation. And yet there was virtually no way to escape state organised solidarity, for the Solidarity Committee created an environment of opportunity for charitable giving, mainly by organising solidarity collections in factories, schools, the military, public places and the street.[52] Obviously, the all-encompassing system of this nanny state undermined private initiative, which probably also partly explains why the wider GDR population was seldom proactive in initiating such fundraising events. Still, there were strong feelings of solidarity with the people of the Third World in their struggle against neo-colonialism, imperialism and racism. It is therefore important to acknowledge that empathy with the liberation struggles in southern Africa was, more often than not, genuine. In this

---

[50] See PAAA, MfAA, C 1428/75, 1971–1973, Rolle und Bedeutung Afrikas im revolutionären Weltprozess, speziell im Hinblick auf die Systemauseinandersetzung zwischen Sozialismus und Imperialismus – politisch, ökonomisch, strategisch [no date].
[51] Van der Heyden, *GDR International Development*, 65–70.
[52] Witkowski, 'Between Fighters', 73–77.

context, the international solidarity of the workers' movement, the FDGB, tried to cultivate links with African unions, and many in the GDR's workers' movement believed that solidarity was the ideal tool for creating a better society and thus a better world.[53]

The GDR was, however, not simply an ideological apparatus dictated by ideological principles. A small ruling elite and influential thinkers drove forward the GDR's solidarity movement. Although the state came before everything else in the GDR, there was still room for individualism. This was particularly so when an individual's motivation furthered the objectives of the state. For some of the main activists within the GDR's solidarity movement, and the SED in general, supporting southern Africa's liberation struggles was also grounded in a more personal motive, which had its origins in Germany's fascist past.[54] Various members of the ruling party viewed South Africa's policies in southern Africa as a continuation of European fascism and thus Pretoria as a 'fascist regime'.[55] It is also worth noting here that the Nazi ideology had not only influenced the ideological fabric of apartheid South Africa; the South African National Party (NP) had openly supported Hitler and Nazi-Germany during the Second World War.[56] Hence, it is perhaps not surprising that West Germany's reluctance to cease co-operating with South Africa's National Party was a persistent thorn in the side of the SED and the Solidarity Committee.[57] The southern African liberation struggle had personal significance for some SED members. Given that the KPD, the Communist Party of Germany, was ruthlessly persecuted by Hitler's henchmen, it seems plausible to conclude that the existence of South Africa's apartheid state was, for the former KPD cadres within the SED, a vivid reminder of the ills of Nazi Germany and thus a focal point in the fight against fascism.

---

[53] Schleicher, *Zwischen Herzenswunsch*, 6.
[54] See also Schleicher/Schleicher, *Special Flights*, 9–44.
[55] See Babing, *Gegen Rassismus*, 1949–1977, Rede des DDR-Vertreters Bernhard Neugebauer vor dem UN- Sicherheitsrat zur Namibiafrage, 05.06.1975, 467; Ibid, Rede des Botschafters Peter Florin, Stellvertreter des Ministers für Auswärtige Angelegenheiten und Ständiger Vertreter der DDR bei den Vereinten Nationen, vor der XXXI. Tagung der UN-Vollversammlung zur Apartheidpolitik der Regierung Südafrikas, 03.11.1976, 637. Peter Florin, the permanent representative of the GDR at the United Nations, for example, called Pretoria's apartheid policy 'fascist terror': Babing, *Gegen Rassismus*,1977–1982, Rede des Botschafters Peter Florin, Stellvertreter des Ministers für Auswärtige Angelegenheiten und Ständiger Vertreter der DDR bei den Vereinten Nationen, vor dem UN Sicherheitsrats zur Aggressionspolitik des Apartheidregimes von Südafrika, 06.06.1980.
[56] For an assessment of South Africa's relations with Nazi-Germany, see J. Peires, *Ruling by Race: Nazi Germany and Apartheid South Africa*, eBook, 2008. See also Dedering, 'Ostpolitik', 12.
[57] For a detailed analysis of the GDR's accusation that fascism continued to be part of West Germany, see B. Niven, 'The Sideways Gaze, The Cold War and Memory of the Nazi Past, 1949–1979', in T. Hochscherf, C. Laucht and A. Plowman (eds.), *Divided but not Disconnected: German Experiences of the Cold War*, New York, Berghahn Books, 2010, 49–62.

That Heinrich Eggebrecht, one of the co-founders of the Solidarity Committee and a former KPD member, experienced, as many KPD members did, Nazi brutality first-hand during his imprisonment in a concentration camp might, to some extent, explain his unwavering dedication to the liberation struggle in southern Africa. As Ilona Schleicher points out, Eggbrecht's understanding of solidarity, as a crucial component of the anti-imperial class struggle, derived partly from his personal experience of the anti-fascist resistance struggle in Nazi-Germany.[58] Hence, it is reasonable to suggest that a complex web of shared experiences established a personal bond between leading policy makers in the GDR and liberation fighters in southern Africa. Consequently, the influence of individuals on the GDR's solidarity movement cannot be underestimated, although the Solidarity Committee was deeply interwoven in the power structures of the GDR, and the committees' actions were subject to SED approval.[59]

Importantly, however, the GDR did not indiscriminately support national liberation struggles in southern Africa. Ideological considerations determined the GDR's involvement with liberation movements. The more committed the socialist orientation of the liberation movement and the stronger the struggle against the imperialist class enemy, the better its chances of it receiving East Berlin's support.[60] Thus, the GDR's solidarity with liberation movements was propelled forward by the dynamics of the Cold War.

By the mid-1960s, the Third World had developed into a major battlefield of the Cold War, a new theatre in the conflict between the United States and the Soviet Union, between capitalism and communism. In this context, the GDR's foreign policy was in line with the Soviet Union's striving after ideological dominance in strategically significant territories throughout the Third World. Needless to say, the capitalist West was determined to counter communist advances in the Third World – even if it implied supporting a regime that was in clear violation of human rights. This can be partly explained by the fact that the Cold War took place within a context of extreme paranoia. While the capitalist West feared that if one country in a region came under the control of communism, the neighbouring countries would follow in a domino effect, the communist East was paranoid about capitalist infiltration and subversion.

In summary, East Berlin never fully came to terms with the fact that in most parts of the world the GDR remained the second German state, the less powerful and less influential little brother.[61] That the GDR continued to stay in the shadow of West Germany affected

---

[58] Schleicher, *DDR-Solidarität*, 9–17.
[59] It seems worth noting here that denazification and anti-fascism were also integral aspects of the GDR's cultural programme.
[60] See also Schulz, 'The politics of East-South relations', 159.
[61] See also H. Bortfeldt, 'In the Shadow of the Federal Republic, Cultural Relations Between the GDR

East Berlin's foreign policy and decision-making process, particularly during the Honecker era. The image conscious elite in East Berlin was all too aware of the GDR's standing in the eyes of the international community and thus aligned many of their decisions, particularly with regard to foreign policy, on the perceived need to step out from under West Germany's shadow. Thus it is hardly surprising that the UN mandate to observe Namibia's first free elections in 1989 was welcomed by the GDR's ruling elite. The opportunity of improving the GDR's international image was a compelling enough reason for sending National People's Army (NVA) officers, under the umbrella of the UN, to Namibia.[62] Hence, the GDR's international image remained a concern in the minds of the ruling elite right through until the collapse of the GDR in 1990. Ultimately, East Berlin's attempts to improve the GDR's international image were predestined to fail, for the GDR was largely built on pretence and thus ultimately collapsed under the weight of reality. The lingering discontent of the wider East German population could not be subdued, for it had its roots in the day-to-day reality of living under an oppressive regime. Lofty ideological concepts could not block out the tangible lack of fulfilment of human rights, correlated with the absence of self-determination.

Ostpolitik: The two German states' rivalry in Namibia

Between 1945 and 1991, West Germany's political landscape was dominated by two major parties, the Social Democratic Party (SPD) and the Christian Democratic Party (CDU), with its sister party, the Christian Social Union (CSU), and two minor parties, the Free Democratic Party (FDP). The Greens, a relatively new political party, entered the *Bundestag* in 1983.[63]

In 1969, Brandt implemented the policy of 'change through rapprochement', which became eventually known as *Ostpolitik* and signalled a sharp departure from the Hallstein Doctrine.[64] The policy was introduced to improve relations with the Soviet bloc, particularly with East Germany.[65] Yet, although Brandt indicated that Bonn was prepared to recognize

---

and the United States', in D. Junker (ed.), *The United States and Germany in the Era of the Cold War, 1945–1990,* Vol. 2, 1968–1990, Cambridge, Cambridge University Press, 2004, 305–306.

[62] BStU, MfS, HAI Nr. 13985, Vorgesehener Einsatz von Offizieren der NVA bei der UNO, 11.09.1989.

[63] All five parties were closely linked to foundations: the SPD to the Friedrich-Ebert Foundation; the CDU to the Konrad-Adenauer Foundation; CSU to the Hans-Seidel Foundation; the FDP to the Friedrich-Naumann Foundation and the Greens to the Heinrich Böll Foundation.

[64] Egon Bahr, the head of the planning staff of the Foreign Office, was the intellectual force behind *Ostpolitik.* Although Bahr did not invent *Ostpolitik*, he figured out how to put *Ostpolitik* into practice.

[65] For a wide-reaching analysis of *Ostpolitik*, see, e.g., E. Griffith, *The Ostpolitik of the Federal Republic of Germany,* Massachusetts, Cambridge, MIT Press, 1978; S. Tetsuji, *Ein Irrweg zur deutschen Einheit? Egon Bahrs Konzeptionen, die Ostpolitik und die KSZE 1963–1975,* Frankfurt am Main, Peter Lang GmbH, 2010.

the GDR as a sovereign state, he also strongly emphasised that East and West Germany were one nation. Hence, Brandt strongly stressed that 'the right to self-determination embodied in the Charter of the United Nations applies also to the German people'.[66] In stark contrast to the isolationist approach of the Hallstein Doctrine, *Ostpolitik* sought German unification by building bridges between East and West.[67] It was, therefore, crucial to gain Soviet support for *Ostpolitik*, not least for fear that rapprochement between Bonn and East Berlin would be wrongly interpreted as a conspiracy against Moscow.

In 1973, the implementation of the Basic Treaty, which emphasised the development of good neighbourly relations on the basis of equality, further improved diplomatic relations and cooperation between the two German states. Bonn recognised the GDR as a sovereignty, which paved the way for the two German states to become full members of the United Nations. Yet, the admission of the two German states into the United Nations did not necessarily change the dynamic between them. This was partly due to the fact that both states attempted to increase their political weight in the eyes of the international community. International platforms such as the UN gave both Germanys valuable political and diplomatic exposure, making it possible to demonstrate solidarity with Third World struggles and play an active role in the wider efforts to formulate and negotiate solutions.[68]

However, the wider reality of the Cold War needs to be considered here, which, in the case of West Germany, was significantly affected by the quest for German reunification. Although the division of Germany moved into the background in the 1970s, the political dynamics between the two states did not alter significantly. While East Germany intensified its effort to further underline and strengthen the GDR's sovereignty, independence and international standing, West Germany's ultimate aim remained the reunification of Germany.

Importantly, however, *Ostpolitik* and ultimately the Basic Treaty gave both German states greater freedom in their relations with African countries. The GDR experienced the most dramatic changes, for African countries were finally able to establish diplomatic relations with the GDR without having to fear reprisals from Bonn. Between 1970 and 1987, the

---

[66] Brandt strongly stressed that 'the right to self-determination embodied in the Charter of the United Nations applies also to the German people': Deutscher Bundestag, 6. Wahlperiode, 5. Sitzung, 28.10.1969, 21–31.

[67] The concept of 'building bridges between East and West through trade, exchange, aid and mutual trust' was developed by J.F. Kennedy and L.B. Johnson. In the late 1960s, E. Bahr and W. Brandt based *Ostpolitik* on similar ideas: A. Etges, 'Western Europe', in R. H. Immerman and P. Goedde (ed.), *The Oxford Handbook of the Cold War*, Oxford, Oxford University Press, 2013, 166–167.

[68] See also R. Hofmeier, 'Five decades of German-African relations: limited interests, low political profile and substantial aid donor', in U. Engel and R. Kappel (eds.), *Germany's Africa Policy Revisited: Interests, Images and Incrementalism*, Muenster, LIT, 2002, 45–55; Blumenau, *The United Nations*, 5.

number of Third World countries that established economic relations with the GDR grew from 23 to 64.[69] Yet, West German foreign policy towards Africa also benefitted from the developments after the implementation of *Ostpolitik*, as Genscher emphasised in retrospect: 'Our political activity in Africa did not have to focus any longer on inhibiting countries to maintain or assume relations with the GDR'.[70] Yet, although *Ostpolitik* removed many barriers and thus gave both German states greater freedom in their relations with African countries, clashes of interest between the two states in Africa became increasingly likely.

It would thus be naïve to assume that *Ostpolitik* eradicated most differences between East and West Germany. Although relations improved on many levels, it was nearly impossible to achieve détente in the realm of ideology.[71] The ideological rivalry between the communist East and the capitalist West was particularly intense in southern Africa, largely because of the region's strategic importance. Thus, the dynamics of Cold War rivalry for ideological supremacy, especially in countries engulfed in unpredictable independence struggles, provoked at times a volatile mixture of insecurities and hostilities between the two Germanys. Hence, southern Africa's liberation struggles provided considerable opportunity for conflict between East and West Germany, not least because the two Germanys stood at opposite ends of the ideological spectrum. After all, East-West rivalry in southern Africa had clear strategic and ideological underpinnings. Overall, the impossibility of achieving ideological rapprochement was a key factor that undermined trust between the two Germanys.

This can be explained, in part, by the following factors. First, the two German states were ideologically incompatible. After the Second World War, West Germany's prestige and significance was largely based on its growing status as one of the most successful capitalist economies. The GDR, on the other hand, derived its identity largely from its ideological commitment to Marxism-Leninism and thus its participation in the historical struggle against capitalism. Hence, the ideological differences between the two German states provided a breeding ground for populist rhetoric, confrontation, rivalry and distrust. Second, the GDR's ideological orientation played a central role in East Berlin's effort to distinguish

---

[69] Van der Heyden, 'GDR Development', 255. Overall, 19 countries recognized the GDR between 1969 and 1972. In the years following the signing of the Basic Treaty a further 68 countries recognized the GDR: G. Swain and N. Swain, *Eastern Europe since 1945*, New York, Palgrave Macmillan, 2009, 168. For further information on the success and failure of the Hallstein Doctrine in deterring Third World countries from developing diplomatic relations with the GDR and recognizing its sovereignty see Winrow, *The Foreign Policy*, 60–74.

[70] H.-D. Genscher, 'Germany's role in Namibia's independence', Genscher speech at the Humboldt University of Berlin, 13.04.2010, 53. Accessed online December 2015. Accessed online December 2015, available from: www.kas.de/upload/Publikationen/2014/namibias_foreign_relations/Namibias_Foreign_Relations_genscher.pdf

[71] See also M. J. Sodaro, *Moscow, Germany, and the West from Khrushchev to Gorbachev*, London, Cornell University Press, 1990, 228–231.

the GDR from West Germany. The division of Germany into two separate states did not obliterate the common history and culture of the pre-1945 unified German state. Thus, the cultural affinity between the two German states remained reasonably intact throughout the Cold War period. Undeniably, however, the GDR was ideologically distinct from both West Germany and the former unified Germany. Therefore, the GDR had little interest in becoming ideologically more compatible with West Germany, for East Berlin was determined to establish a distinct and independent German state.[72] Finally, ideology also helped to further East Berlin's perceived need to differentiate the GDR from West Germany in the eyes of the international community. In that regard, the GDR's ideological orientation served, inter alia, as a foreign policy compass. Thus, the GDR's solidarity with Third World nations struggling against capitalist exploitation, imperialism and racism supported East Berlin in its quest to establish the GDR on the international stage as profoundly different from West Germany.

Crucially, however, although *Ostpolitik* improved relations between the two Germanys, rivalry over influence in southern Africa continued to increase in the 1970s. Even though the GDR's influence grew in the region through solidarity with liberation movements, East Berlin's efforts to improve diplomatic relations in Africa remained largely unsuccessful during the early 1970s.[73] Bonn's success in undermining East Berlin's efforts to establish a foothold in Africa caused substantial frustration in East Berlin. This became increasingly evident in the GDR's campaign to discredit West Germany in Africa – a development the Foreign Office observed with considerable concern: 'The GDR's increasing propaganda and smear campaign, based on our economic and/or political relations to South Africa, Portugal and Rhodesia, has a detrimental effect on our relationship to Africa. This development must be counteracted'.[74]

However, the Foreign Office was not overly concerned about the GDR's solidarity with liberation movements, mainly because the communist bloc was not yet in an influential enough position to shape events in southern Africa. The Foreign Office concluded that 'communist attempts to thrust the African states on the road to revolution have so far failed'.[75] However, things started to intensify drastically after both German states' relationship with Namibia underwent significant changes in the late 1970s. Given the significance of these developments, this book will begin its analysis of West Germany's policy towards Namibia

---

[72] See also 'DDR: Das Millionen-Spiel', *Der Spiegel*, 1/1973, 01.01.1973; P. Bender, 'Kommunismus heute', *Der Spiegel*, 25/1977, 13.06.1977; 'Verlorene Zeit', *Der Spiegel*, 45/1980 03.11.1980; 'DDR: Wandel durch Abgrenzung?', *Der Spiegel*, 26/1982, 28.06.1982.

[73] PAAA, AV Neues Amt, Bd. 7897, 1969–1976, *Leitgedanken zur deutschen Afrika-Politik*, August 1973, 2.

[74] Ibid.

[75] Ibid., 4.

from the late 1970s onwards. This analysis will be organised by changes in policy set against the backdrop of the two German states competition for influence in Namibia.

Importantly, however, tensions between the two German states over Namibian issues continued mainly on a non-confrontational and overall intangible level. One reason for this was that West Germany's attitude towards the GDR's foreign policy was based on diplomatic prudence rather than confrontation. In the early 1970s, the Foreign Office outlined this approach in a *Gesamtplan für auswärtige Kulturpolitik*: 'Only where it is apparent that the GDR is looking for confrontation or displacement, it is necessary to counter with adequate methods'.[76] The aim was to move away from Adenauer's policy of confrontation and replace it with competition.[77] Furthermore, instead of focusing on differences between the two German states, the aim was to emphasise the historical and cultural commonalities.[78] However, considering that the GDR was actively trying to distinguish itself from West Germany, it seems hardly surprising that Bonn's change in approach towards East Berlin did not produce the desired results. In 1971 already, the Foreign Office reported to Brandt the following:

> The GDR doesn't want competition, but confrontation. Its totalitarian structures make it possible to concentrate quickly and effectively on areas that seem especially beneficial, particularly when it means to fight us. The GDR's weakness lies in the narrow direction of its foreign *Kulturpolitik*, because it avoids cultural exchange out of fear of outside interference. This situation needs to be exploited.[79]

Concerns over GDR advances in developing countries were real and mirrored Brandt's view of West Germany's challenges abroad. Already in 1969, Brandt argued in a letter to the then Finance Minister Franz-Josef Strauß that Berlin needed to counter GDR advances in developing countries: 'Our own endeavours are required, not least because the GDR translates its good specialist books into the languages of the world. If we don't want to lose difficult-to-reclaim terrain, especially in developing countries, we must intensify our efforts now'.[80] Yet, Brandt strongly emphasised competition over confrontation, which also became apparent in the fundamental idea behind *Ostpolitik*, namely to achieve change in socialist countries through rapprochement and not confrontation. Not surprisingly, therefore, Bonn was careful not to

---

[76] PAAA, Zwischenarchiv, Bd. 178680, 1974–1975, *Gesamtplan für Auswärtige Kulturpolitik*.
[77] See also H. Preisgert, 'Das Bonner Aschenputtel', *Die Zeit*, 09.10.1970.
[78] Leitsätze für die auswärtige Kulturpolitik, Dezember 1970, 7. Accessed October 2015, available from: www.ifa.de/fileadmin/pdf/aa/akbp_leitsaetze1974.pdf. See also PAAA, B1 Band 388, 1968–1972, 15 Thesen zur internationalen Kultur-, Wissenschafts- und Gesellschaftspolitik, 18.06.1970.
[79] PAAA, B 1 Band 388, 1968–1972, Erhöhung des Kulturhaushalts des Auswärtigen Amts, 12.03.1971, 6.
[80] Ibid., Brief Brandt an Strauß, 30.08.1969.

be drawn into a confrontational struggle with the GDR: 'Our attitude towards the GDR is based on the concept of active competition instead of confrontation'.[81]

East Berlin, on the other hand, was not overly concerned about confrontation with the other Germany in Third World countries. In fact, the GDR orientated itself on Bonn's presence abroad, aiming to establish ties that had the potential to undermine Bonn's position in the host country.

Instruments of Foreign Policy

In the 1970s, the Brandt government began to regard cultural exchange with Third World countries as a central pillar of foreign policy and thus also as a central aspect of the policy of détente.[82] In 1967, the significance of cultural exchange in foreign policy was vividly expressed by Brandt, the then Vice Chancellor and Foreign Minister of the 'grand coalition' between CDU/CSU and SPD: 'Our own endeavours for peace will be easier if we can trustworthily show the world our desire for peace. Foreign *Kulturpolitik* plays a significant role here'.[83] Brandt argued that cultural work abroad, that is, foreign *Kulturpolitik*, 'often can better win the trust and respect abroad, for the new Germany, then the utterances and actions of the government'.[84] The notion that soft power was potentially more effective than coercive power was a central aspect of Brandt's approach to foreign policy issues.

During the first two decades after the Second World War West Germany was understandably cautiously reserved when it came to overseas enterprises. In the late 1950s, West Germany slowly increased its influence around the world, and greater political weight was attached to cultural exchange abroad. Despite all this, foreign *Kulturpolitik* remained its own entity separate from the government's foreign policy. Still, a possible marriage between foreign *Kulturpolitik* and foreign policy seemed to develop an aura of inevitability in the late 1960s, and was finally approved when Brandt became chancellor in 1969. The SPD-led government, and subsequently *Ostpolitik* and *Kulturpolitik*, promoted a soft approach to foreign policy challenges, especially under circumstances that indicated a potential conflict with the Eastern bloc.

---

[81] Ibid., Leitgedanken für Ausführungen Staatssekretäre im Bundestagsausschuss für Bildung und Wissenschaft, 14.10.1970.
[82] PAAA, B1 Band 388, 1968–1972, 15 Thesen zur internationalen Kultur-, Wissenschafts- und Gesellschaftspolitik, 18.06.1970. It is also worth noting here that foreign *Kulturpolitik* was also viewed as a vehicle to improve West Germany's image and standing in the world: PAAA, B1 Band 388, 1968–1972, Leitgedanken für Ausführungen Staatssekretäre im Bundestagsausschuss für Bildung und Wissenschaft, 14.10.1970, 4.
[83] PAAA, B1 Band 388, 1968–1972, Entwurf Geleitworts BM für Jahresbericht Abt. IV, 1967/68.
[84] Ibid.

Suspicions of an underlying Western imperialist agenda remained, however, prevalent in Third World countries. Understandably perhaps, the two main ideological blocs tried to increase their influence through either direct interference or the establishment of alliance systems, which often generated resistance and scepticism in Third World countries – not least because Cold War rivalry divided the world along narrowly defined ideological lines: communism versus capitalism. Hence, in the 1980s, southern African countries increasingly tried to avoid alignment with either side. This line of thought was based on the principles and goals of the Non-Aligned Movement (NAM).

Although in theory the member states of the Non-Aligned Movement refused to enter the military and political alliances of the great bloc powers, the realities were much more complex. The objective was to avoid being pulled into new forms of subordination after the achievement of independence. Hence, newly independent states were careful not to align themselves to the political and military alliances of one of the two superpowers. The ultimate aim was national self-determination and freedom of action. In theory, non-aligned states did not accept any form of subordination to the leadership of another power. However, growing anti-Americanism by the vast majority of non-aligned states challenged the principles of non-alignment in the early 1970s. The American War in Vietnam promoted widespread support for the North Vietnamese pro-Communist and anti-American campaign, which was closely linked to the Soviet Union and the People's Republic of China.[85] Although the NAM was not a neutralist movement and thus encouraged active participation in world affairs, growing anti-American sentiments promoted increasingly strong ties to Eastern partners.[86] Therefore, it remains open to debate whether or not the polarizing nature of the Cold War undermined the principles and ideals of non-alignment in the 1970s and 1980s.

The South African apartheid regime was skilful in exploiting Cold War polarization. In order to ensure support from the capitalist West, Pretoria rarely missed an opportunity to emphasise the ANC and SWAPO's close relations with communist countries. Cold War paranoia made an unbiased dialogue between the West and southern Africa's liberation movements nearly impossible. Given that the majority of the non-white population supported the liberation struggle, winning over the hearts and minds of the black majority was, indeed, a challenge. With the African continent an ideological battleground of the Cold War, foreign policy towards southern Africa was never straightforward. The Cold War alliances, and subsequently polarization of the world, contributed not only to conflict on the African

---

[85] L. Lüthi, 'The Non-Aligned: Apart from and still within the Cold War', in N. Miskovic, H. Fischer-Tine and N. Boskovska (eds.) *The Non-Aligned Movement and the Cold War*, New York, Routledge, 2014.

[86] R. Petkovic, *Non-Alignment – An Independent Factor in the Democratization of International Relations*, Belgrade, STP, 1979, 16–25.

continent, it made it also difficult to find solutions for the most pressing issues of the era of decolonization.

West Germany's cultural exchange with South Africa and Namibia aroused considerable controversy, mainly because critics, including East Berlin, accused Bonn of assisting the structures of apartheid through cultural exchange.[87] In general, East and West Germany's *Kulturpolitik* was not a cause for serious conflict, although the presence of cultural institutions of both Germanys in a host country occasionally led to competitiveness, misunderstandings and tensions between the two states.[88] Namibia, however, was for both German states a special case, although the former German colony was perceived differently on either side of the Wall. Although there was no cultural exchange between the GDR and South Africa, and subsequently Namibia, the existence of cultural exchange between West Germany and South Africa was a cause for friction between the two German states.

Bonn's focus on a less confrontational exchange with the GDR grew significantly in importance during the Brandt era. Hence, the avoidance of confrontation became also observable in Bonn's position toward the GDR's involvement in Namibia. It is crucial to note, however, that East Berlin's relationship with Namibia was somewhat straightforward and one-dimensional, while West Germany's was encumbered by a complex set of political, economic, cultural and therefore historical considerations. In particular, the future of the approximately 30,000 Namibian Germans was a central concern of successive West German governments and the Foreign Office.[89] The GDR, on the other hand, was able to pursue a policy towards Namibia that was unburdened by most factors West Germany had to consider. Thus, concerns expressed by the German minority in Namibia did not affect East Berlin's solidarity with SWAPO.

The SPD-led government's emphasis on cultural exchange, *Kulturpolitik*, led, inter alia, to an increased focus on German citizens overseas.[90] Regions with a significant number of German immigrants could expect greater attention from the Foreign Office. Not surprisingly, therefore, in July 1970, the German Embassy in Windhoek emphasised in a letter to the Foreign Office that investment in cultural endeavours received wide approval in Namibia:

---

[87] See Wenzel, *Südafrika-Politik*, 89–93.
[88] O. Griese, Auswärtige Kulturpolitik und Kalter Krieg, Die Konkurrenz von Bundesrepublik und DDR in Finnland 1949–1973, Wiesbaden, Harrassowitz Verlag, 2006, 16.
[89] See, e.g., AAPD, 1977, Band I, Gespräch des Bundesministers Genscher mit dem amerikanischen UNO-Botschafter Young, 19.06.1977, 1005; PAAA, AV Neues Amt, Bd. 16413, Gespräch des UN-Kommissars für Namibia, Brajesh Chandra Mishra, am 31.01.1983 im Auswärtigen Amt, 02.02.1983; Deutscher Bundestag,10 Wahlperiode, Stenographischer Bericht, 54. Sitzung, 10.02.1984, 3865.
[90] See PAAA, B1 Band 388, 1968–1972, Grundsätze der auswärtigen Kulturpolitik; hier: Artikel des Herrn Ministers zu veröffentlichen im Bulletin, 03.12.1970.

In proportion to South-West Africa, it seems that a methodological diversification and refinement of our cultural information policy is less important than the fact that we represent the growing cultural credible 'we group' of the common cultural space, despite political reservations. In South-West Africa, our cultural self-expression, unlike in many other parts of the world, continues to be gratefully welcomed because the Afrikaans- and English-speaking population display appropriate openness and demand.[91]

The German Embassy had no illusions about the fact that cultural work could not simply be aligned to the receptiveness of the white minority, but had to recognise the wider political reality in Namibia: 'The black population would get the impression that we try, with this emphasised form of German self-representation, to overcome remnants of our political past, which could generate adverse effects'.[92] A report of the 'conference of the cultural attaché in Nairobi' (1974) was even more critical, leaving little doubt about Bonn's real dilemma in South Africa and Namibia:

> There is no real alternative to our policy toward South Africa. The margin for the cultural co-operation remains narrow and can only be extended with utmost caution. The possible impact on the apartheid and Namibia problem needs to be examined in each case. A possible improvement of our cultural commitment is dependent on the politics of South Africa. The promotion of German schools remains, in South Africa, a special case because of the strong number of German children there. The German element in Namibia does not in itself justify the strengthening of cultural contacts.[93]

Although Brandt's emphasis on a non-invasive exchange was potentially beneficial for deepening the exchange with the wider South African and Namibian black majority, South Africa's apartheid system presented a moral predicament for Bonn. The substantial number of Germans living in both African countries promoted, at times, a justification for strengthening cultural exchange and investment; the overall approach was, however, conservative and cautious. Nonetheless, the GDR viewed West Germany's *Kulturpolitik* as part of its imperial and neo-colonial agenda in Africa.[94] East Berlin expressed strict opposition to any form of cultural cooperation with West Germany, both in Germany and abroad.[95] The GDR believed

---

[91] PAAA, AV Neues Amt, Bd. 7959, 1959–1975, Betr.: Informierung über kulturelle Fragen, Windhuk, 27.07.1970.
[92] Ibid.
[93] PAAA, Zwischenarchiv, Bd. 178610, 1973–1974, Konferenz der Kulturattachés in Afrika vom 9. bis 11. September 1974, 24.09.1974, 4.
[94] H. Lindemann and K. Müller, *Auswärtige Kulturpolitik der DDR*, Bonn-Bad Godesberg, Verlag Neue Gesellschaft GmbH, 1974, 78–79.
[95] See PAAA, B1 Band 388, 1968–1972, Sitzung des Kulturpolitischen Beirats am Freitag, den 22. Januar 1971, 11.00 Uhr, im Restaurant Tulpenfeld, Ansprache des Herrn Ministers anlässlich der Sitzung des Kulturpolitischen Beirats, 15.01.1971, 3.

that West Germany used cultural exchange for the sole purpose of infiltrating Third World countries in order to subsequently promote change from within.[96] This could, for example, include the promotion of Western ideas and concepts in a socialist Third World country. The evidence seems to suggest that West Germany did indeed regard foreign *Kulturpolitik* as a tool to push back GDR's influence in the Third World.[97]

Importantly, however, East Berlin's perceived need to distinguish the GDR from West Germany must also be considered here. There was, of course, no denying that the two German states shared a common history, language and past culture, yet, East Berlin declared that 'the GDR's socialist culture has nothing in common with the imperialists' lack of culture'.[98] Thus, East Berlin's opposition to any form of cultural cooperation with Bonn was part of the GDR's desire to culturally dissociate itself from West Germany.[99] This also became apparent in the GDR's endeavour to disassociate itself from Namibia's German past and subsequently from any cultural commonalities with the Namibian Germans. For West Germany Namibia was not merely another African country. A deeply intertwined past with the former colony gave Namibia a special position in Bonn.[100]

Though Bonn kept a watchful eye on GDR activities on the African continent, and Namibia in particular, West Germany was in the early 1970s not overly concerned about East Berlin's policy towards Africa, as, for example, the report of the 'conference of the cultural attaché in Nairobi' (1974) indicates:

> So far the GDR is only sparsely present in Africa, but selectively very active. The cultural work of the GDR is ideologically pronounced, but also responsive to different local circumstances. The GDR's cultural policy is not aggressive towards us. There is a perception that the regime will not increase their cultural activities in Africa spontaneously, but acts with caution where there is an ideological or other positive starting point. In regards to the GDR, we can follow in Africa, with elevated attention, our previous general line.[101]

---

[96] See MfAA, ZR 2495/86, Abt. OZA /SA II, 1980–1982, Zu imperialistischen Aktivitäten im Bereich der kultur-wissenschaftlichen Zusammenarbeit mit der VR Angola, 16.03.1981.

[97] See PAAA, B1 Band 388, 1968–1972, Letter Brandt to Strauß, 30.05.1969, 4.

[98] Ibid., Sitzung des Kulturpolitischen Beirats am Freitag, den 22. Januar 1971, 11.00 Uhr, im Restaurant Tulpenfeld, Ansprache des Herrn Ministers anlässlich der Sitzung des Kulturpolitischen Beirats, 15.01.1971, 3.

[99] See PAAA, B1 Band 388, 1968–1972, Sitzung des Kulturpolitischen Beirats am Freitag, den 22. Januar 1971, 11.00 Uhr, im Restaurant Tulpenfeld, Ansprache des Herrn Ministers anlässlich der Sitzung des Kulturpolitischen Beirats, 15.01.1971. See also Lindemann and Müller, *Auswärtige Kulturpolitik*, 6.

[100] See, e.g., BPA-Nachrichtenabteilung, Interview Hans Dietrich Genscher, Bundesminister des Auswärtigen, zum Namibia-Problem, 11.10.1978; PAAA, Zwischenarchiv, Bd. 108202, 1975–1976, Haltung der Bundesregierung zur Erklärung der Windhuker Verfassungskonferenz, 18.08.1976.

[101] PAAA, Zwischenarchiv, Bd. 178610, 1973–1974, Konferenz der Kulturattaches in Afrika vom 9. bis 11. September 1974, 24.09.1974, 4.

Ideology played a central role in the GDR's cultural exchange with African countries, which helped to further underline the notion that the GDR was culturally distinct from West Germany. Obviously, cultural exchange played a strong role in the GDR's agenda to spread socialism throughout the world. *Kulturpolitik* supported East Berlin's foreign policy objectives. This was also true with respect to West Germany's foreign *Kulturpolitik* after 1969. As a central pillar of foreign policy, cultural exchange supported the advancement of West Germany's objectives abroad. However, throughout the Cold War era, Bonn followed a policy of non-intervention in Africa, which was based on the conviction that a country's internal conflicts needed to be resolved without foreign interference.[102] Cultural exchange was seen as one of the less invasive approaches for promoting change in African countries.[103] However, in stark contrast to the GDR, West Germany's foreign *Kulturpolitik* objectives included also emphasising the common cultural heritage of the two German states.[104]

From West Germany's perspective, the culture of the two German states remained fundamentally one. Therefore, the continuing competition between the two Germanys was for West Germany not necessarily taking place in the cultural realm but rather in the two states' diverging social order.[105] In short, both German states believed in the possibility of influencing societies to such a degree that the social order could be refined into either a capitalist or a communist society. Thus, culture contained in its broader context elements that promoted tension between the two German states, both domestically and abroad. The division of Germany into two separate states and its wider political, cultural and ideological implications need to be considered as a central cause for East and West German competition at the south-western tip of Africa. Therefore, this book examines some of the controversies surrounding West Germany's cultural relations with South Africa and Namibia in the late 1970s. However, as *Kulturpolitik* did not attempt to interfere directly in Namibia's internal affairs, the focus is on a more invasive foreign policy instrument, namely, non-governmental organisations (NGOs). To what extent did factions within the Federal Government attempt to influence Namibia's path to independence through NGOs in the 1980s?

West Germany's policy towards Namibia was, at the turn of the decade, strongly aligned with the efforts of the so-called Western Contact Group (WCG). In early 1977, three of the

---

[102] Ibid., Bd. 138103, 1984, Wirtschaftliche Zusammenarbeit mit Namibia vor der Unabhängigkeit, Anlage, 14.11.1984.

[103] For an in-depth assessment of the foreign *Kulturpolitik* of West Germany and the GDR, see Griese, *Auswärtige Kulturpolitik*.

[104] See also PAAA, B1 Band 388, 1968–1972, Sitzung des Kulturpolitischen Beirats am Freitag, den 22. Januar 1971, 11.00 Uhr, im Restaurant Tulpenfeld, Ansprache des Herrn Ministers anlässlich der Sitzung des Kulturpolitischen Beirats, 15.01.1971, 3.

[105] PAAA, B1 Band 388, 1968–1972, Erster Gesamtplan zur auswärtigen Kulturpolitik (1973–1976), 07.05.1973.

five permanent members of the UN Security Council (United States, France and the United Kingdom), plus two non-permanent members (Canada and West Germany), embarked on a diplomatic mission to end the deadlock over some of the most potentially explosive issues in southern Africa: apartheid, Rhodesia and Namibia.[106] The Five, as the WCG was also called, were among South Africa's closest allies, which seemed a promising constellation in terms of increasing pressure on Pretoria.[107] Thus, between 1977 and 1983, West Germany's involvement in solving the Namibia question took place predominantly within the wider framework of the WCG. In the broadest sense, the WCG was also an instrument of foreign policy, which promoted a concerted Western effort to resolve some of southern Africa's most pressing problems.

---

[106] On the WCG's role in Namibia's path to independence Hans-Joachim Vergau's book *Negotiating the Freedom of Namibia, The diplomatic achievement of the Western Contact Group* (Basel: Basler Afrika Bibliographien, 2010) should be consulted for an in-depth analysis. Vergau was the deputy permanent representative of Germany to the United Nations and the expert on Genscher's side in the WCG. Vergau's personal role in the WCG underlines the importance of his account.

[107] See Vergau, *Negotiating the Freedom*, 1.

2 Political Parties and SWAPO

This chapter examines the relationship between East and West German political parties and SWAPO. Attention will be given particularly to the divergent views of the different political parties with regard to the South West Africa People's Organisation (SWAPO), founded in 1960. Sam Nujoma, the president of SWAPO, was in 1962 the driving force behind the establishment of the party's military wing, the South West Africa Liberation Army (SWALA). After the International Court of Justice (ICJ) in The Hague repeatedly refused to declare South Africa's occupation of South West Africa illegal, SWAPO's leadership felt pushed towards one of the few remaining options: armed resistance. On 26 August 1966, SWAPO formally launched its armed struggle against South African occupation at Ongulumbashe near the Namibian-Angolan border. After South West Africa was officially renamed by the United Nations Namibia in 1968, SWAPO began to refer to its military wing as the Namibian People's Army (NPA). In 1973 it was renamed to the People's Liberation Army of Namibia (PLAN). For much of the 1970s and 1980s, SWAPO was forced underground, with its leadership coordinating the movements' armed resistance and diplomatic campaign from exile.[1]

West Germany

Social Democratic Party of Germany (SPD)

The SPD was originally a Marxist political party. In 1933, Adolf Hitler prohibited the SPD under the Enabling Act, which led to the imprisonment and murder of many SPD party officials.[2] After the Second World War, the SPD established itself as a moderate socialist party. The Social Democrats consisted of a traditional working-class constituency and held strong links with the trade unions. The SPD advocated policies that called for the fair distribution of wealth within society. In the 1970s, the SPD-led government took a relatively relaxed attitude towards the East-West Cold War rivalry in Africa, although it agreed with the notion that it was necessary to counter Soviet advances in southern Africa. The SPD argued that the previous CDU-led government's failure to engage in constructive dialogue with southern African states left liberation movements with no option but to seek help from the communist

---

[1] For a more detailed account of SWAPO, see L. Dobell, *Swapo's Struggle for Namibia, 1960–1991: War by Other Means*, Basel, P. Schlettwein Publishing, 2000.

[2] The Enabling Act gave Hitler the power to enact laws without the consolidation of the Reichstag.

bloc.³ Thus, in order to prevent SWAPO from moving even closer to Eastern bloc countries, the SPD grew increasingly comfortable with reaching out to liberation movements.⁴

In 1969, when the SPD gained power under the leadership of Willy Brandt, Bonn gradually altered its attitude towards liberation movements. The principles of 'change through rapprochement', as outlined in Brandt's *Ostpolitik*, represented a fundamental change in foreign policy. Thus, the question needs to be asked whether the political dynamics behind *Ostpolitik*, namely bridge building, influenced the SPD-led government's move towards SWAPO.⁵

In 1973 already, the SPD expressed solidarity with liberation movements and promised humanitarian assistance. In 1975, the SPD-led government demanded the end of minority rule and announced, supported by the *Bundestag*, its intention to provide aid to liberation movements for 'peaceful purposes', mainly in the field of education and for Namibian refugees.⁶ The overall attitude was, however, one of caution.⁷ During this period, the SPD related Friedrich Ebert Foundation (FES) was instrumental in establishing contacts with SWAPO, leading to a first meeting between Brandt and Sam Nujoma, the leader of SWAPO, in 1973.⁸ However, in 1975, after Helmut Schmidt replaced Brandt as chancellor, bad judgment on the part of the new foreign minister, Hans-Dietrich Genscher, threatened to destroy what little progress had been made. In 1975 he secretly met Andreas Shipanga, SWAPO's secretary of information. At the time, Shipanga and Nujoma were in a power struggle over the leadership of SWAPO, which generated the suspicion that Bonn was trying to divide and

---

3 See Deutscher Bundestag, Stenographischer Bericht, 54. Sitzung, 10.02.1984, 3866.
4 See, e.g., Ibid, 70. Sitzung, 03.12.1981, 4079; Brenke, *Die Bundesrepublik*, 163–164.
5 Bridge-building was encouraged by US President Lyndon Johnson in 1964. In the late 1960s, Bahr and Brandt translated the concept of bridge building into *Ostpolitik*.
6 Deutscher Bundestag, 8. Wahlperiode, Drucksache 8/1185, 52–53.
7 H. & L. Helbig, *Mythos Deutsch-Südwest, Namibia und die Deutschen*, Weinheim and Basel, Beltz Verlag, 1985, in G. Brenke, *Die Bundesrepublik*, 190. See also Deutscher Bundestag, 7. Wahlperiode, Stenographischer Bericht, 80. Sitzung. 15.02.1974, 5252. It is important to note here that Western countries, including West Germany, supported the UN Namibia Institute (UNNI) in Lusaka financially. The Institute was established in 1976 to provide Namibians with education that would give them the skills to administer an independent Namibia. SWAPO provided the main bulk of the institute's students.
8 See, e.g., PAAA, Zwischenarchiv, Bd. 138100, 1982–1984, Namibia-Initiative; hier: Nujoma-Besuch in Bonn, 27.05.1982; Deutscher Bundestag, 8. Wahlperiode, Drucksache 8/1185, 52–53. Nujoma visited West Germany for the first time in 1973: PAAA, Zwischenarchiv, Bd. 108202, 1975–1976, Namibia/Südwestafrika; hier: Maßnahmen, die geeignet sind, der afrikanischen Kritik an unserer Haltung entgegenzuwirken, 10.07.1979, 17. In January 1978, during a visit to southern Africa, Brandt and SWAPO met again: PAAA, Zwischenarchiv, Bd. 116802, 1977–1978, Afrika-Reise einer Delegation des SPD Parteivorstands, 20.11.1978.

ultimately destroy SWAPO.⁹ Nujoma even went so far as to brand West Germany 'the archenemy of the Namibian people'.¹⁰

In an attempt to defuse tensions between Bonn and SWAPO, Hans Jürgen Wischnewski (SPD), a state secretary in the Foreign Office, recognised SWAPO as the sole representative of the Namibian people, which was in accordance with the UN General Assembly declaration in 1973.¹¹ Nonetheless, the SPD still voted against giving SWAPO permanent observer status at the UN.¹² Thus, perhaps not unexpectedly, relations between the SPD-led government and SWAPO remained cool.

In 1976, in the face of Pretoria's scheming in Namibia, the SPD-led government stated that it sought to work, in an independent Namibia, with all political parties, 'of which SWAPO will probably play the most important role'. The Federal Government also expressed regret that its 'relations with SWAPO were still burdened by misunderstandings and obstacles'.¹³ In early 1977, Egon Bahr (SPD), the Federal Minister for Special Affairs, offered to establish contact between SWAPO and the Federal Government. The proposal remained unanswered.¹⁴ Despite all this, evidence clearly indicates that, under the surface, some trusting relationships emerged between high-ranking members of the government and SWAPO in the mid-to-late 1970s.

By October 1976, the Foreign Office was actively trying to engage in conversation with the SWAPO leadership through the Foreign Minister of Zambia. Despite SWAPO's defensive attitude, the Foreign Office continued to seek ways in which to engage SWAPO.¹⁵ In this respect, the upcoming Socialist International (SI) in Lusaka in March 1977 was viewed as a potentially favourable platform for approaching the liberation movement. The SI was a political platform that blurred the boundaries between capitalism and communism, for it brought together people with a wide range of ideologies under the banner of socialism. However, the venue seemed ideal mainly because Nujoma had expressed his 'deep respect'

---

9   See also S. Nujoma, *Where Others Wavered: The Autobiography of Sam Nujoma*, London, Panaf Books, 2001, 246.
10 Bley/Schleicher, 'Deutsch-Deutsch-Namibische', 278–282.
11 For more information about the United Nations role in the Namibian independence struggle, see J. Krasno, 'Namibian Independence: A UN Success Story', in I. Shapiro and J. Lampert (eds.), *Charter of the United Nations*, London, Yale University Press, 2014, 174–191.
12 Engel, *Die Afrikapolitik*, 157.
13 PAAA, Zwischenarchiv, Bd. 108202, 1975–1976, Haltung der Bundesregierung zur Erklärung der Windhuker Verfassungskonferenz, 18.08.1976.
14 Bley/Schleicher, 'Deutsch-Deutsch-Namibische', 280.
15 The objective was, as outlined by the Foreign Office, 'to reduce the at times hostile distance between us [the Federal Government] and SWAPO': PAAA, Zwischenarchiv, Bd. 116841, 1977–1978, Hausbesprechung unter der Leitung des Herrn Ministers am 21. Januar 1976, 04.01.1977.

for Brandt, who had become the President of the SI in late 1976.[16] Ultimately, Brandt used the SI to express his own views, not necessarily to engage SWAPO, but seemingly to challenge Bonn's attitude towards SWAPO.

In November 1978, Brandt argued at the SI in Vancouver that 'it can sometimes be necessary to use violence against regimes that live by violence'.[17] It should come as no surprise that the statement inflamed the opposition's passion. Friedrich Zimmerman, the deputy chairman of CDU/CSU, would even go so far as to discredit Brandt's foreign policy success: 'Statements like this ought to be understood by terrorists as a justification [for armed struggle] ... Brandt is an unworthy Nobel Peace Prize holder and should return the award'.[18] Although Brandt expressed already in February 1978 that he would like to see SWAPO in power, the rhetoric remained conservative until Vancouver.[19]

Wischnewski, who accompanied Brandt to Vancouver, was more in line with the government's official position, stating that 'those organisations [liberation movements] need our protection, so that they are not discriminated against and simply labelled as communist organisations'.[20] However, Wischnewski also promised the ANC and other liberation movements' political and humanitarian support.[21] Though Wischnewski assured the press that his position was 'not at all in disagreement with German policy', evidence seems to suggest that Bonn's position was not as straightforward.[22]

Even though Brandt was no longer chancellor in 1978, as the head of the SPD and president of the SI, he was still in a position of significant political influence. Wischnews-

---

[16] PAAA, Zwischenarchiv, Bd. 116841, 1977–1978, Hausbesprechung unter der Leitung des Herrn Ministers am 21. Januar 1976, 04.01.1977.

[17] Ibid, Bd. 116840, 1977–1978, Gespräch StS van Well mit Vertretern des Parteivorstandes der SPD am 10. November 1978; hier: angebliche Äußerung von StM Wischnewski und Willy Brandt auf der Sozialistische Internationale in Vancouver, 09.11.1978. Importantly, Brandt continued to make similar statements in the 1980s. For example, he argued in 1980 that 'after numerous desperate attempts to drive forward reforms, the people of South Africa had no other option but to resort to counter violence': B. Loff, 'Wer den falschen Eingang benutzt, wird barsch zurechtgewiesen', *Frankfurter Rundschau*, 24.03.1986. During his last visit to South Africa in 1988, Brandt more or less repeated his Vancouver statement, arguing that 'obstinate resistance' was justifiable against an apparatus of oppression. See, e.g., W. Brandt, 'Die Apartheid muss überwunden werden', SPD im Deutschen Bundestag, 13.06.1988; H. Schreitter-Schwarzenfeld, 'Brandt: Mit Zureden ist in Südafrika nichts zu erreichen', *Frankfurter Rundschau*, 14.06.1988; 'Brandt: Ruf nach Sanktionen nicht überhörbar', *Unsere Zeit*, 14.06.1988.

[18] PAAA, Zwischenarchiv, Bd. 116840, 1977–1978, Report 132/2.

[19] Brenke, *Die Bundesrepublik*, 192. See also BStU, MfS-HA II, Nr. 28977, Südafrikanische Volksorganisation (SWAPO) von Namibia, [no date], 169.

[20] PAAA, Zwischenarchiv, Bd. 116840, 1977–1978, Speech Wischnewski Socialist International, 5.

[21] 'Ein Schritt voraus', *Der Spiegel*, 46/1978, 13.11.1978.

[22] PAAA, Zwischenarchiv, Bd. 116840, 1977–1978, SPD Pressekonferenz Nr. 123/78, 6.11.1978; 'Eklat um Ecevit: würden sie Pinochet aufnehmen', *Frankfurter Allgemeine Zeitung*, 15.11.1978.

ki, who was Helmut Schmidt's close friend and crisis manager, established himself as a political heavyweight in the 1970s.[23] He was Minister of State at the Federal Chancellery from 1976 to 1979, where he was also responsible for relations with the GDR. Therefore, although neither Brandt nor Wischnewski represented the SPD at the SI, the political significance cannot be underestimated, not least because of the political status and influence of both men. Ultimately, Brandt only put into words what many in West Germany had been thinking for a while. Though Brandt had met Nujoma in 1973, and the SPD-affiliated FES had cultivated good relations with SWAPO since the early 1970s, Vancouver was the first time that a high-ranking member of the *Bundestag* publicly expressed understanding for SWAPO's armed struggle. Wischnewski had already criticised the government's policy on South Africa for being 'too hesitant' before Vancouver, but it was the global platform of the SI that provided the necessary political weight to call into question Bonn's attitude towards SWAPO.[24]

No wonder, therefore, that the GDR viewed the SI as a platform that tried to 'ideologically manipulate' African states and movements; an organisation that attempted to 'put illusions' into SWAPO.[25] From the GDR's perspective, it was disturbing to observe that influential political personalities of the class enemy presented views that were not unlike those of the socialist SED.[26] The GDR viewed the SI as an instrument of ideological manipulation. That Brandt made additional efforts to contact Nujoma via written correspondence was viewed as part of the SPD's broader effort to exert influence over SWAPO.[27] SWAPO had no difficulty in believing that the SPD actively tried to gain influence over it through the SI.[28]

In West Germany, however, for those at the forefront of negotiations with Pretoria, Vancouver represented a leadership challenge. The Foreign Office showed little sympathy for Brandt and Wischnewski's solo actions. Wischnewski interpreted Genscher's criticism as the defence of a failing status quo: 'The party goes a step forward – that should be allowed'.[29]

---

[23] Brandt remained Schmidt's close advisor after 1979 and continued an advisory role under Kohl in 1982.
[24] 'Ein Schritt voraus', *Der Spiegel*, 46/1978, 13.11.1978.
[25] PAAA, MfAA, ZR 1133/87, 1976–1985, Vermerk über ein Gespräch mit dem Sekretär des sowjetischen afro-asiatischen Solidartätskomitees, Genossen Schubin, 17.10.1977. See also PAAA, MfAA, ZR 439/86, 1976–1981, Abt. Auslandsinformation, Konzeption für die auslandsinformatorische Arbeit der DDR gegenüber den sozialistisch orientierten Ländern Afrikas und im arabischen Raum, 19.01.1981.
[26] Obviously, the SPD was a socialist party, but operated within a capitalist context.
[27] BStU, MfS-ZAIG Nr. 6147, Zu neuen BRD-Aktivitäten gegenüber der 'Südwestafrikanischen Volksorganisation von Namibia' (SWAPO), 27.06.1980.
[28] PAAA, MfAA, ZR 2765/84, 1977–1984, Vermerk Gespräch mit Genossen O.T. Emvula, Leiter der Vertretung der SWAPO in der DDR am 07.11.1980.
[29] 'Ein Schritt voraus', *Der Spiegel*, 46/1978, 13.11.1978.

Critics within the SPD accused Genscher of 'considering at every step the Namibian with a German passport'.³⁰ In their view, this would ultimately 'evoke multi-layered problems' for West Germany in post-independent Namibia, for signs pointed towards a SWAPO-led Namibia.³¹ Ultimately, Vancouver led to a meeting between Günther van Well, Secretary of the State in the Foreign Office, and an executive committee of the SPD.³² Seemingly irritated, van Well stressed that Genscher had made it clear that Bonn sought talks with liberation movements 'in order to convince them to abandon violence and strive for peaceful change, not to strengthen their will to use violence'.³³ Evidently, the Foreign Office and Genscher were frustrated that they had not been consulted beforehand. In October 1978, Genscher tried to negotiate a date for Namibia's first free elections with Pretoria and it is probably reasonable to assume that Genscher's failure to come to an agreement with Pretoria compromised his objectivity towards Brand's statements in Vancouver. It seems, therefore, that Genscher was more frustrated about Pretoria's stubbornness in the face of his efforts to negotiate a solution to problems afflicting Namibia than about Brandt's statement concerning the liberation struggles in southern Africa.³⁴ In fact, Genscher agreed widely with the SPD's changing attitude towards SWAPO. Even before Brandt expressed his understanding for the African armed struggle, Genscher came close to expressing similar views during a *Bundestag* debate in 1977:

> In order to find a peaceful solution in southern Africa we promote there, as everywhere, the renunciation of force. We are, however, concerned that our demand is seen by increasing numbers of the black majority as disguised support of racial

---

[30] Importantly, however, these accusations do not stand up to scrutiny, for Namibian Germans did not feel represented by Genscher's policy towards Namibia in 1978: 'Bei den Gemäßigten gilt Genscher als Feind Nummer eins', *Münchner Merkur*, 16.10.1978.

[31] BStU, MfS-ZAIG Nr. 8357, Informationen über einige Tendenzen in der Afrika-Politik der BRD, 06.10.1978. The report stated that Genscher 'was fighting for his political survival and his foreign policy focused on the electorate'. Thus, in this view, Genscher did not focus on whatever strategy seemed to present the best long-term approach to Namibia, but on ensuring that he would receive political credit for his efforts in Namibia.

[32] PAAA, Zwischenarchiv, Bd. 116840, 1977–1978, Gespräch StS van Well mit Vertretern des Parteivorstandes der SPD am 10. November 1978; hier: angebliche Äußerung von StM Wischnewski und Willy Brandt auf der sozialistischen Internationale in Vancouver, 09.11.1978. See also 'Ein Schritt voraus', *Der Spiegel*, 46/1978, 13.11.1978.

[33] Ibid, 2–3. It is worth noting here that the *Bundestag* motivated the government to use all its resources to stop further 'bloodshed' in southern Africa: Deutscher Bundestag, 8. Wahlperiode, Drucksache 8/1185, 14.11.1977, 52–53.

[34] In fact, Genscher praised Wischnewski's efforts in Namibia retrospectively, particularly his commitment to solve the controversy over the West German consulate in Windhoek: H.-D. Genscher, 'Germany's Role in Namibia's Independence', Genscher speech Humboldt University of Berlin, April 2010, 55. Accessed online December 2015, available from: www.kas.de/upload/Publikationen/2014/namibias_foreign_relations/Namibias_Foreign_Relations_genscher.pdf

discrimination, because the white minority does not show any willingness for fast and drastic change.³⁵

Ultimately, Genscher acknowledged that in the face of the white minorities' reluctance to change the status quo, it was unrealistic to demand the renunciation of violence from the black majority.³⁶

Before Brandt's Vancouver speech, Genscher had tried to drive forward the Foreign Office's initiative to improve relations with SWAPO. In early 1978, Genscher spoke in private with Nujoma on the side-lines of talks between SWAPO and the WCG in New York. The post-meeting report by the Foreign Office stated that Kenneth Kaunda, the President of Zambia, called on Nujoma 'to do the first step towards improving relations with the Federal Government'. The report concluded that given SWAPO's 'hostile comments' in the past and that practically no official contact existed prior to the meeting, it was 'remarkable' that the meeting took place in a 'friendly, almost warm atmosphere'.³⁷ That Genscher invited Nujoma to come to Bonn further underlined the positive undertone of their first private meeting.³⁸ Moreover, it also indicated that Genscher was eager to wipe the slate clean and start anew after the crisis over his meeting with Shipanga in 1975.

In 1978, little more than a month after Nujoma's Bonn visit, Hans-George Stelzer, the former SPD ambassador, and Gerhard O. Kleinstes, SPD advisor for international relations, met SWAPO representatives in Lusaka.³⁹ However, neither Genscher nor the Foreign Office was informed by the SPD of the steps it was taking. Yet, the meeting was positive enough to

---

[35] PAAA, Zwischenarchiv, Bd. 116840, 1977–1978, Gespräch StS van Well mit Vertretern des Parteivorstandes der SPD, 09.11.1978. The intention to strive towards dialogue with SWAPO was also grounded in the Foreign Office's changing perception of the liberation struggle, based on the acknowledgment that 'those who resist peaceful change through violence and oppression provoke violence by the oppressed': Ibid, Hausbesprechung unter der Leitung des Herrn Ministers am 21. Januar 1976, 04.01.1977.

[36] Ultimately, Genscher's view was in line with the Foreign Office's position in the late 1970s: PAAA, Zwischenarchiv, Bd. 116841, 1977–1978, Hausbesprechung unter der Leitung des Herrn Ministers am 21 January 1976, 04.01.1977.

[37] AAPD, 1978, Band I, Begegnung Bundesminister – Sam Nujoma, Präsident der SWAPO, in New York am 12.02.1978, 20.02.1978, 273–276; Ibid, Namibia-Initiative; hier: Ministergespräche der Fünf mit Südafrika und SWAPO, 12.02.1978.

[38] Upon his return from New York, Genscher informed Brandt about the invitation, and that the Friedrich-Ebert or Friedrich-Nauman Foundation would be available to host Nujoma's visit: AAPD, 1978, Band I, Begegnung Bundesminister – Sam Nujoma, Präsident der SWAPO, in New York am 12.02.1978, 20.02.1978, 276. In mid-1978, the Foreign Office also encouraged further talks with SWAPO. See AAPD, 1978, Band II, Aufzeichnung des Ministerialdirigenten Gorenflos, 08.08.1978, 1193.

[39] The meeting was arranged to test the waters with SWAPO before agreeing to officially meet ten days later.

encourage the SPD to proceed with plans to officially meet with SWAPO.[40] When Genscher asked questions about the exact purpose of the SPD delegation's consultation with SWAPO, he only received 'evasive answers', the Foreign Office noted, clearly irritated.[41] Although both the Foreign Office and the SPD expressed in the late 1970s the opinion that it was necessary to improve relations with SWAPO, the SPD did not necessarily push the Foreign Office into achieving such objectives. Hence, given that the SPD had bypassed the Foreign Office in its efforts to engage with SWAPO, it is reasonable to conclude that the exclusion of the Foreign Office from the decision-making process contributed to Genscher's disapproving attitude.

The SPD's first official meeting with SWAPO, under the leadership of Wilhelm Roth, chairman of the committee for developmental policy questions, took place in Zambia in November 1978, shortly after Brandt's Vancouver speech. Probably more than anything else, the meeting showed that the GDR had considerable influence over SWAPO, for East Berlin had cautioned SWAPO against relations with West Germany. Hence, SWAPO was concerned that closer relations with the SPD were explicitly linked to demands with regard to its relationship with the GDR. The delegation, however, made it clear that there was no interest in interfering in SWAPO's internal affairs.[42] Furthermore, Roth promised SWAPO humanitarian aid in the educational and social field, which confirmed promises made by Wischnewski at the SI.[43] The SPD delegation concluded that the Federal Government should seek out contacts with SWAPO in order to keep the liberation movement from drifting further towards Moscow. The group based its recommendation also on the impression that SWAPO was not 'unequivocally fixed towards Marxism'.[44]

However, there were some indications that a move towards SWAPO was not as straightforward as it might have seemed at the time. In June 1978, the West German Embassy in Lusaka reported to the Foreign Office, after a meeting with an unnamed SWAPO member who had received a scholarship from the SPD-affiliated FES, that 'SWAPO was currently not interested in a political rapprochement or co-operation with the Federal Government

---

[40] PAAA, Zwischenarchiv, Bd. 116802, 1977–1978, Gespräche einer Delegation des SPD-Parteivorstandes mit SWAPO, 10.11.1978.
[41] Ibid.
[42] Ibid, Bd. 116802, 1977–1978, Afrika-Reise einer Delegation des SPD Parteivorstands, 20.11.1978. After Genscher's meeting with Nujoma in early 1978, the Foreign Office assumed that the GDR had prompted SWAPO to adopt a cautious attitude vis-à-vis Bonn. See AAPD, 1978, Band I, Begegnung Bundesminister – Sam Nujoma, President der SWAPO, am 12.02. 1978, 20.02.1978, 276.
[43] See also 'Ein Schritt voraus', *Der Spiegel*, 46/1978, 13.11.1978.
[44] PAAA, Zwischenarchiv, Bd. 116802, 1977–1978, Afrika-Reise einer Delegation des SPD Parteivorstands, 20.11.1978.

because it could lead to difficulties with the Soviets and their allies, who are the only ones that supply SWAPO with weapons'.[45] Thus, SWAPO would continue to occupy such a position as long as it was embroiled in an armed struggle against foreign occupation, as the SWAPO cadre explained further. Consequently, SWAPO had 'to pay lip service to Marxism-Leninism', although there was little commitment to such 'complex and difficult to understand theories'. Hence, in the final analysis, he came to the conclusion that 'any endeavour to establish closer ties with SWAPO was bound to fail'.[46] Thus, all of this indicated that the SPD-led government was bound to face substantial challenges from the GDR in its endeavour to improve relations with SWAPO.[47]

In summary, it has become apparent that the SPD and the Foreign Office were in some kind of struggle for dominance with regard to West Germany's policy towards Namibia. Given that Genscher was also the head of the FDP in a SPD/FDP coalition government, it was likely that policy disagreements would produce some rivalry between the coalition partners. In the Schmidt-Genscher government there had been disagreements about the most effective way to continue *Ostpolitik*.[48] With regard to Genscher's attempt to gain Pretoria's support for free elections in Namibia, the newsmagazine *Der Spiegel* assumed that Genscher's objective was to 'make his mark in a chancellor-like manner as a crisis manager'.[49]

Furthermore, it seems reasonable to assume that the South African airborne assault on a SWAPO base in Angola in May 1978, contributed to both Brandt's open sympathy for SWAPO's armed resistance and the government's push towards improving relations with the liberation movement. Although Cassinga did not receive much attention in the *Bundestag*, the atrocity, which killed and wounded more than 500 SWAPO combatants and civilians, led to a further deterioration of attitude vis-à-vis Pretoria.[50]

Additionally, in 1971, Angostinho Neto, the head of the People's Movement for the Liberation of Angola (MPLA), had approached the SPD-led government for support in the liberation war against Portugal. Bonn declined the MPLA's request, except for Wischnewski

---

[45] Ibid., Bd. 116802, 1977–1978, Gespräch mit SWAPO-Vertreter, Lusaka, 15.06.1978.
[46] Ibid.
[47] After Genscher's meeting with Nujoma in early 1978, the Foreign Office came to a similar conclusion, stating that the GDR had prompted SWAPO to adopt a cautious attitude vis-à-vis Bonn. See AAPD, Band I, 1978, Begegnung Bundesminister – Sam Nujoma, President der SWAPO, am 12.02. 1978, 20.02.1978, 276.
[48] A. Pittman, *From Ostpolitik to Reunification: West German-Soviet Political Relations since 1974*, Cambridge, Cambridge University Press, 1992, 41.
[49] 'Ein Schritt voraus', *Der Spiegel*, 46/1978, 13.11.1978.
[50] Cassinga was mentioned only twice in the Bundestag (1978 and 1989): Deutscher Bundestag, 8. Wahlperiode, Stenographischer Bericht, 100. Sitzung, 22.06.1978, 7968; Ibid, 11. Wahlperiode, Stenographischer Bericht, 164. Sitzung, 05.10.1989, 12433. Cassinga was seen as an attempt by Pretoria to undermine the willingness of SWAPO to agree to UN-monitored elections.

who was in favour of supporting the MPLA. Neto eventually found a willing supporter in the Soviet Union, and steered his country on a communist course after independence. Horst Ehmke, the deputy party leader of the SPD, made it clear that it was in West Germany's interest to prevent Namibia from following the same path: 'We have learnt from our Angola mistakes'.[51]

Thus, a complex set of factors motivated the SPD-led government to improve relations with SWAPO in the late 1970s. However, it seems safe to conclude that progressive thinkers, such as Brandt, Bahr and Wischnewski, had not only been behind West Germany's rapprochement with the Eastern bloc countries, but had also been the driving force behind the government's move towards SWAPO. Brandt and Bahr's strategic concept of change through rapprochement was based on bridge-building, which ultimately improved relations with both the GDR and SWAPO. Obviously, ideology, a major hurdle to good relations, was not given much importance, as will be discussed in the next chapter.

Importantly, however, there is no evidence to suggest that the SPD's move towards SWAPO was propelled forward by the establishment of the WCG. The SPD's gradual improvement of relations with SWAPO began before the establishment of the WCG in 1977. However, given that the WCG was led by the foreign ministers of the five member countries, it seems reasonable to assume that the rivalry between the Foreign Office and the SPD was a factor that motivated the Schmidt government to intensify its involvement in Namibia. That Genscher and the Foreign Office were repeatedly excluded from the SPD's initiatives in Namibia seems to support this assertion. Ultimately, however, the combined efforts of various SPD members, the SPD-government as a whole and the Foreign Office laid the groundwork for better relations between SWAPO and West Germany. In the early 1980s, Genscher voiced his conviction that diplomatic engagement and not political isolation changed SWAPO's attitude: 'SWAPO was very radical but changed and moderated its position during the process of integration into international talks'.[52] That the initiatives for better relations coming from within the Federal Government brought about a favourable change in SWAPO's attitude, albeit variable and unstable, confirmed the value of engagement with SWAPO.[53] In 1981, Brandt promised Nujoma that the SPD would use its influence to advance Namibia's independence. True to Brandt's promise, the SPD's efforts increased in the early 1980s, but lost momentum after the SPD-led government was removed from power in October 1982.

---

[51] 'Ein Schritt voraus', *Der Spiegel*, 46/1978, 13.11.1978.
[52] AAPA, 1983, Band II, Ministerialdirigent Schauer, z. Z. Helsinki an das Auswärtige Amt; Betreff: BM-Besuch in Helsinki, 03.11.1983, 1616–1620.
[53] See also Ibid., 1616–1620.

Free Democratic Party (FDP)

Formed in 1948, the FDP was essentially an amalgam of several liberal parties from the Weimar era. Consequently, the Free Democrats represented a liberal and politically progressive party line. From 1961 to 1983, only three political parties were represented in the West German parliament, the *Bundestag*: the SPD, the CDU/CSU and the much smaller FDP.

By the time of Namibia's independence in 1990, Hans Dietrich Genscher was the Western world's longest serving Foreign Minister (1974–1992). For the most part, the FDP supported the Namibia-policy of its chairman and head of the Foreign Office. However, Genscher at times faced strong opposition from both inside and outside his party, particularly in the 1980s. The critics of Genscher's approach to the Namibia question generally followed two principal lines of arguments. One set of critics painted a picture of Genscher as unassertive and cautious, to the point of pusillanimity, in his engagement with Pretoria.[54] The other accused Genscher of gradually subordinating his 'claim for a genuine West German Namibia policy' to the Reagan administration's approach to the Namibia question.[55] But these arguments only partially stand up to scrutiny as criticism of Genscher's approach towards the Namibia problem had its origins in more general causes. Essentially, most arguments against the foreign minister were closely linked to the two main issues that hindered rapid progress in Namibia. First, there was a general reluctance of Western powers to challenge South Africa seriously throughout the 1970s and 1980s. Second, the Western powers were willing to accept a subordinate role to US-leadership in the Namibia question, particularly in the 1980s. It is therefore not surprising that even his critics had to concede that Genscher was 'accepted as an honest broker and person of high moral integrity' in his negotiations with SWAPO.[56]

In more general terms, Genscher's approach to the Namibia question was never aimed at forcing Pretoria to release its grip on Namibia, for Genscher took the view that 'only free and fair elections, involving all relevant political powers, can bring about lasting peace'.[57] In other words, Namibia could only become truly independent from South Africa by means

---

[54] See AGG, Petra Kelly, Akte: 1473, Brief Kelly an Genscher, 13.01.1986.
[55] See, e.g., H. Melber, 'Federal Republic of Germany and Namibia, West German support to continued Occupation – with special reference to the Ministry for Economic Cooperation', paper submitted on the behalf of the Anti-Apartheid-Movement in the Federal Republic of Germany on occasion of EC-summit, December 4th and 5th, *Anti-Apartheid-Movement* (AAM), 1987; H. Melber, 'Namibia-Politik: Umgang mit einer "historischen" Hypothek', *Frankfurter Rundschau*, 22.06.1987.
[56] See Melber, 'Federal Republic', 8.
[57] AAPD, 1980, Band I, Genscher-Nujoma Gespräch in Salisbury, 17.04.1980, 634. See also PAAA, AV Neues Amt, Bd. 16413, 1983, Brief Genscher an Heinz Georg Binder, President of the Ecumenical Commission for Church and Society in the European Communities.

of a democratically organised political process.⁵⁸ On this basis, Genscher believed in West Germany's moral obligation to assist peoples under colonial rule or foreign domination to exercise their rights to self-determination and independence, as declared in General Assembly resolution 1514 (XV).⁵⁹ Genscher's strong commitment to finding a negotiated solution to Namibian independence raises questions about his personal motives.

Genscher became foreign minister under Helmut Schmidt, who claimed foreign policy responsibility for both West Germany's relations with its Western allies and its policy towards the Eastern bloc. Thus, Genscher had limited options for leaving a mark in his new role as foreign minister in the mid-1970s.⁶⁰ However, the Namibia question and the growing crisis in southern Africa generated considerable national and international interest. Thus, it seems reasonable to suppose that Genscher saw potential opportunities in southern Africa to establish himself as foreign minister and leave a mark in foreign policy.⁶¹ In that regard, Genscher benefited greatly from West Germany's new membership in the UN, for it offered a platform for exposure at an international level and allowed him to actively participate in world affairs. Perhaps understandably, therefore, the formation of the WCG was welcomed by Genscher. Some critics have argued that Genscher hoped to 'make a name for himself as an attorney of African interests'.⁶² However, there is no reason to discredit Genscher's commitment in seeking a solution to the question of Namibia's independence. Behind his personal objectives lay an unquestionable belief in the right of national self-determination and a strong disapproval of apartheid. Within this context, Genscher probably also viewed his commitment in the Namibia-Initiative as an opportunity to give his party a 'liberal Africa profile', as Engel points out.⁶³

---

⁵⁸ See also PAAA, AV Neues Amt Bd. 16413, 1983, Genscher statement at the Namibia debate of the Security Council, 26.05.1983.
⁵⁹ General Assembly resolution 1514 (XV) of 14 December 1960: Declaration on the Granting of Independence to Colonial Countries and People. See also Genscher, 'Germany's role in Namibia's', 54–55. At the Humboldt University, Genscher stated the following: 'We claimed the right of self-determination for us Germans in order to reunite peacefully. How could we have denied the right of self-determination to the Namibian people?'
⁶⁰ Genscher occupied the post of interior minister from 1969 to 1974. Genscher became foreign minister under Helmut Schmidt in 1974. For more information about Genscher and his foreign policy approaches, see K. Brauckhoff und I. Schwartz (eds.), Hans-Dietrich Genschers Außenpolitik, Wiesbaden, Springer, 2015.
⁶¹ Telephone interview with Klaus Freiherr von der Ropp, 28.04.2016. Klaus Freiherr von der Ropp, an expert on West Germany's relations with South Africa, was an active observer of the events in southern Africa during the Cold War. See also Brenke, *Die Bundesrepublik*, 71; Engel, *Die Afrikapolitik*, 159.
⁶² 'Genscher's Namibia-Politik', Namibia Information Office, Nr. 24, Januar 1984. See also PAAA, Zwischenarchiv, Bd. 125282, 1981, Eine afrikanische Lösung für Namibia? Die deutsche Namibia Politik nach Genf, Volker Stolz, 14.02.1981.
⁶³ Engel, *Die Afrikapolitik*, 159.

The foreign minister's opinion about Pretoria was undoubtedly shaped during his early years at the helm of the Foreign Office. It seems reasonable to suggest that his first meeting with the South African Prime Minister Balthazar Johannes Vorster and Foreign Minister Hilgard Muller in Bonn set the course for Genscher's approach towards both Pretoria and Namibia. On 23 June 1976, Vorster and Muller held talks with US Secretary of State Kissinger in Bonn. Although the Federal government declined Vorster an official state visit, Schmidt and Genscher agreed to the talks being held at the Palais Schaumburg in Bonn. The Palais was a deliberate choice, allowing the delegation to meet away from demonstrations against the apartheid regime, as Schmidt explained to Vorster during the meeting.[64] The meeting was from the outset highly controversial, not only provoking strongly negative reactions from the press, but also from the wider West German population, with Pretoria's draconian policies in South Africa and Namibia at the centre of the controversy. The Soweto Youth Uprising, which started on 16 June 1976 as a peaceful protest against the compulsory use of Africaans as a medium of instruction in black schools in the Transvaal, further inflamed the controversy over Vorster's visit. The youth protests were met with ruthless police repression. By 23 June 1976, at least 176 students had been killed.[65] Yet, it was primarily the Anti-Apartheid Movement (AAB) that expressed its disapproval of the Vorster government in the form of street protests. Not unexpectedly, SWAPO also voiced considerable criticism about Vorster's Bonn visit. Ben Amathila, the SWAPO representative to the Federal Republic of Germany, urged Helmut Schmidt and his government 'to not have anything to do with the visit of Mr Vorster'.[66]

Critics objected to such visits because they appeared to condone Pretoria's policies in South Africa and Namibia. Although the SPD-led government was genuinely opposed to the oppressive policies of the apartheid regime, the Vorster visit indicated, despite the emphasis on the unofficial function of the meeting, that West Germany was not prepared to participate in an international boycott against South Africa. Between diplomacy and sanctions, the former naturally took precedence over the latter as the main instrument for the promotion of change in southern Africa. In point of fact, the SPD-led government justified the Vorster visit by arguing that it was an 'opportunity to present the federal government's views': 'The Federal Government did so because it believes that full use must be made of all possibili-

---

[64] PAAA, Zwischenarchiv, Bd. 108220, 1975–1976, Report Schmidt-Vorster, 25.06.1976.
[65] For a detailed analysis of the Soweto Youth Uprising, see, e.g., S. M. Ndlovu, 'The Soweto Uprising', in *The Road to Democracy in South Africa, Vol 2, 1970–1980*, Pretoria, Unisa Press, 2006.
[66] PAAA, Zwischenarchiv, Bd. 108220, 1975–1976, Brief Ben Amathila an Helmut Schmidt, 2.06.1976, 2.

ties to achieve a peaceful solution in southern Africa and to eliminate the last remnants of colonialism and racial discrimination in that area'.[67]

Nonetheless, a minute of the meeting reveals that Schmidt was rather confrontational towards Vorster, warning the South African prime minister that the regimes current course was unsustainable: 'South Africa is risking that the free world is seeing South Africa less and less as part of the free world'.[68] Against this background, Bonn urged Pretoria, in a statement following Vorster's visit, to approve elections that will include 'all relevant forces and political parties in Namibia, including SWAPO'.[69] The following summary was forwarded after the meeting to Ben Amathila, the SWAPO representative to the Federal Republic:

> The Federal Government has always made it plain that it strongly condemns the policy of apartheid. It has restated this in the Luxemburg Declaration of the Nine and made it known worldwide by endorsing the resolution adopted on 19 June 1976 by the UN Security Council pointing out on that occasion that it views the policy of racial discrimination as violating fundamental human rights and disturbing peace and stability. Proceeding from this basic position, the Federal Government pointed out the following in its recent talks with Prime Minister Vorster and Foreign Minister Muller.
>
> The Federal Government, in conformity with a number of African Governments, considers it imperative that a date be set for Namibia's independence now or in any case before the next session of the UN General Assembly so as to accelerate the process of independence. In its talks with the South African leaders, the Federal Government also stressed the fact that, without the participation of all relevant political forces and parties in Namibia (including SWAPO) and of international bodies, there seems to be the possibility of securing a safe and stable future for the country. The Federal Government therefore urgently calls for such participation and considers it necessary that an active role accorded to the United Nations and the OAU in the process of Namibia's attaining independence. The Federal Government hopes in spite of the ever louder call for the use of force that its policy for a peaceful settlement of the conflict will meet with understanding and have the support of the OAU and its member States.[70]

---

[67] Ibid., Besuch PM Vorsters und Außenminister Mullers; hier: Unterrichtung afrikanischer Staaten, 28.06.1976, 2.
[68] PAAA, Zwischenarchiv, Bd. 108220, 1975–1976, Vermerk über das Gespräch des Bundeskanzlers mit Premierminister Dr. B. J. Vorster, 25.06.1976, 8. The minute of the meeting was signed by Jürgen Ruhfus, Head of Department II and Helmut Schmidt's personal foreign policy and security adviser. The Department II of the Chancellery corresponds to the Foreign Office and was responsible for foreign, security and development policy.
[69] Ibid, Position of the Federal Republic of Germany on Problems of Southern Africa, 01.07.1976, 4.
[70] Ibid., Letter Foreign office to Ben Amathila, the SWAPO representative to the FR, 15.07.1976, 2–4. An almost identical statement was presented to the United Nations on 1. July 1976: PAAA, Zwischenarchiv, Bd. 108220, 1975–76, Position of the Federal Republic of Germany on Problems of Southern Africa, 01.07.1976.

With the consideration that the 31st UN General Assembly was scheduled for September, a few months after Vorster's Bonn visit; Schmidt's openness can be understood as a briefing of Pretoria on Bonn's position before the upcoming UN session. Despite Schmidt's outspokenness, Bonn appeared careful not to undermine the dialogue with Pretoria by criticising the apartheid regime too harshly, or to put Vorster in an embarrassing position. Genscher, in particular, continued to emphasize the need for an open dialogue with all parties. He repeated Bonn's criticism at the 31st UN General Assembly, but avoided addressing Pretoria directly: 'We can only expect peaceful development in southern Africa; see peace as secure where nobody tries to hinder historically necessary change. In this world is no place for racism and colonialism anymore'.[71] Genscher also emphasised that the UN has a vital role to play in Namibia's transition to independence.[72]

In September 1978, Genscher reassured Nujoma, on the side-lines of the UN General Assembly in New York, that the Federal Government's position was not immutably fixed: 'Namibia will not knock in vain at the Federal Government's door, should it require help'. In return, Nujoma made it clear that SWAPO had, contrary to widespread assumption in the West, no intention to expel the Namibian Germans from Namibia, nor did SWAPO stand for expropriation.[73] By 1981, there could no longer be any remaining doubt about Nujoma's sympathies for the foreign minister, as he openly expressed that Genscher 'seemed to us [SWAPO] very likeable'.[74] Although Genscher harboured some reservations about Nujoma's leadership prowess, the relationship between Genscher and Nujoma grew stronger throughout the 1980s.[75]

---

[71] H. D. Genscher, *Erinnerungen*, Berlin, Siedler Verlag, 1995, 333.
[72] Ibid., 333.
[73] PAAA, Zwischenarchiv, Bd. 116802, 1977–1978, Gespräch des Bundesministers mit dem Präsidenten der SWAPO, Sam Nujoma, in New York, 29.09.1978. See also AAPD, 1978, Band II, Gespräch des Bundesministers Genscher mit dem Präsidenten der SWAPO, Nujoma, in New York, 29.09.1978, 1429–1430.
[74] Ibid., Bd. 127477, 1981, Nujoma-Äußerungen über Ergebnisse seiner Europa-Reise und aktuelle SWAPO-Politik, Luanda, 24.06.1981.
[75] Genscher's concerns were largely based on Nujoma's authority within SWAPO. In this regard, the foreign minister saw in Robert Mugabe, the prime minister of Zimbabwe, a stronger leader. Genscher feared that Nujoma might fail to adopt a constructive approach with regard to Resolution 435. The question was whether Nujoma would be able to accept a compromise without being pushed into isolation within SWAPO: PAAA, Zwischenarchiv, Bd. 138102, 1984, Deutschbritische Konsultationen am 02.05.1984; hier: Gespräch BM mit AM Howe, 03.05.1984, 5. The evidence indicates that Nujoma trusted Genscher. In 1984, for example, Nujoma wrote to Genscher the following: 'I wish to take advantage of the good relationship and good communication contacts that exists between us to bring to your attention an issue which has created some concern in me and my SWAPO colleagues': PAAA, Zwischenarchiv, Bd. 138098, 1984, SWAPO; hier: Brief von Präsident Nujoma an BM Genscher wegen angeblicher Äußerungen von MDB Rumpf in Windhoek, Lusaka, 21.03.1984.

Yet, both SWAPO and Pretoria proved tough to deal with, as both parties repeatedly obstructed the negotiation process. During his first visit to South Africa in late 1978, Genscher already received a first glimpse into the negotiation challenges that lay ahead. The Foreign Minister discussed with Pieter W. Botha, the new South African Prime Minister, and Cyrus Vance, the Foreign Minister of the United States, the need for free elections in Namibia. The meeting exposed – contrary to Genscher's claim that his mission had been 'successful' – the stubborn resolve of the apartheid regime.[76] As contemporary observers might have expected, Pretoria repeated its main argument, emphasising South Africa's role as a buffer state against communism in the region, which was also the justification for denying 'communist SWAPO' the right to participate in elections. Seen in this light, it becomes apparent why Genscher repeated with almost religious zeal two fundamental conditions for solving the Namibia question: the need to ensure a free and fair election and the observance of human rights.

While Genscher was accustomed to criticism from opposition parties, opposition to his approach towards the Namibia question in his own party was a new phenomenon in the 1980s. The FDP parliamentarian Wolfgang Rumpf was one of the most vocal opponents of Genscher's policy towards Namibia. In 1981, Rumpf, who only recently had become a member of the *Bundestag*, travelled with fellow FDP parliamentarian Manfred Vohrer on a fact-finding-tour to Namibia and Zimbabwe. Upon their return, the duo expressed their support for the Democratic Turnhalle Alliance (DTA).[77] The DTA received widespread support from Namibia's white minority and was the main political opposition to SWAPO. In late 1981, Rumpf went for a second time to Namibia. Back in Germany, he praised with seemingly growing enthusiasm the DTA as a model for progress. Rumpf apparently detected signs of Namibia's progress in an increase in the standard of living and a decrease in racial discrimination. Yet, he still urged the apartheid regime to make substantial concessions with regard to the occupation of Northern Namibia, to eliminate the remnants of racial discrimination in schools and to hand over the Tinten Palace to the council of ministers.[78] Rumpf soon became one of the most reliable DTA supporters in the *Bundestag*, continuing to argue that the DTA political model had been instrumental in promoting a mixed race and integrated society in Namibia.[79]

Although Genscher's policy on Namibia encountered increasing disapproval within the FDP in the mid-1980s, the opposition inside the FDP did not necessarily support the South

---

[76] 'Genscher-Mission: Dritte Dimension', *Der Spiegel*, 43/1978, 23.10.1978.
[77] fdk tagesdienst, Nr. 178/81, 9.3.1981, in Brenke, *Die Bundesrepublik*, 207.
[78] fdk tagesdienst, Nr. 956/81, 27.11.1981, in Brenke, *Die Bundesrepublik*, 208.
[79] See Namibia-Pressedienst, Nr.30/1983, 17, in Brenke, *Die Bundesrepublik*, 208.

African apartheid regime.[80] For some FDP parliamentarians, Genscher was too accommodating towards Pretoria. For example, Wolfgang Gerhardt, the FDP vice chairman, urged in 1985 the implementation of sanctions against South Africa. In conformity with Genscher's position, the call for sanctions received an unmistakably clear response from Friedhelm Ost, the government spokesman: 'The Federal Government rules out any boycott'.[81]

With almost stubborn determination, Genscher rejected any opposition by repeating the three pillars of his Namibia policy. First, the apartheid regime could not be forced into changing the status quo. Consequently, using sanctions as a means of applying pressure on Pretoria was not a viable option. Second, elections needed not only to be free and fair, but also based on the principle of 'one man, one vote'. Hence, elections excluding SWAPO or sections of the black majority could not lead to stability and peace. Yet, SWAPO could not expect to be considered a legitimate candidate without giving up the armed struggle. According to Genscher's analysis, Bonn supported, in principal, the liberation movement's goals, but full support required one essential concession: the renunciation of violence.[82] Third, elections needed to take place under the umbrella of the UN. Governments installed by the apartheid regime were 'null and void'. Perhaps unsurprisingly, Pretoria thought the Foreign Office was occupied with enemies of South Africa. 'At the top of our list stands the name Genscher', an employee of the presidential office told *Der Spiegel* in 1988.[83] Genscher's frustration about the lack of progress in the Namibia question sharply increased in the later 1980s. This became particularly apparent in his growing criticism of Pretoria. The complex set of factors that prevented progress towards Namibia's independence and led to Genscher's deteriorating influence with regard to the Namibia question will be investigated in the second part of this book.

In reality, Genscher's approach to the Namibia question was rather conservative. Clearly, the political dynamics during Genscher's first few years as foreign minister, including his encounters with Pretoria and the crisis with SWAPO in 1975, significantly shaped his policy towards Namibia. With regard to Pretoria's insistence that South Africa was a bulwark against communism in southern Africa, Genscher showed little support for this line of reasoning. His attitude derived partly from the understanding that the origins of the conflicts in southern Africa could be found in Europe. In his opinion, 'the contagion of the East-West

---

[80] Brenke, *Die Bundesrepublik*, 209.
[81] 'Tiefe Sorge', *Der Spiegel*, 31/1985, 29.07.1985. For information on the demand for a consumer boycott by the anti-apartheid movement, see J. Bracia and D. Leidig, *"Kauft keine Früchte aus Südafrika": Geschichte der Anti-Apartheid-Bewegung*, Frankfurt/M., Brandes & Apsel, 2008. It is worth noting here that Genscher's position towards sanctions changed in the late 1980s.
[82] Genscher, *Erinnerungen*, 3; See also PAAA, Zwischenarchiv, Bd. 108220, 1975–76, Erklärung der Bundesregierung nach dem Besuch von P.M. Vorster, New York, 19.07.1976.
[83] 'Mann für Männer', *Der Spiegel*, 4/1988, 25.01.1988.

conflict to the Third World could not be stopped from the periphery but from its core'.[84] In other words, an easing of tension in Europe would also improve the situation in southern Africa. Nonetheless, Genscher had no illusions about the ongoing East-West conflict in southern Africa. He acknowledged that the Soviet Union harboured ambitions 'to increase its influence through the exploitation of conflicts in the region'. Consequently, the Soviet Union posed a threat to West Germany's security and economic interests in southern Africa, as Genscher pointed out.[85] However, Genscher stressed that it was important 'to find peaceful solutions to the conflicts in southern Africa', emphasising that 'peace and stability can only be achieved by eliminating the root causes'.[86] Thus, although Genscher acknowledged that West Germany and the Eastern bloc were actively competing for influence in southern Africa, he saw little strategic reason to try to push back the Eastern bloc in the region, for the East-West divide in Europe was the most likely cause for an escalation of the conflict in southern Africa.[87]

Thus, the GDR's solidarity with SWAPO was in Genscher's view not a reason for concern. On the contrary, the situation was in part of the West's own making. Western powers repeatedly declined SWAPO's request for aid in the early and mid-1970s, which left the liberation movement with no option but to seek the support of socialist states, as Genscher explained.[88] Thus, SWAPO's relationship with Moscow and East Berlin was not based on ideological conviction, but on the need for reliable allies in the national independence struggle. Genscher saw in the relationship between SWAPO and the GDR an opportunistic alliance brought together by Cold War rivalry on African soil. His understanding that the West had failed liberation movements in Africa seems to have become even clearer in retrospect, as Genscher's oral presentation in 2010 at the Humboldt University of Berlin indicates: 'Why did liberation movements in Africa rather go to Moscow than to any other capital in the West? It was because the West was not on their side, because the West had not said in absolute clarity: Africans are entitled to independence as much as we are'.[89] The Cold War division of the world into ideological camps made it nearly impossible for liberation move-

---

[84] Genscher, *Erinnerungen*, 337.
[85] PAAA, Zwischenarchiv, Bd. 116841, 1877–1978, Deutsch-südafrikanische Beziehungen; hier: Antwort des BM auf das Fernschreiben des MdB Dr. Marx vom 07.02.1978, 09.02.1978.
[86] Ibid.
[87] Obviously, the superpowers' competition for supremacy was the root cause of the conflict. The Soviet Union's allies in Eastern Europe and the US allies in Western Europe stood at the centre of this power struggle. Thus, it was 'widely believed that the boundary between Eastern and Western Europe was the most likely locus for the outbreak of a major conflict', as Holdren points out: J. P. Holdren, 'North-South Issues and East-West Confrontation', *Bulletin of the Atomic Scientists*, Vol. 41, No 7, Chicago, Foundation for Nuclear Science, August 1985, 98–99.
[88] Genscher, *Erinnerungen*, 333.
[89] Genscher, 'Germany's role in Namibia's', 58.

ments to establish meaningful relations with the West. Hence, easing Cold War tensions between the superpowers in Europe was instrumental in softening the East-West competition for influence in southern Africa.[90] Thus, there was no strategic reason to build a buffer zone against the Eastern bloc in southern Africa or be concerned about liberation movements' alliance with communist states, for only an improvement in relations between East and West could resolve these issues.

Christian Democratic Union (CDU) and Christian Social Union (CSU)

Based on Christian values, the conservative CDU and its Bavarian sister party, the CSU, were established after the Second World War. Both parties focused on Western cultural values and held conservative policy positions such as anti-communism. In the 1970s, the CDU/CSU was in the role of the opposition to the SPD-led coalition government. Although at times, CDU and CSU seemed to approach the Namibia question from opposite ends of the political spectrum, there was sufficient consensus across party lines to show a united front in the *Bundestag*. While the CSU was firmly established in its opposition to SWAPO, the CDU took a slightly less hardline position, believing that SWAPO would eventually move from armed struggle towards political negotiation. Nonetheless, the CDU encountered, as Gabriele Brenke points out, greater discrepancies in agreeing on a coherent Namibia policy than the CSU.[91] The exchange of diverging opinions between the two parties was, however, a logical expression of a policy in transition, shaped by their role as the opposition to the government.

Although the conservatives were still in the process of shaping their Namibia policy, they agreed on two issues: support for the Democratic Turnhalle Alliance (DTA), the main political opposition to SWAPO, and unwavering opposition to sanctions against South Africa.[92] In the late 1970s, the CDU/CSU support for the Pretoria-backed DTA became increasingly apparent and was filtered mainly through the two parties' political foundations: the Konrad Adenauer Foundation (CDU) and the Hanns Seidel Foundation (CSU). Logically, therefore, both the CDU and the CSU supported the DTA financially through their foundations in the mock election of 1978.[93] 4.5 million deutsche marks of this money was used to buy the *Allgemeine Zeitung* in Windhoek, which fulfilled the strategic purpose of influencing

---

[90] Genscher explained in his Humboldt speech that 'countries outside of Europe were not spectators but victims of the East-West-Conflict. This East-West-Conflict was not limited to Europe, but affecting the whole world. Africa, too, was a victim in this power struggle for zones of influence'. See Genscher, *Germany's role in Namibia's independence*, 2.
[91] Brenke, Die Bundesrepublik, 164–173.
[92] See Deutscher Bundestag, 8. Wahlperiode, Drucksache 8/2748, 11.04.1979, 2.
[93] G. Wellmer, 'Background Paper on Relations between Federal Republic of Germany and Namibia', presented at the International Seminar on the Role of Transnational Corporations in Namibia, *Anti-Apartheid Movement (AAM)*, Federal Republic of Germany, 1982, 2.

opinion in Namibia.⁹⁴ Overall, the CDU/CSU supported the improvement of conditions in Namibia that had the potential to move the DTA into a favourable light, especially in the eyes of the black majority. Supporting the DTA through foundations was potentially politically less controversial than direct political lobbying and financial support.

Despite all this, the diversity of opinion was greater in the CDU, with some parliamentary members even voicing understanding for the armed struggle against oppressive regimes, as the CDU's youth league, *Die Junge Union*, concluded after a symposium on the North-South conflict in 1978.⁹⁵ Nonetheless, concern about the militarized nature of liberation movements and their affiliation to Moscow and East Berlin was dominant in both parties.

Consequently, CDU and CSU questioned SWAPO's suitability as political party in power, which undermined any call for a rational dialogue between CDU/CSU and SWAPO in the 1970s. Both CDU and CSU believed that SWAPO's claim to power was threatening Namibia's path to democracy, as it might lead to a centralised state, not unlike the GDR.⁹⁶ The CDU and CSU based a possible improvement of relations with SWAPO on the fulfilment of two main demands: to renounce violence and give up the notion that SWAPO was the sole representative of the Namibian people. The apparent aim was to create equal opportunities for all parties.⁹⁷ However, neither SWAPO nor the CDU/CSU were willing to conform to any standards of suitability for improved relations.

Hence, the CDU/CSU expressed serious objections to the Federal Government's rapprochement with both the GDR and SWAPO.⁹⁸ Hans Graf Huyn, CSU member of the *Bundestag*, argued that rapprochement with the GDR 'has not served détente and peace in the World. Today, the so called advisors of the SED-regime, advisor of the National People's Army and others support Moscow's neo-colonialism in Ethiopian, in south Yemen, in Mozambique and Angola'.⁹⁹ In 1980, Hans H. Klein, CDU Member of Parliament, complained about the government's apparent 'double moral standards'. Klein accused the Schmidt government

---

⁹⁴ Wellmer, 'Background Paper', 2. See also H. Melber and G. Wellmer, 'West German Relations with Namibia', in A. D. Cooper (ed.), *Allies in Apartheid: Western Capitalism in Occupied Namibia*, Hampshire and London, The Macmillan Press LTD, 1988, 92.
⁹⁵ Brenke, *Die Bundesrepublik*, 178.
⁹⁶ In the 1970s, it was not uncommon to believe that a SWAPO-led Namibia would lead to a centralised one party state: PAAA, Zwischenarchiv, Bd. 108202, 1975–1976, Betr.: SWAPO, Entwurf einer Aufzeichnung über die SWAPO, 18.11.1976, 8.
⁹⁷ Brenke, *Die Bundesrepublik*, 183. See also Deutscher Bundestag, 8. Wahlperiode, Drucksache 8/2748, 11.04.1979.
⁹⁸ See, e.g., U. Holtz, 'Die SPD und die SWAPO', Deutschland Union Dienst (DUD), Pressedienst der CDU und CSU, Nr. 182, 31. Jhg., 22.09.1977; 'Der Sprecher der CDU/CSU-Bundestagsfraktion, Dr. Eduard Ackerman, teilt mit', CDU/CSU Fraktion im Deutschen Bundestag, Pressedienst, 27.05.1981.
⁹⁹ Deutscher Bundestag, 8. Wahlperiode, Stenographischer Bericht, 79. Sitzung, 10.03.1978, 6215.

of intentionally remaining silent on controversial issues such as the SED-regime's human rights violations in the GDR, Soviet Union's genocide in Cambodia and SWAPO's terror acts.[100] Basically, Klein called into question the moral compass of the government.

Among West German political parties, the CDU and CSU were especially swayed by the highly emotive terms of the Cold War. Although Adenauer's Hallstein Doctrine was replaced by *Ostpolitik* in 1969, the policy of isolation continued to provide the concepts on which the CDU/CSU established its foreign policy in the 1970s. Hence, interactions with both the GDR and SWAPO were still conditioned by a policy that intended to achieve change through isolation as opposed to rapprochement. Thus, it is unsurprising that the GDR harboured largely negative views of the CDU and CSU, particularly regarding their relations with Pretoria and the German Namibian minority. That Franz Josef Strauß, the leader of the Bavarian CSU, had once been an active Nazi Party member explained – in the view of Julius Mader, who held close relations to the SED and Stasi – his passionate support for Germans in Namibia and the government in South Africa.[101] The objective of this 'Neo-Nazi union' was to maintain their dominant position in the region.[102] Although this was a particular outlandish charge, it was not uncommon for the GDR propaganda machine to make discrediting claims about German politicians' apparent Nazi-past.[103] Not unexpectedly perhaps, the CDU/CSU's criticism of the GDR was, at times, equally harsh. For example, Heiner Geissler, the General Secretary of the CDU, compared the GDR leadership with the apartheid regime in Pretoria in 1988. The GDR's restrictions on the Western press and religious freedom led to such a comparison.[104] In the same year, Bonn major Hans Daniels (CDU) also provoked outrage in East Berlin, after comparing the GDR's relentless pursuit of critics with human rights abuses in South Africa.[105]

In 1983, the CDU/CSU regained power, which led to a more coherent party line.[106] However, the rivalry between Helmut Kohl, the newly elected Chancellor, and Strauß generated an atmosphere of unpredictability in the 1980s. The Bavarian traditionalist was a staunch

---

[100] DUD, Nr. 12, 34. Jahrgang, 17.01.1980.
[101] Mader's relationship with the SED changed in the 1980s, for he started to present a more balanced view in his publications on issues concerning the Soviet Union and the Eastern bloc countries.
[102] 'Ehemalige Hitleroffiziere und deutsche Millionäre helfen den Apartheid-Faschisten in Namibia', *Panorama DDR*, 1980.
[103] M. F. Scholz, 'Active Measures and Disinformation as Part of East Germany's Propaganda War, 1953–1972', in K. Macrakis, T. W. Friis and H. Müller-Enbergs (eds.), *East German Foreign Intelligence: Myth, Reality and Controversy*, New York, Routledge, 2010, 113–126 and 141.
[104] 'Geißler vergleicht DDR mit Südafrika', *Frankfurter Rundschau*, 11.10.1988.
[105] 'Zwischen Bonn und Potsdam knirscht es', *Das Parlament*, 26.08.1988.
[106] See also R. von Lucius, 'Die künftige Politik Bonns gegenüber dem südlichen Afrika gewinnt Konturen', *Frankfurter Allgemeine Zeitung*, 25.04.1983.

critic of Brandt's *Ostpolitik* and fierce opponent of Genscher. Strauß' opposition to Genscher was further aggravated by his desire to become foreign minister under Kohl. However, Kohl made an election-pact with the FDP out of concern that the CDU/CSU could not win a majority in the *Bundestag*.[107] Also, the coalition with the FDP made it easier for Kohl to keep Strauß out of his cabinet by keeping Genscher at the helm of the foreign ministry, for Strauß had emphasised that he would be only available for the post of foreign minister. However, Genscher made the continuation of his policy towards Namibia a precondition for a coalition between the FDP and CDU. This was a thorn in Strauß' side, for he strongly objected to Genscher's uncompromising support for achieving Namibia's independence via the channels of the UN, and his efforts to improve relations between SWAPO and the German-speaking minority.[108]

Strauß' disagreement with the Kohl government's policy towards Namibia was most strongly reflected in attempts to pursue an alternative policy via the CSU-led Federal Ministry of Economic Cooperation and Development (BMZ), which led to extended 'tussles' between the BMZ and the Foreign Office in the 1980s.[109] The rivalry between Strauß and Genscher became particularly noticeable with regard to disagreements on appropriate aid policies and other African issues.[110] Strauß also embarked on a fierce rhetorical campaign against Genscher's foreign policy approaches, particularly with regard to Namibia and South Africa.[111] The Bavarian hardliner approached the Namibia question from a less inclusive perspective, which can be summed up in a statement Strauß made in 1985: 'The white culture must survive'.[112]

Strauß continued his unrelenting campaign against SWAPO until his sudden death in 1988.[113] As a professed anti-communist, Strauß had no difficulty connecting SWAPO to So-

---

[107] Only a political party with a clear majority of seats in parliament was allowed to govern. The seats a party received in the *Bundestag* were determined by the percentage of votes a party received in the election. The coalition with another political party fulfilled the purpose of securing a majority of seats in the *Bundestag* and thus the right to govern.

[108] V. Jabri, *Mediating conflict: Decision-making and Western intervention in Namibia*, Manchester and New York, Manchester University Press, 1990, 145.

[109] Deutscher Bundestag, 10. Wahlperiode, Stenographischer Bericht, 54. Sitzung, 10.02.1984, 3863.

[110] R. Hofmeier, 'Five decades of German-African relations: limited interests, low political profile and substantial aid donor', in U. Engel and R. Kappel (eds.), *Germany's Africa Policy Revisited: Interests, Images and Incrementalism*, Münster, LIT, 2002, 49.

[111] See, e.g. 'Strauß: Südafrika im globalen Konzept Moskaus', *Die Welt*, 02.04.1982; 'Strauß passt Afrika-Kurs nicht', *Frankfurter Rundschau*, 07.03.1983; 'SWAPO-Chef ruft nach Strafe', *Frankfurter Rundschau* 17.09.1985; 'Treuer Anhänger', *Der Spiegel*, 32/1986, 04.08.1986. Despite strong opposition, particularly by Strauss, the continuity of Genscher's policy towards South Africa was firmly confirmed in early-1984: 'Kontinuität der Südafrika-Politik bestätigt', *Frankfurter Allgemeine Zeitung*, 11.02.1984.

[112] 'Tiefe Sorge', *Der Spiegel*, 31/1985, 29.07.1985.

[113] In early 1988, SWAPO complained about Strauß' continued support of Pretoria and the interim government in Namibia: ISSA, Akte: Namibia 1986–1990, Franz-Josef Strauß im südlichen Af-

viet strategic ambitions in Africa.[114] Although solidarity with the South African apartheid regime was not unique to Strauß, his flamboyant personality and political status made him the most conspicuous West German spokesperson for the white minority in South Africa and Namibia. With this in mind, Strauß declared during a visit to South Africa in 1988: 'Never, in my 40 years in politics, have I witnessed such an unfair treatment of a country'.[115] His resilient support for Pretoria was not received without controversy in both Germanys. For the press, however, Strauß was more than simply a communist-hater; he was a reliable source for controversial headlines.

Kohl was never entirely comfortable with Strauß' political style or policies, which was also rooted in their rivalry for the leadership of the CDU/CSU throughout the late 1970s. In the heated campaign for the top position, Strauß rarely missed an opportunity to publicly demean Kohl, which in turn led to a godfather caricature of Strauß on the front-page of Der Spiegel, a West German news magazine, in 1976.[116] The rivalry persisted even after Kohl won the early general election in 1983.[117] Strauß tried to expose Kohl's foreign policy insecurities by aggressively pursuing alternative approaches. However, the constant interfering in foreign policy was also the strategic continuation of the CSU leader's quest for a leadership role beyond Bavaria. While Strauß was passionate about international politics, Kohl was mocked by critics on the subject of foreign policy as a 'provincial novice', guided by instinct rather than knowledge and experience.[118] Strauß was confident, outspoken and opinionated. His continuous meddling in foreign policy earned him the title 'auxiliary foreign minister'.[119] Indeed, Strauß saw himself better qualified than Kohl and Genscher, who were in his eyes 'foreign policy dilettantes'.[120]

---

rika, SWAPO of Namibia, Pressedienst, Luanda, 29.01.1988. Strauß died of a heart attack on 3 October 1988.

[114] See Deutscher Bundestag, 8. Wahlperiode, Stenographischer Bericht, 52. Sitzung, 27.10.1977, 4041–4050.

[115] 'Das macht ihm keiner nach', *Der Spiegel*, 5/1988, 01.02.1988. In 1977 already, Strauß warned of civil war and the 'exodus of whites' in Namibia and Zimbabwe. See Deutscher Bundestag, 8. Wahlperiode, Stenographischer Bericht, 52. Sitzung, 27.10.1977, 4051.

[116] 'Strauß: Der Mann, der Kohl regiert', *Der Spiegel*, 39/1976, 20.09.1976.

[117] J. Gedmin, 'Helmut Kohl, Giant', Hoover Institution, Stanford University, 1999.

[118] 'Genscher: Der Kanzler denkt genau wie ich', *Der Spiegel*, 45/1983, 07.11.1983. For example, in 1983, Kohl spoke very little during the first official state visit of Dirk Mudge, the DTA Chairman, as stated in the Foreign Office report of the meeting. Whether this was a further reflection of Kohl's insecurity with regard to foreign policy matters remains open to interpretation: PAAA, Neues Amt 16414, 1983, Namibia Initiative; hier: Gespräch BK mit DTA-Vorsitzendem Mudge, Bonn, 15.06.1983.

[119] See, e.g., 'Genscher: Der Kanzler denkt genau wie ich', *Der Spiegel*, 45/1983, 07.11.1983; 'Außenpolitisch untragbare Kraftmeierei', *Vorwärts*, 15.03.1983; 'Tiefe Sorge', *Der Spiegel*, 31/1985, 29.07.1985.

[120] 'Genscher: Der Kanzler denkt genau wie ich', *Der Spiegel*, 45/1983, 07.11.1983.

Strauß was Pretoria's most outspoken ally in Bonn, and his commitment to defend Pretoria against any criticism coming from within the government frequently challenged Genscher's diplomatic efforts. In line with Pretoria's perception of Genscher, Strauß slammed the foreign minister's policy towards Africa in 1985 as 'blind to the African reality' and consisting of nothing more than 'insubstantial drivel made of UN-resolutions'.[121] Genscher's disapproval of the South African regime was a particularly bitter pill for the Bavarian firebrand to swallow. In 1987, Strauß had had enough of Genscher's policy towards South Africa, accusing the seasoned foreign minister of putting Pretoria 'constantly in the dock'.[122] With great passion, Strauß presented South Africa in West Germany as a bulwark against communism in southern Africa. He even spoke favourably of some of Pretoria's most controversial policies, such as apartheid and the homelands.[123] Genscher, however, soon came to the conclusion that Strauß' opposition to the Kohl-Genscher foreign policy was not necessarily based on political conviction but the desire to 'ridicule the unloved duo'.[124]

In the 1980s, Kohl's attitude toward SWAPO was based on the notion that SWAPO had to play a pivotal role in solving the Namibia question. Kohl was committed to solving the Namibia question via UN resolutions, which were critical of the apartheid regime in Pretoria. Yet, Kohl only played a constructive behind-the-scenes role, relying on Genscher's considerable experience in foreign affairs to fulfil Bonn's role as mediator in the Namibia question. Occasionally, Kohl made headlines with regard to southern Africa, for example when he granted a divisive figure such as the South African Prime Minister P.W. Botha an official state visit.[125]

From the West German perspective, it was of course desirable that the GDR would not establish strong diplomatic and economic relations around the world. The less successful the GDR was as a sovereign state, the higher were the chances that East Berlin would seek close relations with West Germany; ideally, even seek reunification.[126]

---

[121] 'Tiefe Sorge', *Der Spiegel*, 31/1985, 29.07.1985.

[122] 'Im Busch', *Der Spiegel*, 1/1987, 29.12.1986.

[123] See, e.g., 'Das macht ihm keiner nach', *Der Spiegel*, 5/1988, 01.02.1988; B. Grill, 'Ein Ministerpräsident auf Extratouren, "Ich bin hier, das ist viel"', *Die Zeit*, 29.01.1988. The homelands were racially segregated areas in South Africa, established to separate Blacks from Whites. The homelands were built around the idea that the black majority should have their separate living areas, with their own independent governments and away from the predominantly white urban areas. In total, the apartheid state established 10 homelands in South Africa.

[124] '*Genscher:* Der Kanzler denkt genau wie ich', *Der Spiegel*, 45/1983, 07.11.1983.

[125] See, e.g., 'Frostiger Empfang fuer Botha in Bonn', *General Anzeiger*, 06.06.1984; A. Nacken, '"Mal ist das Sofa drinnen und mal draußen", Botha zeigt sich in Bonn unbeirrbar', *Frankfurter Allgemeine Zeitung*, 07.06.1984.

[126] The West German constitution demanded from the government to seek reunification.

The Green Party

The Green Party was West Germany's first environmentalist political party. The principles of green politics, such as environmentalism and anti-nuclearism, but also social-democratic economic policies, social justice and non-violence, became the party's political pillars. A number of the Greens' first members achieved political prominence during the so-called '68 movement. Frustrated with the survival of an influential right-wing political order in West Germany after the demise of Nazi-Germany, the '68 student movement challenged the long-established status quo of government establishments and educational institutions. Although unsuccessful in overthrowing the status quo in the late 1960s, the '68 movement paved the way for moderate left-wing political ideas to re-enter mainstream politics in West Germany.

With just 27 of the 520 seats, the Greens finally entered the *Bundestag* in 1983. Although the youngest party in the *Bundestag*, many members of the Green Party could look back to over a decade of campaigning against poverty in developing countries. Petra Kelly, one of the founders and leading theoretician of the Greens, showed particular concern for the African continent.[127] Convinced of the power of protest, Kelly used her growing celebrity status to encourage global political action, especially in South Africa and Namibia. However, it was probably the Greens' lack of concern about ideological affiliations that promoted their dispassionate approach to the Namibia question. The Green Party regarded both the capitalist and the socialist approach as fundamentally deficient and supported neither side wholeheartedly, or, in Kelly's words: 'We are neither left nor right, but different'.[128]

Consequently, the Greens were not concerned about SWAPO's flirtation with Marxist-Leninist theories, but acquired a realistic view of SWAPO's ideological orientation: 'SWAPO has asked the UN and especially the West to support an independent Namibia – in the case of the latter without any result. You cannot reject an organisation over and over again and then expect that they would not fall back on other offers'.[129] The Greens understood SWAPO's alliance with the Soviet bloc in relative rather than absolute terms. While all West German political parties struggled with SWAPO's revolutionary and pro-Soviet attitude, the Green Party's solidarity with SWAPO was almost undivided and absolute. Hence, the Greens found little reason to question whether SWAPO fulfilled all the criteria of a legitimate political party.

---

[127] See, P. Kelly, 'Neither Red nor Blue', *Financial Mail*, 20.09.1985.
[128] Ibid. During the interview, Kelly also stated that 50 percent of the Greens were willing to form a coalition with the SPD, while those against it argued that a coalition would compromise its views and compromise the Greens identity. Kelly also explained that the Greens envisioned 'a non-aligned European belt of states, including the countries of the East, with no exploitive relations with the Third World'.
[129] AGG, Petra Kelly, Akte 1473, 1983–1986, Michael Vesper, Namibia-Hearing, September 1985.

For the Greens, Bonn's Namibia policy was fundamentally flawed. One factor was the refusal of successive governments to acknowledge that Germany's colonial past in Namibia had contributed to the country's predicament, as outlined by Michael Vesper, managing director of the *Bundestag* faction of the Greens, in 1984 at the UN Symposium '*A Century of Heroic Struggle of the Namibian People*' in New York: 'The Germans are partly responsible for the causes that led to the Namibian nations' 100-year liberation struggle; also for it to still not be successfully finalised and for an internationally recognised independence of the country to be a long way away'.[130]

Indeed, there was a fundamental problem inherent in Bonn's relationship with Namibia: objectivity. Questions of post-colonial guilt and the ensuing responsibility towards Namibia made it difficult to make decisions on the basis of rational criteria concerning the common interest of the Namibian people. Therefore, controversial issues were usually filtered out of the decision-making process. Bonn tried, for example, to evade the question of Germany's historical responsibility towards all the people of Namibia. The quality of Bonn's decision-making was, to some extent, compromised by its concerns for the future of the German-speaking minority in Namibia.

Furthermore, the Greens accused Bonn of actively undermining Namibia's independence by failing to engage in a critical dialogue with Pretoria. Bonn's support for UN resolutions was perceived as insincere and only a diversion from the real aim, namely 'to modernise apartheid without having to give up the entitlement of white supremacy'.[131] However, the Greens went even a step further, accusing successive governments of being partially responsible for SWAPO's armed resistance: 'Through its collaboration with South Africa, the Federal Government has to bear some blame for the escalation of the war in Namibia, Angola and Mozambique. Through the Federal Government's support, the militarised white state terror has been enabled to survive until violent liberation appears the only solution'.[132]

Yet, the Greens did not condone violent resistance. They saw SWAPO's struggle against the apartheid regime rather pragmatically, as becomes apparent in a statement by Annemarie Borgmann, speaker of the Green Party in the *Bundestag*, during a visit to Namibia in 1986: 'We do not agree with everything that SWAPO does; the use of violence, for example, would never come into question for us – but this is a different country and SWAPO has tried to achieve things in a peaceful way before it took up arms'.[133] Although the Greens and

---

[130] Ibid., Symposium on a century of heroic struggle of the Namibian people, 01.11.1984
[131] 'Die Namibia-Politik der Bundesregierung', Grünes Bulletin, Sonderheft, Sep/Okt. '85. See also Deutscher Bundestag, 10. Wahlperiode, Stenographischer Bericht, 243. Sitzung, 06.11.1986, 18857–18859.
[132] Ibid.
[133] See R. A. Bevan, 'Petra Kelly: The Other Green', *New Political Science*, Vol. 23, Nr. 2, 2001, 181–202.

the SPD agreed on many issues concerning Namibia, the Green Party argued that the SPD's policy record suggested that it lacked a strategic vision of how to advance the Namibia question. For the Greens, the SPD-led government had been, although critical, too accommodating towards South Africa, or, in Vesper's words: 'The Schmidt government was in no way unpleasant for the apartheid regime'.[134]

In all of the above, it is necessary to consider that the Greens were, in the 1980s, in the role of the opposition and saw themselves as a radical parliamentary opposition force, not prepared to form a coalition for the sole purpose of entering government.[135] It seems, therefore, reasonable to suggest that the Greens tried to make a name for themselves, perhaps not unlike in the case of the FDP. As a new political party, and with a long history of activism regarding African issues, the Namibia question seemed probably ideal for establishing a party profile in foreign affairs. It is also important to note that West Germany's relationship with SWAPO had already improved when the Greens entered the *Bundestag* in 1983. Nonetheless, the Green Party's relationship with SWAPO was, within a West German context, still exceptional – a fact Sam Nujoma verified with frustration during the 'Namibia-Hearing' in 1985: 'We salute them [Green Party and members of the public] for their courage and express our hope that other legislators and the government will not remain indifferent to the un-abating carnage against the black people of Namibia and South Africa'.[136] Clearly, Nujoma's speech was more of a plea to the Federal Government to take a harder stance against South Africa than an expression of praise for the Green Party, for SWAPO could feel quite certain of the Greens' support.

The liberation movement's perception of West Germany's political parties was similar to that of the Greens. At times, only the tone – descending into diplomatically unacceptable language – exposed SWAPO's revolutionary background. Obviously, Nujoma's sharply polemical attitude vis-à-vis the West was not helpful in strengthening relations with West German political parties. There is, however, no evidence to suggest that the Greens at any time doubted their solidarity with SWAPO. Yet, the Greens did not fail to express their disappointment in SWAPO when it became apparent that prisoners had been tortured in SWAPO camps in Angola.[137]

Ironically perhaps, in the wide diversity of opinion concerning the Namibia question, the Green Party coincided more with the GDR's Socialist Unity Party (SED) than with their

---

[134] 'Vesper Bundestag, 3', Grünes Bulletin, Sonderheft Sep/Okt. '85.
[135] See Bevan, 'Petra Kelly', 181–202.
[136] S. Nujoma, 'SWAPO tritt kompromisslos für freie Wahlen ein', in ISSA wissenschaftliche Reihe 21(ed.), *Im Brennpunkt: Namibia und die Bundesrepublik Deutschland*, Köln, MVR, 1987, 50.
[137] AGG, Akte 2127, 1989, Die Grünen im Bundestag, Offener Brief der Grünen im Bundestag an die SWAPO in Namibia, 08.08.1989.

West German counterparts. Long-range objectives of both the Greens and the SED were, in theory, determined by the collective interest of the Namibian majority. The Namibian German minority received little consideration from both the Greens and the SED. Consensus on the direction in which Namibia should progress after the achievement of majority rule did not, of course, exist: for ideological reasons. When it came to the SED, the Greens followed a double strategy, namely to actively support the opposition, while simultaneously keeping good relations with the SED government. The SED's Namibia policy did not leave much room for friction because of a wide range of similarities in both parties' approach. The Green Party frequently voiced its concerns about human rights issues in the GDR, but with regard to southern Africa, both parties seemed to have settled into silent agreement. The Greens found fault mainly in the Western powers' approach, particularly in the reluctance to seriously challenge the status quo in southern Africa.

Although the Greens had limited political influence, their solidarity with SWAPO was characterized by a strong commitment to champion SWAPO's cause in West Germany. In 1985, the Greens affirmed their solidarity with SWAPO by donating 15,000 deutsche marks, half of the latest parliamentary allowance increase, to the SWAPO refugee camp in Nyango in Zambia.[138] Furthermore, the Green Party was the only party that openly campaigned in Namibia and South Africa against Pretoria. In the 1980s, the Green Party was a typical protest party that relied on public protest to capture widespread attention. In 1985, for example, a small group of Green Party members, including Kelly, staged a 48 hour sit-in in the West German embassy in Pretoria. The objective of their campaign was two-fold: to urge Bonn to put pressure on the apartheid regime to release political prisoners; and to demand a West German economic boycott of South Africa.[139] The Greens initiative was based on the notion that only substantial external political and economic pressure against Pretoria could ward off the danger of civil war amid a backdrop of growing civil unrest.[140] The Federal government was, in the Greens' view, partly responsible for the atrocities committed under apartheid, as a statement following the embassy sit-in emphasised: 'The Federal government's current political goodwill towards South Africa is partially responsible for violence, terror and murder against the black population'.[141] Almost exactly one year later, in late 1986, a delegation of the Greens, including Vesper and Bergman, were arrested during a

---

[138] AGG, Petra Kelly, Akte 1473, 1983–1986, Pressemitteilung Nr. 109/85, Politische Solidarität mit der SWAPO.

[139] See, e.g., 'Petra Kelly and the Greens stage embassy sit-in in Pretoria', *The Times London*, 11.09.1985; AGG, B.II.1, Die Grünen im Bundestag, Signatur 3, 1983–1990, Pressemitteilung Nr.562/85, 12.09.1985.

[140] AGG, B.II.1, Die Grünen im Bundestag, 1983–1990, Signatur 3, Pressemitteilung Nr. 562/85, Erklärung zur Beendigung der Botschaftsbesetzung in Pretoria.

[141] Ibid.

fact-finding visit to Katutura, a township near Windhoek. Anton Lubowski, a Namibian German human rights lawyer and SWAPO activist, and various SWAPO members were also detained.[142] Indisputably, the Green Party showed strong commitment to the promotion of the principle of equal rights and self-determination for peoples in southern Africa in the 1980s.

In light of the above, what was the main criterion for Cold War alliance – ideological conviction, strategic calculation, national interests or perhaps even moralistic principles? Considering that all sides took the liberty to form alliances with those whom they had previously denounced, the answer cannot be straightforward. Today, when the world is no longer polarised between two antagonistic camps, it is hard to recapture the paranoia and rivalry that determined East and West relations around the globe for more than four decades. The Third World seemed strange, fragile and explosive: a seemingly unpredictable arena in which neither side could judge with certainty the other's resolve and intentions. Ideological affiliations often seemed the only safe reference point, and the projection of strong leadership was, more often than not, firm ideological affiliation with either of the two camps rather than political vision. Thus, in the 1970s, the CDU/CSU's policy towards Namibia seemed firmly aligned with anti-communist sentiments, while the SPD's position was less definite. Attitudes and actions changed, but there was a strong tendency to view events in southern Africa through the ideological prism of the Cold War. By the turn of the decade, however, there was a clear move away from such hardened positions. By the time the Greens entered the *Bundestag*, it was no longer controversial to establish close relations with liberation movements.

East Germany

The Socialist Unity Party of Germany (SED)

The solidarity movement in the GDR was largely controlled by the governing party, the SED. Although the GDR had incorporated some elements of multi-party system, the SED always held the majority. Thus, the National Front, an association which comprised all parties and political organizations in the GDR, was firmly controlled by the SED. The regular elections were designed to display unity and underline the SED's legitimate rule. Though in theory a separation between party and state existed, the hierarchical system of government and administration was deeply controlled by the party.[143] Ultimately, the SED stood above all other

---

[142] See AGG, Petra Kelly, Akte 1473, 1983–1986, Die Grünen im Bundestag, Protest gegen die Festnahme der Grünen Delegation in Namibia, Pressemitteilung 445/86, 11.07.1986. In the later parts of the 1980s, Lubowski became the only white member of the SWAPO leadership.

[143] Fulbrook, *Anatomy*, 43–55.

organizations in the GDR, which meant that there was little tolerance for legitimate opposition. Thus, although the Solidarity Committee was officially not controlled by the state, it was in reality governed by the secretariat of the SED Central Committee.

In the 1960s, solidarity with the liberation struggles in southern Africa assisted the SED in its efforts to overcome the Hallstein Doctrine, but was also an opportunity to accentuate the GDR's credentials in the 'class struggle' against the West.[144] In the 1970s, the GDR was free from the restrictions of the Hallstein Doctrine, allowing the SED to redirect available resources to the reinforcement of the GDR's sovereignty and the promotion of the world revolutionary process in southern Africa. The Central Committee of the SED and the Foreign Ministry had a vision to further strategically relevant developments in southern Africa, perhaps even help establish 'new Cubas' in the region.[145] In this respect, the SED's interaction with SWAPO grew steadily in the 1970s, and intensified most substantially between 1977 and 1982.[146]

In the 1960s, the Solidarity Committee was the prime contact for liberation movements and commissioned to co-ordinate solidarity campaigns, immediate humanitarian aid, material assistance and scholarships. The Solidarity Committee's funds came from private donations, fund raisers, civil organisations and ministries and public funds.[147] Although the Solidarity Committee was not involved in supplying arms to liberation movements, the SED leadership used solidarity funds to finance such requests.[148] In the mid-1970s, the SED established direct party relations with liberation movements and took over the coordination responsibilities of the Solidarity Committee.[149] From then on, the Ministry of State Security (MfS) became increasingly involved in southern Africa. The formation of newly independent states and the intensification of the liberation struggles in southern Africa promoted a stronger involvement of the MfS in the region. The MfS was especially active in the education of military instructors, bodyguards, military intelligence officers, as well as in personal protection and underground work.[150]

---

[144] See also H.-G., Schleicher, 'Waffen für den Süden Afrikas. Die DDR und der bewaffnete Befreiungskampf', in U. van der Heyden, I. Schleicher und H.-G., Schleicher (ed.), *Engagiert für Afrika: Die DDR und Afrika II*, Münster, LIT, 1994, 13. The recipients were ZAPU, FRELIMO, PAIGC and MPLA.

[145] Bley/Schleicher, 'Deutsch-Deutsch', 10.

[146] BStU, MfS-HA II, Nr. 28977, Südafrikanische Volksorganisation (SWAPO) von Namibia, [no date], 169.

[147] Van der Heyden, 'GDR Development', 73.

[148] Schleicher, *DDR Solidarität*, 53.

[149] H.-G. Schleicher, 'GDR Solidarity: The German Democratic Republic and the South African Liberation Struggle', in *The Road to Democracy in South Africa: International Solidarity*, Volume 3, Pretoria, Education Trust, 2008, 1092.

[150] For more information regarding the role of the Ministry of State Security in the GDR's policy

Either the Politbüro of the Central Committee of the SED or the General Secretary of the Central Committee, Erich Honecker, commissioned MfS assignments in southern Africa. However, once an assignment was given to the MfS, the preparation and realization of the project took place autonomously. Yet, there was a significant interaction between the MfS and the Ministry of Foreign Affairs and the International Relations Section of the Central Committee of the SED.

In 1982, the GDR's foreign policy strategy in South Africa and Namibia was, as outlined by the MfS, strongly influenced by the intensification of East-West confrontation in the region, focussing on the following objectives. First, support the national and social liberation struggle of the people of Namibia and South Africa against colonialism, imperialism, neo-colonialism and racism. Second, consolidate and deepen alliance relationships with leading liberation movements. Third, repel the attacks of imperialism, the apartheid regime, the leaders of Peking and other reactionary powers against the developing alliance between the ANC, SWAPO and the socialist community of states. Fourth, actively support the ANC and SWAPO in the complete liquidation of the apartheid regime, in ending the reign of terror, in the respecting of human rights and in realising self-determination. Fifth, expose and hinder the manoeuvring of imperialism in trying to impose a neo-colonial solution on the Namibian nation. Finally, contribute to the development, improvement and strengthening of the revolutionary security apparatus of both liberation movements, the ANC and SWAPO, so that they can defend the attacks against their organisations.[151] Obviously, the GDR's efforts reflected unease about Western power and influence in southern Africa.

The MfS outlined, however, only factors that supported the notion that solidarity with SWAPO was an expression of altruism, with the sole purpose of helping Namibia achieve independence. Undeniably, although the SED genuinely supported SWAPO's cause, the underlying objective of this solidarity was based on strategic and tactical calculations, influenced by the reality of the East-West conflict.[152] The SED's objectives in southern Africa were, in the late 1970s, based on promoting the spread of socialism and consolidating the

---

towards Africa, see H.-G. Schleicher und U. Engel, 'DDR-Geheimdienst und Afrika-Politik', *Außenpolitik, Zeitschrift für Internationale Fragen*, Jg. 47, 4. Quartal, Hamburg, Interpress Verlag GmbH, 1996, 399–409. It is worth noting here that the training of cadres took place mainly in the GDR, largely to avoid overstretching resources.

[151] BStU, JHS Potsdam, Mikrofilmstelle, VVS JHS o001–110/82, Lehrkonzeption für Grundlehrgänge auf dem Gebiet der politisch-operativen Sicherung von Befreiungsorganisationen des südlichen Afrika, 01.09.1982, 4–5. (This is a slightly paraphrased version of the original text.)

[152] The GDR's early relations to anti-colonial movements in Africa had indeed altruistic components, as Schleicher points out. See H.-G. Schleicher, 'Afrika in der Außenpolitik der DDR', in U. van der Heyden, I. Schleicher and H.-G. Schleicher (eds.), *Die DDR und Afrika: Zwischen Klassenkampf und neuem Denken*, Münster, LIT, 1993, 14.

gains already made. It is noteworthy in this respect that West Germany actively tried to improve relations with SWAPO during that same period.

Thus, the SED recognised in the developments in southern Africa an opportunity to ignite the world revolutionary process by supporting liberation movements.[153] The ultimate aim was, as outlined by Marx, to unite the proletarian revolutionary forces of the advanced European countries with the national liberation movements in the Third World, for the national liberation struggles were part of the broader world revolutionary process. The national liberation struggle in southern Africa presented, therefore, an opportunity for the SED to establish its revolutionary credentials. Though it may be doubted whether the GDR's policy-makers harboured the strong convictions that the GDR had the ability to influence events on such a large scale through the support of liberation movements, the GDR leadership demanded that the GDR take an active part in the 'world revolutionary process'.[154]

SWAPO greatly appreciated the solidarity of the GDR, which became apparent in the increasingly close relationship between SWAPO and the SED.[155] In 1976, Nujoma expressed his wish to visit the GDR with a SWAPO delegation, which came to fruition in late 1977 and led to the establishment of a SWAPO representative office in the GDR in 1978.[156]

In order to strengthen ideological affinity, the SED actively tried to influence southern African countries to adopt a communist system modelled on the USSR. The aim was to spread 'real socialism' and bind newly independent African countries to the Eastern bloc. Given that the Cold War divided the world along ideological lines, the SED had reason to expect some kind of loyalty from liberation movements, particularly SWAPO, after the achievement of independence. In a SWAPO-led Namibia, the GDR, and not West Germany, would receive favourable treatment in both political and economic spheres. The GDR's objective to gain greater political and economic influence in southern Africa was not built on coercive power, but largely on establishing close ties and ideological bonds.

SWAPO had no reason to fear that the GDR secretly harboured geostrategic ambitions, mainly because of East Germany's limited economic strength and military scope.[157] Per-

---

[153] Van der Heyden, 'GDR Development', 143–144.
[154] Schleicher, 'GDR Solidarity', 1070.
[155] See Babing, *Gegen Rassismus, 1977–1982*, Gemeinsame Kommuniqué über den Besuch einer Delegation der Südwestafrikanischen Volksorganisation (SWAPO) von Namibia in der DDR, 20.12.1977, 110–112.
[156] BStU, MFS-HAII, Nr. 28977, 14. See also Babing, *Gegen Rassismus, 1977–1982*, Gemeinsame Kommuniqué über den Besuch einer Delegation der Südwestafrikanischen Volksorganisation (SWAPO) von Namibia in der DDR, 20.12.1977, 110–112.
[157] Van der Heyden points out the following: 'To accuse the GDR of having geostrategic interests in southern Africa would mean to misinterpret her economic and military powers': Van der Heyden, 'GDR Development', 147. See also Schleicher, 'Interessenlage', 254.

haps ironically therefore, the GDR's relative weakness gave the SED's anti-imperialist claims credibility.[158] However, the GDR's attitude towards liberation movements was the most convincing factor. Interactions between the SED and liberation movements took place 'on an equal footing' and without interference in internal affairs, which was invaluable in building mutual trust.[159]

Within this context, Joshua Nkomo, a close friend of Honecker and the leader of the Zimbabwe African People's Union (ZAPU), stated that Zimbabwe would not have any obligations to the GDR after independence, when the country's focus would be on economic development.[160] As it became apparent in the late 1970s that socialist Mozambique was plunging ever deeper into economic crisis, excessive dependence on the economically weak Soviet bloc countries came to be regarded as undesirable. In fact, there emerged a growing desire to seek economic relations with the West. Moreover, there were grounds for suspicions about the Soviet Union's long-term intentions.

Even though the Soviet Union was not an imperialist power in a conventional sense, the pathology of superpowers, namely imposing their will on weaker states, was an undeniable aspect of Soviet power. In 1979, the Soviet Union's invasion of Afghanistan accentuated Moscow's unpredictable, perhaps even imperialist tendencies.[161] Kenneth Kaunda, the first President of Zambia, told Horst Ehmke, SPD member of the *Bundestag*, that the invasion had 'gripped him to the marrow'.[162] Similarly, Peter Corterier, SPD member of the *Bundestag*, pointed out that the Soviet Union's invasion of Afghanistan not only 'shocked African countries', but also made them 'realize that a very close liaison with the Soviet Union threatens their independence'.[163] There was great concern that both the Soviet Union and the US might sharply escalate their intervention in southern Africa should they feel that their

---

[158] See also 'Wir haben euch Waffen und Brot geschickt', *Der Spiegel*, 10/1980, 03.03.1980. Moscow's intervention in Afghanistan 'greatly tarnished the Soviet Union as an anti-imperialist supporter of national liberation movements'. See R. B. Rais, *The Indian Ocean and the Superpowers: Economic, Political and Strategic Perspectives*, New Jersey, Barnes & Nobel, 1987, 125–126.

[159] Interview Hans-Georg Schleicher, Berlin, 20.02.2016. Schleicher also stated that East Berlin had no power political ambitions, although the GDR actively supported Soviet ambitions in southern Africa. In this context, the GDR viewed its support of Soviet objectives in southern Africa as part of the world revolutionary process. Graca Machel, the wife of former South African President Nelson Mandela, noted in a conversation with Schleicher that the GDR distinguished itself positively from both the Soviet Union and China because it had no power political ambitions. See also Schleicher, 'Afrika in der Außenpolitik', 23.

[160] 'Wir haben euch Waffen und Brot geschickt', *Der Spiegel*, 10/1980, 03.03.1980.

[161] See also Rubinstein, *Moscow's Third World*, 3–38.

[162] 'Wir haben euch Waffen und Brot geschickt', *Der Spiegel*, 10/1980, 03.03.1980. See also Deutscher Bundestag, 8. Wahlperiode, Stenographischer Bericht, 197. Sitzung, 18.01.1980, 156987.

[163] Deutscher Bundestag, 8 Wahlperiode, Stenographischer Bericht, 197. Sitzung, 18.01.1980, 15697.

interests were threatened. In the face of Cold War rivalry, both superpowers acted dangerously unpredictably, especially when it came to defending strategic interests. This became apparent when the US Military started to intervene in the Vietnam War in 1961 and the Soviet Union invaded Afghanistan in 1979.[164]

Although the GDR might not have relied on coercive policy instruments or harboured geostrategic ambitions, there were underlying, unspoken expectations. First, the GDR's aim was to advance its international standing as a sovereign state and an equal member of the community of nations. Second, East Berlin was determined to enhance the GDR's influence and standing within the Eastern bloc countries. Third, the GDR had an interest in enhancing its influence outside of Soviet-controlled states. Fourth, it wanted to establish favourable economic relations with newly independent countries, particularly with those countries that had received GDR assistance during the liberation struggle. Finally, the GDR expected to gain privileged access to natural resources after the achievement of independence.[165] As expected, West Germany was concerned about the GDR's growing involvement in southern Africa.[166] By the 1980s, few in West Germany doubted that East Berlin was actively trying to direct SWAPO's ideological and political orientation into a direction that was favourable to the GDR.

In 1981, the Research Institute for Political Science at the University of Cologne, in a study about the SED's relationship with SWAPO, came to the conclusion that a SWAPO-led Namibia would 'in the best case lead to an African-GDR and in the worst case to a second Uganda'.[167] Though SWAPO was never truly committed to communist ideology, the GDR's centralised one-party system seemingly presented to SWAPO an attractive political concept for post-independence Namibia. Hence, from the GDR's perspective, West German infiltration into SWAPO was a realistic concern.

In 1982, the Institute for International Relations (IIB) at the academy of the Ministry of State Security in Potsdam developed a detailed guideline for its teaching staff for the education of liberation movements. In the case of SWAPO, the education of cadres was a central aspect of GDR solidarity.[168] The GDR provided various political and ideological

---

[164] See also M. A. Lawrence, 'The Rise and Fall of Nonalignment', in R. J. McMahon (ed.), *The Cold War in the Third World*, Oxford, Oxford University Press, 2013, 149.

[165] See, e.g., Schulz, 'The politics of East-South', 159; H.-G. Schleicher, 'Afrika in der Außenpolitik der DDR', in U. van der Heyden, I. Schleicher und H.-G. Schleicher (eds.), *Die DDR und Afrika, Zwischen Klassenkampf und neuem Denken,* Münster, LIT, 1993, 12–13.

[166] This will be discussed in more detail in the next chapter.

[167] 'SED bildet Bürgermeister fuer Windhoek aus', *Welt am Sonntag,* 25.03.1981.

[168] See BStU, JHS Potsdam, Mikrofilmstelle, VVS JHS o001–110/82, Lehrkonzeption für Grundlehrgänge auf dem Gebiet der politisch-operativen Sicherung von Befreiungsorganisationen des südlichen Afrika, 01.09.1982, 4.

educational programmes for the cadres of liberation movements.[169] This particular educational programme, however, focussed 'on supporting the construction, development and strengthening of a revolutionary security apparatus within SWAPO and ANC'. The academy's programme was based on the GDR's foreign policy strategy toward national liberation movements in southern Africa. Considering that Western countries, especially Germany, gradually changed their attitude towards liberation movements in the late 1970s, it seems less surprising that the GDR emphasised the need for SWAPO to combat subversive activities, particularly infiltration attempts.[170]

From the SED's perspective, such concerns were not unfounded, for the IIB found reason to believe that the SPD-led government's increasing contacts with SWAPO was an attempt to infiltrate and divide the liberation movement.[171] Hence, it was of paramount importance to establish a security apparatus that was capable of protecting liberation movements 'against enemy activities'. To achieve this objective, there was an especially strong focus on political and ideological education. From the GDR's perspective, it was instrumental 'for the trainees to realise that real socialism was their main ally in the struggle for national and social liberation'.[172] Thus, one of the main objectives was 'to deepen the trainee's emotional bond towards socialism'.[173] East Berlin was concerned that SWAPO was ideologically fickle and thus susceptible to ideological influences from Western sources. The concern about SWAPO derived also from the accurate assessment that West Germany, and other Western countries, tried to increase their influence in southern Africa by manipulating public opinion through educational programmes, cultural exchange, sport and media.[174]

---

[169] See Schleicher, 'GDR Solidarity', 1090–1094 and 1126–1127. The GDR, for example, educated SWAPO children in East Germany, offered vocational training for older students and provided opportunities for university education.

[170] BStU, JHS Potsdam, Mikrofilmstelle, VVS JHS o001–110/82, Lehrkonzeption für Grundlehrgänge auf dem Gebiet der politisch-operativen Sicherung von Befreiungsorganisationen des südlichen Afrika, 01.09.1982, 4.

[171] BStU, MfS Hauptverwaltung Aufklärung Nr. 65, Zum Stellenwert des südlichen Afrika in der gegenwärtigen Afrika-Politik der imperialistischen Staaten, 15.06.1977, 200.For example, O.T. Emvula, the Head of the SWAPO representatives in the GDR, assessed Nujoma's first visit to Bonn rather critically, stating during talks in the Ministry of State Security that the Federal Republic's aim was to 'gather direct information about SWAPO and 'separate SWAPO from its friends (SSG)': PAAA, MfAA, ZR 2765/84, 1981, Vermerk Gespräch mit Genossen O.T. Emvula, Leiter der Vertretung der SWAPO in der DDR, 07.11.1980, 3.

[172] BStU, JHS Potsdam, Mikrofilmstelle, VVS JHS o001–110/82, Lehrkonzeption für Grundlehrgänge auf dem Gebiet der politisch-operativen Sicherung von Befreiungsorganisationen des südlichen Afrika, 01.09.1982, 9.

[173] Ibid., 9.

[174] See PAAA, MfAA, ZR 2495/86, 1980–1982, Abt. OZA /SA II, Zu imperialistischen Aktivitäten im Bereich der kultur-wissenschaftlichen Zusammenarbeit mit der VR Angola, 16.03.1981.

However, such concerns were not an Africa-specific phenomenon, for East Berlin harboured similar concerns about the possible infiltration of Western ideas into the minds of the general population in the GDR. In fact, Brandt's *Ostpolitik* was viewed as an attempt to infiltrate the GDR through rapprochement.[175] Thus, it seems that the GDR's fundamental fear of West German infiltration was, to some extent, projected onto SWAPO. SWAPO's first official visit to West Germany in 1980 and the opening of a SWAPO office in Bonn in mid-1982 further fanned these concerns. In fact, the IIB released its educational concept for SWAPO cadres in September 1982. Importantly, however, the *Bundestag* acknowledged already in mid-1978 that the GDR actively tried to undermine West Germany's ability to implement its policies in Africa through the development of intelligence and security services in African countries.[176]

It thus made sense for the IIB to have precise ideas about the objectives of the programme. There were even clear guidelines as to which character traits were required to attain the standard of a 'revolutionary fighter' – 'discipline, dedication, willingness to make sacrifices, unwavering loyalty and devotion to the organisation, hatred against the enemy and strong affinity with the working class and other strata of the working people of South Africa and Namibia'. Obviously, the programme was not geared towards preparing SWAPO cadres for combat, but aimed at educating cadres of liberation movements in the main principles of socialism. The ultimate goal was, therefore, to consolidate liberation movements against the encroachment of Western influences.

The NVA, the GDR's National Volksarmee, provided extensive training for cadres of liberation movements at various military academies in the GDR.[177] Importantly, however, the SED had a strong interest in keeping the GDR's military undertakings in Africa under wraps, for there was little international tolerance concerning German military activities after 1945.[178] Moreover, Moscow viewed the GDR's considerable armed forces as a bulwark against the North Atlantic Treaty Organization (NATO), a Western military alliance. Con-

---

[175] For a more detailed assessment of East Berlin's concerns about 'political and ideological diversion', see A. Glaeser, *Political Epistemics: The Secret Police, the Opposition and the End of East German Socialism,* Chicago, University of Chicago Press, 2011, 465–527.

[176] Deutscher Bundestag, 8. Wahlperiode, Stenographischer Bericht, 100. Sitzung, 22.06.1978, 7967.

[177] See, e.g., Winrow, *The Foreign Policy*, 121–150; Van der Heyden, *GDR International Development,* 121–148; Schleicher, 'GDR Solidarity', 1104 and 1130–1132.

[178] See also S. Lorenzini, 'East-South relations in the 1970s and the GDR involvement in Africa', in M. Guderzo and B. Bagnato (eds.), *The Globalization of the Cold War: Diplomacy and Local Confrontation, 1975–85*, New York, Routledge, 2010, 111. However, East Berlin agreed with this view and therefore saw 'international military engagement as politically not intolerable': H.-G. Schleicher, 'Waffen für den Süden Afrikas. Die DDR und der bewaffnete Befreiungskampf', in U. van der Heyden, I. Schleicher und H.-G. Schleicher (eds.), *Engagiert für Afrika: Die DDR und Afrika II,* Münster, LIT, 1994.

sequently, the NVA was firmly embedded in Moscow's defence strategy along the western borders. Unlike Cuba, the GDR never became Moscow's instrument for fighting proxy wars in the Third World.[179]

Whenever possible, Moscow and Washington relied on proxy armies, not least because 'they were burnt in Afghanistan and Vietnam'.[180] The Eastern and Western blocs provided mainly military assistance in advisory, training and aid, which of course exacerbated conflict. In southern Africa, Moscow was mainly responsible for supplying arms, while Havana provided manpower and East Berlin advisory and technical support, military training, education and medical care for liberation fighters wounded in battle.[181] In 1967, the SED Politbüro granted southern African liberation movements various types of small arms and ammunition. In the early 1970s, SWAPO received, for the first time, non-lethal military equipment. As part of the intensification of relations between the GDR and SWAPO, the first delivery of weapons arrived in early 1978. In the following years, SWAPO received a substantial amount of small arms, with a total value of several million East German marks.[182] However, these efforts were also undertaken with one eye on the Kremlin. The SED had reason to please the big brother in Moscow, for it needed to maintain the Kremlin's support on the German question and secure favourable economic relations with the Soviet Union.[183]

Consequently, from the perspective of East and West German rivalry in Namibia, the GDR's military assistance neither led to direct confrontation nor rivalry between the two Germanys in Africa. That West Germany prohibited arms exports to 'areas of tension' was, of course, a crucial factor. Nonetheless, West Germany's economic cooperation with South Africa, including in military and nuclear areas, was repeatedly criticised by the GDR and thus opened another front in the ongoing propaganda war between the two states.[184] East and West German rivalry in southern Africa was largely fought out on four fronts: propaganda, political action, ideological interference, and economic relations and support. Rivalry

---

[179] It is debatable whether or not Cuba was a proxy of Moscow in Africa. Some evidence indicates that Cuba was not a proxy of the Soviet Union in Angola. In Ethiopia, however, Havana seemed to have followed Moscow's lead: A. Z. Rubinstein, *Moscow's Third World Strategy*, Princeton, Princeton University Press, 1988, 173–174.

[180] R. Forsberg, 'Toward a nonaggressive world', *Bulletin of the Atomic Scientist*, Vol. 44, No.7, Chicago, Foundation for Nuclear Science, September 1988, 54. Accessed online January 2015, available from: www.tandfonline.com/doi/abs/10.1080/00963402.1988.11456202?journalCode=rbul20

[181] See also van der Heyden, 'GDR Development', 174–175; Schleicher, *DDR-Solidarität*, 26.

[182] Schleicher, 'Waffen für den Süden', 24. In 1978, for example, SWAPO received 135 tons of small arms, with a value of 1.15 million East German marks.

[183] Winrow, *The Foreign Policy*, 121. In 1975 already, Honecker signed a 'Treaty of Friendship' with the Soviet Union, which further underlined East Berlin's position on the side of Moscow.

[184] See Jabri, *Mediating Conflict*, 65.

between the two German states on Namibia played itself out through intangible rather than tangible forces.

The SED's Politbüro was responsible for the GDR's propaganda efforts against the West. The GDR showed great determination to discredit West Germany in Africa and at the UN, particularly in the late 1970s and early 1980s.[185] East Berlin hardly ever missed an opportunity to point out that West Germany's extensive economic relations with South Africa informally assisted Pretoria's policies and dominance in southern Africa.[186] Overall, West Germany expected in the late 1970s that the GDR's propaganda efforts would affect intra-German relations.[187] As the two German states' rivalry in Namibia played itself out through intangible rather than tangible forces, it made sense for the IIB to regard the political and ideological training of SWAPO cadres as a prime concern. Particular attention was paid to the Marxist-Leninist theories of imperialism.[188] However, the IIB's educational programme for SWAPO cadres was not designed simply to serve as a guide to the principles of socialism, but to achieve a particular objective. In 1982, the IIB observed that 'imperialist intelligent agencies' increased subversive measures against liberation movements in southern Africa. Most alarmingly, the Western agencies came to the conclusion that Marxism-Leninism was starting to gain a firm foothold in southern Africa. Thus, the agencies underlined the importance of increasing 'political-ideological diversion' against national liberation.[189] The 'enemy's objective' was, as the institute explained, 'to take the fighters'

---

[185] See also Schleicher, 'GDR Solidarity', 1078–1080.
[186] See, e.g., PAAA, Zwischenarchiv, Bd. 138104, 1984–1985, 39.Un-GV; hier Top 29 – Namibia-Debatte, New York, 07.12.1984; Ibid., Statement by the Deputy Minister of Foreign Affairs and Permanent Representative of the German Democratic Republic to the United Nations, Ambassador Harry Ott, in the Plenary Meeting of the thirty-ninth session of the United Nations General Assembly on agenda item 29 entitled: 'Question of Namibia', on 30 November 1984.
[187] AAPD, 1979, Band II, Aufzeichnung des Ministerialdirigenten Lücking, Gegen uns gerichtete Aktivitäten der DDR in Afrika, 19.12.1979.
[188] BStU, JHS Potsdam, Mikrofilmstelle, VVS JHS o001–110/82, Lehrkonzeption für Grundlehrgänge auf dem Gebiet der politisch-operativen Sicherung von Befreiungsorganisationen des südlichen Afrika, 01.09.1982, 11. It is worth noting here that the SED's central dogma was embedded in Marxism-Leninism and, therefore, was also integrated into the educational programme for liberation movements.
[189] BStU, JHS Potsdam, Mikrofilmstelle, VVS JHS o001–110/82, Lehrkonzeption für Grundlehrgänge auf dem Gebiet der politisch-operativen Sicherung von Befreiungsorganisationen des südlichen Afrika, 01.09.1982, 16. The *Stasi* applied similar measures within the GDR, attempting to prevent the secret services of the West to target the socialist system of the state through 'political-ideological diversion'. It was believed that the West tried to 'destroy the socialist consciousness of the people' through 'political underground activities'. Hence, 'the enemy' tried to instil Western ideological ideas into the minds of the East German population: H. Labrenz-Weiss, 'Stasi at Humboldt University: State Security's Organizational Structures and Control Mechanism in the University, in B. Becker-Cantarino, *Berlin in Focus: Cultural Transformations in Germany*, Connecticut, Greenwood Publishing Group, Inc., 1996, 55–70.

confidence in victory, corrupt the leadership, to divide the organisation and thus paralyse it through inner conflicts'.

To counter further imperialist advances, the IIB stressed the importance of ideological education for the cadres of liberation movements: 'It needs to be pointed out [to the cadres of liberation movements] that ideological diversion is supposed to build the foundation for subversive and other crimes against liberation movements, and that the impact of these measures are used for the acceleration of hostile ideological attacks'.[190] Hence, it seems reasonable to suggest that the educational programme for liberation movement cadres was based on East Berlin's own counterintelligence measures against the infiltration of Western security agencies into the GDR.

Considering the GDR's extensive counter-espionage apparatus and enormous domestic surveillance capacity and reach, the Ministry of State Security was exceptionally well qualified to educate liberation movements in espionage, counter-espionage and ideological warfare. The education of ANC and SWAPO cadres was an ongoing effort to develop a unified and independent security apparatus that would be capable of repelling the 'subversive activities of the security services of South Africa and the main bodies of the imperialist powers'.[191] In the assessment of the IIB, the ANC and SWAPO's security measures were inadequate and too widely spread and thus posed a threat to the cohesion of the movements.

Between 1979 and 1984, SWAPO military cadres received training, in groups of about 12 to15 men, in the GDR, mainly in the areas mentioned above. The training courses were for 3 to 4 months. In preparation for Namibia's independence, a substantial number of SWAPO cadres also received training in 1987/88.[192] The educational programme can be divided in two categories: political and ideological warfare, and defence and reconnaissance countermeasures. The IIB outlined the two main focal points as follows: firstly, to detect and foil with great determination subversive activities against liberation movements, with a special focus on infiltration attempts and other hostile plans and machinations; secondly, to organise offensive and effective protection of the various political, military and other combat activities, and of leading personalities and facilities of liberation movements.[193]

East Berlin invested considerable effort into corroborating the ANC and SWAPO's affinity with Marxism-Leninism. The aim was to strengthen the two liberation movements' ideological conviction in socialism and their affinity with Eastern bloc countries. The underlying

---

[190] Ibid., 16–17.
[191] Ibid., 6–10.
[192] Schleicher/Engel, *DDR-Geheimdienst*, 407–408.
[193] BStU, JHS Potsdam, Mikrofilmstelle, VVS JHS o001-110/82, Lehrkonzeption für Grundlehrgänge auf dem Gebiet der politisch-operativen Sicherung von Befreiungsorganisationen des südlichen Afrika, 01.09.1982, 6.

motive was to increase the influence of socialism in the Third World, which supported Moscow in realising its great power interests.[194] In countries that had achieved national independence, such as Mozambique, GDR-advisors continued to exert influence largely through police assistance and the construction of a centralised state, with the aim to consolidating independence.[195]

The educational programme for liberation movements, as outlined by the IIB, to some degree resembled the MfS' measures against West German infiltration after the introduction of *Ostpolitik*. Although East Berlin largely welcomed *Ostpolitik*, it feared that West Germany sought to increase contact in order to politically and ideologically manipulate GDR citizens into committing acts against state and society.[196] It, therefore, becomes apparent that from East Berlin's perspective, West Germany's move towards SWAPO was propelled by the same dynamic that motivated the Federal Republic's rapprochement with the GDR. The dominant concern was that West Germany had no sincere desire to improve relations, but was attempting to weaken both SWAPO and the GDR from within. In southern Africa, West Germany was, in the GDR's view, actively trying to undermine the rise of socialism.[197] Further analyses in the following chapters will examine whether the GDR's scepticism about West Germany's efforts to improve relations with SWAPO was unfounded.

It would be wrong to assume, however, that the GDR was merely a well-oiled ideologically controlled apparatus. On the contrary, a shared belief in socialism among the ruling class shaped the GDR's identity. For example, Peter Florin, the GDR's permanent representative to the UN, Herman Axen, a leading member of the SED Politbüro and Oscar Fischer, the GDR's foreign minister, were united in their objective to spread socialism throughout the world. Of course, some in the SED saw the GDR's involvement in Africa as a means to enhance their status within the party and, as Schleicher points out, 'satisfy personal vanities'.[198] Given that the high command of the Warsaw Pact commissioned the GDR with the task of increasing military support in Africa, it seems plausible that the GDR's policy towards southern Africa might have presented opportunities for building a reputation under the watchful

---

[194] See also PAAA, MfAA, ZR 439/86, Abt. Auslandsinformation, 1976–1981, Konzeption für die auslandsinformatorische Arbeit der DDR gegenüber den sozialistisch orientierten Ländern Afrikas und im arabischen Raum, 19.01.1981.

[195] H.-H., Döring, *'Es geht um unsere Existenz': Die Politik der DDR gegenüber der Dritten Welt am Beispiel von Mosambik und Äthiopien*, Berlin, Ch. Links Verlag, 1999, 226.

[196] Glaeser, *Political Epistemics*, 478–479. See also H. Labrenz-Weiss, 'Stasi at Humboldt University', 55–70.

[197] See also Schleicher, 'Interessenlage', 254.

[198] Ibid., 257.

eyes of the eight communist countries that formed the Warsaw Pact.[199] Honecker personally overlooked the international affairs of the GDR, especially with regard to Africa. He was particularly fixated on southern Africa, not least because successes became increasingly visible in the late 1970s and 1980s.[200] Although Honecker sought international recognition as leader, it cannot be denied that solidarity with the African liberation struggles was for him a 'matter of the heart'.[201]

However, despite the compelling strategic reasons for establishing relations with liberation movements, the SED did not indiscriminately offer solidarity. Ideological and political affinity with socialism was a guiding principle for identifying suitable candidates.[202] Although socialism was not always pronounced in liberation movements, the GDR recognised, in most cases, a willingness to embrace socialist theories. Ideological kinship was viewed as an important ingredient for establishing cohesion between nations. In fact, both the Soviet and the Western bloc recognised ideology as an instrument to cement their influence in Third World countries.

While the SED was committed to supporting other nations in realising national independence and self-determination, everyday life for the wider GDR population was neither marked by independence nor self-determination. Those were, of course, liberties most GDR citizens desired for themselves and thus reflected the fundamental contradiction in the GDR's policy towards southern Africa. Yet, despite the GDR's paternalistic control of its citizens, large numbers of people identified with their state's solidarity with southern African liberation struggles. This was the case largely because it promoted a sense of being on the right side of the ideological divide, not least because the other Germany maintained close relations with the apartheid regime.[203] Even for ordinary GDR citizens, solidarity with nations struggling for national self-determination was a 'matter of the heart'.[204] Hence, for the purpose of cultivating a positive national and international image, the SED was eager to publicly emphasise the sincere sympathy of ordinary GDR citizens for the African liberation struggles.[205] Furthermore, the GDR's leadership saw solidarity as a potentially useful tool for

---

[199] J. Nawrocki, 'Hoffmanns "Afrikakorps"', *Die Zeit*, 26.05.1978.
[200] Schleicher, 'Interessenlage', 257.
[201] Interview with Hans-Georg Schleicher, Berlin, 20.02.2016.
[202] B. H. Schulz, 'The politics of East-South relations: The GDR and Southern Africa', in T. A. Baylis, D. Childs, E. L. Collier and M. Rueschemeyer (eds.), *East Germany in Comparative Perspective*, London, Routledge, 1989, 159. See also, Schleicher, 'GDR Solidarity', 1083–1084; Schleicher, *DDR Solidarität*, 13.
[203] See also Schleicher, 'GDR Solidarity', 1101.
[204] Schleicher, 'GDR Solidarity', 1097–1102. See also BArch, DZ8/3a, Baku, 12.–14.6.1976.
[205] See Babing, *Gegen Rassismus, 1977–1982*, Gemeinsame Erklärung des Solidaritätskomitees der DDR und des DDR-Komitees für die UN-Kampfdekade gegen Rassendiskriminierung zum Tag der Solidarität mit dem Volk von Namibia, 26.081977, 83–84.

bringing together the country, which was strongly reflected in a speech by Kurt Seibt, the president of the Solidarity Committee: 'We call on all social organisations and institutions of our republic to deepen the thought of anti-imperialistic solidarity and proletarian internationalism in the minds and hearts of our people'.[206]

In schools, kindergartens and hospitals, the wider GDR population came into contact with the men, women and children of liberation movements living in the GDR. Families went on outings with wounded liberation movement cadres, organised fundraisers for their families and collected toys for the children.[207] Although the wider GDR population largely supported solidarity with liberation movements and, therefore, showed significant 'solidarity potential', 'the centralistic mechanism of society tended to discourage rather than encourage people's own initiatives', as Schleicher points out.[208]

Consequently, the GDR experience of the so-called GDR Kids – the SWAPO children who grew up in East Germany – cannot be compared with the everyday experience of ordinary GDR citizens. Life in the GDR was not necessarily characterised by a feeling of togetherness between the African refugees and the wider GDR population. Winnie Ya-Otto, one of the approximately 400 GDR children of Namibia, and the daughter of SWAPO's Secretary of Labour John Ya-Otto, recollects:

> Most of the time, life took place away from the wider GDR population. Outings with SWAPO parents, who were also educated in the GDR, and older students in general did not involve the wider GDR population, only the relevant government officials. Our life in East Germany was pleasant and we grew up in a well-protected and structured environment.[209]

---

[206] Ibid., Aus der Rede von Kurt Seibt, Vorsitzender der Zentralen Revisionskommission der Sozialistischen Einheitspartei Deutschlands und Präsident des Solidaritätskomitees der DDR in Berlin, 02.05.1977, 69.

[207] Ibid., 60–61. Seibt also pointed out that the working class was the main contributor to the GDR's solidarity fund.

[208] Schleicher, 'GDR Solidarity', 1097–1102.

[209] Interview with Winnie Ya-Otto, Berlin, 15.01.2015. Winnie Ya-Otto grew up in the GDR and is the daughter of the late John Ya-Otto, SWAPO politician, trade-unionist and diplomat. The interviews in this thesis were conducted by the author. Primary source materials regarding the education of SWAPO cadres and children are held in the Bundesarchiv-Lichterfelde. See, e.g., BArch, DQ 4/5433, 1980–1989, Unterstützung der Berufsausbildung von Angehörigen der SWAPO (Namibia); BArch, DR 2/11382, 1979–1984, Zur Entwicklung der Ausbildung namibischer Frauen im SWAPO-Kinderheim in Bellin; BArch DR 2/11434, 1981–1983, Deutschintensivausbildung ausländischer Lehrlinge/Praktikanten. For a detailed account of the life of SWAPO children in the GDR, see C. Kenna (ed.), *Homecoming: The GDR Kids of Namibia*, Windhoek, New Namibia Books, 1999; C. Kenna (ed.), Die "DDR-Kinder" von Namibia: Heimkehrer in ein fremdes Land, Göttingen, Klaus Hess Verlag, 2010.

That does not, of course, mean that GDR citizens did not establish meaningful relationships with their African guests. However, it does imply that the GDR was not a haven for liberation movements, integrating its guests into the deeper layers of ordinary society. Members of liberation movements and their families came to the GDR for medical treatment or education and military training. To fully integrate the cadres of liberation movements and their families into GDR society would have defeated the purpose of their stay, namely to return to Namibia as soldiers, leaders and valuable members of society. Therefore, ideology was also central in the education of SWAPO cadres and children, for the SED hoped that its guests would one day return to Namibia as leaders, grounded in shared ideals with the GDR and a strong affinity with Marxism-Leninism.[210] Yet, the GDR did not force ideological education upon liberation movements. To the contrary, Nujoma, for example, pressed the GDR to ideologically educate SWAPO cadres.[211]

In sum, the SED's close relations with SWAPO was based on genuine support and both national and international interests. The GDR perceived West Germany's improving relations with SWAPO as a threat to its close relations with SWAPO and its wider interests.

---

[210] See, e.g., BArch, DR 2/11382, 1979–1984, Lehrprogramm: Ausgewählte Grundfragen des Marxismus-Leninismus; PAAA, MfAA, ZR 3112/93, 1990, Vermerk über das Gespräch des Ministers für Kultur, Herbert Schirmer mit dem Minister für Bildung, Kultur und Sport der Republik Namibia, Nahas Angula, 31.05.1990. This was also confirmed in interviews. Interview with Winnie Ya-Otto, Berlin, 15.01.2015; Hans-Georg Schleicher, 20.02.2016; Telephone interview with Uwe Zeise, Windhoek, 20.04.2016. Uwe Zeise was the GDR Ambassador to Zimbabwe between 1988 and 1990. He was also ambassador in Kenya and Tanzania. Zeise started his career in Africa in 1971.

[211] BArch-SAPMO, DY 30/5918, Bericht über den Aufenthalt der Delegation des ZK der SED und des Ministeriums für Volksbildung vom 17.10.1979–24.10.1979 bei SWAPO in Angola; Information über das Gespräch der Delegation mit dem Präsident der SWAPO, Genossen Sam Nujoma, 31.10.1979. Hans-Georg Schleicher also stated that cadres of liberation movements were eager to study the ideological theories of Marxism-Leninism. Interview with Hans-Georg Schleicher, Berlin, 20.02.2016.

3 SWAPO: the *Bundestag* and the Foreign Office

The *Bundestag*

Records of the *Bundestag* suggest that leaders and backbenchers of all political parties showed far-reaching interest in Namibia's independence struggle, at least until early 1980.[1] In the *Bundestag* all members had a platform to exercise their right to challenge the government's actions. Written questions, or interpellations, could be submitted and answered in writing by representative ministers of government. Major interpellations were debated further in an ensuing *Bundestag* session, mainly by ministers with experience and expertise in the policy areas under scrutiny. Hence, *Bundestag* debates represent relevant party positions, although limited speaking time allowed only a small and preselected group of parliamentarians to debate the interpellation in the *Bundestag*.[2] Consequently, *Bundestag* debates offer limited insight about backbencher support. But a close examination of mid–and late 1970s *Bundestag* debates offers valuable insight into the extent to which the SPD-led government's foreign policy principles shaped West Germany's policy towards southern Africa until the end of the Cold War in 1990.[3] This paves the way for a more comprehensive understanding of the Kohl government's struggle to articulate a coherent foreign policy toward southern Africa after its election victory in 1983.

After gaining power, the Kohl government was immediately faced with a substantial foreign policy challenge: how to bring the FDP, its indispensable coalition partner, and the CDU/CSU together, despite widely opposing viewpoints? This was especially challenging with regard to finding common ground on foreign policy issues, particularly concerning Africa. In the 1970s, the gulf between the two sides seemed unbridgeable. In early 1977, the CDU/CSU submitted a major interpellation to the government with regard to West Germany's policy on development assistance.[4] The answer to the interpellation was prepared in writing by Genscher and Marie Schlei, the Federal Minister of Economic Cooperation and Development, followed by a *Bundestag* debate in late 1977.[5] The *Bundestag* focused almost

---

[1] Brenke, *Die Bundesrepublik*, 159.
[2] For a detailed study of the *Bundestag*, see T. Saalfeld, 'Germany: Multiple Veto Points, Informal Coordination and Problems of Hidden Action', in K. Strom, W. C. Mueller and T. Bergman (eds.), Delegation and Accountability in Parliamentary Democracies, Oxford, Oxford University Press, 2003, 347–376.
[3] For additional information on *Bundestag* debates on southern Africa in the late 1970s, see also Brenke, *Die Bundesrepublik*, 159–176; Stiers, *Perzeptionen der Entwicklung*, 143–172.
[4] Deutscher Bundestag, 8. Wahlperiode, Drucksache 8/345, 04.05.1977.
[5] Ibid., Drucksache 8/879, 07.09.1977; ibid., Stenographischer Bericht, 52. Sitzung, 27.09.1977.

exclusively on the Federal Government's policy toward Africa; that is, the growing East-West competition over influence in southern Africa.

As the session of 27 September 1977 offers particular valuable insight into the government-opposition divide with regard to the Soviet expansionist strategy in southern Africa, the debate will be examined in detail. Subsequent debates will not be explored in the same depth, but will be discussed to establish to what extent the opposition changed position before and after gaining power in 1983.

The *Bundestag* debate highlighted that all factions within the SPD/FDP coalition government supported the Federal Government's policy to promote change through rapprochement in southern Africa. Though the Schmidt government did not declare the principles of *Ostpolitik* to be the guiding principles of its foreign policy toward southern Africa, the widely-expressed desire for a rapprochement with pro-communist governments and liberation movements in southern Africa invites such comparison. The generally high level of support within the SPD/FDP coalition government for an ideologically non-discriminatory foreign policy toward Africa, particularly southern Africa, seemed to also reflect the growing international understanding that it was impossible to reach a settlement in Namibia without SWAPO.[6] The CDU/CSU parliamentary faction, on the other hand, was divided between the moderates, who emphasised commonalities with the government in the vital foreign policy issues, and the hardliners, who took a more uncompromising position, focussing on fundamental foreign policy differences.[7] However, both factions were united in their opposition to forge ties of solidarity with African countries and liberation movements that maintained close relations with the communist bloc.[8]

In late 1977, most Western countries still thought it controversial to establish relations with southern African liberation movements, although the UN General Assembly endorsed SWAPO's armed independence struggle in 1976. The CDU/CSU hardliners, who were strongly fixated on the East-West conflict, had little sympathy for the actions of liberation

---

[6] See also Ibid, 4004. Furthermore, Genscher left little doubt as to his government's position on ideological proliferation: 'We don't want to export ideologies'. The opposition, however, questioned Genscher's statement, arguing that Western values such as human rights and democracy would not fall within the category of ideology. The CDU/CSU opposition further stated that Genscher's assertion was built on hypocrisy, for the government endorsed freedom and social market economy in international discussions on the world economic order. However, Genscher statement was based on the non-aligned principles and therefore on the idea that nations could establish close and friendly relations with both the East and the West. Hence, there was in principle no need for ideological proliferation or alignment: Ibid., 4064.

[7] See Ibid., 3973–4069.

[8] In the late 1970s, the CDU/CSU maintained fairly uniform perceptions on issues such as liberation movements, developments in Namibia and the engagement of the Eastern bloc in southern Africa, as Werner Stiers points out. See Stiers, *Perzeptionen der Entwicklung*, 156.

movements. During the *Bundestag* debate, Jürgen Todenhöfer, the CDU/CSU parliamentary spokesperson for development policy and a self-proclaimed admirer of Strauß, left little doubt about the CDU/CSU's disapproval of the provision of humanitarian aid to liberation movements: 'We don't give money to terrorists'.[9]

Strauß' position with regard to liberation movements was equally uncompromising. His previous statement that humanitarian assistance to liberation movements was an 'accessory to murder' provoked a strong response from within the SPD. Strauß, who was no stranger to political controversy, maintained his position by arguing that material support of liberation movements, even if unmistakeably given as humanitarian aid, might not be understood by the receiver as such and, therefore, might be used otherwise. Hence, material support might be channelled into the wrong direction, thus assisting murder. Furthermore, Strauß also stressed that liberation movements do not necessarily bring freedom. The conflict in Angola between the three national liberation movements, he argued, had locked the country – fuelled by Soviet and Cuban weapons transfers – in a bloody civil war between late 1975 and early 1976.[10] From the perspective of the conservative coalition, the government failed to recognise that the actions of liberation movements were related to the Soviet Union's imperialist expansion of power.[11]

In this light, the CDU/CSU opposition also criticised the SPD-led government for failing to elaborate on the GDR's support and education of African 'guerrilla groups'. That the Federal Government remained silent on the matter seemed of particular concern to the opposition, for the GDR's activities in Africa threatened international peace.[12] The debate, however, focussed on the growing desire within the SPD-led government to improve relations with liberation movements rather than the GDR's activities and presence in southern Africa. Fundamentally, however, Bonn's changing attitude towards liberation movements was, to a certain extent, interlinked with East Berlin's growing influence in southern Africa. After all, the GDR owed much of its regional influence to its solidarity with national liberation movements. When understood in this light, it becomes apparent that *Bundestag* debates about southern African liberation movements contained underlying intra-German issues, even if only in the broadest sense.

Importantly, however, the SPD-led government under Helmut Schmidt saw no reason to confront the GDR in Africa, for it was the West's lack of support that motivated liberation movements to seek support from the GDR and other Eastern bloc countries. Hence, in re-

---

[9] J. Leinemann, 'Das Büblein stampft und hacket', *Der Spiegel,* 34/1979, 20.08.1979; Deutscher Bundestag, 8. Wahlperiode, Stenographischer Bericht, 52. Sitzung, 27.10.1977, 3978.
[10] Deutscher Bundestag, 8. Wahlperiode, Stenographischer Bericht, 52. Sitzung, 27.10.1977, 4047.
[11] Ibid., 4009.
[12] Ibid, Drucksache 8/879, 07.09.1977, 9.

sponse to the GDR's growing military cooperation with developing countries, the Federal Government envisioned 'to intensify its co-operation with Third World nations for the promotion of independence and peaceful development'. In order to enhance awareness in Third World countries for real independence, the government stressed the importance of information and communication. In this respect, the Schmidt government used its diplomatic and political contacts to emphasise to Third World countries that East Berlin's activities were not altruistic but geared toward expanding the GDR's spheres of influence. The government agreed with the opposition that the GDR's ultimate aim was to alter the global balance of power in favour of the Eastern bloc.[13] However, instead of confronting the GDR in Africa, the SPD-led government argued that helping African nations progress toward economic growth and national independence would ultimately reduce dependency on foreign powers and thus help to achieve non-alignment. In the case of liberation movements, the same conceptual approach applied, namely to loosen the movements' dependency on foreign powers by providing tailored support. At the centre of this strategy stood the conviction that Third World countries were neither interested in capitalism nor communism, but in fulfilling fundamental human needs.[14]

For the Schmidt government, the policy of détente was 'indivisible'.[15] Although Brandt's *Ostpolitik* was geared toward improving relations between East and West Germany on German territory, the government was careful not to let tensions related to the division of Germany spill over into the Third World. It is not surprising, therefore, that the SPD-led government warned repeatedly against transferring the East-West dichotomy to the Third World.[16] In fact, the advocates of détente argued that the East-West rivalry in southern Africa had its origins in Europe and it would, thus, be futile to treat it as an African problem.[17]

The CDU/CSU opposition found it difficult to accept such a policy in the face of Soviet expansionism in the Third World in the late 1970s. Moreover, reality painted a different picture, displaying the full complexity of the rivalry between East and West Germany in Africa. Although *Ostpolitik* improved German-German relations in the early to mid-1970s, foreign policy became an increasing cause for tensions in the late 1970s, particularly with regard to southern Africa. Undeniably, the clear conflict of interest between the two German states in southern Africa also had a negative effect on intra-German relations. However, the SPD-led government seemed, in stark contrast to the CDU/CSU, less susceptible to entanglements in confrontational Cold War rivalries.[18]

---

[13] Ibid., 9.
[14] Ibid., Stenographischer Bericht, 52. Sitzung, 27.09.1977, 4004–4006.
[15] Ibid, Drucksache 8/879, 07.09.1977, 9.
[16] Ibid., 9.
[17] See also Chapter Three, FDP.
[18] In this context, Vohrer criticised the CDU/CSU opposition for prematurely rejecting countries

Brandt's *Ostpolitik* was built on the premise that rapprochement and not confrontation with the Eastern bloc countries would bring about the desired changes. The German-German rivalry in southern Africa was thus unlikely to escalate into a full-scale confrontation under the SPD-led government. The reassuring, albeit moderate, success of *Ostpolitik* in improving intra-German relations gave the SPD-led government reason to believe that rapprochement with communist influenced countries and liberation movements in southern Africa would soften East-West tensions in the region.[19] Following that line of thinking, Manfred Vohrer, the FDP spokesperson for development policy, warned that the West's failure to show solidarity with the black majority of Rhodesia, Namibia and South Africa would only push liberation movements toward the Eastern bloc. Such a process, Vohrer pointed out, had already taken place in the former Portuguese colonies.[20] For the same reason, the Federal Government strongly disapproved of the CDU/CSU attempts to attach the terrorist label to liberation movements. To this effect, Bahr (SPD) stressed that the 'just struggle' of southern African liberation movements cannot be compared with the 'terrorist crimes' committed in West Germany.[21]

Considering that the CDU/CSU strongly opposed *Ostpolitik*, it is not surprising that the coalition criticised the missing linkage between détente in Europe and Soviet expansionism in southern Africa: 'While new versions of détente are explored in Europe, the Soviet Union and Cuba, both foreign to the region, massively enhance their power in Africa', the CDU parliamentarian Werner Marx pointed out'.[22] Obviously, part of his criticism was directed against the Brandt government's failed attempt to promote peaceful change in Angola through economic rapprochement between the Portuguese dictatorship and Europe.[23]

---

and liberation movements for their supposed ideological affiliation. See Deutscher Bundestag, 8. Wahlperiode, Stenographischer Bericht, 52. Sitzung, 27.09.1977, 3984.

[19] The SPD-led government was also influenced and positively motivated by Carter's 'optimism', as Schlei pointed out. See Deutscher Bundestag, 8. Wahlperiode, Stenographischer Bericht, 52. Sitzung, 27.09.1977, 3990. In 1977, Carter was still committed to the policy of détente, despite the Soviet Union's expansionist foreign policy. By 1979, however, Soviet advance in Southeast Asia and Africa led to the re-introduction of containment as the guiding principle of US foreign policy. For a closer look at Carter's policies, see K. E., Morris, *Jimmy Carter, American Moralist*, Georgia, University of Georgia Press, 1969.

[20] Deutscher Bundestag, 8. Wahlperiode, Stenographischer Bericht, 52. Sitzung, 27.09.1977, 3984. For an in-depth account of West Germany's position during the decolonisation of the Portuguese colonial empire in Africa, see L. Lopes, *West Germany and the Portuguese Dictatorship, 1968–1974: Between Cold War and Colonialism*, Basingstoke, Palgrave Mcmillan, 2014.

[21] In the late 1970s, the Red Army Faction and other Marxist-Leninist groups resorted to terrorism to overthrow West Germany's Government, or West Germany's 'system of oppression', as Bahr described the aim of such terrorist groups during the *Bundestag* debate: Deutscher Bundestag, 8. Wahlperiode, Stenographischer Bericht, 52. Sitzung, 27.09.1977, 4052.

[22] Ibid, 4063.

[23] See also Lopes, *West Germany and the Portuguese*, 245.

This line of thinking, which was popular in the CDU/CSU, was also expressed by Strauß: 'What is the meaning of détente, when ... Soviet weapon supplies will fuel one giant bloody civil war after the other'.[24]

Consequently, the CDU/CSU had clear ideas on the requirements and conditions for establishing relationships with African nations. The main principles were laid out in the *Bundestag* by Todenhöfer. Fundamentally, the CDU/CSU's disapproval was centred on the government's efforts to improve the economic development of Third World countries, while the Soviet Union focused predominately on exporting weapons and ideologies. Todenhöfer pointed out that the CDU/CSU took the view that development aid should only be granted if a co-operative partnership was possible and politically acceptable. Thus, it was particularly problematic to provide development assistance to 'communist developing countries; developing countries that integrate themselves into the Soviet global strategy in the Third World; developing countries that are involved in local conflicts and take up peace-endangering radical positions; and countries that promote international terrorism'.[25] Volkmar Köhler, the CDU Vice Chairman for Economic Co-operation and Development, expressed similar views, but added that the CDU/CSU generally agreed with the government on supporting developing countries to achieve 'independence from everyone'.[26] Fundamentally, Köhler and Todenhöfer made the same accusation, namely that the government lacked a strategy against the increasing influence of the communist bloc countries, including the GDR, in Africa. Put most simply, the CDU/CSU viewed the Federal Government's development policy as too undiscriminating

However, the Federal Government deemed it wrong to use development assistance for short-term foreign policy aims, not least because long-term development assistance was intended to benefit both West Germany and underdeveloped countries economically. After all, economic growth in developing countries offered West Germany's national economy the prospect of access to potentially lucrative new markets. That development assistance would also benefit West Germany was difficult to dispute and thus received widespread support among all political parties.[27] This shows that the CDU/CSU's concerns lay entirely with the Soviet Union's growing influence in southern Africa.

---

[24] Deutscher Bundestag, 8. Wahlperiode, Stenographischer Bericht, 52. Sitzung, 27.10.1977, 4046. In 1982, Strauß argued in a similar fashion, declaring that the policy of détente had promoted Soviet arms build-up, particularly in the Third World: 'Strauß: Südafrika im globalen Konzept Moskaus', *Die Welt*, 02.04.1982

[25] Deutscher Bundestag, 8. Wahlperiode, Stenographischer Bericht, 52. Sitzung, 27.10.1977, 3977.

[26] Ibid., 4009. Furthermore, Kohler stressed that the CDU/CSU 'wants that Africa is the continent of the Africans'.

[27] Ibid., 3983–3988.

The SPD-led government was, however, opposed to a foreign policy toward Africa that was based on ideological discrimination, not least because of the underlying polarising consequences. The government, for its part, was committed to replacing confrontation with co-operation.[28] During the *Bundestag* debate, this point of view was most strongly expressed by Schlei: 'We will not allow ourselves to be forced into Cold War-type confrontations in developing countries'.[29] Furthermore, in stark contrast to the CDU/CSU, the SPD-led government rejected any interference in the affairs of other countries. Instead of forcing developing countries to side with either East or West, the objective was to promote independence, through economic development, from both the Western and Soviet blocs. Hence, the Schmidt government argued that 'development assistance was an important element of foreign policy'. In this view, Third World countries had to be part of the economic progress in the world for peaceful development to materialise.[30] Ideological orientation was therefore not an important factor in determining whether or not a country should receive development assistance, for the main objective of development assistance, namely, economic stability and growth, would promote greater ideological independence in Third World countries. Therefore, the wider benefits of being integrated into the Western economy, such as the satisfaction of basic needs through economic growth, would make a unilateral commitment toward the Soviet bloc increasingly unattractive for developing countries.[31]

From the opposition's perspective, the Federal Government's strategy was fundamentally flawed, for the impact of Western economic exchange and assistance remained limited, while communist weapon exports further inflamed conflict in the Third World. Furthermore, Western economic relations with pro-communist regimes in the Third World indirectly benefitted Moscow. Given that the Soviet Union's economic capacity was too limited to provide substantial economic stability to Third World countries under its influence, Western economic assistance to pro-communist countries unintentionally helped to compensate for Moscow's shortcomings on the part of providing economic stability, or in Todenhöfer's words: 'In many countries, the Soviet Union concentrates on military and political influence and views Western help, if given nonpolitically, as an accompanying measure of its own strategy'.[32]

It is, therefore, understandable that the Soviet Union's geopolitical interests in Africa, and not the GDR, took centre stage at the *Bundestag* debate. Evidently, the SPD-led government took the view that the GDR's activities in southern Africa were closely aligned with

---

[28] Ibid., Drucksache 8/879, 07.09.1977, 2–4.
[29] Ibid., Stenographischer Bericht, 52. Sitzung, 27.09.1977, 3989.
[30] Ibid., Drucksache 8/879, 07.09.1977, 2–4.
[31] Ibid., Stenographischer Bericht, 52. Sitzung, 27.09.1977, 3985 and 3990.
[32] Ibid., 3977.

the Soviet Union's foreign policy objectives. Hence, the CDU/CSU's criticism of the Federal Government's failure to elaborate on the GDR's involvement in southern Africa seems to indicate that the opposition credited the GDR with a greater degree of foreign policy independence than the Federal Government, at least in the late 1970s.

As the communist bloc's influence in Africa continued to grow in the late 1970s, it is hardly surprising that the East-West conflict within Africa remained a topic of discussion in the *Bundestag* after the September 1977 debate. In April 1979, the CDU/CSU expressed their mounting frustration with the SPD-led government's Africa policy. The coalition's major interpellation to the *Bundestag* raised questions about, inter alia, SWAPO's position in the upcoming elections and, subsequently, the role of GDR-educated SWAPO cadres in a SWAPO-led Namibia.[33] The Soviet Union's expansionist policy in Africa, however, remained the CDU/CSU's main concern. A further CDU/CSU interpellation, also submitted in April 1979, urged the government to refrain from supporting liberation movements that used violence, which was not justified as a legitimate right to resistance.[34] Moreover, the CDU/CSU, including Helmut Kohl, continued to express their opposition to political and financial support for liberation movements, not least because 'liberation movements depended heavily on the Soviet Union and orientated their actions and goals on the imperialistic and anti-Western foreign policy of the Soviet Union'.[35]

In January 1980, several months before the national election, the *Bundestag* discussed the interpellations submitted by the CDU/CSU opposition, with an intensified focus on Soviet expansionism in Africa.[36] In a passionate *Bundestag* debate, the CDU/CSU essentially continued to accuse the government of lacking an effective strategy against 'Soviet imperialism and neo-colonialism' in Africa. The CDU/CSU pointed out that the Soviet Union and its 'proxies' had caused many conflicts and tensions on the African continent in recent years, and that several African states had also de facto become economically, politically and militarily dependent on Moscow.[37]

Genscher strongly rejected such accusations, emphasising that the Federal Government had always strongly condemned the Soviet Union as well as its 'accessories' from the Warsaw Pact countries and Cuba 'for attempting to gain power and influence on African soil,

---

[33] Ibid., Drucksache, 8/2748, 11.04.1979.
[34] Ibid. In late 1978, the SPD and FDP *Bundestag* faction also submitted a major interpellation with regard to Namibia based on concerns that South Africa might sabotage the efforts of the Western Contact Group and the UN regarding Namibia's independence. The SPD and FDP *Bundestag* faction asked the government to outline its Namibia strategy in the face of Pretoria's lack of cooperation: Deutscher Bundestag, 8. Wahlperiode, Drucksache, 8/2168, 06.10.1978.
[35] Ibid., Drucksache, 8/2728, 02.04.1979.
[36] Ibid., Stenographischer Bericht, 197. Sitzung, 18.01.1980.
[37] Ibid., 15691. Here, Stercken's statement probably referred to Angola and Mozambique.

as well as to bring countries that had only recently gained independence in new forms of political and ideological dependency'. In Genscher's view, it was 'particularly depressing' for West Germany to see that the GDR was an accessory of Soviet interests in Africa. Genscher emphasised, however, that he was not concerned about 'GDR experts who were employed for peaceful assistance and development, but soldiers and military personnel who influence the military education and the security and media sectors of African states'. In this regard, Genscher pointed out that the GDR undermined the cause of self-determination and independence in Africa.[38] Genscher acknowledged that the Soviet Union and its satellites promoted conflict in Africa through military education and aid, while simultaneously undermining the self-determination of newly independent states by ideologically and politically binding them to the communist bloc.

Obviously, Genscher largely agreed with the opposition's concerns about Moscow's policy towards Africa. The foreign minister was, however, careful to stress that it would be a grave mistake to take a narrow view of African countries cooperation with the communist bloc, for his criticism was not aimed at African countries' but at the Soviet Union's policy toward Africa. To this end, Genscher made an impassioned plea for objectivity: 'Let us not discriminate countries because they had at some point worked with the Soviet Union; let us not make the mistake to transfer the East-West conflict to Africa through artificial labels such as 'pro-Soviet' or 'pro-Western', to literally make a change of the domestic and foreign policy position impossible for these countries through premature labels, because they are labelled communist satellites'. Genscher continued to argue that African countries main objective was self-determination, which implied independence from both the capitalist West and the communist East. It would be fruitless, therefore, to try to bind African countries to the West.[39] He pointed out that the Federal Government's objective was to support African countries in achieving economic and social stability through 'expanded assistance', 'co-operative partnership' and 'the strengthening of independence and self-sufficiency'. He remained convinced that, regardless of the opposition's scepticism, such measures would ultimately 'show that the Soviet Union and its allies are not the natural partners of the Third World, but Western democracies, which offer a partnership based on equality and mutual respect'.[40] To this end, Genscher stressed the importance of political co-operation with Afri-

---

[38] Ibid., 15716–15717.
[39] Ibid., 15717. For a critical analysis from the CDU parliamentarian Hans Hugo Klein with regard to the SPD-led government's position expressed during the Bundestag debate, see Deutschland Union Dienst, Nr. 12/34, 6–8. Genscher emphasised the Federal Government's continuing commitment to détente with the Eastern bloc countries in 1980. The question was how to achieve détente throughout the world.
[40] Ibid., 15716–15717.

can countries that had already gained independence and, therefore, wanted to assert their independence. He was against categorically rejecting African countries simply because they maintained close ties with the communist bloc, for it would only drive them further away from the West.[41]

Wolfgang Roth, the chairman of the SPD's Developing Policy Commission, was more confrontational toward the opposition than Genscher, accusing the CDU/CSU of relying on a 'two-step' approach in southern Africa: 'First, they ask: what does the Soviet Union want? And afterwards they say: all right then, we do the opposite; perhaps we will have done something useful'.[42] Essentially, Roth accused the CDU/CSU of turning African conflicts into East-West conflicts. Like Genscher, Roth saw little benefit in discriminating against African countries simply because of their relations with the communist bloc. Roth took the view that African countries sought the support of the Soviet Union, GDR and Cuba because these countries were using 'anti-imperial, anti-colonial verbiage', creating the impression that the communist bloc would be the most reliable partner in the independence struggle.[43] Importantly, Roth acknowledged that the Soviet Union's policy towards Africa exerted a destructive influence on West Germany's Africa policy, but not in the overall context of the East-West conflict. Rather, he argued that the Eastern bloc hindered African countries in achieving the much-desired progress by assisting the build-up of African armies. In this context, Roth stated that 'the 3000 GDR military advisers in Africa do nothing positive, but contribute to the arms build-up on the continent'. In this view, the Soviet Union and the GDR contributed to the perpetuation of conflicts in Africa, which led to Roth's conclusion: 'it makes sense that we fight the expansion of Soviet interests in Africa, not because we seek an East-West conflict there, but because we want to create conditions for positive development in Africa'.[44] The SPD-led government, as well as its foreign minister, remained convinced that this objective could best be achieved through humanitarian aid, as well as through initiatives that promoted economic growth and reform in Africa, particularly with regard to southern Africa.[45]

The CDU/CSU opposition, however, continued to question this approach. Jürgen Todenhöfer, for example, argued that although Moscow sought rapprochement with the West, the policy of appeasement had failed, because the Soviet Union 'rejected a global easing of tensions' and thus continued to compete for influence with the Western powers in Third

---

[41] See also 'Genscher: Entwicklungshilfe verstärken', *Frankfurter Allgemeine Zeitung*, 19.01.1980.
[42] Deutscher Bundestag, 8. Wahlperiode, Stenographischer Bericht, 197. Sitzung, 18.01.1980, 15724.
[43] Ibid., 15724.
[44] Ibid., 15724.
[45] Ibid., 15720–15724.

World countries. In effect, Todenhöfer continued to question the usefulness of détente, for the East-West conflict had merely moved from one part of the world to another. 'To pursue a war policy in the Third World and Africa stands for the Soviet Union not in opposition to the so-called easing of tensions in East-West relations', Todenhöfer explained.[46]

Due to Soviet advances in Africa in the late 1970s, many in the CDU/CSU evidently felt vindicated for the hardline-stance they had taken toward communism in Africa since at least the collapse of the Portuguese empire. With seemingly genuine conviction, the CDU/CSU continued to warn the SPD-led government of the dangers of pursuing an appeasement policy in the face of Soviet expansionism.[47] Todenhöfer pointed out that the appeasement policy of the West had, over the last five years, not changed the Soviet Union's policy towards Africa, but motivated Moscow to intensify its offensive on the continent.[48] In a rather alarmist fashion, Todenhöfer warned again of the potential catastrophic consequences of unrestricted Soviet influence in the Third World:

> Along the Indian Ocean, the Soviet Union has managed to conquer one strategically important position after the other. It stretches from Vietnam, Laos and Cambodia, via Afghanistan, South Yemen, Ethiopia and Mozambique to Angola. You all know – the Foreign Minister surely also knows this – those who control the Indian Ocean, control Africa, control Asia and have in the long run also the chance to control Western Europe.[49]

Concerns over the expansionist Soviet global strategy were relatively widespread in the West at the turn of the decade. Nonetheless, the SPD-led government tried to encourage a positive outlook, although the Cold War offered a vivid background for apocalyptic forebodings. The CDU/CSU, however, dismissed the SPD-led government's optimistic approach as naïve or worse.[50] Seen in this light, it might be expected that hardliners such as Todenhöfer would accuse the SPD-government of 'playing down' the Soviet offensive in the Third World, while simultaneously 'using development aid to indiscriminately support pro-communist guerrilla-organisations and developing countries that are integrated into the Soviet

---

[46] Genscher emphasised the government's continuing commitment to détente with the Eastern bloc countries during a party meeting in 1980 and acknowledged that détente had to reach further: 'It is a matter of realizing this policy beyond Europe, throughout the world': Ibid, 15680.
[47] Ibid., 15718.
[48] Ibid., 15719.
[49] Ibid., 15718. Hans Stercken (CDU) made a similar statement, 15691–15692; see also Volkmar Köhler (CSU), 15731
[50] Deutscher Bundestag, 8. Wahlperiode, Stenographischer Bericht, 197. Sitzung, 18.01.1980, 15723. Interestingly, Carter's critics dismissed Washington's appeasement policy toward Moscow as naïve: M. B. M. B., Brown, *Condi: The Life of a Steel Magnolia, Nashville*, Thomas Nelson Publisher, 2007, 107.

global strategy'.⁵¹ In Todenhöfer's view, it was 'either naïve or dishonest' to believe that it would be possible to separate important pro-Soviet states with economic and development aid from the Soviet Union's global strategy.

Roth claimed that Todenhöfer's hard-line rhetoric was actively damaging the CDU/CSU's international image and stated that the SPD-led government 'appreciated the constructive contributions' of the CDU moderates, Volkmar Köhler and Alois Mertes.⁵² Still, the hardline positions expressed by Todenhöfer and Strauß received vociferous support from within the CDU/CSU in *Bundestag* debates in the late 1970s.⁵³

In the conservative view, 'the Soviet Union had potential influence over the crucial power political sectors, such as the military, security organs and state-run economy and administration, while the Federal Government and other Western powers provide extensive aid in all other areas'.⁵⁴ Thus, although the West provided Third World countries with extensive development assistance, crucial for economic and political stability, the communist bloc had influence over all-important political-military decision-making organs. Consequently, the strategy to loosen the communist grip on Third World countries through development aid was not achieving the desired results. Hence, the CDU/CSU continued to argue that development assistance should not be given to countries that 'integrate themselves into the Soviet Union's global strategy', but to countries that 'undertake serious efforts to bring about a change in the course of foreign policy'.⁵⁵

Basically, the CDU took the view that the military and economic potential of African nations was too limited to deter Soviet interventionism in Africa. Therefore, it was necessary to actively interfere in the political affairs of African nations, or 'risk leaving the field to the Soviet Union', as Todenhöfer put it.⁵⁶ Consequently, Pretoria's interventionist policy received widespread understanding from within the CDU/CSU. The SPD-led government displayed a more critical attitude towards Pretoria. After all, it advocated a non-interventionist foreign policy, which was the opposite of South Africa's self-proclaimed right to interfere in the internal affairs of neighbouring countries.⁵⁷

---

51 Cortier (SPD), for example, pointed out that the 'Cape-route argument', as used by Todenhöfer and others, was part of South African propaganda. See Deutscher Bundestag, 8. Wahlperiode, Stenographischer Bericht, 197. Sitzung, 18.01.1980, 15698–15722
52 Ibid., 15720–15724.
53 Ibid., Stenographischer Bericht, 97. Sitzung, 10.03.1978, 6203–6236.
54 Ibid., Stenographischer Bericht, 197. Sitzung, 18.01.1980, 15720.
55 Ibid., 15720. See also 'Opposition verlangt Engagement in Afrika', *Süddeutsche Zeitung*, 19.01.1980.
56 Ibid., 15720.
57 Noteworthy here, South Africa did not only claim the right to interfere in the internal affairs of its neighbours; it also stated that the West had no right to interfere in South Africa's internal affairs, including apartheid: J. Hanlon, *Beggar your Neighbours: Apartheid Power in Southern Africa*,

It is important to understand that the 1980 *Bundestag* debate took place at a time when the Soviet Union's influence in the Third World seemed to be increasing steadily. The notion that the policy of appeasement was aiding Soviet advances in the Third World became increasingly prevalent among Western conservatives at the turn of the decade. In fact, after years of appeasement under Carter, Reagan built his 1980 presidential campaign on anti-Soviet rhetoric and the apparent need to roll back communist advances in the Third World.[58] The Reagan administration's policy of 'rollback' eventually became known as the Reagan Doctrine. The policy was an energetic effort to undermine Soviet influence in the Third World by supporting anti-communist insurgencies and regimes, rather than directly challenging the Soviet Union militarily.

Seen in this light, it becomes apparent that the CDU/CSU's approach to the Soviet Union's growing influence in the Third World was a reflection of contemporary strategic thought, found predominantly within conservative parties. It is not altogether surprising, then, that the CDU/CSU argued that it was necessary to push back the influence of the communist bloc in the Third World. Todenhöfer criticised the SPD-led government's policy of non-interference in the internal affairs of other countries, arguing that 'there probably wouldn't be a communist Ethiopia, a refugee problem in Cambodia and an occupied Afghanistan' had the West acted decisively against the Soviet Union in Angola.[59] Overall, 'the appeasement policy of the West has not weakened the Soviet offensive; on the contrary, it has intensified it', Todenhöfer concluded.[60] In this context, the Soviet Union was viewed as a colonial power in Africa, aiming to establish, in the widest sense of the word, a colonial empire. In fact, Richard Jaeger, CSU member of the *Bundestag*, argued that the Soviet Union and its satellites, including the GDR, were the only powers that practised colonialism in South Africa [he probably meant southern Africa].[61]

With regard to liberation movements, the CDU/CSU continued to oppose strongly any cooperation with liberation movements that used violence to achieve national independence. The Federal Government, however, censored the opposition for their apparent double

---

Indiana, Indiana University Press, 1987, 60.

[58] See C. Adams, *Ideologies in Conflict: A Cold War Docu-Story*, Lincoln, iUniverse, Inc., 2001, 488.

[59] Carter's appeasement policy came under similar criticism in the late 1970s, which became increasingly attacked for being too soft on the Soviet Union. See Morris, *Jimmy Carter*, 274.

[60] Deutscher Bundestag, 8. Wahlperiode, Stenographischer Bericht, 197. Sitzung, 18.01.1980, 15719

[61] Ibid., 15736. The implementation of socialist structures in countries that came under the Soviet sphere of influence was often interpreted as an indication that Moscow harboured neo-colonial ambitions and thus was returning to Russia's pre-revolutionary era: B. Apor, 'Sovietisation, Imperial Rule and the Stalinist Leader Cult in Central and Eastern Europe', in R. Healy and E. Dal Lago (eds.), *The Shadow of Colonialism on Europe's Modern Past*, Hampshire, Palgrave Macmillan, 2014, 234.

standards with regard to liberation movements. The government pointed out that, although the CDU/CSU saw no problem in talking with the Pretoria-backed liberation movement, UNITA, in Angola, conservatives continued to identify SWAPO as 'terrorists and gangs of murderers'. With seemingly growing conviction, the SPD-led government emphasised that the right to resist applied in the face of terror and oppression, just as laid down in West Germany's constitution. For the SPD-led government, this position also implied violent resistance.[62]

The SPD-led government claimed that, in the CDU/CSU policy towards Africa, an overly narrow focus on the Soviet Union's actions in Africa was predominant. Corterier, for example, accused the CDU/CSU of seeing Africa 'only through the glasses of the East West conflict', while Helmut Schäfer, FDP spokesman for Foreign Affairs, compared CDU/CSU hard-line positions with the foreign policy doctrine of the 'obsolete Hallstein Doctrine'.[63] In the same breath, he also praised *Ostpolitik* for improving West Germany's relations with Africa.[64] The CDU/CSU, on the other hand, argued that the government's policy of détente was not a viable and effective strategy in the face of Soviet expansionism in Africa. Given that the Soviet Union saw Africa, Asia and South America through the prism of 'world revolution and global dominance', it was impossible to separate the challenges in southern Africa from the East-West conflict, as Jaeger pointed out.[65] Despite these fundamental disagreements, the government and opposition agreed in principle that the communist bloc had a negative impact on Africa.

However, the CDU/CSU strongly disagreed with the SPD-led government on how to loosen the communist grip on Africa. While the SPD-led government believed that economic progress and national independence would promote in African nations the desire to implement the principles of non-alignment, the CDU/CSU doubted that progress and independence alone would bring about such a positive outcome, especially if a strong communist influence had already existed during the pre-independence period. The SPD-led government disagreed with this line of reasoning, pointing out, quite rightly, that in many countries a

---

[62] Ibid., 15701–15702. Brandt's statement at the Socialist International was based on similar conclusions, which, however, caused outrage amongst the CDU/CSU opposition in 1978. By 1980, such a position had become less controversial, not least because there was greater support for SWAPO's cause in the West.

[63] Ibid., 15698.

[64] Ibid., 15703–15705. Schäfer pointed out that the Hallstein Doctrine denied diplomatic relations to countries that didn't follow Bonn's 'demand for good conduct'; that is, countries that established diplomatic relations with the GDR. Hence, the CDU/CSU demand for declining support to countries and liberation movements with close ties to the Communist bloc was, in Schäfer's view, comparable to the Hallstein Doctrine.

[65] Deutscher Bundestag, 8. Wahlperiode, Stenographischer Bericht, 197. Sitzung, 18.01.1980, 15734–15737.

slow loosening of the alliance relationship with the Soviet Union was taking place.[66] Indeed, it became increasingly apparent in the early 1980s that the Soviet Union's expansionist moves into the Third World had failed to yield the desired results. Moscow could not hold on to Afghanistan, and newly independent countries such as Mozambique and Zimbabwe increasingly sought the assistance of Western powers.[67] Despite these early indications of change, the CDU/CSU remained in favour of applying the carrot and stick approach; that is to reward only countries and liberation movements that were willing to embrace the social market economy and stop helping to fulfil Soviet geostrategic objectives in Africa.[68] Despite these differences, both the government and the opposition supported African countries in exercising their right to self-determination and independence from all foreign powers. Ultimately, the government and the opposition were trying to achieve roughly the same objective; the approach was fundamentally different. All this, of course, raises the question of how the GDR interpreted West Germany's political landscape at the turn of the decade. The Ministry of State Security's intelligence-gathering provided, through the infiltration of West German government agencies, a relatively accurate picture of Bonn's foreign policies. In the late 1970s, the foreign-intelligence-gathering department (HV A) of the Ministry of State Security assessed the broad range of foreign policy approaches presented by the main West German political parties. Logically, East Berlin had a keen interest in gathering information about West German views on the communist bloc's growing presence in the Third World.

In early 1977, the GDR's intelligence service reported that the Federal Government authorised governmental entities to conduct an assessment on the 'socialist countries infiltration into African countries'. According to the GDR's foreign-intelligence gathering department, West Germany was seriously concerned that the communist bloc was gaining ground in southern Africa:

> Since the countries in southern Africa and the liberation movements in Rhodesia, Namibia and the South African Republic will be top priority for Soviet activities, an increased direct threat to NATO will result out of this. Especially those countries are affected that are essential for the feedstock supplies of NATO, particularly the EG countries. The control over the Cape route would put the Soviet Union in the position to seriously disturb the economies of the NATO countries.[69]

---

[66] Ibid., 15725.
[67] See also M. B. Yahuda, 'The Significance of Tripolarity in China's Policy Toward the United States Since 1972', in R. S. Ross, *China, the United States, and the Soviet Union: Tripolarity and Policy Making in the Cold War*, New York, M. E. Sharpe, Inc., 1993, 49.
[68] Deutscher Bundestag, 8. Wahlperiode, Stenographischer Bericht, 197. Sitzung, 18.01.1980, 15735–15736.
[69] BStU, MfS-Hauptverwaltung Aufklärung, Nr. 63, Information über das militärische Engagement der sozialistischen Länder in Afrika südlich der Sahara aus BRD-Sicht, 11.04.1977, 182.

The MfS report recited a foreign policy concern predominantly present in the CDU/CSU. Todenhöfer, Köhler and Stercken, CDU members' of the *Bundestag*, made statements along these lines in early 1980. Moreover, the CDU/CSU criticised the SPD-led government for showing little concern about the strategic importance of the Cape route.[70] It is, nonetheless, quite likely that government agencies still emphasised the Soviet Union's strategic interest in the Cape route, for it was a widely-held concern in the late 1970s. However, the Federal Government's policy of rapprochement envisioned an easing of the East and West rivalry and thus probably dismissed the issue as unhelpful in achieving this objective. The CDU/CSU, on the other hand, held the view that Western success or failure in Africa depended on strong countermeasures to Moscow's growing influence in the Third World. Hence, the strategic importance of the Cape route remained a relevant issue for the CDU/CSU. In this context, it becomes apparent why several leading members of the CDU/CSU faction advocated an interventionist approach in southern Africa, while a majority of the SPD/FDP faction came out in support of the government's non-interference policy. Overall, the GDR's intelligence service seemed to concern itself to a greater degree with West Germany's perception of Moscow's strategic aims in the Third World than with West Germany's perception of the GDR's aims in Africa. This can be explained by the SPD-led government subordinating the GDR's objectives in Africa to Moscow's strategic interests in Africa.

From the GDR's perspective, the Western bloc countries, particularly the US, Great Britain, West Germany and France, 'worked against a possible progressive development in southern Africa'. This accusation was based on the allegation that Western powers continued predominantly to support Pretoria's interests. Hence, the HV A accused Western powers of trying to 'hinder in Africa a change in the balance of power to their disadvantage'.[71] In this respect, the foreign-intelligence gathering department pointed out that, 'although they [the West] verbally condemn the ruling class in Pretoria and Salisbury and recognise the right of the African majority to self-determination, they are not prepared to support the liberation struggle of the African people'. Instead, Western powers actively tried to infiltrate liberation movements for the purpose of dividing them and hindering efforts to reach agreements.[72] In this respect, the HV A reported that the heterogeneous character of liberation movements offered, in the opinion of progressive African politicians, ample starting points for fragmentation. In this view, West European social democratic parties, especially the SPD,

---

[70] Deutscher Bundestag, 8. Wahlperiode, Stenographischer Bericht, 197. Sitzung, 18.01.1980, 15735.
[71] Worth noting here again, West Germany accused the communist bloc countries of trying to change the balance of power in southern Africa to their advantage, as pointed out above.
[72] BStU, MfS-Hauptverwaltung Aufklärung, Nr. 65, Zum Stellenwert des südlichen Afrika in der gegenwärtigen Afrika-Politik der imperialistischen Staaten, 15.06.1977, 188–189.

used its close contacts with SWAPO politicians to divide and weaken the movement. For the sole purpose of weakening SWAPO, the former information secretary of SWAPO, Andreas Shipanga, had received extensive financial support from within West Germany. The documents found during his arrest in April 1977 showed that Shipanga was planning to create a new leadership within SWAPO, the HV A had pointed out.[73]

However, the HV A also reported that the Federal Government denied these accusations, stressing that the call for a new beginning in relations with SWAPO was gaining momentum within the SPD-led government. Furthermore, the Federal Government also stated that it was in favour of solving issues such as the consulate in Windhoek and the cultural agreement with South Africa in a way that was satisfactory for both West Germany and SWAPO. To this end, West German diplomats made the 'confidential proposal' that leading SWAPO politicians should 'take advantage of the opportunity' to meet Brandt in an African country.[74] However, the HV A report failed to give any indication of SWAPO's position regarding the Federal Government's desire to improve relations. Instead, the report stated that it was paramount for SWAPO 'to secure unity within the movement, prevent the interference of imperial powers and focus on the intensification of the armed struggle to force the Vorster regime to the negotiation table'.[75]

Clearly, the HV A's report provided East Berlin with an accurate account of the Federal Government's changing views concerning SWAPO in 1977. However, the report was formulated rather generically, leaving room for alternative interpretations. For example, the HV A report made the generalised accusation that Western powers actual objective was to infiltrate, fragment and weaken African liberation movements.[76] Thus, it also underlined SWAPO's increasingly critical stance toward the West.[77] Yet, the HV A failed to give some insight into SWAPO's view on the government's efforts to work toward a rapprochement, or Bonn's desire to increase contacts with SWAPO representatives in New York. Instead, the report indicated that SWAPO believed that West Germany supported the splinter group around Shipanga for the sole purpose of 'undermining the fighting power of the liberation movement'. Although the Federal Government denied these allegations, as the GDR's foreign intelligence service stated, it seems impossible not to project some negative aspects of this accusation on the SPD-led government's move towards SWAPO. The fact that the HV A

---

[73] Ibid., 200.
[74] Ibid., 201.
[75] Ibid., 200. Similar assessments can be found in the following documents: BStU, MfS-HA II, Nr. 28977, Südwestafrikanische Volksorganisation (SWAPO) von Namibia, [no date], 169; PAAA, Zwischenarchiv, Bd. 116840, 1977–1978, Beziehungen DDR – Südafrika, 27.11.1978, 2.
[76] Ibid., 189.
[77] Ibid., 201.

mentioned that the Federal Government had apparently developed strong convictions about the need to improve relations with SWAPO does not necessarily remove the accusation that Bonn was trying to infiltrate SWAPO for its own sinister purposes.[78] Consequently, the report left little scope for a positive view of Bonn's efforts to improve relations with SWAPO in 1977. What the HV A report indicates is that, in 1977, the GDR was already concerned about West German infiltration into SWAPO, which led to counterintelligence and anti-espionage programme that was tailored to SWAPO's particular circumstances in 1980, as discussed previously.

This is not surprising when it is remembered that, in the late 1970s, a sharp increase in East-West rivalry for influence in Africa made it increasingly difficult to find common ground and a realistic compromise, as positions in general became more entrenched. There is, of course, the possibility that the intelligence was represented with a negative undertone for political reasons. According to SED ideology, despite *Ostpolitik*, West Germany remained the GDR's class enemy, although rapprochement with West Germany made it increasingly difficult for East Berlin to present 'the West German leaders as class enemies, imperialists and warmongers'.[79] Hence, West Germany's ties with South Africa presented an opportunity for the SED to paint a picture of the other Germany as a neo-colonial power that supported racism and economic exploitation in Africa. Moreover, West Germany's policy towards southern Africa presented an opportunity for the GDR to underline its claims to sovereignty by seeking to distance radically itself from West Germany's foreign policies in Africa: 'The GDR has nothing in common with the colonialist and neo-colonialist practices of the German imperialism as they are known by the African peoples sufficiently', as a GDR delegate declared at a UN conference in Maputo in early 1977.[80]

The SPD-led government's move toward both the GDR and SWAPO, and its changing attitude toward Pretoria, challenged East Berlin's portrayal of the GDR as the better Germany, one that occupied the moral high ground in its relations with Africa. Ironically perhaps, the SPD-led government's policy toward southern Africa was, in the crudest sense, closer to the views espoused by East Berlin than the CDU/CSU in the late 1970s.

In mid-1977, the HV A also assessed the CDU/CSU foreign policy approach toward southern Africa. The report was unambiguous with regard to the CDU/CSU's attitude to-

---

[78] Ibid., 200–201.
[79] D. Childs, 'The SED faces the challenges of Ostpolitik and Glasnost', in T. A. Baylis, D. Childs, E. L. Collier and M. Rueschemeyer (eds.), *East Germany in Comparative Perspective*, London, Routledge, 1989, 7.
[80] PAAA, MfAA, C 3000, 1977, Statement by the head of the delegation of the German Democratic Republic at the United Nations Conference in Support of the peoples of Zimbabwe and Namibia, Maputo, 16 to 21 May 1977, 2.

ward national liberation movements. Not only did the CDU/CSU's approach toward liberation movements leave little room for interpretation, the CDU/CSU and East Berlin also held fundamentally different views on national liberation movements. Thus, the CDU/CSU's foreign policy approach toward southern Africa was in line with East Berlin's portrayal of the two German states as fundamentally different. The CDU/CSU's critical attitude toward liberation movements and a generally favourable attitude toward Pretoria presented conspicuous differences in their foreign policy objectives toward southern Africa. With regard to Namibia, the foreign-intelligence-gathering department emphasised the CDU/CSU's opposition to a SWAPO-led government. Actually, the HV A claimed that it was, in the CDU/CSU's view, 'necessary to prevent SWAPO from taking power' in Namibia. Furthermore, the CDU/CSU saw Namibia as part of South Africa and thus considered the continued existence of the South African Republic a main objective. However, the CDU/CSU expected strong opposition to this objective from foreign powers such as the Soviet Union, Cuba and the GDR, largely through this support of guerrilla activities within the two countries. The HV A also indicated that the overall economic and geostrategic significance of southern Africa played an important role in the CDU/CSU's strategic thinking. Overall, the HV A assessment predominantly reflected the hardline positions within the CDU/CSU. Rightly so, perhaps, given that the hardliners were the loudest voices in the *Bundestag* in the late 1970s.[81]

The Kohl government in the *Bundestag* in the early 1980s

After Strauß' electoral disaster in late 1980, the CDU/CSU's concerns about Soviet expansionism in Africa lost some momentum in the *Bundestag*. The disastrous defeat at the polls led to a more inward-looking period for the conservative coalition. Overall, domestic issues such as increase in unemployment and inflation were generally more prominent in the early 1980s. These economic issues also led to growing friction within the SPD-FDP coalition government, which was further exacerbated by economic differences between Schmidt and Genscher and the ongoing debate over the placement of U.S. missiles on West German territory to counter the nuclear threat emanating from the Soviet Union.[82] Ultimately, the protracted crisis over the stationing of Intermediate-Range Nuclear Forces (INF) in Ger-

---

[81] BStU, MfS-Hauptverwaltung Aufklärung, Nr. 87, Auffassung von CDU/CSU-Politikern zur westlichen Südafrika-Politik, 22.08.1977, 390–393.

[82] Schmidt recognised that Europe could only negotiate an arms deal with the Soviet Union from a position of strength. This approach was not in contradiction with détente, as many would have argued at the time, for it was not a contradiction to strengthen the position of Europe while seeking to reduce tensions with the Soviet Union: R. L. Garthoff, *A Journey through the Cold War: A Memoir of Containment and Coexistence*, Washington, D. C., The Brookings Institution, 2001, 286.

many for the purpose of restoring the equilibrium of power led to Schmidt's downfall.[83] All of these factors together, and the economic downturn in particular, contributed to the SPD's political decline.[84] A vote of no confidence in October 1982 removed Schmidt as chancellor and voted Helmut Kohl in and Kohl also emerged victorious in the 1983 national election. Although Genscher's reappointment to the post of foreign minister promised the continuation of the SPD-led government's foreign policy toward southern Africa, Kohl still needed to appease the hardliners within CDU and CSU. That Genscher was a strong critic of Soviet expansionism made it slightly easier for Kohl to argue in favour of the seasoned foreign minister, for the Eastern bloc's geopolitical aims in underdeveloped countries continued to be a central concern within CDU/CSU. However, Kohl was in a stronger position than in previous years. He no longer needed to adjust his policies to suit the hard-line positions within the conservative union. The 1983 election victory allowed Kohl to argue that Strauß' uncompromising attitude led to election defeat in 1980. Hence, Kohl was in the fortunate position of being able to speak from a position of strength when he proposed to build the government's policies on a 'coalition of the middle'. The logic behind the coalition of the middle was that moderate policies would appeal to a wider electorate.[85]

In the 1983 election, the Green Party won twenty-eight seats in the *Bundestag*, which created competition with the SPD in the role of opposition.[86] Soon, the Green Party became the leading opposition to the Kohl government's policy toward southern Africa, while the SPD's campaign in southern Africa lost momentum after the election debacle in 1983. In late 1983, during Question Hour, the Greens expressed their strong opposition to the government's plans to officially receive P.W. Botha in West Germany, and in early 1984, the Bundestag debated the Green Party's major interpellation regarding the government's policy toward southern Africa.[87] A few months later, in May 1984, the SPD also submitted a minor interpellation regarding Botha's forthcoming visit to Bonn, which was discussed in the *Bundestag* in June 1984.[88] At this point, the Greens had also submitted a minor inter-

---

[83] R. C. Eichenberg, 'Dual Track and Double Trouble: The Two-Level Politics of INF', in P. B. Evans, H. K. Jacobson and R. D. Putnam (eds.), *Double-Edged Diplomacy: International Bargaining and Domestic Policies*, California, University of California Press, 1993, 45–77.

[84] Worth mentioning here, Genscher's decision to switch sides led to many FDP resignations in the early 1980s. See 'Der Kanzlersturz – Die Wende von 1982', ZDF (TV documentary film). Accessed online March 2015, available form: www.youtube.com/watch?v=D4pfC48kr9o&spfreload=10

[85] McAdams, *Germany Divided*, 154. See also *Der Spiegel*, Die Wende ist perfect, 10/1983; J. M. Markham, 'Kohl and his Coalition Win Decisively in West Germany', *New York Times*, 07.03.1983.

[86] Saalfeld, *Germany: Multiple*, 361.

[87] Deutscher Bundestag, 10. Wahlperiode, Stenographischer Bericht, 54. Sitzung, 10.02.1984 During Question Hour, the *Bundestag* allows government representative to answer previously submitted questions. *Bundestag* members can also ask question related to the issue under discussion.

[88] Ibid., Drucksache 10/1508, 25.05.1984; Ibid., Stenographischer Bericht, 73. Sitzung, 06.06.1984.

pellation concerning Botha's visit, which the *Bundestag* included in the debate. It became apparent that the Green Party was eager to establish itself as the leading opposition party in the *Bundestag*, particularly with regard to issues concerning southern Africa.

Although the post-election period was marked by infighting and disagreements over policy directions, Kohl's dissociation from the uncompromising right-wing positions of Strauß seemed to have some effect on the *Bundestag*. One particularly striking aspect was the fact that *Bundestag* debates on southern Africa cooled down somewhat. Even though Reagan's anti-communist foreign policy increased East-West tensions, the *Bundestag* was less susceptible to Cold War populism in the early 1980s.[89] The *Bundestag* discussed the continuing crisis in southern Africa without the strong focus on the Soviet Union that was so characteristic of the late 1970s. While hardliners, such as the CSU parliamentarian Graf Huyn, changed neither their views nor tone, others, such as Stercken (CDU), were more moderate tone after the election.[90] Strauß never compromised or aligned his political tone to changes coming from Bonn. But some changes, such as the interpretation of liberation movements' allegiance toward communism, became apparent in the *Bundestag* soon after the 1983 election. Thus, although Guenther Verheugen, who became a SPD member after the FDP changed coalition partners, criticised the Kohl government for reducing SWAPO to an important conversational partner, he also stated that 'it could have come worse', for the CDU/CSU had still demanded 'the immediate termination of any support for the pro-communist terrorist SWAPO' in March 1983.[91] Indeed, the attitude towards SWAPO changed in favour of the liberation movement. Although the CDU/CSU remained rather critical, a new openness became increasingly apparent. Yet, the previous government's move towards SWAPO was still widely viewed as too one-sided a commitment to the liberation movement, so the more open-minded strategy was to establish relations with both SWAPO and the DTA.[92] Obviously, this was a clear break from the one-sided support of the DTA that was prevalent in the conservative coalition throughout the 1970s and early 1980s.[93]

Kohl faced considerable challenges regarding Bonn's policy toward Namibia and South Africa. The formation of foreign policies that drew closer to those of the previous SPD-led government generated significant opposition from the CDU/CSU hardliners, particular Strauß. His election victory gave Kohl sufficient positive momentum to formulate a foreign

---

[89] Ibid., Drucksache 10/1544, 05.06.1984. Reagan's anti-communist foreign policy was nowhere more vividly reflected than in his 'evil empire' speech in 1983.
[90] Deutscher Bundestag, 10. Wahlperiode, Stenographischer Bericht, 54. Sitzung, 10.02.1984, 3885–3887; Ibid., 3867–3869.
[91] Ibid., 3866.
[92] Ibid., 3868–3869.
[93] Ibid., 8. Wahlperiode, Stenographischer Bericht, 197. Sitzung, 18.01.1980, 15694–15695.

policy that steered widely clear of hardline positions. In retrospect, Genscher acknowledged that Kohl's achievements during the immediate period after winning the 1983 election were quite remarkable: 'Kohl's effort to bring his party in from the cold regarding foreign policy, particularly *Ostpolitik*, and lead it on the road to progress and success has not received sufficient appreciation'.[94] Had Strauß won the election in 1980, West Germany would have steered in an entirely different direction, particularly with regard to the Namibia question and South Africa. In 1971, Strauß had already promised Pretoria deliveries of arms in case of a CDU/CSU victory in the next national election.[95] With regard to Namibia, after the election, the CDU/CSU was far less engaged in the *Bundestag* than before the election. This can be explained by the conservative union having strongly opposed the Namibia policy of the FDP, its new coalition partner, in the late 1970s and early 1980s, as Brenke points out.[96] Given that Kohl backed Genscher on foreign policy issues, there was only one way forward for the CDU/CSU, particularly after an intense period of pre-election infighting, and that was to support, or at least accept, Kohl's foreign policy changes. Equally noteworthy perhaps, Kohl's foreign policy alignment to the previous socialist democratic government signalled a break with the policies of his conservative counterparts in London and Washington. In fact, the Kohl-Genscher government actively tried to commit Reagan to an East-West détente policy in the mid-1980s.[97]

The Foreign Office

Perceptions of SWAPO's role in Namibia's independence struggle underwent a slow but undeniable change in the early 1970s. In 1971, the Organisation of African Unity (OAU) condemned Western imperial powers, including West Germany, for their continuing support of the apartheid regime in Pretoria.[98] Although Brandt sympathised with the OAU's concerns, the chancellor was not in a position to break fundamentally with the previous conservative governments' policies because of extensive economic relations with South Africa, as Ken-

---

[94] 'Hans-Dietrich Genscher: Ein Politikerleben', Spiegel TV, 08.10.2014 (TV program). Accessed online August 2015, available from: www.youtube.com/watch?v=94xj_1BnK70.
[95] Brendel, "*Freiheit fuer Mandela*", 57.
[96] Brenke, *Die Bundesrepublik*, 160.
[97] G. Niedhart, 'The Federal Republic of Germany Between the American and Russian Superpowers: 'Old Friend' and 'New Partner'', in D. Junker, P. Gassert and W. Mausbach (eds.), *The United States and Germany in the Era of the Cold War, 1945–1990: A Handbook*, Cambridge, Cambridge University Press, 2004, 24.
[98] PAAA, MfAA C 1428/75, Abteilung Afrika, Konferenz der Organisation für afrikanische Einheit (OAU), 05.07.1971, 3.

neth Kuanda, the president of Zambia, explained after talks with Brandt in 1970.⁹⁹ For the GDR, West German economic relations with South Africa presented something of an Achilles heel in its policy towards Africa. By the time the GDR was formally admitted into the UN in 1973, East Germany could look back to more than a decade of active opposition to Western cooperation with the South African apartheid regime.¹⁰⁰

In 1973, the General Assembly recognized SWAPO as the 'authentic representative of the Namibian people', which was upgraded in Resolution 31/146 to in the status of 'sole and authentic representative of the Namibian people' in 1976. Resolution 31/146 declared further that the General Assembly supported SWAPO's armed independence struggle, making it increasingly difficult for Pretoria to portray SWAPO as a terrorist organisation.¹⁰¹ However, Pretoria had no difficulty in portraying SWAPO as Moscow's ally in southern Africa. In early 1976, SWAPO developed a constitutional proposal for Namibia, outlining its firm commitment to the United Nations and non-aligned countries. Only a few months later, SWAPO's political program underlined the need to 'strengthen SWAPO's anti-imperialist international solidarity with socialist countries'.¹⁰² Even though the West could find comfort in SWAPO's apparent commitment to a peaceful settlement through the diplomatic channels of the UN, SWAPO's apparent allegiance to revolutionary change raised considerable doubts about its true intentions. These developments did not go unnoticed in West Germany.

In June 1977, the Foreign Office acknowledged that, after years of stagnation in Namibia, 'the last six months marked an almost dramatic acceleration of the political development'.¹⁰³ The Foreign Office identified, among other factors, increased international pressure on South Africa, increased efforts of the West in Namibia, change of government in the United States and international rejection of discrimination and apartheid as the driving force behind these changes.¹⁰⁴ In this context, the question of whether or not to increase contact with SWAPO came up for consideration in the Foreign Office in early 1977. In January, the Foreign Office asked Western countries to provide information regarding their relation-

---

99   Ibid., 3.
100 See BArch, DZ 8/33, Letter from the Afro-Asian Solidarity Committee of the GDR to the Anti-Apartheid Committee of the United Nations, 12.10.66.
101 At the thirty-first session on 20 September 1976, the General Assembly declared in Resolution 31/146 that it 'recognizes that the national liberation movement of Namibia, the South West Africa People's Organization, is the sole and authentic representative of the Namibian people; and that it 'supports the armed struggle of the Namibian people, led by the South West Africa People's Organization, to achieve self-determination, freedom and national independence in a united Namibia'.
102 See PAAA, Zwischenarchiv, Bd. 115782, Ideologische Orientierung der namibischen Befreiungsorganisation SWAPO, 08.02.1978, 2.
103 Ibid., Bd. 116802, Politischer Halbjahresbericht Südwestafrika/Namibia, 01.06.1977.
104 Ibid.

ship with SWAPO.[105] Within the framework of a fundamental review of West Germany's Namibia policy, the main objective was to inquire into issues such as frequency of official and unofficial contacts and first-hand impressions of SWAPO representatives. The survey revealed that only Britain and Italy maintained frequent contact with SWAPO. Most governments, including Washington, had little or no contact with the liberation movement in early 1977.[106] This indicates that the recognition of SWAPO by the UN did not promote greater interaction between Western governments and SWAPO and that the SPD-led government's move towards the Namibian liberation movement was neither influenced by the UN nor by other Western governments.[107]

Furthermore, in late 1977 the Political Directorate-General 3 of the Foreign Office, responsible for relations with countries and regions in Asia, Latin America, Africa and the Middle East, assessed SWAPO's ideological orientation.[108] SWAPO's interactions with East Berlin and Moscow became the centre of this investigation. In late 1977, SWAPO representatives paid a four day official visit to the GDR at the invitation of the Central Committee (ZK) of the SED. The SWAPO representatives were also received by Honecker. Both parties used the visit to underline close political affiliations and common ideological orientation, with an emphasis on the joint struggle against neo-colonial solutions in southern Africa. The meeting concluded with the signing of a declaration of cooperation between SED and SWAPO, which promised to increase cooperation over the next two years.[109] In addition, the Foreign Office analysed two speeches made by Nujoma, one held in Moscow and one in East Berlin, leading to the following conclusion:

> ...the Marxist-Leninist orientation outlined in SWAPO's party programme of 1976 has not only continued but also been strengthened. Thus, SWAPO has become an organisation that commits itself ideologically to Moscow's course...It can be expected that in Germany the political opponents of the government's Namibia-policy will confront the government about the evermore apparent ideological orientation of SWAPO.[110]

---

[105] Ibid., Teleprinted communications between Foreign Office and USA, France, Great Britain, Ireland, Italy, Belgium, Netherlands, Denmark, Luxemburg regarding relations with SWAPO, January 1977.
[106] Ibid., Chart summarizing Teleprinted communications.
[107] The survey did not include Sweden and Norway, which both maintained close relations with SWAPO in the 1970s. For Sweden's relationship with SWAPO, see T. Sellström, *Sweden and National Liberation in Southern Africa: Solidarity and Assistance 1970–1994*, Volume II, Stockholm, Uppsala, Nordiska Afrikainstitutet, 2002, 238–247. For Norway's relationship with SWAPO, see T. L., Eriksen, *Norway and National Liberation in Southern Africa*, Stockholm, Elanders Gotab, 2000, 98–103.
[108] PAAA, Zwischenarchiv, Bd. 116802, Ideologische Orientierung der namibischen Befreiungsorganisation SWAPO, 08.02.1978.
[109] Ibid., 1–5.
[110] Ibid., Ideologische Orientierung der namibischen Befreiungsorganisation SWAPO, 27.12.1977, 6.

Evidently, the Foreign Office came to believe in the late 1970s that SWAPO was moving ever-closer toward the communist bloc and subsequently turning into an affiliated organ of Moscow. Under these circumstances, it was thought unlikely that a SWAPO-led government would consider West Germany's interests in Namibia.[111] Nonetheless, the Foreign Office was dedicated to gathering sufficient information before coming to a final conclusion.

In early 1978, the Political Directorate General 3 reassessed SWAPO's ideological orientation, after Baron Rudiger von Wechmar, the West German ambassador to the UN in New York, expressed doubts about SWAPO's Marxist-Leninist orientation.[112] Wechmar argued that Western reluctance to support SWAPO promoted an 'African socialism' in Namibia. From this perspective, SWAPO's rhetoric was simply aligned to the ideological orientation of those powers that supported the liberation struggle. Thus, Wechmar warned the Foreign Office not to underestimate the 'pragmatic nationalists' within SWAPO, who are 'ideologically indifferent and accept everything that serves the seizure of power' without any meaningful commitment to ideologies. In the final analysis, Wechmar stated that the West German representatives in New York recommended – also for the benefit of the Namibian Germans – to 'build an atmosphere of cooperation with SWAPO', even if SWAPO was a Marxist-Leninist movement.[113]

The Foreign Office disagreed with Wechmar's assessment, citing Nujoma's unmistakeably strong criticism of the Western powers' apparent 'dishonest and neo-colonial' ambitions in southern Africa and the apparent necessity for a joint struggle with socialist countries to 'liberate Namibia, the African continent and all humanity from colonial and imperial dominance'. SWAPO's economic ideas for Namibia, as outlined in the National Program of 1976, were largely in line with socialist economic principles such as public ownership of property.[114] Nonetheless, the Foreign Office agreed that although African liberation movements are, in general, inclined to use strong ideological rhetoric during the liberation struggle, 'this ideological overload often does not continue after the fighting objectives are achieved'.[115] 'African socialism' did not apply to Namibia.[116] Like Mozambique and Angola,

---

[111] Ibid., 6.
[112] Ibid.; Ibid., Bd. 115782, Ideologische Orientierung der South West Africa People's Organization (SWAPO), 21.01.1978.
[113] Ibid., 1–4.
[114] Ibid., 6.
[115] Ibid.
[116] For a more detailed study on Marxism in the Third World, see M.N. Katz (ed.), *The USSR and Marxist Revolutions in the Third World*, Canada, Woodrow Wilson International Center for Scholars, 1990.

Namibia was driven by a nationalism that aspired to change the status quo radically.[117] Thus, the General Directory 3 came to the following conclusion:

> A peaceful solution in Namibia is not feasible without the inclusion of SWAPO ... The West cannot have an interest that the ever more apparent ideological orientation will be followed by a determined foreign policy on communist course. Consequently, we have to convince SWAPO with great determination and effort that its long-term interests are not in the East but in the West. It is in our interest to strengthen SWAPO's trust in us by intensifying and cultivating interactions with all leading SWAPO representatives.[118]

The Foreign Office proposed a meeting between Genscher and Nujoma on the side-lines of the Namibia debate in New York on 11 and 12 February 1978. Genscher's view of SWAPO seemed more in line with the UN representative in New York than the Directorate General 3 of the Foreign Office. In October 1978, Genscher warned of 'a thoughtless transmission *[Übertragung]* of East-West antagonism onto the Third World through premature labelling and random association'. He stressed that it would be a mistake 'to divide developing countries into pro-West and pro-East'.[119] Despite all this, he indicated that Bonn was concerned about the Communist bloc's growing influence in southern Africa:

> A peaceful solution for Namibia would have a signal effect, making it easier to solve other problems in southern Africa peacefully. A peaceful solution would also avert the danger that extra-regional powers intervene militarily and establish zones of predominance, as they have done in other parts of Africa.[120]

Seemingly timed with the Foreign Office assessment of SWAPO, Genscher indicated, at the 32rd UN General Assembly in New York, Bonn's willingness to improve relations with SWAPO: 'We are for the independence of the African states and equality of races. The Federal republic of Germany agrees with all those who champion, in liberation movements and anywhere else, self-determination and human rights through non-violent means'.[121]

So Genscher indirectly offered Bonn's support to SWAPO. According to Genscher's analysis in *Erinnerungen*, Bonn supported, in principal, the liberation movement's goals, but full support required a major concession: the renunciation of violence.[122] However, al-

---

[117] Ibid., Bd. 115782, Ideologische Orientierung der namibischen Befreiungsorganisation SWAPO, 08.02.1978.
[118] Ibid., 10.
[119] H.-D. Genscher, *Deutsche Außenpolitik, Ausgewählte Reden und Aufsätze 1974–1985*, Bonn, Verlag Bonn Aktuell GmbH, 1985, 187.
[120] Genscher, *Deutsche Außenpolitik*, 186.
[121] Genscher, *Erinnerungen*, 333.
[122] Ibid., 334.

though Genscher and the Foreign Office were of the opinion that West Germany needed to seek to increase interactions with SWAPO, the overall interpretation of SWAPO's ideological orientation could not have been more different. Like Wechmar, Genscher understood SWAPO's ideological orientation as an opportunistic manifestation, which was limited to the duration of the liberation struggle, while the Foreign Office recognized in the late 1970s a more permanent ideological orientation, with the potential to shape the political future of a SWAPO-led Namibia.[123] Thus, although there was an agreement in the Foreign Office about SWAPO's ideological orientation, fundamental differences existed about long-term ramification of the liberation movement's relationship with the Eastern bloc. Despite those differences, there was general consensus that West Germany should seek to improve relations with SWAPO.

Hence, when Nujoma visited Bonn in 1980, the Foreign Office saw an opportunity to reduce SWAPO's mistrust of Germany and to collaborate with the liberation movement in advancing the cause of Namibian independence through the UN. At the same time, it aimed to promote a more objective and favourable perception of SWAPO among the West German public. After Nujoma's visit, the Foreign Office expressed confidence that these objectives had been achieved. This did not mean that SWAPO would stop criticising West Germany or become a less impressionable target for the GDR, but SWAPO stated that its Bonn visit 'marked a new chapter in the relations' with West Germany. Nujoma and his delegates even spoke of 'friendship'.[124] SWAPO's one main ambition was to gain control over Namibia, using whatever means were necessary and its ideological affiliation with Marxism-Leninism was largely opportunistic. Its rhetoric became predominantly militant and Marxist-Leninist whenever negotiations stalled and Namibia's independence seemed unattainable.

---

[123] The accusation that Nujoma was a 'political opportunist' was not uncommon among both Western and African observers. Furthermore, SWAPO often increased its Marxist rhetoric after claims that it was not a communist movement. See PAAA, AV Neues Amt, Bd. 16413, 1983, Namibia-Initiative; hier: Kommunistische Partei Namibias –Angriffe gegen SWAPO als 'nicht-kommunistisch', 27.04.1983.

[124] PAAA, Zwischenarchiv, Bd. 127747, 1981, Besuch des SWAPO-Präsidenten Sam Nujoma vom 23. bis 27. Oktober 1980 in der Bundesrepublik Deutschland; hier: Ablauf und Wertung, 27.10.1980.

4 The decision-making process regarding Namibia

The GDR's national interests in southern Africa have received considerable scholarly attention, and West Germany's economic relations with Namibia and especially with South Africa have been examined in relative detail.[1] This book concentrates on the influence of West Germany's economic power on the strategic direction of foreign policy.

In 1979, West Germany was, after the US, the second biggest importer of South African goods.[2] In the late 1970s, the newsmagazine *Der Spiegel* pointed out that German business in South Africa 'could expect 15 to 20 percent annual return, plus high political stability'. However, the president of the Committee and the Delegation of German Industry and Commerce (DIHT), Otto Wolff von Amerongen, did not see low wages as the main benefit for West German business in South Africa, but the easy access to natural resources.[3] This was also true with regard to West Germany's economic relations with Namibia. However, West German business relations with Namibia were insubstantial compared to Great Britain and the United States. In 1976, the Foreign Office reported that the UN considered only six West German companies in Namibia as noteworthy, and the total investment in the industrial sector amounted to less than three million deutsche marks.[4] Still, potential for growth in trade and investment was considerable.

From the GDR's perspective, there was little doubt that West Germany's interest in Namibia, and southern Africa as a whole, was based predominantly on economic considerations. In the late 1970s, the MfS believed that the changing balance of power in southern Africa since the end of the Portuguese empire and the intensification of the liberation struggle made it impossible to postpone Namibia's independence any longer. As a result, the main investors in Namibia, Great Britain, France, West Germany, the United States and Canada drastically increased their efforts in 1977. In this view, the Western powers' real interests lay

---

[1] See, e.g., U. van der Heyden, *GDR International Development Policy Involvement, Doctrine and Strategies between Illusions and Reality 1960–1990, The example (South) Africa*, Berlin, LIT Verlag, 2013; Schleicher/Schleicher, *Special Flights*; Winrow, *The Foreign Policy*; Van der Heyden, *Zwischen Solidarität*. See, e.g., Wenzel, *Südafrika-Politik*, 31–42; 83–89 and 158–172; Brenke, *Die Bundesrepublik*, 64–67 and 255–260.

[2] Study Commission on US Policy toward Southern Africa (ed.), *South Africa: Time Running Out*, Los Angeles, University of California Press, Ltd, 1981, 304. For an assessment of Namibia by West German representatives to the United Nations, see PAAA, AV Neues Amt, Bd. 7906, Sitzung des Entkolonisierungsausschusses, 06.08.1973, 3–4.

[3] 'Mehr Weltoffenheit gegenüber Südafrika', *Der Spiegel*, 43/1978. See also Jabri, *Mediating Conflict*, 64–65.

[4] PAAA, Zwischenarchiv, Bd. 108204, 1975–1976, Namibia: deutscher Einfluss, Lusaka, 27.08.1976.

in safeguarding their economic interests in Namibia and subsequently in hindering change. After all, most of Namibia's economic profits were drained away by foreign investors, and foreign trade was entirely in the hands of Pretoria and the white minority, for Namibia was still built on 'typical colonial structures', as the MfS explained.[5] For this reason, West Germany had little interest in increasing pressure on Pretoria, as Peter Florin, the GDR's permanent representative to the UN, pointed out in 1981.[6]

Logically enough, West Germany, as a major economic power, had substantial interest in Namibia's vast wealth in natural resources.[7] Although the country imported mainly uranium and blister copper from Namibia, there was significant potential for expanding natural resource-based imports, considering West Germany's extensive national economy.[8] In 1978, the Foreign Office pointed out in its half-yearly report on Namibia that the country's huge uranium resources were attracting a growing number of West German and US industrialists. The report stated that 'it can be expected that the country will experience an unparalleled economic boom after independence, as a direct consequence of its huge wealth in natural resources. It was believed that such an upsurge could also be the catalyst for a growing manufacturing industry in Namibia.[9]

Given the trade potential between West Germany and Namibia, Namibia should not become economically inaccessible. It was in the interest of West Germany that Namibia would remain an integral part of the world capitalist market after independence. In fact, in the late 1970s, the possible loss of sustained and unhindered access to southern Africa's natural resources was a commonly voiced concern.[10] For the same reasons, West Germany

---

[5] BStU, MfS-HA II, Nr. 28977, Südwestafrikanische Volksorganisation (SWAPO) von Namibia [no date], 160.

[6] A. Babing (ed.), *Gegen Rassismus,* 1977–1982, Rede des Stellvertreters des Ministers für Auswärtige Angelegenheiten und Ständigen Vertreters der DDR bei den Vereinten Nationen, Peter Florin auf der XXXV Tagung der UN Vollversammlung zu Namibia, 03.03.1981, 462–464.

[7] West Germany never denied its interest in Namibia's natural resources. In fact, Genscher even emphasised the interest of German businesses in Namibia at the Security Council special meeting on Namibia in 1978. Importantly, however, Genscher emphasised that the Federal Government would especially support economic exchange in areas that promote the development of Namibia. See PAAA, Zwischenarchiv, Bd. 178773, 1978, Erklärung der Bundesrepublik Deutschland in der Sonder-Generalversammlung über Namibia, 21.04.1978.

[8] Jabri, *Mediating Conflict*, 50. See also Babing, *Gegen Rassismus*, 1949–1977, Rede des DDR-Vertreters Heinz Knobbe im Vierten Komitee der XXXI. Tagung der UN Vollversammlung zur Namibiafrage, 29.11.1976, 651–656.

[9] PAAA, Zwischenarchiv, Bd. 116802, 1977–1978, Politischer Halbjahresbericht Südwestafrika/Namibia, 01.03.1978, 5.

[10] See, e.g., Deutscher Bundestag, 8. Wahlperiode, Stenographischer Bericht, 197. Sitzung, 18.01.1980, 15791–15737; PAAA, Zwischenarchiv, Bd. 116841, 1877–1978, Deutsch-südafrikanische Beziehungen, hier: Antwort des BM auf das Fernschreiben des MdB Dr Marx vom 07.02.1978, 09.02.1978, 3.

strongly opposed sanctions against South Africa. But, despite West German and British objections, the newly elected Carter administration showed sympathy for the idea of applying economic pressure on South Africa. In the late 1970s, the issue was taken up at the Foreign Office. The Political Directorate-General 3 of the Foreign Office argued that it had become increasingly apparent that the United States' priority lay with black Africa, not least because of its own black constituency. Hence, the Foreign Office warned that West Germany must give greater consideration to Washington's position on South Africa, for African nations might in future not only exert determined pressure through the diplomatic channels of the UN, but directly via the United States. The Foreign Office also observed that the thought of 'punishing' South Africa for its inactivity was slowly gaining momentum, for the US and Canada were losing patience with Pretoria.[11]

Sanctions against South Africa were widely supported by African countries.[12] Considering that African opinion increased in importance under the Carter administration, it seems warranted to assert that the Foreign Office was concerned that growing pressure from African states might push Carter towards sacrificing Western economic interests in South Africa for the cause of human rights. The tone and language used by the Foreign Office seems to support this assumption. That the West German ambassador in New York, Freiherr von Wechmar, also expressed concerns about the Carter administration's apparent willingness to apply sanctions against South Africa indicates how widespread such concerns were in the late 1970s.[13] Furthermore, Carter adopted a human rights-oriented foreign policy, which probably created the impression during his first year in office that his administration's South Africa policies differed from those of previous administrations. It soon became apparent, however, that strategic and economic interests were still given greater priority, despite the rhetoric of opposition to apartheid and support of racial equality.[14] However,

---

[11] PAAA, Zwischenarchiv, Bd. 116841, 1977–1978, Washingtoner Expertengespräche über wirtschaftliche Massnahmen gegenüber Südafrika, 29.03.1978.

[12] 'South Africa: Time Running Out', *The Report of the Study Commission*, 297.

[13] Washington submitted a draft for a new resolution that contained the following passage: 'We call upon all states to review their economic relations with South Africa, in particular to review commitments to funding the export of goods and services to South Africa, and for guaranteeing private credit'. See PAAA, AV Neues Amt, Bd. 7920, 1978, Sicherheitsrat-Sanktionen und sonstige westliche Druckmittel gegen Südafrika, 25.01.1978.

[14] For a detailed assessment of the conflicting views of Carter's policy towards South Africa, see S. Stevens, '"From the Viewpoint of a Southern Governor": The Carter Administration and Apartheid, 1977-1981', *Diplomatic History* 36(5) (November 2012). Accessed online February 2015, available from: www.researchgate.net/publication/259550725_From_the_Viewpoint_of_a_Southern_Governor_The_Carter_Administration_and_Apartheid_1977–81 Some scholars argue that the Carter administration gave human rights priority over economic interests. See A. Thomson, *U.S. Foreign Policy Towards Apartheid South Africa, 1948–1994*, London, Palgrave Macmillan, 2008, 91–100.

although the Carter administration encouraged US companies to adopt 'enlightened employment practises' in South Africa, the policy was laid out in such a way that it did not hurt US economic interests.[15]

Without a doubt, the threat of more severe measures against South Africa gave Bonn an incentive to lobby for Pretoria's compliance to elevate the looming threat. After all, West Germany's extensive economic relations with South Africa would have been hard hit by more severe measures.

There was some support within the SPD-led government for an economic boycott against South Africa, but the conservative opposition unanimously opposed it, on the grounds that it 'would cost seven million German workers their jobs', as Todenhöfer argued in the *Bundestag*.[16] Genscher explained that a policy of 'all or nothing will in the end lead to nothing'.[17] He opposed the application of economic pressure that might bring South Africa's economy to its knees. The aim was to politically and economically stabilise the African continent and to achieve change by initiating incentives for change rather than forcing change. To that end, West German long-term strategy in southern Africa concentrated on three objectives: 'maintenance of peace, implementation of human rights and unimpeded economic exchange'. Implicit in this view was the assumption that West Germany's economic interests in southern Africa would also benefit the interests of African countries in the region.[18]

In the late 1970s, the SPD-led government argued that economic assistance had the potential to promote greater independence of socialist African nations from the Soviet bloc.[19] This could then pave the way for an effective implementation of the policy of non-alignment. In 1980, Rainer Offergeld (SPD), Federal Minister for Economic Cooperation (BMZ), argued in the *Bundestag* that West Germany's economic assistance to Third World countries was superior to Eastern assistance, because 'it does not demand an alliance, it demands no subjugation and it demands no subordination into an alliance system'.[20] This approach was broadly based on the principle of non-interference into the internal affairs of other states.[21] The aim was to promote the independence of developing countries from

---

[15] Stevens, *From the Viewpoint*, 876.
[16] Deutscher Bundestag, 8. Wahlperiode, Stenographischer Bericht, 197. Sitzung, 18.01.1980, 15722–15723.
[17] Ibid., 10. Wahlperiode, Stenographischer Bericht, 54. Sitzung, 10.02.1984, 3877.
[18] Both the SPD-led government of the 1970s and the CDU-led government of the 1980s embraced the following guideline for its Africa policy: 'The German Africa policy is part of our peace politic. Our policy wants to contribute, in both our and Africa's interest, to a political and economic stabilisation of our neighbouring continent': Deutscher Bundestag, 10. Wahlperiode, Stenographischer Bericht, 54. Sitzung, 10.02.1984, 3876.
[19] See Chapter Three, The *Bundestag*.
[20] Deutscher Bundestag, 8. Wahlperiode, Stenographischer Bericht, 197. Sitzung, 18.01.1980, 15727.
[21] Ibid., 15714. The principle of non-interference into the internal affairs of other states was also

both the Eastern and Western blocs through economic relations and economic development aid.[22] Although such a policy had many proponents in the government, including Genscher, it was viewed as not yet applicable to the Namibian case, for Namibia was effectively still governed by South Africa. Consequently, economic assistance would not have promoted greater independence in the Namibian case, but strengthened and perpetuated minority rule. Hence, the SPD-led government determined that development assistance should only be made available to Namibia after independence:

> The West can most convincingly assure a fair constitutional order in Namibia and a policy of non-alignment by giving credible assurance that it will provide substantial tangible aid for consolidating Namibia after its independence and especially for developing its economy. The Federal Government is not only prepared to do so, but has already initiated preparatory planning.[23]

Nonetheless, there were still different levels of pre-independence assistance not at government level. Some was provided via non-governmental organisations (NGO's) and foundations. The SPD-affiliated Friedrich Ebert Foundation, for example, offered scholarships and educational training for SWAPO cadres, and also financed SWAPO's office in Bonn in late 1982.

The CDU/CSU had argued in favour of development assistance to strengthen the South Africa installed Democratic Turnhalle Alliance (DTA) government and, therefore, Pretoria's 'internal solution' for Namibia. In fact, the CSU-affiliated Hanns Seidel Foundation (HSS) actively supported the DTA since 1978.[24] Also, in early 1978, the HSS applied for funding at the Federal Ministry for Economic Cooperation and Development (BMZ) to establish an institute for political education for the DTA. The Foreign Office was strictly against the project, mainly because it would breach the government's commitment to political neutrality in Namibia. The HSS went ahead with its plan regardless, which led to the accusation that the BMZ supported the HSS in Namibia. These allegations were, however, unfounded, as the Foreign Office revealed.[25] Unsurprisingly, therefore, the HSS also maintained close relations with Pretoria.[26]

---

outlined by the Commission on Security and Cooperation in Europe (CSCE), an independent US Government agency, which was founded to improve relations between East and West.

[22] Ibid., 15720.

[23] PAAA, Zwischenarchiv, Bd. 125282, 1981, Position of the Government of the Republic of Germany on Namibia, July 1981, 3.

[24] See 'Spiegelbild der Entwicklungspolitik', *Namibia Nachrichten*, 7. Juni 1989, 7. It is also noteworthy that the HSS organised a seminar for the DTA in Bonn in 1984: PAAA, Zwischenarchiv, Bd. 138099, 1982–1984, Demokratische Turnhallen-Allianz (Namibia); hier: Bonn-Besuch Kaura, 10.04.1984.

[25] PAAA, Zwischenarchiv, Bd. 116841, 1977–1978, Pressegespräch über Südafrika am 02.11.1978; hier: Aktivitäten der Hanns Seidel Stiftung in Namibia, 31.10.1978.

[26] AAPD, 1984, Band II, BM-Treffen mit AM Botha am 10.11.1984 in Frankfurt, 12.11.1984. Yet,

Thus, although the SPD-led government put great emphasis on the political value of helping African countries achieve economic development, the economic approach had little value in a country that was still engulfed in a war of independence. Consequently, the Federal Government had limited possibilities for directly influencing Namibia's independence process and, therefore, tied its efforts largely to the diplomatic process. West Germany considered the wider geopolitical realities in the region. While the SPD-led government started to move closer to SWAPO in the late 1970s, few harboured any illusions that Namibia's independence was achievable without Pretoria's consent. There was no question that a radical, even revolutionary, change had to come from above, from those who had established a firm grip on Namibia. Thus, the SPD-led government's approach to the Namibia question also considered measures that seemed to have the potential to change South Africa from within.

Considering West Germany's extensive economic relations with South Africa, there was always the lingering possibility of trying to force Pretoria, through economic pressure, to change course in Namibia. However, there was a general reluctance in Bonn to use economic coercion to achieve political objectives, and a widespread scepticism about the effectiveness of economic sanctions against South Africa.[27] Importantly, it is also necessary to consider that Bonn was under pressure from domestic firms to support measures and policies that would ensure the continuation of unhindered business with South Africa.[28] Yet, Bonn saw little contradiction in protecting West German economic interests in southern Africa while simultaneously trying to promote change in Namibia and South Africa, for economic co-operation was a viable option in achieving political objectives, as Genscher pointed out:

> We have always been of the opinion that economic sanctions are not the right measure to assert influence, but that economic co-operation also offers the possibility to assert influence. How else can we justify that we have worldwide relations with countries which are not democracies, and neither claim to be it nor want to become it.[29]

Clearly, West Germany wanted to present itself as a just state that had given up its imperialist ambitions. There was a strong desire to erase the negative attributes associated with Germany by building a positive reputation, and ultimately present West Germany as the 'good

---

despite the fact that foundations supported both SWAPO and the DTA, the level of assistance provided by foundations in the 1970s should not be overrated.

[27] Wenzel, *Südafrika-Politik*, 83.
[28] PAAA, Zwischenarchiv, Bd. 108220, 1975–1976, Deutsch-südafrikanische Beziehungen, 14.01.1975, 3.
[29] Deutscher Bundestag, 10. Wahlperiode, Stenographischer Bericht, 54. Sitzung, 10.02.1984, 3879. See also BPA-Nachrichtenabteilung, Rundfunk-Auswahl Deutschland, Ref. II R2, Hans Dietrich Genscher, Bundesminister des Auswärtigen, zum Namibia-Problem, 11.10.1978.

Germany'.[30] Obviously, a favourable reputation was also viewed as a precondition for good economic relations with developing nations. Hence, West Germany's considerable economic power also provided an incentive to promote good international relations.

By the late 1970s, the notion that West German economic influence in southern Africa could be used as a potential instrument of foreign policy received increasing support. Genscher was a strong advocate of using his country's economic reach to promote political change at the southern tip of Africa. During the early years of his tenure as foreign minister, he already proposed the introduction of a code of conduct for West German businesses in southern Africa, which reflected his confidence in achieving change through reform rather than coercive political measures and economic sanctions.[31]

West Germany's economic relations with Namibia cannot be investigated in isolation, for Namibia's economy and natural resources were largely under South African control. West Germany's foreign policy towards Namibia was interwoven with its economic interests in South Africa and the region as a whole. South Africa's occupation of Namibia made progress almost entirely dependent on Pretoria's willingness to make concessions. Thus, Namibia's independence was deeply interlinked with South Africa's preparedness to accept a change of the status quo in Namibia. Considering that West Germany maintained extensive economic relations with South Africa throughout the 1970s and 1980s, it is necessary to question whether Bonn could have intervened in South African affairs through economic means and subsequently promote a change in Pretoria's attitude towards Namibia.

The concept of promoting reform through economic cooperation was also taken up by the Foreign Office, which indicates that there was a general understanding that West Germany needed to step up its efforts in South Africa to prevent more severe consequences such as growing civil unrest followed by war and revolution. In early 1977, the Foreign Office discussed with the German Federation of Trade Unions (DGB) the implementation of a 'code of conduct', as already introduced to British firms in South Africa by the House of Commons in 1976.[32] The Foreign Office pointed out that German companies such as Siemens already followed a code of conduct, while other companies found excuses in restrictions imposed by apartheid.[33] Rather alarmingly, the Foreign Office encouraged West German companies in southern Africa 'to push, in their own well-intended interest, for a legislative reform, before

---

[30] B. Blumenau, *The United Nations and Terrorism: Germany, Multilateralism & Antiterrorism Efforts in the 1970s*, New York, Palgrave Macmillan, 2014, 202.
[31] PAAA, Zwischenarchiv, Bd. 116845, 1977–1978, Deutsche Unternehmen im südlichen Afrika, 14.02.1977.
[32] Ibid.
[33] See also 'Mehr Weltoffenheit gegenüber Südafrika', *Der Spiegel*, 43/1978.

the pressure of reality will seek release in a revolutionary explosion'.[34] Unambiguously, the Foreign Office demanded that the West German business community in southern Africa take greater social responsibility, and show a greater commitment to forge sustainable economic relations in the region, going beyond merely cosmetic measures.

The Foreign Office justified its reluctance to impose guidelines on West German companies by pointing towards the government's foreign policy and economic principles: first, the SPD-led government's dogmatic separation between economics and politics, which was a central pillar of *Ostpolitik*; second, the foreign policy principle of non-intervention in the affairs of sovereign states; and third, the industries' rejection of state paternalism, which reflected the liberal economic regulations in West Germany. From the perspective of West German businesses, the continuation of the status quo in southern Africa guaranteed unhindered business activities in the region, while any attempt to pressure South Africa into implementing reforms would on ly make Pretoria more unpredictable.[35] Yet, the Foreign Office's suggestion to implement reforms without Pretoria's approval seemed even less appealing.

In late 1977, in talks with the West German Embassy in Pretoria, West German businesses in South Africa expressed their unease about implementing economic reforms that might oppose the legal requirement of South Africa's economic policies:

> All firms have one thing in common, namely the fear that such measure would in this increasingly sensible atmosphere strain the current right to hospitality. To annoy the government would only lead to further losses, for the business conditions are already weakened by depression. Anyhow, some of the 'principles', named in a different context, are in conflict with local laws.[36]

However, West German companies agreed on supporting a code of conduct that would be established within the framework of the European Community. Such a proposal would allow German businesses in southern Africa to argue that the parent companies in West Germany implemented these measures and thus take the responsibility off firms operating in southern Africa.[37] In late 1977, the European Community's foreign ministers accepted the proposal and established a formal code of conduct for firms operating in South Africa.[38] Still, the Federation of German Industry (BDI) held the view that such guidelines

---

[34] PAAA, Zwischenarchiv, Bd. 116845, 1977–1978, Deutsche Unternehmen im südlichen Afrika, 14.02.1977.
[35] See 'Mehr Weltoffenheit gegenüber Südafrika', *Der Spiegel*, 43/1978. See also PAAA, Zwischenarchiv, Bd. 116845, 1977–1978, Gespräche zwischen Botschaft und Vorstand der Deutsch-Südafrikanischen Handelskammer, 16.11.1978.
[36] PAAA, Zwischenarchiv, Bd. 116845, 1977–1978, Überlegungen zur Abgabe einer Prinzipienerklärung, 01.09.1977.
[37] Ibid.
[38] Ibid., Code of Conduct for Companies with Subsidiaries, Branches or Representation in South

were unnecessary, arguing that West German companies had already followed similar principles since 1976, as provided by the Organisation for Economic Co-operation and Development (OECD).[39] The DGB and other unions were equally critical.[40] In the end, the West German companies in South Africa accepted the code of conduct, mainly because of concerns about public criticism.[41] For Bonn, however, the code of conduct was also 'a means to justify West Germany's business relationship with South Africa to the Third World'. In the eyes of the West German business community in South Africa, this argument was flawed, for the code of conduct might not only lead to demands for further concessions at a later date, Pretoria's uncompromising attitude regarding the Namibia question could still lead to sanctions against South Africa.[42]

Nonetheless, both the SPD-led government of the 1970s and the CDU-led government of the 1980s adopted a two-pronged strategy. First, both governments in essence maintained that it was necessary for Pretoria to recognise apartheid as a cause of regional instability, internal conflict in South Africa and Namibia, and international isolation.[43] Only then would it be possible to help solve the growing regional conflicts. Second, Bonn defended its economic relations with South Africa on the grounds that it allowed West Germany to change the apartheid system from within: 'The Federal government promotes the use of existing economic relations with South Africa to contribute to an evolutionary development in South Africa that will lead to the social and ultimately political equality of all races'.[44]

In sum, the threat of sanctions remained by far the greatest peril to West German business in South Africa. Furthermore, despite the best efforts of Bonn's policy-makers to improve West Germany's image in Africa, the code of conduct had little positive effect, for it was a mere cosmetic alteration rather than a far-reaching reform that could have threatened the very fabric of the apartheid state. In fact, there seems little evidence to suggest that the

---

Africa, 20.09.1977.
[39] Ibid., Erklärung des BDI zum Verhalten der Industrie in Südafrika, 22.09.1977.
[40] Ibid., DGB-Brief an das Auswärtige Amt, 05.11.1977. See also Wenzel, *Südafrika-Politik*, 159–160. Wenzel assumed that the Ministry for Economics and Technology (BMWi) and the Ministry of Finance (BMF) hindered the Foreign Office from imposing further reforms on West German companies operating in South Africa. However, as outlined above, evidence suggests that the Foreign Office's reluctance to impose a code of conduct on West German businesses in South Africa did not come as a result of outside pressure. Thus, it seems unlikely that the Foreign Office had any intention to introduce further measures, apart from the EU code of conduct.
[41] See also Wenzel, *Südafrika-Politik*, 159.
[42] PAAA, Zwischenarchiv, Bd. 116845, 1977–1978, Gespräche zwischen Botschaft und Vorstand der Deutsch-Südafrikanischen Handelskammer, 16.11.1978.
[43] Ibid., Brief Genscher an Hans-Günther Sohl, 23.11.1977. Hans-Günther Sohl was a West German industrialist.
[44] Ibid., Elemente für das Gespräch mit der EKD, 21.02.1978.

code of conduct had any real impact on companies' treatment of non-white workers.⁴⁵ Nonetheless, Genscher argued in the *Bundestag* in 1984 that the code of conduct showed, after only four years of implementation, signs of positive improvements for non-white workers. Expectedly, the statement received a number of sceptical interjections from the opposition parties.⁴⁶ SWAPO had already expressed its general scepticism about the effectiveness of a code of conduct in late 1978.⁴⁷ Yet, despite Genscher's overly optimistic assessment of the code of conduct, he had little illusion about West Germany's ability to change the apartheid state, and contain or reverse Soviet influence in southern Africa. Hence, Genscher argued that Pretoria needed to implement far-reaching social, educational and industrial reforms in preparation for 'the distribution of political power to all population groups and as a means to counter extremist-revolutionary tendencies'. In the foreign minister's view, these reformative steps would most likely also benefit West German economic interests in southern Africa.⁴⁸

Genscher firmly believed that 'the core issue of Germany's policy towards South Africa, and the West's in general, lies in not letting this politically and economically important country fall under communist control'.⁴⁹ He acknowledged that further communist advances in southern Africa had the potential to pose a threat to the capitalist market system in the region, and consequently to German economic interest in southern Africa.⁵⁰ However, the responsibility of countering such threats lay primarily with Pretoria, for apartheid served, in Genscher' view, as a breeding ground for communism.⁵¹

Pretoria agreed, of course, with Genscher that communism was a threat to the Western economic system in southern Africa, but was reluctant to see any link between apartheid and communism, for Pretoria defended its policies by arguing that South Africa was the last bulwark against communism in the region.⁵² In the face of Pretoria's intransigence, the SPD-

---

45 Wenzel, *Südafrika-Politik*, 88 and 160.
46 Deutscher Bundestag, 8. Wahlperiode, Stenographischer Bericht, 54. Sitzung, 10.02.1984, 3877.
47 PAAA, Zwischenarchiv, Bd. 116802, 1977–1978, SPD – Abt. Ausland-Referat II, Namibia: SWAPO, 03.11.1978.
48 Ibid., Brief-Genscher an Hans-Günther Sohl, 23.11.1977.
49 Ibid. However, Genscher disagreed on most issues with Sohl, who supported extreme views such as finding a place for a white state in Africa, 'comparable to Israel in the Arabic world'.
50 Indeed, Genscher had no doubts about the Soviet Union's objectives in southern Africa. He repeatedly emphasised that Moscow's main ambition was 'to increase Soviet influence in the region through the exploitation of conflicts'. Consequently, the Soviet Union posed a threat to West Germany's security and economic interests in southern Africa, as Genscher explained: PAAA, Zwischenarchiv, Bd. 116841, 1877–1978, Deutsch-südafrikanische Beziehungen, hier: Antwort des BM auf das Fernschreiben des MdB Dr Marx vom 07.02.1978, 09.02.1978, 3.
51 This view was also represented by the WCG. Wischnewski expressed similar views at the Socialist Internationale in Vancouver in 1978: PAAA, Zwischenarchiv, Bd. 116840, Wischnewski speech at the Socialist Internationale in Vancouver in 1978.
52 Ibid. Bd. 108220, 1975–1976, Vermerk über das Gespräch des Bundeskanzlers mit Premierminister Dr. B. J. Vorster, 25.06.1976, 7.

led government argued that the regime's policies would determine the success or failure of the communist bloc in southern Africa.

The Soviet Union argued that capitalist exploitation was the cause of underdevelopment in the Third World. Consequently, the removal of the capitalist market system was instrumental in advancing overall development in Third World countries. The support of liberation movements and relations with anti-imperialist regimes was part of the Soviet agenda to overcome colonial capitalism in southern Africa.[53] Hence, the possibility that the communist bloc countries would gain control over southern Africa indeed presented a threat to the long-established capitalist market system in the region. In the early 1980s, it became increasingly apparent that the Eastern bloc's economic community was not in a position to provide southern African countries with an attractive alternative to Western economic power. The self-described Marxist-Leninist republics of Angola and Mozambique headed towards economic disaster, which motivated Mozambique to mend ties with the West in the early 1980s.[54] Moscow quickly ruled out military intervention, for the Soviet resources in the region were too limited to risk a military confrontation with South Africa over Mozambique.[55] Additionally, Soviet resources were already heavily stretched in Afghanistan, contributing to Moscow's cautious approach in southern Africa. Generally speaking, however, Moscow would not tolerate a breakaway from its sphere of influence. In the case of the GDR, for example, Moscow repeatedly clamped down on Honecker's attempts to establish good neighbourly relations with West Germany.[56] However, while geographic proximity allowed the Soviet Union to impose its will on its European satellites, the Soviet Union's sphere of influence in southern Africa was too limited to hinder countries under its influence to establish ties with the West, or even break from Moscow. Yet, despite the Soviet Union's relative weakness and limited reach in southern Africa, the Soviet-Cuban military cooperation in Angola and the GDR's support of liberation movements fed into Western concerns that Moscow might try to extend its military presence in the region.

From the perspective of West German business interests in southern Africa, the worst-case scenario envisaged that greater Soviet influence would cut off large parts of the region from the capitalist world. The presence of an estimated 35,000 Cuban troops and mili-

---

[53] E. Schmidt, 'Africa', in R. H. Immerman and P. Goedde (eds.), *The Oxford Handbook of the Cold War*, Oxford, Oxford University Press, 2013, 267–268.

[54] P. Duignan and L. H. Gann, *The Cold War: End and Aftermath*, Stanford, Hoover Institution Press, 1996, 15.

[55] See also C. Saunders and S. Onslow, 'The Cold War and southern Africa, 1976–1990', in M. P. Leffler and O. A. Vestad (eds.), *The Cambridge History of the Cold War: Volume 3, Endings*, Cambridge, Cambridge University Press, 2010.

[56] C. Clemens, 'West Germany and New Superpower Détente', in M. Cox (ed.), *Beyond the Cold War: Superpowers at a Crossroads*, Lanham, University Press of America, Inc., 1990, 160.

tary advisers on the Namibian border amplified West German insecurities. The conservative camp, most of all CSU chairman Franz Josef Strauß, and numerous business-related groups and industries, as pointed out above, further fuelled fears of subversion by using anti-communist rhetoric. However, West Germany believed, correctly, that the communist-bloc countries, including the GDR, had no real interest in gaining an immediate foothold in the regional economy. This was mainly because the communist bloc countries understood that granting military support opened up more possibilities for gaining influence than economic support or by political means.[57] This does not, of course, imply that the communist bloc had no economic interest in southern Africa, but gaining greater influence in the region could not be achieved by economic means due to the communist bloc's limited economic power.[58]

Importantly, however, the Soviet Union was against direct military involvement in southern Africa. Yet, after some initial concerns, Moscow looked with favour on Cuba's military presence in Angola, for the Cuban troops increased the Soviet Union's military influence in the region, while Moscow provided only logistical support. Cuba's ambition to play a major international role materialised in southern Africa mostly in favour of Soviet ambitions. This generally also holds true with respect to the GDR. The Soviet Union supported overseas involvement of its satellite states, for their efforts helped Moscow to portray the Soviet Union as a true superpower with global reach and influence. Hence, despite the Soviet Union's limited resources, the GDR's solidarity with southern African liberation struggles and Cuba's troops in Angola supported Moscow in building up a formidable presence in the region between 1975 and 1985.[59] However, the fact that East Berlin supported Moscow's power ambitions in southern Africa does not imply that the GDR did not pursue its own national interests in the region.

In 1979, at a time when intra-German rivalry in southern Africa reached an unprecedented peak, leading to an intensification of the GDR's support of liberation movements in southern Africa, Bonn evaluated East Berlin's objectives as follows:

> The GDR does not rely on visually effective campaigns directly on the battlefield. Nonetheless, the GDR's activities in the political-military infrastructure of strategically important states such as Mozambique, Angola and Zambia, as well as Ethiopia

---

[57] BStU, MfS-Hauptverwaltung Aufklärung, Nr. 63, Das militärische Engagement der sozialistischen Länder in Afrika südlich der Sahara aus BRD-Sicht, 11.04.1977, 178.

[58] In the late 1970s, economic considerations become increasingly important in the GDR's policy towards southern Africa. See also B. H. Schulz, *Development Policy in the Cold War era: The two Germanies and Sub-Saharan Africa, 1960–1985*, Münster, LIT, 1995, 17.

[59] For a contemporary assessment of Moscow's power strategy during the Cold War, see J. Steel, *Soviet Power, The Kremlin's Foreign Policy – Brezhnev to Cherenkov*, New York, Simon & Schuster, Inc., 1983.

need to be taken very seriously. The aim is to increase those countries' political, economic and military dependency on the GDR through the concentration on ideological education, and the establishment of economic and military entanglements.[60]

According to the GDR's foreign intelligence service, the overall objective of the communist bloc countries in southern Africa was, in West Germany's view, to influence the political development and gain increasing military control over the strategically important Cape route and the region's natural resources and raw materials.[61] The Soviet Union's objective was to gain political and military influence over southern Africa rather than to rely on costly economic competition with the West in the region. The GDR and Cuba played an active role in helping the Soviet Union to realise its geopolitical ambitions in southern Africa.

Until the late 1980s, the Soviet Union ruled out the possibility of establishing extensive economic relations with South Africa. However, the Soviet Union had a long history of co-operating with South Africa on the marketing of natural resources, for the two countries dominated the production of minerals that were critical for manufacturing industries, including the industrial production of the Eastern bloc countries.[62] The GDR only maintained official trade relations with South Africa until 1963, although some evidence seems to indicate that limited unofficial trade continued until at least the early 1970s. However, it is impossible to determine whether the GDR was directly involved in such trade, for GDR goods reached South Africa mainly via third countries. The 1963 decision to boycott trade with South Africa was more strictly adhered to in the 1970s and 1980s. To give up access to an attractive foreign market was a substantial sacrifice for the GDR's struggling economy, as Van der Heyden points out.[63] Thus, East Berlin was, in stark contrast to Bonn, convinced that economic pressure would finally force Pretoria to change course in South Africa and Namibia. However, the GDR's decisive policy against apartheid and the regime in Pretoria was not grounded in altruistic considerations, but on a long-term economic planning which was also in line with the Soviet strategy in southern Africa.

Although Moscow's interactions with Pretoria provided opportunities for intensifying further economic cooperation between the two countries, which could have led to the crea-

---

[60] BStU, MfS-HVA, Nr. 84, Aktuelle Informationsübersicht Nr. 40/79, 5.10.1979, 111–112.
[61] BStU, MfS-Hauptverwaltung Aufklärung, Nr. 63, Das militärische Engagement der sozialistischen Länder in Afrika südlich der Sahara aus BRD-Sicht, 11.04.1977, 179. Although the SPD-led government agreed widely with the notion that it was necessary to reverse the steady increase of Soviet influence in southern Africa, the views outlined by the MfS represented largely the views of the CDU/CSU's position: Deutscher Bundestag, 8. Wahlperiode, Stenographischer Bericht, 197. Sitzung, 1980, 15701–15737.
[62] K. M. Campbell, 'Southern Africa in Soviet Foreign Policy', *The International Institute for Strategic Studies* (IISS), Adelphi Papers, 227, Winter 1987/8, 175.
[63] Van der Heyden, *Zwischen Solidarität*, 92–113.

tion of a mineral cartel, the Soviet Union had little interest in increasing its influence in the region through economic means. Moscow believed that supporting SWAPO and ANC would put the Soviet Union, from a strategic rather than a moral point of view, on the right side of history. The Kremlin believed that, once these liberation movements gained power, the Soviet Union would gain control over some of the world's largest mineral resources, insofar as the ANC and SWAPO could be controlled after independence.[64] Moscow assumed that the liberation movements' gratitude for Soviet support would translate into greater consideration of Soviet interests in the pre-independence era; an assumption that was also held by East Berlin.[65] Hence, the belief that these liberation movements would eventually gain power was unquestionably one of the reasons that Moscow and East Berlin threw their support behind the liberation struggle in southern Africa. In the face of the GDR's ailing economy, the prospect of lucrative future business and unhindered access to natural resources motivated East Berlin, at least in mid-to-late 1970s and 1980s, to further strengthen its already good relations with liberation movements in southern Africa.[66]

Although the Soviet bloc had neither the ambition nor the economic capacity to enter into economic competition with the West in southern Africa, economic rivalry took place at the level of propaganda. While West German politicians and journalists accused the GDR of failing to observe its declaration to boycott South Africa diplomatically and in trade, West Germany's co-operation with South Africa presented an even bigger target for GDR propaganda.[67] In fact, the GDR's efforts to discredit West German business in Africa further highlighted Bonn's dilemma of trying to steer a course between economic interests in southern Africa and its historic and moral obligation to support majority rule, equal rights and self-determination. Hence, the GDR's criticism of West Germany's economic relations with South Africa and Namibia on international platforms such as the United Nations and the International Solidarity Conference offers considerable insight into the general dynamics of the two German states' rivalry in southern Africa.

Obviously, the Federal Republic's extensive economic relations with South Africa caught the attention of the GDR's propaganda offence against West Germany in Africa.[68] Although *Ostpolitik* considerably improved relations between the two German states, rivalry on the

---

[64] See also C. Saunders and S. Onslow, 'The Cold War and southern Africa, 1976–1990', in M. P. Leffler and O. A. Vestad (eds.), *The Cambridge History of the Cold War: Volume 3, Endings*, Cambridge, Cambridge University Press, 2010, 222–243.
[65] See Chapter Two, The Socialist Unity Party (SED).
[66] See also BStU, MfS-HA XVIII, Nr. 8379, Beschluss über vorläufige Grundsätze für eine mögliche Beteiligung der DDR an der Bildung und Tätigkeit gemischter Gesellschaften in Entwicklungsländern Afrikas, Asiens, bzw. Lateinamerikas, 04.05.1978, 216.
[67] Van der Heyden, *Zwischen Solidarität*, 101.
[68] See BArch-SAPMO, DZ 8/39, International Solidarity Conference in Addis-Ababa, 30.10.1976.

African continent, especially in southern Africa, continued almost unabated until at least the mid-1980s. Throughout the 1970s, the GDR never missed an opportunity to talk about the 'exploitive' practises of West German businesses in southern Africa. From the perspective of the GDR-style state socialism, international monopolies were geared toward 'looting the African people and natural resources of South Africa and Namibia'.[69] With regard to West Germany's economic interests in Namibia, the Ministry of Foreign Affairs came to the following conclusion in 1971: 'It is apparent that the Federal Republic of Germany also supports the South African racist-regime and its colonial policy in Namibia. West German monopolies are actively involved in the exploitation of the Namibian people and natural resources'.[70]

The GDR pointed out that Namibia's great wealth benefitted only international monopolies and the Namibian white minority.[71] The introduction of the code of conduct was viewed simply as an attempt to 'conceal' such practises.[72] The argument that 'transnational monopolies can become instruments for the promotion of freedom and equality through economic investment in South Africa' was seen as a 'pretext for legitimising existing and new investment' and 'to perpetuate the system of apartheid'.[73] West Germany's economic success was a source of frustration for East Berlin. While West Germany's economic power helped its leaders to further their broader international political and economic objectives and improve the country's overall international standing, the GDR was economically too weak to rely on economic power to advance East Berlin's international standing and ambitions.

Nonetheless, although the GDR's economic power was far too limited for it to have an impact on African countries' overall economic situation, the GDR compensated for this relative weakness by making available a wide range of educational programmes to African states that sought to gain economic independence from the West. The aim was 'to advance economic independence by strengthening the scientific and technological potential of de-

---

[69] See, e.g., Babing, *Gegen Rassismus*, 1977–1982, Rede des DDR-Vertreters Gerhard Schröter im Vierten Komitee der XXXV. Tagung der UN-Vollversammlung, 02.10.1980, 416–417 and 72; ibid., Rede des Leiters der DDR Delegation, Hans-Jürgen Weitz, auf der UN Konferenz für die Unterstützung der Voelker Simbabwes und Namibias von 16.5.1977 bis 21.5.1977 in Maputo, 16.04.1977.

[70] Ibid., 1949–1977, Erklärung eines Sprechers des Ministeriums für Auswärtige Angelegenheiten der DDR zum Gutachten des Internationalen Gerichtshofes in der Namibiafrage, 29.06.1971. 197.

[71] BStU, MfS-HA II, Nr. 28977, Informationsmaterial über die Südwestafrikanische Volksorganisation Namibias (SWAPO), March 1981, 181.

[72] Babing, *Gegen Rassismus*, 1977–1982, Rede des DDR-Vertreters Gerhard Schröter im Vierten Komitee der XXXV. Tagung der UN-Vollversammlung, 02.10.1980, 417.

[73] Ibid., Die Rolle transnationaler Monopole in Südafrika, 08.11.1979, in Rede des DDR-Vertreters Gerhard Schröter im Vierten Komitee der XXXV. Tagung der UN-Vollversammlung, 02.10.1980, 417.

veloping countries'.⁷⁴ Seen from this perspective, it becomes apparent that the GDR made good use of the limited economic power it had available. East Berlin was not against using economic power to further its interests, but its economic strength was too limited to do that effectively.

Western capitalism represented everything the GDR stood against. There was a general consensus among the GDR's ruling class that from the perspective of the GDR's socialist economy, which was based on centralised state planning and, in theory, around improving the lives of the working class, West Germany's economy had little to offer, for it represented the old capitalist economic order. From the GDR's perspective, the primary objective in the West's economic activities in Africa was to achieve an economic exchange in which African states would be integrated into the 'imperialist world economic system'.⁷⁵ Evidently, the GDR's viewpoint derived from the Marxist-Leninist understanding that the capitalist economic system needs to constantly open up new economic markets in search of resources and profits.⁷⁶ The West's main objective in southern Africa was therefore the creation of new capitalist markets, with the purpose of growing economic influence in the region. The GDR believed that West Germany pursued three particular policy objectives in southern Africa: 'to promote capitalistic tendencies within the 'middleclass' to create favourable conditions for the long-term expansion of a neo-colonial strategy'; 'to strangle in African states the revolutionary process from within'; and 'to officially acknowledge the legality of the liberation struggle in order to gain influence over the liberation movement, while simultaneously continue the close co-operation with the racist colonial regime, which was a pillar of capitalism in Africa'.⁷⁷ West Germany's economic success was based on imperialist exploitation.⁷⁸ In fact the GDR's economy depended on subventions from West Germany in the 1970s and to an even greater extent in the 1980s. Bonn soon realised that Honecker was prepared to make concessions in return for economic assistance and the GDR's dependency on West Germany slowly undermined the one-party state at its foundation.⁷⁹ In some

---

74 BStU, MfS-HA II, Nr. 29532, Hilfeleistungen der DDR für Entwicklungsländer und nationale Befreiungsbewegungen, 22.07.1984, 34.
75 PAAA, MfAA, C 1426/75, 1971–1973, Einschätzung der gegenwärtigen Situation in Afrika, Einfluss des Imperialismus, [no date], 8.
76 For a more detailed assessment of the Marxist-Leninist view on capitalist expansionism, see W. H. Mott, *The Economic Basis of Peace, Linkages between Economic Growth and International Conflict*, Connecticut, Greenwood Press, 1997, 53–57.
77 PAAA, MfAA, C 1426/75, 1971–1973, Einschätzung der gegenwärtigen Situation in Afrika, Die Afrika-Politik der BRD, [no date], 9.
78 B. Byg, 'Solidarity and Exile, Blonder Tango and the East German Fantasy of the Third World', in E. Rueschmann (ed.), *Moving Pictures, Migrating Identities*, Jackson, University Press of Mississippi, 2003, 59.
79 K. Cosgrove, 'Erich Honecker', in D. Wilsford (ed.), *Political Leaders of Contemporary Western*

respect, West Germany contributed, through the exchange of economic aid for concessions, to a slow dismantling of some of the GDR's totalitarian structures.[80] Ultimately, East Germany's dependence on West German economic assistance made it increasingly difficult for the centralised state to resist Bonn's efforts toward unification in the late 1980s.

In regards to South Africa's apartheid state, West Germany followed a similar approach – or at least, so it seems, given that consecutive governments and the Foreign Office supported the notion that measures such as the code of conduct had the potential to change apartheid from within. The example of the GDR showed that it was not entirely unrealistic to believe that states with totalitarian structures could be reformed through economic relations. Yet, the continuous deterioration of the situation in South Africa presented a daunting challenge for the West and its interests in southern Africa. In 1986, the GDR's Ministry of State Security observed that the West saw in the face of growing domestic unrest against the Botha regime an urgent need to calm and influence the situation. Although there was a general consensus that the apartheid system could no longer be maintained, there was also a general consensus that a 'change in the capitalist power structures could not be allowed', as the MfS pointed out.[81] In the 1980s, Western concerns over the general political situation in southern Africa remained subservient to larger interests in the region, among which economic factors were paramount.

Hence, by the mid-1980s, West Germany 'was actively engaged in committing SWAPO for the future', as the MfAA reported. West Germany saw in the ever-deepening crisis in South Africa the urgent need to ensnare the likely future leaders of Namibia.[82] Indeed, while the GDR and SWAPO had a long-standing relationship of mutual trust built up between them, West Germany's relationship with the liberation movement was still characterised by grave fluctuations between trust-based co-operation and suspicion-based hostility. Moreover, West Germany's extensive economic ties with South Africa and its reluctance to support sanctions against the apartheid regime had harmed West Germany's international image.

Europe: A Biographical Dictionary, Westport, Greenwood Press, 1995, 200. See also H.-H., Hertle, 'Germany in the Last decade of the Cold War, in O. Njolstad, *The Last Decade of the Cold War: From Conflict Escalation to Conflict Transformation*, New York, Routledge, 2004, 221–227. Talks between Bonn and East Berlin slowly led to concessions that loosened some of the restrictions imposed on GDR citizens after the erection of the Berlin Wall.

[80] While the GDR lifted, for example, some travel restrictions to West Germany, the infamous State Security apparatus, the Stasi, drastically stepped up its surveillance of GDR citizens.

[81] BStU, MfS-Hauptverwaltung Aufklärung Nr. 40, Die Entwicklung in der Südafrikanischen Republik, 06.01.1986, 417.

[82] BStU, MfAA-ZR 2763/84, 1981–1984, Bericht über die Konsultation der Abteilung Ost- und Zentralafrika mit den sowjetischen Außenministerium, 21.06.1984, 9.

The MfAA concluded that in the mid-to-late 1980s West Germany was, in stark contrast to South Africa, no longer concerned about a SWAPO-led Namibia. Bonn was convinced that 'once Namibia has achieved independence, the West could secure the desired political influence over the country through additional economic aid and economic engagement'.[83] It is not surprising that the MfAA arrived at such a conclusion, considering that Bonn frequently discussed the possibility of using West Germany's economic influence in southern Africa to promote change.[84] In other words, there seemed little reason to doubt that West Germany would try to use its economic strength to influence post-independent Namibia.[85] Furthermore, firsthand experience had taught East Berlin that West Germany was willing to use its economic power to achieve political influence.

Interestingly, however, it was during talks with the Soviet Union that West Germany apparently indicated it was actively engaged in binding SWAPO to West Germany as a preparation for smooth future cooperation. In mid-1984, this information was then passed on to the East-Central Africa Department of the MfAA.[86] Though it is impossible to determine why West Germany might have provided such information to the Soviet Union, it seems likely that Bonn wanted to underline, at a time of rapidly deteriorating US-Soviet relations, the Western powers' commitment to undermine Moscow's efforts to bring the region under its control. The emphasis was evidently on Western economic superiority.[87] No doubt West Germany could feel confident that a SWAPO-led Namibia would not automatically give Moscow and East Berlin greater influence in Namibia, for even decades of uncompromising solidarity and ideological affinity with SWAPO could well be considered as less of a decisive factor in SWAPO's post-independence decision-making than realpolitik.[88]

---

[83] Ibid., 9.

[84] Deutscher Bundestag, 10. Wahlperiode, Stenographischer Bericht, 54. Sitzung, 10.02.1984, 3879–3882. See also PAAA, Zwischenarchiv, Bd. 125282, 1981, Position of the Government of the Republic of Germany on Namibia, July 1981; BPA-Nachrichtenabteilung, Rundfunk-Auswahl Deutschland, Ref. II R2, Hans Dietrich Genscher, Bundesminister des Auswärtigen, zum Namibia-Problem, 11.10.1978; Ibid., Bd. 116845, 1977–1978, Deutsche Unternehmen im südlichen Afrika, 14.02.1977, 4.

[85] Both Kohl and Genscher found it necessary to take measures against Soviet influence in southern Africa. The aim, however, was to achieve this objective through political solutions and economic development, and not by turning southern Africa into an ideological battleground between East and West. See also PAAA, AV Neues Amt, Bd. 16413, 1983, UN-Rat für Namibia; hier: Bericht an die 37. GV, 11.12.1982.

[86] BStU, MfAA-ZR 2763/84, 1981–1984, Bericht über die Konsultation der Abteilung Ost- und Zentralafrika mit den sowjetischen Außenministerium, 21.06.1984, 9.

[87] Ibid., 9.

[88] There was general confidence that West Germany's economy was superior to the economies of the Eastern bloc countries. Consequently, it was widely believed that West Germany was in a better position to support southern African countries. Already in 1980, the SPD-led government argued that West German economic aid had the potential to sway independent African states away

Whatever the case, West Germany had good reasons to envisage such developments in a post-independence Namibia. In 1978, after West Germany's first official meeting with SWAPO in Lusaka, an SPD delegation reported that 'political and economic realism' was noticeable in the liberation movement.[89] Furthermore, Nujoma stated in New York in 1983 that the West should think about Namibia's need for international economic and technical support.[90] Also in 1983, Nujoma made it clear, during a meeting with the West German Ambassador to Angola, that SWAPO had no intention of flying the 'red flag' over Windhoek, for he advocated the policy of non-alignment and saw Namibia as a future member country of the World Bank and International Monetary Fund (IMF).[91] Obviously, SWAPO had to think about post-independence Namibia from a rational perspective. In this light, Western countries were in an overall stronger position to offer economic rewards for post-independence cooperation than the Eastern bloc countries. Overall, the attractiveness of the free market system, which the Eastern bloc countries were not linked to, cannot be underestimated here.[92]

Thus, East and West German competition for influence in southern Africa contained a strong economic component. Although the GDR's presence in Africa was, before the introduction of *Ostpolitik*, dominated by the objective of breaking free from the constraints imposed by the Hallstein Doctrine, after the removal of these restrictive measures in 1969, the GDR was free to become an 'active partner of the Soviet power strategy', particularly in Africa.[93] In southern Africa, East Berlin's overall objective was to support Moscow's agenda to gain control and influence over the region and its natural resources. Although the GDR's own economic interests moved further into the foreground in the mid-1970s, there was no dichotomy between the GDR's economic interests in southern Africa and the Soviet Union's strategic objectives in the region.[94] Both East Berlin and Moscow's aim was to secure access to natural resources and new export markets.[95] Hence, if anything,

---

from the Soviet bloc and promote self-determination and non-alignment: Deutscher Bundestag, 8. Wahlperiode, Stenographischer Bericht, 197. Sitzung, 18.01.1980, 15727–15729.

[89] Nujoma declared in mid-1981 that SWAPO will after independence establish, similar to Angola, extensive trade relations with the West. See AAPA, 1981, Band 1, SWAPO; hier: Nujoma-Besuch in Bonn vom 25. bis 27.05.1981, 29.05.1981, 873.

[90] PAAA, AV Neues Amt, Bd. 16414, 1983, Gespräche der fünf Außenminister in Paris, 08.06.1983.

[91] Ibid., Ambassador Wand, lunch mit SWAPO-President Nujoma, Luanda, 12.07.1983.

[92] See also B. Hocking and M. Smith, *World Politics*, New York, Routledge, 2014, 249–250.

[93] 'Wir haben euch Waffen und Brot geschickt', *Der Spiegel*, 10/1980, 03.03.1980.

[94] U. van der Heyden, 'GDR Development', 29. See also BStU, MfS-HA XVIII, Nr. 8379, Beschluss über vorläufige Grundsätze für eine mögliche Beteiligung der DDR an der Bildung und Tätigkeit Gemischter Gesellschaften in Entwicklungsländern Afrikas, Asiens, bzw. Lateinamerikas, 04.05.1978, 216.

[95] See, e.g., BStU, MfS-HA XVIII, Nr. 8379, Beschluss über vorläufige Grundsätze für eine mögliche Beteiligung der DDR an der Bildung und Tätigkeit Gemischter Gesellschaften in Entwicklungsländern Afrikas, Asiens, bzw. Lateinamerikas, 04.05.1978, 216; 'Wir haben euch Waffen und Brot

the GDR's own economic interests emphasised the benefit of supporting the Soviet Union's aims in southern Africa.

It is apparent that the GDR's solidarity with liberation movements was partly driven by economic considerations. There is also some evidence that indicates that the growing interaction between West Germany and SWAPO was, to some degree, also motivated by economic objectives, at least in the mid-1980s. Given that SWAPO was clearly by far the most significant force in Namibia's struggle for national independence in the 1980s, it seems only logical that Bonn saw the liberation movement increasingly as the government-in-waiting and thus responsible for Namibia's political and economic orientation after independence. Smooth economic co-operation was therefore necessarily linked to good relations with SWAPO. However, West Germany's position toward South Africa was infinitely more complex.

Although West Germany grew increasingly critical of South Africa in the late 1970s, a complex set of economic and political considerations prevented Bonn from breaking off its relations with Pretoria. As a result, Bonn maintained a cooperative relationship with Pretoria throughout the 1970s and most of the 1980s. Ipso facto, West Germany's economic considerations dealt predominantly with the reality of keeping extensive economic relations with a country that grew increasingly isolated on the world stage as a consequence of its apartheid policy and its illegal occupation of Namibia. While West Germany wanted to avoid a politicisation of its economic relations with southern Africa, consecutive governments, including the Foreign Office, agreed that German businesses in southern Africa could potentially contribute to the gradual dismantling of the long-established apartheid structures. In essence, West Germany's policy toward South Africa was geared towards finding a compromised solution that would not challenge its economic interests in Namibia and South Africa. Obviously, no government – no matter how idealistic, no matter how well-intending – could afford to disregard West Germany's extensive economic relations with South Africa. In any event, West Germany was not influential enough to pressure Pretoria into changing course.[96]

The GDR, on the other hand, put itself firmly on the side of the oppressed majority in southern Africa, repeatedly pointing out the exploitative intentions of the capitalist West in the region, which was viewed as the GDR's duty in the struggle against racism, apartheid and colonialism. However, with newly independent states such as Mozambique and liberation movements such as SWAPO forging strong relations with both the East and the West, relationships became less polarised in the 1980s. The increasing interest in improving relations with the West was, however, largely motivated by economic considerations. Thus, the

---

geschickt', *Der Spiegel*, 10/1980, 03.03.1980.
[96] 'South Africa: Time Running Out', *The Report of the Study Commission*, 305.

role of crisis in propelling a shift in allegiance cannot be underestimated, which added a further element of complexity and unpredictability to East-West rivalry in Africa.

Both the GDR and West Germany's Green Party were also very critical of West German uranium trade with Namibia and South Africa, as well as the apparent exchange of nuclear-know-how. The credit transactions with South Africa and Namibia by West German banks also faced repeated criticism from both East Berlin and the Green Party.[97] All these issues were taken up by the Green Party in the *Bundestag*.[98] Opposition to West Germany's economic relations with Namibia and South Africa became increasingly stronger in the mid-1980s. While the CDU-led government agreed with applying economic power to further West Germany's interests in southern Africa, the Green Party voiced strong concerns about Bonn's apparent lack of economic consciousness.[99] West Germany's extensive economic relations with South Africa supported the repressive apartheid regime and South Africa's economic well-being and foreign military aid were instrumental for the occupation of Namibia. The Greens were especially concerned that some of the largest German companies such as Mercedes-Benz and Siemens, were involved in deals that directly benefitted South Africa's military, regardless of Bonn's commitment to the UN arms embargo against South Africa. Consecutive governments defended West German economic relations with South Africa and Namibia on the grounds that economic co-operation offered possibilities to promote reforms and, thus, influence the apartheid regime from within.[100] Though East Berlin never wavered in its strong support for SWAPO's cause, the GDR was not in a position to guarantee a steady stream of material and financial support to SWAPO's struggle for national liberation. This is particularly true for the early 1980s when the East German economy was in a dire condition.

---

[97] Babing, *Gegen Rassismus*, 1977–1982, Rede des DDR-Vertreters Gerhard Schröter im vierten Komitee der XXXV. Tagung der UN-Vollversammlung, 02.10.1980, 415–417. See also BStU, MfS ZAIG Nr. 11115, Babing A, Die Zusammenarbeit imperialistischer Staaten mit Südafrika und Rhodesien, 22.05.1973, 141–179; BStU, MfS-Hauptverwaltung Aufklärung, Nr. 12, Außenpolitischer Informationsbericht Nr. 4/81, BRD-Beteiligung an der Ausbeutung der Uranvorkommen in Namibia, 26.01.1981.

[98] Deutscher Bundestag, 10. Wahlperiode, Stenographischer Bericht, 54. Sitzung, 10.02.1984, 3874.

[99] It is worth noting that the SPD parliamentarian Lenelotte von Bothmer, a strong advocate of developing closer relations with SWAPO, was also a strong critic of West German economic relations with South Africa, particularly in the late 1970s. See, e.g., PAAA, Zwischenarchiv, Bd. 116840, 1977–1978, Wirtschaftliche Maßnahmen gegen Südafrika, 06.03.1978; 'Rüge für deutsche Firmen', *Frankfurter Rundschau*, 16.02.1978.

[100] See PAAA, Zwischenarchiv, Bd. 116841, 1977–1978, Elemente für das Gespräch mit der EKD, 21.02.1978; Deutscher Bundestag, 10. Wahlperiode, Stenographischer Bericht, 54. Sitzung, 10.02.1984, 3876–3882. For a more detailed account of West German companies in South Africa during the Schmidt years, see 'South Africa: Time Running Out', *The Report of the Study Commission*, 304–305.

To the surprise of contemporary observers, Strauß, the communist hater and passionate advocate of strict distancing from the GDR, was the mastermind behind the deal for two unrestricted loans to the GDR in 1983.[101] The GDR was under acute balance of payment problems and Honecker proposed, in exchange for loans, to reform the GDR's intra-German border policy.[102] While Genscher's reappointment into the position of foreign minister justified Kohl's continuation of Genscher's policy towards Namibia, the Strauß-Honecker deal paved the way to further rapprochement between the two German states. Hence, Strauß came under heavy criticism for his deal with Honecker, particularly from CSU hardliners. Theo Waigel, CSU chairman, later explained that the deal was not controversial from Strauß' perspective, as, in the 1960s, he had already proposed to negotiate a financial settlement with Moscow for Soviet withdrawal from East Germany.[103] Thus, Strauß' deal with Honecker can be understood as an attempt to financially free the GDR from the Soviet Union, while simultaneously strengthening its ties to West Germany.[104] Ironically, Strauß never accepted a similar approach towards SWAPO, although the SPD argued along these lines. However, the Strauß-Honecker deal was important with regard to the GDR's solidarity with SWAPO's cause.

In 1981/82, the GDR's commitment to the Namibian liberation struggle became apparent, when Nujoma asked East Berlin to provide further food aid and weapons urgently, as well as take in further refugee children.[105] Although the GDR's economy was in a dire state, Honecker personally ensured that SWAPO received extensive aid. In fact, the GDR more than doubled its material support for SWAPO, and deepened the political and conceptual co-operation, as Schleicher points out.[106] In the early 1980s, SWAPO received between one

---

[101] The first loan was for more than one billion deutsche marks and the second for 950 million. A further loan of more than 200 million deutsche marks for postal services was secretly added. See H. Haftendorn, *Coming of Age: German Foreign Policy since 1945*, Maryland, Rowan & Littlefield Publishers, 2006, 146.

[102] Border policy changes included to ease restrictions on tourist and visitor visas, including permits for urgent family matters, as well as the removal of spring-guns along the German-German border. See also Chapter Two, CDU/CSU.

[103] See, e.g., F. J. Strauß, *Die Erinnerungen*, Berlin, Siedler Verlag, 1989, 470–475; H. Kohl, *Erinnerungen, 1982–1990*, München, Droemer Verlag, 2005, 175–183. See also 'Millardenkredit für den Feind, Der Aufsehen erregende Strauß-Deal mit der DDR', ARD (TV documentary film). Accessed online October 2014, available from: www.youtube.com/watch?v=KwtfD04qVZg

[104] To argue that Strauß' deal strengthened the GDR in 1983, and subsequently undermined the possibility of German reunification for almost another decade, fails to consider Moscow's strategic interest in keeping the GDR within the influence of the Eastern bloc. See, e.g., H. M. Kloth, 'Kalter Krieg, Milliardenspritze für den Mauerbau', *Der Spiegel*, 22.07.2008.

[105] H.-G., Schleicher, 'Die Haltung der DDR zu Befreiungsbewegungen am Beispiel der SWAPO Namibias', in S. Bock, I. Muth, and H. Schwiesau (eds.), *Alternative deutsche Außenpolitik? DDR-Außenpolitik im Rückspiegel (II)*, Münster, LIT, 2006, 122.

[106] Schleicher, 'Die Haltung der DDR zu Befreiungsbewegungen', 122–123.

and three million German marks annually in military aid, as well as extensive military training for SWAPO cadres in the GDR.[107] Not surprisingly, therefore, Nujoma mentioned in a conversation with Schleicher in November 1989, at the time the Berlin Wall fell, that 'if that had happened earlier, we [SWAPO] would not be here today'.[108] Next to the Soviet support, the GDR's solidarity was indispensable to SWAPO. Had the GDR support dried up in the early 1980s, Namibia's path to independence might have taken a different route. Hence, it is rather ironic that Strauß, SWAPO's strongest antagonist in Bonn, contributed – in the broadest sense – to the liberation movement's survival in the 1980s. Without the Strauß-Honecker deal, the GDR would not have been in a position to continue supporting SWAPO in the 1980s, let alone increase food aid and provide military aid into the millions.

The Germans of Namibia

The de facto white population of Namibia in the 1980s was about 117,000, of whom 30,000 were of German origin.[109] During the same period, international political attention focused increasingly on the future of Namibia, which subsequently further increased pressure on Bonn to not only accept Namibia as a special responsibility but proactively support initiatives that might lead to an internationally accepted independence.[110] The Namibian Germans, however, showed little support for West German efforts, although consecutive governments put the German minority's interests before the interests of the black majority.[111]

In the mid-1970s the Foreign Office became increasingly preoccupied with the German-speaking minority's position in post-independence Namibia.[112] The Ministry of the Interior even discussed with the Foreign Office the naturalisation of Namibian Germans, pointing out that, although possible in theory, financial questions and foreign policy issues required further careful consideration. After all, such an undertaking would be substantial in scope.[113] The Foreign Office was equally critical and therefore opposed measures that

---

[107] Ibid., 125.
[108] Ibid., 134–135.
[109] The estimate was given by Chancellor Schmidt in 1976: PAAA, Zwischenarchiv, Bd. 108220, 1975–1976, Vermerk über das Gespräch des Bundeskanzlers mit Premierminister Dr. B. J. Vorster, 25 June 1976. For more information about the German-speaking Namibian minority, see M. Oldhaver, *Die deutschsprachige Bevölkerungsgruppe in Namibia: Ihre Bedeutung als Faktor in den deutsch-namibischen Beziehungen*, Hamburg, Verlag Dr. Kovak, 1997.
[110] See also Engel/Kappel, *Germany's Africa Policy*, 48.
[111] See also Brenke, *Die Bundesrepublik*, 125.
[112] The following Foreign Office file offers particular valuable insight into West German concerns regarding the Namibian Germans future in Namibia: PAAA, Zwischenarchiv, Bd. 108204, 1975–1976.
[113] See PAAA, Zwischenarchiv, Bd. 108204, 1975–1976, Einbürgerung ehemaliger Deutscher in Na-

would contribute to a rush toward naturalisation among Namibian Germans. The Foreign Office explained that it was not in the interest of West Germany's Namibia policy 'to initiate a mass exodus of the former Germans', for it would only expose West Germany's domestic and foreign policy to criticism. In terms of domestic policy, the Foreign Office was concerned that critics would accuse the government of 'failing to stand up for the rights of former German citizens in Namibia'.[114] With regard to foreign policy, it was feared that West Germany would be accused of 'wanting to rob Namibia of a section of its population that was important for the economic existence of the country'. However, the Foreign Office also emphasised that a 'mass exodus' was rather unlikely, unless Namibia would plunge into an 'acute crisis situation', for most Namibian Germans had no intention of leaving an independent Namibia.[115] Hardly surprising therefore, the Foreign Office dismissed reports that the Federal government was actively making arrangements to resettle Namibian Germans to South America in the event that the black majority gained power.[116]

In the 1970s, the SPD-led governments agreed with the Foreign Office. The Development Minister Egon Bahr urged the government to contemplate giving the German minority in Namibia the same juridical rights as Germans returning from the former Eastern territories of Germany.[117] In any event, Schmidt reassured Vorster that West Germany was willing to take in Namibian German refugees, although such a scenario did probably not weigh heavily in Bonn's calculations, for it was unlikely that Namibian Germans would emigrate in significant numbers to Germany.[118] In fact, the SPD-government was of the opinion that Namibians of German origin could play a central role in the development of the country after independence. Hence, to prepare for a mass exodus would have been hypocritical, for Bonn's Namibia policy envisioned 'an independent Namibia in which different races enjoy equal rights and live together in peace'.[119]

Sceptics within the CDU/CSU pressed hard to make the government confirm that it 'grants all Germans, at home and abroad, the protection they need, including those living in Namibia'.[120] Namibia carried, of course, greater emotional weight for Germany than any other country in

---

mibia, 19.08.1976.
[114] Ibid., Wiedereinbürgerung ehemaliger deutscher Staatsangehöriger, 02.11.1976, 3.
[115] Ibid., 3.
[116] Deutscher Bundestag, 8. Wahlperiode, Stenographischer Bericht, 29. Sitzung, 26.05.1977.
[117] 'Jeder nimmt zehn Schwarze mit ins Grab', *Der Spiegel* 45/1976. See also PAAA, Zwischenarchiv, Bd. 108204, 1975–1976, Wiedereinbürgerung ehemaliger deutscher Staatsangehöriger, 02.11.1976, 3.
[118] PAAA, Zwischenarchiv, Bd. 108204, 1975–1976, Wiedereinbürgerung ehemaliger deutscher Staatsangehöriger, 02.11.1976, 3.
[119] Deutscher Bundestag, 8. Wahlperiode, Stenographischer Bericht, 29. Sitzung, 26.05.1977, 2072. See also Ibid., Stenographischer Bericht, 30. Sitzung, 27.05.1977, 2194.
[120] Ibid., Stenographischer Bericht, 31. Sitzung, 15.06.1977, 2268.

Africa. In the 1970s and 1980s, this has often led to emotional evaluations of the liberation struggle waged by SWAPO and its potentially wider consequences for Namibia. In 1976, for example, Bahr warned that the decolonisation of Namibia would bring with it unprecedented emotional turmoil: 'Now for the first time, it is about the decolonization of a region where German emotions will come to the surface. Nothing that we have witnessed in terms of decolonization created as much uproar as will Namibia. Vietnam will be nothing in comparison'.[121] With emotions often running rampant, West German newspapers, particularly the newsmagazine *Der Spiegel*, adeptly used first-hand accounts from Namibia to tap into its readers' emotional affinity with the former German colony.[122]

German Namibians disregarded Bahr's Vietnam comparison as scaremongering, which was a reflection of their unrelenting attitude in the early 1970s. The rhetoric was often militant and expressed with bravado. 'Everyone takes ten blacks to one's grave', a German farmer assured the German news magazine *Der Spiegel* in 1976.[123] The *Allgemeine Zeitung*, a Windhoek based newspaper, was equally militant in its rhetoric. In the early 1970s, Kurt Dahlmann, the Chief Editor of the *Allgemeine Zeitung*, challenged his fellow German Namibians 'to demonstrate that they are made of steel'.[124] Regardless, the militant rhetoric was unlikely ever to lead to collective violent actions, as the Foreign Office concluded in 1978: 'Farmers who would want to fight to the last bullet are a clear minority'.[125] In later years, the rhetoric lost its militancy and became more reflective, expressing the concerns of the white minority regarding their future in an independent Namibia.[126]

Overall, attitudes within the Namibian German community changed in the late 1970s, becoming more accepting of the inevitable: an independent Namibia governed by SWAPO.[127] In the 1980s, the overwhelming majority of Namibian Germans adopted a progressively positive attitude toward Namibia's future. Of course, this attitude was also a healthy component of the German minority's survival instinct. In 1978 already, the news magazine *Der Spiegel* reported that most German-speaking Namibians 'would rather renounce apartheid and share government with blacks than risk losing their homeland'.[128] This change in at-

---

[121] 'Die Stunde kommt, da man dich braucht', *Der Spiegel*, 37/1981; 'Jeder nimmt zehn Schwarze mit ins Grab', *Der Spiegel*, 45/1976.
[122] See, e.g., 'Jeder nimmt zehn Schwarze mit ins Grab', *Der Spiegel*, 45/1976; 'Die Stunde kommt, da man dich braucht', *Der Spiegel*, 37/1981; 'Namibia: Großer Gewinn', *Der Spiegel*, 6/1984; 'Namibia: Weihnachten am Kavango', *Der Spiegel*, 44/1989; 'Auf Kante', *Der Spiegel*, 2/1991.
[123] 'Jeder nimmt zehn Schwarze mit ins Grab', *Der Spiegel*, 45/1976, 01.11.1976
[124] Ibid.
[125] PAAA, Zwischenarchiv, Bd. 116802, Politischer Halbjahresbericht, Namibia/Südwestafrika, 01.03.1978.
[126] Ibid.
[127] See Ibid., Politischer Halbjahresbericht, Namibia/Südwestafrika, 01.06.1977, 8.
[128] 'Vor der Katastrophe noch ein Karneval', *Der Spiegel*, 9/1978, 27.02.1978.

titude can be partly explained by developments in the late 1970s that helped to empower German-speaking Namibians. In mid-1977, the German-speaking minority in Namibia established the *Interessengemeinschaft deutschsprechender Südwester* (IG), the interest group for German-speaking Southwest Africans, which was an important step toward overcoming the 'political abstinence' of the Namibian Germans.[129] Additionally, the white-led DTA was also formed in late 1977, giving the white minority further confidence that minority interests would receive fair representation in a political process towards independence. The DTA's controversial landslide election victory in 1978 further strengthened the white minority's confidence.

The relationship between the IG and SWAPO improved slowly but consistently after several meetings in the early 1980s.[130] Nujoma reassured the IG that SWAPO would not introduce nationalisation and confiscate white-owned farms, as there was 'enough land in this sparsely populated land'. Nujoma also warmed to the idea of bringing 'German experts from Namibia' together with SWAPO people to plan for the future in areas such as agriculture, management and industry.[131] SWAPO also argued that because of the wider repercussions of the German colonial past in Namibia, West Germany had a moral responsibility toward the black population of Namibia.[132] This view resonated strongly among some members of the *Bundestag*. In 1984, the FDP parliamentarian Günther Verheugen underlined Germany's 'historic responsibility' towards Namibia, stating that 'the effects of Germany's colonial past in this part of the world still unfolds, and will do so until Namibia is finally independent'. Verheugen also took responsibility for Germany's past atrocities: 'Our responsibility does not only exist in our concern about the fate of the Germans and those of German origins in Namibia. Our responsibility also derived from the injustice that has happened there in our name. It is also a special responsibility toward the black majority'.[133] Both the SPD and the Green Party also underlined Germany's historic and moral responsibility for crimes committed under German colonial rule in Namibia.[134]

---

[129] Brenke, *Die Bundesrepublik*, 125. The National Archives of Namibia hold a collection of IG documents, which can be found under the following signature: AACLRS.004.

[130] See AAPD, 1983, Band 1, Mein Antrittsbesuch bei AM Botha am 18.05.1983, Botschafter Lahusen, Pretoria, 18.05.1983, 769.

[131] PAAA, Neues Amt, Bd. 16414, Positive Äußerung Nujomas über Harare-Treffen, Luanda, 13.06.1983. In late 1978 already, SWAPO urged the SPD-government to 'inform the Namibian Germans that SWAPO honestly wished to continue the dialog'. SWAPO was concerned that the Namibian Germans perception of SWAPO was largely influenced by South Africa's propaganda: PAAA, Zwischenarchiv, Bd. 116802, Afrika-Reise einer Delegation des SPD-Parteivorstands, Pretoria, 20.11.1978, 3.

[132] PAAA, Zwischenarchiv, Bd. 116802, Britische Haltung zur Namibiafrage, London 10.05.1976, 8.

[133] Deutscher Bundestag, 10. Wahlperiode, Stenographischer Bericht, 54. Sitzung, 10.02.1984, 3865.

[134] See, e.g., Ibid., 3865; P. Kelly, 'Namibia: the first genocide in the history of the Germans', in ISSA

The Foreign Office, however, always had a more critical perception of the Namibian Germans, as, for example, becomes apparent in a 21 page report concerning the possible closure of the West German consulate in 1975:

> The German minority (15,000) and the German citizens (5000) don't play a decisive role in the political transitory process. They are a heterogeneous [*heterogene*] group, who on the one hand stand in a certain opposition to the Boers, and on the other hand build together (with the Boers) the white unity front against the blacks. The 'Germans' are not more racist than the other whites. They are conservative, but not Nazis. They don't feel that they are Germans but as German South Westerners, who had to take up the South African citizenship against their will. The South Africans consider the Germans as politically unreliable because they would strike a deal with the blacks if this would save their existence. The Germans have because of their strong paternalism a better reputation among the blacks than the South Africans. The black functional elite, who hoped the Germans would make with them common front against the Boers to establish an independent Namibia; see in them worse enemies than the South Africans.[135]

Indeed, Namibian Germans were a relatively isolated minority group in Namibia and, therefore, too dependent on Western support to ignore the SPD-led government's move towards SWAPO in the late 1970. Hence, the German-speaking Namibians had to adjust their attitudes accordingly.

Yet, the CSU/CSU hardliners instrumentalized the concerns of the Namibian Germans to justify their opposition to SWAPO. When the SPD-led government closed the West German consulate in Windhoek in 1977, Strauß expressed especially strong concerns:

> In a SWAPO ruled Namibia there is no longer a place for whites – except in prisons, concentration camps or in cemeteries ... One's mind does anguish, one is revolted by the fact, that for the sake of SWAPO the government of the Federal Republic of Germany has closed the German consulate in Windhoek leaving German citizens residing there without legal protection.[136]

The motivation behind Strauß' unyielding solidarity with the Namibian Germans can probably also be explained by his contempt for Genscher. After all, Strauß found in Namibia's German-speaking community keen allies against the foreign minister and his policies.[137]

---

wissenschaftliche Reihe 21(ed.), *Im Brennpunkt*, 42–45.
[135] PAAA, Zwischenarchiv, Bd. 108202, *Namibia politische Berichte, allgemein*, Abteilung 3, 13.07.1975.
[136] Africa Post 25 (1978) 6, in G. Wellmar, 'Background Paper on Relations between Federal Republic of Germany and Namibia', presented at the International Seminar on the Role of Transnational Corporations in Namibia, *Anti-Apartheid Movement*, Federal Republic of Germany, 1982, 163.
[137] Genscher's relationship with the Namibian Germans had always been difficult, partly because of his good relations with Nujoma. See 'Die Stunde kommt, da man dich braucht', *Der Spiegel*

Strauß' populist rhetoric and his good relations with Namibian hard-liners made him an easy target for GDR propaganda.[138] The GDR accused Bonn of supporting Pretoria's policy of racial segregation and oppression in Namibia. This accusation was largely based on the SPD-led government's reluctance to support UN recommendations in the 1970s that seemed to challenge the Namibian Germans' interests. For instance, West Germany did not recognize SWAPO as the sole representative of the Namibian people, as declared by the UN in 1972, nor did Bonn follow UN recommendations to dissolve the West German consulate in Windhoek, until 1977. West Germany's perceived responsibility towards the Namibian Germans had been one of the motives behind Bonn's opposition.[139]

The GDR's uncompromising solidarity with SWAPO virtually ruled out the possibility of also considering the concerns of Namibian Germans. Therefore, the GDR's link forged with SWAPO in the 1970s was based on the regionally exclusive support of the liberation movement's interests. While West Germany assumed a protectionist role over Namibian Germans, this was a role the GDR would never assume. In 1976, Peter Florin, the GDR's representative to the UN in New York, made it clear that East Berlin wanted nothing to do with Namibian Germans because their patriotism was still anchored in the past:

> The people of the GDR have nothing in common with those reactionary forces of German origin in Namibia, who still march on the Kaiserstrasse in Windhoek to places that are named after notorious fascists such as Goering und Goebbels; who still get inspired by Goebbels racial laws and other Nazi ideas.[140]

The GDR prided itself on its anti-fascist legacy, claiming to have extinguished fascism in the GDR.[141] Thus, the undisguised affinity with the former German Reich by some German Namibians made it impossible for the GDR to regard the German-speaking minority as partners in the future Namibia.[142]

31/1981, 07.09.1981.

[138] See Chapter Two, CDU/CSU.

[139] 'Genschers Schwenk', *Der Spiegel*, 21/1977, 16.05.1977.

[140] Babing, *Gegen Rassismus*, 1949–1977, Rede des Botschafters Peter Florian vor dem UN Sicherheitsrat zur Namibiafrage, 13.10.1976. 634. See also Ibid., Rede des DDR-Vertreters Heinz Knoppe im Vierten Komitee der XXXI. Tagung der UN-Vollversammlung zur Namibiafrage, 29.11.1976; Ibid., 1977–1982, Rede des Botschafters, Peter Florin, Stellvertreter des Ministers für Auswärtige Angelegenheiten und ständiger Vertreter der DDR bei den Vereinten Nationen, vor der wiederaufgenommenen XXXIII. Tagung der UN-Vollversammlung zur Namiabiafrage, 25.05.1979, 288.

[141] See also M. Stibbe, 'Fighting the First World War in the Cold War, East and West German Historiography on the Origins of the First World War, 1949–1959', in T. Hochscherf, C. Laucht and A. Plowman (ed.), *Divided but not Disconnected: German Experiences of the Cold War*, New York, Berghahn Books, 2010, 38.

[142] See also, J. Mader, 'Ehemalige Hitleroffiziere und deutsche Millionäre helfen den Apartheid-Faschisten in Namibia', *Panorama DDR*, Berlin, 1980.

A few German-speaking Namibians actively supported SWAPO's liberation struggle despite the risks involved. The most prominent supporter of SWAPO was Anton Lubowski, a lawyer and active SWAPO member. Lubowski, who was born in Namibia to South African-German parents, was assassinated in late 1989. Although the Lubowski case has never been solved, some evidence seems to suggest that the death squad of the South African Defence Force (SADF), the Civil Cooperation Bureau (CCB), was involved in the murder.[143]

---

[143] R. Dale, *The Namibian War of Independence*, Jefferson, NC, McFarland, 2014, 108–109.

5 East and West German rivalry: the mid-to-late 1970s

The controversy over West Germany's consulate in Windhoek

In mid-1970, the Security Council asked all states to terminate their consular and diplomatic relations with Namibia.[1] As a result, West Germany came under increasing international pressure, particularly from African and Eastern bloc countries, to close its consulate in Namibia, for many perceived the maintenance of the consulate as an 'approval of South African supremacy over the territory'.[2] In the mid-1970s, West Germany remained the only country still maintaining a consulate in Namibia, which became increasingly difficult to justify.[3] West Germany's perceived responsibility towards Namibia's German minority made it, however, difficult to decide the fate of its consulate.[4] Germany's historical affiliation with Namibia, its post-colonial moral obligation to the country, the cultural affinity with approximately 30,000 German-speaking Namibians and the geopolitical importance of a representative office in Windhoek – especially in Cold War terms – placed the consulate in a unique position.[5]

In the mid-1970s, in response to growing international pressure, the Foreign Office debated the different scenarios regarding the consulate's future.[6] The debates ranged from officially closing the consulate to letting it slowly 'dry out' by not appointing a new consul after the retirement of Consul Leonard Kremer in mid-1975.[7] However, finding a solution

---

[1] See PAAA, Neues Amt, Bd. 7987, 1969–1976, OAE-Konferenz 1972, 02.06.1972, 4. It is worth mentioning here that, in 1974, South Africa intensified its military campaign against SWAPO, pushing Pretoria further into isolation.

[2] See, e.g., Deutscher Bundestag, 8. Wahlperiode, Stenographischer Bericht, 52. Sitzung, 27.10.1977, 4062; PAAA, Zwischenarchiv, Bd. 108202, 1975–1976, Namibia, New York UNO, 19.06.1976; PAAA, Neues Amt, Bd. 7987, 1969–1976, Grundzüge unserer Afrikapolitik; hier: Anpassung an veränderte politische Daten, 26.02.1973, 7.; PAAA, Zwischenarchiv, Bd. 108202, 1975–1976, Sitzung des Auswärtigen Ausschusses des Bundestages am 07.04.74; hier: Südliches Afrika-Konsulat Windhuk, 06.04.1976; Ibid., Konsulat Windhuk, New York UNO, 08.10.1976, 7; Genscher, 'Germany's role in Namibia's independence', 55.

[3] See, e.g., PAAA, Zwischenarchiv, Bd. 108202, 1975–1976, Konsulat Windhuk, New York UNO, 08.10.1976; PAAA, Neues Amt, Bd. 7987, 1969–1976, Grundzüge unserer Afrikapolitik; hier: Anpassung an veränderte politische Daten, 26.02.1973, 7.

[4] PAAA, Zwischenarchiv, Bd. 108202, 1975–1976, Sitzung des Auswärtigen Ausschusses des Bundestages am 07.04.74; hier: Südliches Afrika-Konsulat Windhuk, 06.04.1976.

[5] See, e.g., PAAA, Neues Amt, Bd. 7987, 1969–1976, Grundzüge unserer Afrikapolitik; hier: Anpassung an veränderte politische Daten, 26.02.1973, 7; Ibid., OAE-Konferenz 1972, 02.06.1972, 5.

[6] See PAAA, Zwischenarchiv, Bd. 108202, 1975–1976, Namibia politische Berichte, 1975/76.

[7] Ibid., Politische Berichte Namibia, 1975/76, Procedere und Zeitpunkt, 2–3. It seems apparent that this proposal was built on the knowledge that Consul Leonard Kremer would retire from his post in June 1975, although his name was not mentioned in the document.

to the consulate question was further aggravated by two opposing concerns. First, the Foreign Office had to consider South Africa's economic and geopolitical importance for West Germany, for closing the consulate had a potentially detrimental effect on relations with Pretoria.[8] Second, the Foreign Office was concerned about the 'possible long term impairment of German interests in Namibia, if the consulate would remain open until the achievement of independence'.[9] Obviously, the continuation of good economic relations with both South Africa and Namibia was a top priority. West German industry expressed its grave concern that the closure would hamper business in South Africa and Namibia, emphasising West Germany's dependency on both natural resources and export markets, West Germany was one of Namibia and South Africa's biggest suppliers in the 1970s.[10] Although economic relations with South Africa were considered crisis-proof, economic relations with Namibia seemed less predictable.[11]

The Foreign Office was sceptical about whether the consulate's closure would have a positive impact on West Germany's image in Africa.[12] It was even questioned whether closing the consulate would have important benefits for West Germany, particularly within the UN.[13] There was strong interest on the part of the Federal Government in gaining support from African countries in the UN, particularly with regard to the German question but also concerning southern Africa:

> In future we will compete in many separate questions [*Einzelfragen*] with the GDR and need to defend ourselves in international organisations. In regards to Africa, we are in an especially difficult situation: the GDR can always stand unconditionally on the side of Africa in UN polls on questions regarding relations with the minority regime in southern Africa (demands for sanctions against South Africa, Namibia resolution etcetera), while we have to abstain from voting because of our interests (trade, investment, NATO-alliance with Portugal).[14]

---

[8] See Ibid., Konsulat Windhuk, New York UNO, 08.10.1976, 2.
[9] Ibid., Sitzung des Auswärtigen Ausschusses des Bundestages am 07.04.74; hier: Südliches Afrika-Konsulat Windhuk, 06.04.1976.
[10] Ibid., Gründe, die gegen eine Schließung des Konsulats Windhuk sprechen, 31.07.1975.
[11] See also Brenke, *Die Bundesrepublik*, 121. It is also worth noting, however, that from Pretoria's perspective the closure of the consulate was not seen as particularly problematic. On the contrary, Pretoria saw the consulate as a hindrance to the integration of Namibian Germans into the South African culture ('South Africaness'): PAAA, Zwischenarchiv, Bd. 108202, 1975–1976, Namibia/Südwestafrika; hier: Massnahmen, die geeignet sind, der afrikanischen Kritik an unserer Haltung entgegenzuwirken, 10.07.1975, 22.
[12] See PAAA, Zwischenarchiv, Bd. 108202, 1975–1976, Konsulat Windhuk, New York UNO, 08.10.1976, 4.
[13] Ibid., 312-312.20 NAM, 08.07.1975, 5.
[14] PAAA, AV Neues Amt, Bd.7897, 1969–1976, Empfehlungen der Reformkommission des Auswärtigen Amtes, die Zahl der kleinen Auslandsvertretungen zu reduzieren; hier: Afrika, 15.07.1971, 3–4.

The GDR's economic relations with southern African countries were negligible, giving East Berlin the autonomy to back resolutions that challenged the economic status quo in the region. West Germany, on the other hand, was restricted in voting options due to its economic interests in Africa, especially South Africa.[15]

With regard to East and West German rivalry in Africa, the consulate in Windhoek played, as all West German embassies and consulates in Africa, a central role in defending West Germany's image against GDR propaganda.[16] East Berlin saw Bonn's reluctance to close its consulate as further proof that the SPD-led government supported Pretoria's oppressive apartheid policies.[17] Predictably, the controversies surrounding the consulate became propaganda fodder for the GDR. In late 1974, for example, Radio DDR 1, a popular GDR radio station broadcast a lengthy propaganda piece about the consulate. The polemical broadcast challenged West Germany to follow other nations in closing its consulate, or at least take responsibility for the fascist tendencies of the German nationals in Namibia.[18] As already discussed, demonising the Federal Republic as fascist – or in the case of the Namibian Germans as supporters of fascism overseas – was an integral aspect of GDR attempts to discredit West Germany within the GDR, as well as in Africa and other Third World countries.[19] Considering, however, that West German embassies in Africa established themselves in the 1960s as a bulwark against GDR propaganda; it seems somewhat ironic that, in the 1970s, the consulate in Windhoek provided the context for GDR propaganda against West Germany.[20]

However, individual opinion varied within the Foreign Office debate, with some staff arguing that the closure of the consulate would diminish West Germany's exposure to criticism, particularly from SWAPO and Sub-Saharan countries.[21] In general, proponents in

---

[15] In 1975, the Foreign Office viewed the consulate in Windhoek as potentially useful for improving relations with Namibia's liberation movements. The objective was to 'establish the foundation for our [West Germany's] connection to the future governing circles of Namibia': PAAA, Zwischenarchiv, Bd. 108202, 1975–1976, Betr.: Namibia, New York, 28.04.1975.

[16] PAAA, AV Neues Amt, Bd.7897, 1969–1976, Empfehlungen der Reformkommission des Auswärtigen Amtes, die Zahl der kleinen Auslandsvertretungen zu reduzieren; hier: Afrika, 15.07.1971, 3–4.

[17] 'Genschers Schwenk', *Der Spiegel*, 21/1977, 16.05.1977.

[18] ISSA, Akte: Namibia 1972–86, Monitor Dienst (DW), Oktober 1974 (Radio DDR 1), *Kritik aus der DDR an der Aufrechterhaltung des Bonner Konsulates in Windhuk*.

[19] M. F. Scholz, 'Active Measures and Disinformation as Part of East Germany's Propaganda War, 1953–1972', in K. Macrakis, T.W. Friis and H. Müller-Enbergs (eds.), *East German Foreign Intelligence: Myth, Reality and Controversy*, New York, Routledge, 2010, 120–125.

[20] PAAA, AV Neues Amt, Bd.7897, 1969–1976, Empfehlungen der Reformkommission des Auswärtigen Amtes, die Zahl der kleinen Auslandsvertretungen zu reduzieren; hier: Afrika, 15.07.1971, 3–4.

[21] PAAA, Zwischenarchiv, Bd. 108202, 1975–1976, politische Berichte Namibia, Februar 1975.

Bonn argued that the consulate's closure would improve West Germany's relations with SWAPO.[22] As far as Sam Nujoma was concerned, that was indeed the case. In 1976, he made it clear that SWAPO 'will have nothing to do with West Germany' until 'the West Germans withdraw their consulate'.[23] In May 1977, the Foreign Office made it official that the Federal Government was considering the closure of the consulate in Windhoek. SWAPO leader Sam Nujoma was briefed about the decision on the side-lines of the Namibia-Initiative in New York in mid-1977. Nujoma's responded as follows:

> There was no hatred from SWAPO's side against the Federal Government or German nationals in Namibia. However, West Germany's reluctance to close the consulate in Windhoek had to be interpreted as a veto against SWAPO and for South Africa. However, there would be no longer a reason not to establish normal relations once those obstacles are eliminated.[24]

It was, however, unavoidable that closing the consulate in Windhoek would only partially improve relations between West Germany and SWAPO, mainly because Bonn continued its co-operation with Pretoria, the very regime that consistently blocked Namibia's independence.

The CDU/CSU, however, expressed strong feelings against closing the consulate, accusing the government of caving in to outside pressure and 'blackmail-demands of the militant, communist ruled SWAPO'.[25] The Foreign Office refuted these allegations by arguing that improving relations with SWAPO played only a secondary role:

> Essentially, we are welcoming an improvement in our relationship with SWAPO, which we recognise as an important political power in Namibia. However, the Federal Government does not consider closing the consulate with SWAPO in mind [Seitenblick auf SWAPO]. The Federal Government decision is solely influenced by the assessment of long-term German interests. Its motive is to improve the protection of (Namibian) Germans. In the perception of the Federal government, this can be better and more reliably achieved from outside Namibia during the transitional period.[26]

---

[22] See Ibid., Konsulat Windhuk, New York UNO, 08.10.1976, 5.
[23] Ibid., Namibia, New York UNO, 19.06.1976.
[24] Ibid., Bd. 116802, 1977–1978, UNO an Bonn AA, Nr. 1775, August 1977. Two years earlier, however, Nujoma's relationship with the Federal Government, particularly Genscher, was less than friendly. In May 1975, Nujoma declared that he would like 'to drive all Germans out of Namibia, because he has no use for them'. Hence, Nujoma's change in tone was a result of the improved relations between the SPD-led government and SWAPO in the late 1970s: Deutscher Bundestag, 8. Wahlperiode, Stenographischer Bericht, 52. Sitzung, 27.10.1977, 4075.
[25] KAS Archive, Bestand: 07-001/16073, *Die Politik der CDU/CSU-Bundestagsfraktion gegenüber dem südlichen Afrika*, 1978, 8. See also Deutscher Bundestag, 8. Wahlperiode, Stenographischer Bericht, 52. Sitzung, 27.10.1977, 4062–4075.
[26] PAAA, Zwischenarchiv, Bd. 116802, 1977/1978, AZ: 312.320 NAM, September 1977.

Two years earlier, however, the Foreign Office and the SPD-led government had argued that the requirements of the German minority in Namibia warranted the maintenance of the consulate.[27] Although the consulate had, by then, already turned into a diplomatic liability, it was still considered indispensable.[28] The main argument against closing the consulate was based on the notion that German citizen and those of German origin would have to depend on the South African authorities in Namibia.[29] Given that Namibia had a rather substantial German-speaking community, the consulate in Windhoek occupied a unique position in Bonn, not comparable to other West German consulates and embassies in Africa. In the mid-1970s, it became increasingly apparent that SWAPO would play a pivotal role in Namibia's future. Thus, in the light of Bonn's difficult relationship with SWAPO, many in Bonn feared that West Germany might be denied diplomatic relations in a SWAPO-led Namibia, which would have a potentially negative effect on the Namibian Germans' future in Namibia. Thus, many viewed the closure of the consulate as a vital step towards improving relations with SWAPO.[30] The GDR state security also concluded that concerns about West German standing in post-independence Namibia was the main motivation behind Bonn's decision to close the consulate:

> To guarantee the protection of the Federal Republic's nationals and German speakers' interests, the Federal Government aspires to establish, at the time of Namibia's independence, the best possible diplomatic and consular presence in Namibia, which makes it necessary to come to an arrangement with SWAPO, but also to establish contact with the Turnhallen-Alliance (DTA).[31]

Much more important than the Namibian Germans, however, was to insure the continuation of close economic and diplomatic relations between the two countries in the post-independence era. In this respect, Bonn perceived the GDR's solidarity with SWAPO as a guarantor of robust relations in a SWAPO-led Namibia. The SPD-government acknowledged that no

---

[27] Ibid., Bd. 108202, 1975–1976, Konsulat Windhuk; hier: Eventuelle Schliessung der Vertretung unter Gesichtspunkten der Abt. 1, 06.11.1975. See also Deutscher Bundestag, 8. Wahlperiode, Stenographischer Bericht, 52. Sitzung, 27.10.1977, 4074–4075.

[28] The Foreign Office expected that 'the closure [of the consulate] will face strong inner-political criticism and will be interpreted as political weakness'. It was expected that critics would argue that the closure would leave Namibian Germans 'unprotected': PAAA, Zwischenarchiv, Bd. 108202, 1975–1976, Konsulat Windhuk, New York UNO, 08.10.1976.

[29] Deutscher Bundestag, 8. Wahlperiode, Stenographischer Bericht, 52. Sitzung, 27.10.1977, 4075. See also Brenke, *Die Bundesrepublik*, 119–120.

[30] PAAA, Zwischenarchiv, Bd. 116841, 1977–1978, Hausbesprechung unter der Leitung des Herrn Ministers, 21.01.1976.

[31] BStU, Zentralarchiv, MfS – Hauptverwaltung Aufklärung, Nr. 69, April 1978, Auskunft über Probleme des antiimperialistischen Befreiungskampfes in Zimbabwe und Namibia, 18.

such reassurance existed for West Germany.³² Thus, closing West Germany's consulate in Windhoek was indeed an onerous conclusion, but it became increasingly difficult to defend the consulate against mounting international criticism. The decision to close the consulate was finally made at the end of October 1977.

In 2010, Genscher acknowledged in retrospect that the support of his 'co-fighter', Hans-Jürgen Wischnewski, was vital in reaching a decision amidst considerable disagreement within the SPD-FDP coalition government and spirited resistance from the opposition. However, Genscher did not specify that the consulate's closure was related in any way to improving relations with SWAPO, nor did he acknowledge concerns about the GDR's advantageous standing in a SWAPO-led Namibia. In Genscher's account, the consulate was dissolved predominantly because it reflected negatively on West Germany's image in the Third World, particularly in Africa. Genscher thus explained further that the closure 'was a decisive step in Germany's Africa policy and mainly in its credibility vis-à-vis states still waiting for their independence and the abolition of apartheid'.³³

In 1963, Pretoria approved the consulate on condition that it be part of the German embassy in South Africa.³⁴ Although the consulate gained independence from West Germany's Embassy in Pretoria in 1970 amd placed under the direct administration of the Foreign Office, West Germany's economic and political cooperation with South Africa invited the impression that West German institutions in Namibia were an extension of the Bonn-Pretoria alliance.³⁵ Hence, the political deadlock over Namibia's independence led to widespread misrepresentations of Pretoria's agreement with West Germany, as Genscher recollects:

> Pretoria saw this position as a confirmation that the Federal Republic of Germany would consider Namibia as being under the sphere of influence of South Africa. In reality, it was interpreted as the acknowledgement of ongoing South African dominion in Namibia. This is why it was urgently necessary to take courageous steps to dissolve this consulate.³⁶

---

32 See also Brenke, *Die Bundesrepublik*, 120–121.
33 Genscher, 'Germany's Role', 55.
34 Ibid.
35 The assumption that Bonn had secret alliances with Pretoria was not uncommon. In 1967, for example, the Afro-Asian Solidarity Committee of the GDR published a memorandum under the tile: 'The Bonn-Pretoria Alliance'. The memorandum claimed to prove that Pretoria was conspiring with Nazis in post-war Germany. Accessed December 2014, available from: www.sahistory.org.za/sites/default/files/DC/Acn3167.8/Acn3167.8.pdf. The so-called Nuclear Axis between West Germany and South Africa made headlines in the late 1970s. For a detailed analysis of West Germany's nuclear co-operation with South Africa, see Z. Cervenka and B. Rogers, *The Nuclear Axis: Secret collaboration between West Germany and South Africa*, London, Julian Friedmann Books Ltd, 1978.
36 Genscher, 'Germany's Role', 55.

For Pretoria, the implications of such a misinterpretation were positive, for it gave the impression that Bonn agreed with its policy towards Namibia. The reality was, however, that the SPD-led government had always stressed that the continuation of the consulate did not in any way imply that West Germany approved of South Africa's administration of Namibia.[37] For the consulate in Windhoek to be associated with Pretoria's agenda in Namibia was a serious concern in Bonn. These growing concerns became even more evident after the establishment of the WCG.

In 1977, Genscher and the Foreign Office repeatedly emphasised that closing the consulate in Windhoek would give West Germany's involvement in the WCG greater credibility.[38] After all, the five Western countries involved in the Namibia Initiative were trying to negotiate a compromise between South Africa and SWAPO. West Germany was the only member still maintaining a consulate in Namibia, which raised questions about its allegiance to South Africa. Furthermore, while East Berlin's solidarity with liberation movements established the GDR's credibility in southern Africa, Bonn's cooperation with Pretoria undermined West Germany's credibility in the region and beyond.

In summary, Bonn's concern about West Germany's position in a SWAPO-led Namibia was a dominant factor behind the decision to close the consulate. Within this context, the GDR's good relations with SWAPO were perceived as a threat to West Germany's influence in post-independence Namibia. It was feared that the GDR's solidarity with SWAPO would guarantee East Germany a favourable position in a SWAPO-led Namibia. The Foreign Office hoped that closing the consulate would improve West Germany's image in Africa. However, the Foreign Office saw the West German embassies and consulates in Africa as effective voices against GDR propaganda on the continent. The decision to close the consulate was ultimately based on the conviction that it would improve West Germany's image in Africa. The Federal Government's decision to close the consulate removed it as a target for GDR propaganda, international criticism and the assumption that the consulate was an approval of South Africa's control over Namibia.

West Germany's cultural programme with South Africa and Namibia

In 1977, the SPD-led government terminated West Germany's cultural agreement, *Kulturabkommen*, with South Africa as part of an effort to build the country's credibility in Africa. The decision was not taken lightly, for the *Kulturabkommen* with South Africa also included

---

[37] Brenke, *Die Bundesrepublik*, 119–120.
[38] AAPD, 1977, Band I, Gespräch des Bundesministers Genscher mit dem amerikanischen UNO-Botschafter Young, 19.06.1977, 1005. See also Brenke, *Die Bundesrepublik*, 121.

Namibia.[39] Both the *Kulturabkommen* and the consulate in Windhoek were established with the purpose, inter alia, of connecting with the German speaking minority in Namibia. German schools, and institutions such as the Goethe institute, on the other hand, provided a platform to build cultural relations between Germany and Namibia's non-white majority. However, the *Kulturabkommen* generated increasing criticism, leading to accusations that West Germany promoted racial discrimination by granting predominantly white pupils access to cultural programmes and German schools.[40] The problem lay, however, not in West German policies but in South Africa's racial laws. In the case of West German private schools, for example, law prohibited the education of non-white pupils.[41]

Genscher was among the first to demand the opening of German schools to non-white students.[42] Considering that the West increased its efforts in Namibia in 1977, it seems reasonable to assume that Genscher was propelled by concerns about his credibility as an honest broker in the WCG. After all, West Germany's efforts seemed hypocritical as long as German schools in southern Africa carried the stigma of being an 'instrument of apartheid'.[43] However, in 1975 Genscher worked towards the opening of German schools to non-white students, which shows that the West's growing commitment to resolve the crisis in Namibia did not propel the foreign minister towards this position. In 1975, the inexperienced foreign minister still needed to prove his grasp on global affairs and build a credible reputation. Genscher probably saw racial issues as an opportunity to show that his foreign policy approach was guided by an inner moral compass. In 1977, he emphasised during a meeting with the South African Foreign Minister Hilgard Muller that 'racial discrimination in the German co-financed schools was a continuing serious problem' and not in accordance with West Germany's 'principals and beliefs'.[44] Genscher asked Muller and Vorster for the removal of racial laws, leading to the gradual dismantling of discriminatory policies on German schools in Namibia.[45]

---

[39] See PAAA, Zwischenarchiv, Bd. 108202, 1975–1976, Kulturabkommen mit Südafrika; hier: Anwendung auf Namibia, 11.08.1975.
[40] See Ibid., Rassenpolitik in der von uns geförderten Deutschen Höheren Privatschule Windhuk (DHPS), 26.08.1976.
[41] See Ibid., Namibia/Südwestafrika; hier: Einseitige Kündigung des Kulturabkommens mit Südafrika bezüglich seiner Geltung für Südwestafrika seitens der Bundesrepublik Deutschland, 01.08.1975.
[42] Not for the first time in 1977: Witte, *Deutsche Schulen*, 35.
[43] Witte, *Deutsche Schulen*, 33.
[44] PAAA, Zwischenarchiv, Bd. 108202, 1975–1976, Südafrika, politische Beziehungen zur BRD, 424/75 VS-NFD, 09.09.1975, 1–5.
[45] See Ibid., Genscher Brief an Muller, 27.11.1975; Ibid., Betr.: Unsere Politik bezüglich Namibia, 04.08.1976.

In the mid-1970s, after the General Assembly had recognized SWAPO as the sole legitimate representative of the Namibian people, there was a renewed intensity of critical debate in the UN about the Namibia problem. The sudden collapse of the Portuguese colonial empire in southern Africa gave the Namibia question further urgency.[46] In this connection, West Germany's relationship with South Africa became increasingly the focal point of outside scrutiny, while the consulate in Windhoek and the *Kulturabkommen* with South Africa became the focus of much international criticism. Needless to say, the growing international demand for West Germany to dissolve its consulate in Windhoek moved the Namibia question further into the focus of the *Bundestag*.[47] In the late 1970s, West Germany was the last country to maintain a cultural agreement with the apartheid state. Apart from growing international reproach, there was also a rising tide of criticism from SWAPO. In particular, the German-only white schools in Namibia and South Africa came under the scrutiny of the liberation movement.[48] Although the SPD-led government choose to rescind its cultural agreement with Namibia in 1977, cultural exchange with South Africa remained widely intact.[49] As cultural exchange programmes between West Germany and South Africa targeted the educational and professional sector, which was deeply interwoven with the economic and commercial cooperation between the two countries, terminating cultural exchanges between West Germany and South Africa had little effect as long as economic and commercial exchanges continued unabated.[50] Logically, therefore, critics argued that both cultural exchange and economic relations strengthened the structures of apartheid and South Africa's economic and military dominance in southern Africa.[51]

Yet, Genscher was reluctant to give up West Germany's *Kulturabkommen* with South Africa. In 1981, he argued during a meeting with Desmond Tutu, the Secretary General of the South African Council of Churches, that the '*Kulturabkommen* was an important chan-

---

[46] See Deutscher Bundestag, 7. Wahlperiode, Drucksache 7/3637, 15.05.1975, *Bundestag* report 29th UN General Assembly.
[47] See, e.g., Ibid., Stenographischer Bericht, 206. Sitzung, 04.12.1975, 14219–14220; Ibid., 8. Wahlperiode, Stenographischer Bericht, 52. Sitzung, 27.10.1977, 4062–4064. See also Engel, *Die Afrikapolitik*, 147–177.
[48] See also PAAA, Zwischenarchiv, Bd. 108202, 1975–1976, Betr.: SWAPO, Entwurf einer Aufzeichnung über die SWAPO, 18.11.1976, 10.
[49] See, e.g., Deutscher Bundestag, 10. Wahlperiode, Drucksache 10/833, 21.12.1983, 14; Ibid., Drucksache 10/3166, 11.04.85, 2.
[50] See M. O. Anda, *International Relations in Contemporary Africa*, Maryland, University Press of America, 2000, 54. See also PAAA, Zwischenarchiv, Bd. 116840, 1977–1978, Kulturpolitische Zusammenarbeit mit der nichtweißen Bevölkerung Südafrikas, 20.02.1978.
[51] See PAAA, Zwischenarchiv, Bd. 108202, 1975–1976, Rassenpolitik in der von uns geförderten Deutschen Höheren Privatschule Windhuk (DHPS), 26.08.1976. See also Wenzel, *Südafrika-Politik*, 89–93.

nel for providing black South Africans with West German aid'.[52] Genscher believed that dissolving the programme would produce more harm than good, as it would have only a limited effect on the political situation in South Africa. Although Tutu agreed in principle with Genscher, he was still convinced that suspending the *Kulturabkommen* would send out 'a morally important signal'.[53] However, the Foreign Office viewed cultural exchange as an instrument of foreign policy.

In order to promote peaceful change in South Africa, for example, the department for cultural relations in the Foreign Office launched, with the support of all political parties, the *Special Program Southern Africa* in 1980.[54] Under the leadership of Hildegard Hamm-Brücher, the former State Secretary for the Federal Ministry of Education, the program supported gifted non-white students, promoted crafts and trades training, artistic exchange, and financial support of projects initiated by West German foundations that sought to improve the situation of non-whites.[55] The program was geared in particular towards opening schools to non-white students. Overall, however, the programme promoted little change in the ratio of non-white students to the total number of students.[56]

In late 1981, the *Kulturabkommen* with South Africa became for the first time the focal point of a press conference. Karl Theodor Paschke, the press spokesman of the Foreign Office, echoed Genscher's position, which did not go down well with the press. There was little acceptance of the notion that the cultural exchange benefited non-white South Africans as much as white South Africans. In late 1983, a considerable number of prominent individuals associated with film, sport, literature and academia voiced in an open letter to Genscher their concerns about West Germany's *Kulturabkommen* with South Africa. Although the press widely ignored the letter, the issue was taken up by the *Bundestag* in early 1984.[57] In

---

[52] AADA, 1981, Band I, Gespräch zwischen Genscher und Tutu, 11.03.1981, 371.
[53] Ibid., 371.
[54] See also Deutscher Bundestag, 10. Wahlperiode, Drucksache 10/833, 21.12.1983, 14; Witte, *Deutsche Schulen*, 34.
[55] For further information concerning West German educational programmes and financial support, see Deutscher Bundestag, 10. Wahlperiode, Drucksache, 10/833, 21.12.1983, 13–14.
[56] The Private German Higher School Windhoek offered seven German courses for 160 non-white pupils in 1982. Nine non-white pupils enrolled as fulltime students. The German School Karibib also offered language courses. Furthermore, foundations, such as the Otto Benecke Foundation, offered non-white pupils scholarships for study at West German or South African universities: Deutscher Bundestag, 10. Wahlperiode, Drucksache 10/833, 21.12.1983, 14. That German schools taught in German made it impossible to enrol large numbers of non-white students. Bonn was aware of this problem. In 1977, the Foreign Office planned the launch of a special language exchange programme for non-white South African students. The programme envisioned to send non-white students for 5 weeks on an exchange programme to Germany, starting in 1979: PAAA, Zwischenarchiv, Bd. 116840, 1977–1978, Kulturpolitische Zusammenarbeit mit der nichtweißen Bevölkerung Südafrikas, 20.02.1978.
[57] The Bundestag debate was called by the SPD already in mid-1983, addressing concerns about the

late 1983, the Kohl government declared in the *Bundestag* that the *Kulturabkommen* with South Africa will continue, although it was widely criticised that it was predominantly catering to the needs of the white minority. The argument for continuation was based on the notion that past experiences showed that cultural exchange can contribute toward dismantling racial discrimination and, therefore, promoted racial equality and the improvement of the living conditions of the black population.[58] Genscher gave cultural exchange, with the approval of the Kohl government, a positive evaluation in late 1983.[59]

The Green Party was, however, not convinced, demanding the termination of West Germany's *Kulturabkommen* with South Africa in 1985.[60] The Greens pointed out that in 1982 there had been less than 0.2 percent of black students at German schools in South Africa and Namibia, while the government had paid 8 million deutsche marks in school subsidies in 1976, and 12 million in 1982. Furthermore, the Greens argued that the *Kulturabkommen* promoted an undesirable exchange of scientific know-how, for it gave South Africa the basic knowledge on how to build and design nuclear weapons.[61] In this regard, they opposed all cultural education in Namibia, including the 'well intended crafts and trades training', for it was an approval of South Africa's illegal occupation of Namibia.[62] The main concern was that it created the impression that West Germany supported apartheid and the occupation of Namibia.[63] Both the Green Party and the SPD viewed *Kulturabkommen* as a vehicle that intentionally or unintentionally consolidated Pretoria's position in Namibia.[64]

However, to some degree, the rivalry between the two German states over influence in Namibia also played itself out in the realm of cultural exchange. The Ministry of Foreign Affairs (MfAA) claimed in the early 1970s that after the Hallstein Doctrine had failed to hinder the GDR to establish relations with African countries, Bonn attempted to undermine East Berlin's possibilities to increase the GDR's influence in Africa by using cultural ex-

---

newly elected government's policy towards southern Africa: Deutscher Bundestag, Drucksache 10/230, 06.07.1983. For an assessment of the position of the German Anti-Apartheid Movement, the church, German artists, scientists and sports associations, see H. Brendel, *"Freiheit für Nelson Mandela!" Wie der Kampf gegen die Apartheid nach Deutschland kam*, Hamburg, Diplomica Verlag GmbH, 2014, 60–77.

[58] Deutscher Bundestag, 10. Wahlperiode, Drucksache 10/833, 21.12.1983, 9. See also PAAA, Zwischenarchiv, Bd. 116840, 1977–1978, Kulturpolitische Zusammenarbeit mit der nichtweißen Bevölkerung Südafrikas, 20.02.1978
[59] Deutscher Bundestag, 10. Wahlperiode, Drucksache 10/833, 21.12.1983, 14.
[60] Ibid., Drucksache 10/3166, 11.04.1985, 2.
[61] See also AGG, B.II.1, Die Gruenen im Bundestag, Signatur 3, 1983–1990, Pressemitteilung Nr. 576/85, 17.09.1985. For further insights into the Green Party's campaign against West German military co-operation with South Africa, see the following file: AAG, Akte 342, Uschi Eid.
[62] Deutscher Bundestag, 10. Wahlperiode, Stenographischer Bericht, 54. Sitzung, 10.02.1984, 3873.
[63] See also ISSA wissenschaftliche Reihe 21 (ed.), *Im Brennpunkt*, 133–158.
[64] See Deutscher Bundestag, 10. Wahlperiode, Stenographischer Bericht, 54. Sitzung, 10.02.1984.

change to undermine its political, cultural and economic capacities on the continent.[65] The GDR viewed cultural-academic exchange, which focused largely on the education of medical personal, teachers, skilled workers and academic cadres, as especially beneficial for building relations with African countries.[66] SWAPO in particular benefited from the GDR's cultural-academic exchange programmes.

Seen from the GDR's perspective, there was one primary objective in the West's cultural activities in Africa, namely, to force civil development models *[bürgerliche Entwicklungsmodelle]* in the realms of culture, education and information exchange upon African states for the sole purpose of furthering Western ideological expansion in Africa.[67] Consequently, East Berlin had little doubt that West Germany actively tried to limit the GDR's political, cultural and economic ability to influence African states.[68] Nonetheless, for the GDR, 'the cultural-academic collaboration proved to be an effective medium for the elaboration of relations with African states'.[69]

In 1980, at a time when East and West German rivalry in Africa reached a new peak, West Germany's foreign intelligence agency, the *Bundesnachrichtendienst* (BND), prepared for the Foreign Office a report on the GDR's educational endowment in the Third World.[70] The report made the following observation:

> The GDR's can establish focal points that can be changed quickly, because its development aid, which is often dressed up in the name of foreign cultural policy, is deployed in accordance to political considerations and carries out political decisions. The GDR influences and indoctrinates. While our offer for cooperation is based on partnership and independent development, and the pluralism of our political, social and cultural reality, the GDR concentrates its engagement on interference and modification, that is, on socialist development in accordance to GDR expectations, and on binding those states or organisations that accept help to the GDR.[71]

The report concluded that West Germany's cultural exchange with Africa was by no means inferior to the GDR's engagement, although the report acknowledged that West Germany could well adopt some aspects of the GDR's educational engagement in Africa. To this end, West Germany should get more involved with African countries that are in a state of up-

---

[65] PAAA, MfAA, C 1428/75, 1971–1973, Einschätzung der gegenwärtigen Situation in Afrika, Die Afrika Politik der BRD, [no date], 9.
[66] Ibid., 14.
[67] Ibid., 8.
[68] Ibid., 9.
[69] Ibid., 14.
[70] AAPD, 1980, Band I, Ausbildungshilfe der DDR an Angehörige aus Ländern der Dritten Welt, 24.06.1980, 980–983.
[71] Ibid., 980.

heaval, as already indicated in the planned *Special Program Southern Africa*. Yet, the report emphasised that increasing development aid and educational endowment should not result into a scramble for influence with the GDR. Instead, West Germany should rest assured of its superiority, for it had greater resources available than the GDR and its assistance was not attached to political demands.[72] The latter was not, of course, entirely true, for both German states expected future gains.

West Germany's cultural agreement with South Africa was, like the consulate in Windhoek, widely viewed as an indirect approval of Pretoria's policies in both South Africa and Namibia. In the late 1970s, it became increasingly difficult for the SPD-led government to support Namibia's independence process without having to justify its *Kulturabkommen* with South Africa. To avoid further criticism, particularly from the GDR and African states, the Federal Government agreed to terminate the cultural agreement with Namibia and close the consulate in Windhoek. The diplomatic importance of these drastic measures was reflected in a statement Genscher made in 1985: 'Without the closure, we would have been condemned to political inactivity.'[73] These actions gave West Germany credibility in the eyes of African countries and allowed Genscher to play a central role in the Western powers' efforts to find a negotiated solution to the Namibia problem.

West Germany's relations with South Africa in the late 1970s

In the mid-1970s, West Germany's relationship with South Africa became ever more challenging. Although both Bonn and Pretoria had a substantial interest in deepening the longstanding bilateral relations between the two countries, the wider reality of apartheid gradually drove a wedge between the two nations, making co-operation increasingly difficult. Domestic political considerations and international pressure encouraged the SPD-led government to overthink its relationship with Pretoria. The communist bloc's growing level of involvement in southern Africa added further complexity to an already complex situation. To understand West Germany's changing relations with South Africa against this backdrop of increasing cooperation between East Germany and SWAPO, it is advantageous to investigate the relationship between Bonn and Pretoria. The developments that led to a meeting between the two heads of states in West Germany in mid-1976 seem ideal for this purpose.[74]

---

[72] Ibid., 980–983.
[73] PAAA, Zwischenarchiv, Bd. 138105, 1985, Brief-Genscher an Kurt. H. P. Jung, 30.04.1985.
[74] Importantly, after the two German states had been admitted into the UN in 1973, it became increasingly difficult for Bonn to politically support Pretoria, particularly with regard to Namibia. The UN General Assembly had declared South Africa's occupation of Namibia illegal in 1970. Hence, the SPD-led government became increasingly openly critical of Pretoria. By the mid-

In 1970, the UN confirmed, in Resolution 276, the illegality of South Africa's presence in Namibia. On request of the Security Council, the International Court of Justice established the legal consequences for South Africa's continued occupation of Namibia. In 1971, the Court of Justice confirmed the illegality of South Africa's presence in Namibia and called upon Pretoria to end South Africa's occupation of Namibia. The UN member states were informed of their responsibility to refrain from supporting South Africa in Namibia. In December 1974 and January 1976, the Security Council challenged South Africa to respect the UN resolution and the ruling by the Court of Justice. Proposed sanctions against South Africa were vetoed by the three permanent UN member states: the USA, France and the United Kingdom. This allowed South Africa to remain unfazed by growing international pressure. Overall, there were good reasons to believe that Western countries would not undermine their own economic and geopolitical interests in southern Africa, and, most importantly, their economic relationship with South Africa.[75] This was particularly true for West Germany.[76]

In September 1975, Pretoria arranged a constitutional conference in Windhoek, inviting the eleven 'population groups' of the `homelands', ten of which participated. SWAPO was neither invited nor wanted to participate, as the liberation movement denounced the delegates as Pretoria's puppets.[77] The change in South Africa's policy towards Namibia in late 1976 came as a surprise. After all, the National Party in Namibia, which was closely linked to the National Party in South Africa, was well-placed to strengthen its already robust position in Namibia. Yet, international condemnation, growing demand for sanctions against South Africa, and increasing pressure from the United States left Pretoria with no alternative but to create the impression of fulfilling some of the UN demands.[78] In the mid-1970s, it became imperative for Pretoria that if Namibia's independence was inevitable, it should at least be on terms favourable to South Africa.

1970s, the relationship between Bonn and Pretoria had become rather frosty. See also Dedering, 'Ostpolitik', 17.

[75] See PAAA, Zwischenarchiv 116841, 1977–1978, Washington experts talk about economic measures against South Africa, 29.03.1978.

[76] See Ibid., Deutsch-südafrikanische Beziehungen; hier: Antwort des BM auf das Fernschreiben des MdB Dr. Marx vom 07.02.1978, 09.02.1978.

[77] Brenke, *Die Bundesrepublik*, 121. The `homelands' were ten traditional areas, divided by South Africa along ethnic lines. Some areas received limited self-governing rights. Overall, however, all remained under Pretoria's control. In fact, the motivation behind dividing the country into homelands was based on the desire to create further dependency on South Africa, especially in economic terms, and subsequently gain greater control over the different ethnic groups: L. Kaela, *The Question of Namibia*, London, McMillan Press Ltd, 1996, 77–90.

[78] See also Ibid., 21.

During that same period, Pretoria intensified pressure on Bonn to invite Foreign Minister Hilgard Muller to pay an official state visit to West Germany. In previous years, the Foreign Office repeatedly evaded the request by diverting meetings to the side-lines of the UN plenary assembly, as a Foreign Office file reveals.[79] Determined to schedule a meeting between Genscher and Muller, South Africa's ambassador to West Germany, Donald Bell Sole, complained to the Foreign Office about the Federal Government's reluctance to meet South Africa's Foreign Minister. Sole spoke in his charm offensive about Muller's German roots and his desire to visit Genscher in Germany.[80] Feeding Bonn's concern over a possible deterioration in bilateral trade relations Sole stated that once German advocates, such as Finance Minister Diedrichs, had left the South African cabinet, 'there will be a stronger tendency towards benefitting France'.[81] Pretoria was evidently aware that many in West Germany were concerned that it might use economic relations as a tool of influence and enforcement to change the Federal Government's position.

Furthermore, although Sole stressed his reluctance to inform Foreign Minister Muller that he 'wasn't welcome in the Federal Republic of Germany', he left no doubt about his intention of using precisely those words at their upcoming meeting in London on 20 January 1975.[82] Nonetheless, Genscher did not give in to South African pressure, agreeing to meet Muller only at the side-lines of the next UN plenary assembly.[83] Upon consultation with Muller, Sole, clearly annoyed, declined Genscher's proposal, pointing out that the foreign minister would not attend the next UN session, for South Africa was temporarily excluded from the General Assembly. Again, Sole tried to change Genscher's attitude through pressure tactics; this time by pointing out that the British Foreign Minister met Muller in London despite domestic and foreign pressures that were stronger than what Bonn would have to expect.[84]

In the end, Pretoria left Genscher with little option but to meet Muller in West Germany, for the Vorster government used the inauguration of South Africa's new embassy in September of the same year to send its Foreign Minister to Bonn, regardless of the SPD-led

---

[79] PAAA, Zwischenarchiv, Bd. 108220, 1975–1976, Deutsch-südafrikanische Beziehungen; hier: Besuchswunsch des südafrikanischen Außenministers, 14.01.1975, 3–4. For example, the then West German Foreign Minister Walter Scheel met Muller in New York in 1973 and 1974, and also in Paris in 1974.
[80] Muller had visited West Germany in 1967 for the funeral of Konrad Adenauer.
[81] PAAA, Zwischenarchiv, Bd. 108220, 1975–1976, Deutsch-südafrikanische Beziehungen; hier: Gespräch des Herrn Bundesministers mit dem südafrikanischen Botschafter am Donnerstag, 16.01.1975.
[82] Ibid.
[83] Ibid.
[84] Ibid., Brief-Sole an Genscher, 23.01.1975.

government's position. Despite all the protestations, Genscher finally agreed to meet Muller in private at the Foreign Office in Bonn.[85] Obviously, the unofficial nature of the meeting, and the fact that Bonn was not directly involved in the foreign minister's visit, helped swing opinion in Muller's favour.[86] Prior to this development, opinions about Muller's long-desired state visit to West Germany varied considerably within the Foreign Office.[87]

Walter Gehlhoff, State Secretary in the Foreign Office, for example, warned that 'a meeting would cause serious embarrassments and therefore one should simply not react to the request'.[88] In early-1975, Political Directory 3 of the Foreign Office, responsible for relations with Africa, also expressed its concern about an official meeting between the two foreign ministers:

> We also share the wish to uphold and broaden our relationship, but this should, in our opinion, happen in relative anonymity. The publicity generated by a visit of Minister Muller would create inner political and foreign policy problems that will not simplify but probably complicate efforts to champion South Africa in international bodies. Should the situation in southern Africa, including Rhodesia and Namibia, develop so that bridge building between black and white will be possible, which is to some extent already the case, we would in future welcome visitor exchanges with friends.[89]

Helga Steeg, the head of foreign economic relations in the Foreign Office, also believed that West German representatives' response on African questions in the UN might have harmed West Germany's economic relations with South Africa.[90] Similarly, a memorandum presented to the Foreign Office by the South African-German Chamber of Commerce came to the conclusion that the Federal Government's political ascendancies, statements and activities have a negative impact on relations with South Africa. The Chamber of Commerce feared that France might gain economic advantages over West Germany in South Africa due to the Federal Government's actions.[91] Evidently, the SPD-led government would have preferred to distance itself from Pretoria, but feared jeopardising West Germany's economic relations with South Africa. Therefore, the extent to which Pretoria used West Germany's

---

[85] Ibid., letter Lothar Lahn, Head of Department Political Directory 3 of the Foreign Office, to Donald Bell Sole, South African ambassador to Germany, 07.02.1975.
[86] Ibid., Besuch des südafrikanischen Außenministers in der Bundesrepublik Deutschland im September 1975, 17.03.1975.
[87] For further correspondence between Bonn and Pretoria regarding Muller's Bonn visit, see Zwischenarchiv, Bd. 108220.
[88] PAAA, Zwischenarchiv, Bd. 108220, 1975–1976, Deutsch-südfrikanische Beziehungen; hier: Besuchswunsch des südfrikanischen Außenministers, 14.01.1975, 2.
[89] Ibid.
[90] Ibid., 3.
[91] Ibid.

economic investments and interests in South Africa to exert pressure on Bonn becomes apparent.[92]

When Genscher finally received Muller in Bonn, he acknowledged West Germany's predicament of being 'caught between its continuing relationship with South Africa and its policies in the UN and towards African states'.[93] Overall, Genscher was not overly squeamish in his dealings with his South African counterpart. Genscher pointed out that Mozambique and Zimbabwe 'were under threat of a radical (also communist) development, if the moderate powers are not sufficiently supported'. He saw similar developments in Namibia, warning Muller that the postponement of a solution only strengthened radicals.[94] Here, his underlying concern outlined the risk of post-independence Namibia being influenced by the more radical elements in SWAPO. However, in Genscher's view, the responsibility lay entirely with Pretoria. Hence, he advised Muller to grant Namibia's majority the right of self-determination. To achieve this aim, Genscher proposed handing over the responsibility for Namibia to the UN.[95]

Less than a year later, the SPD-led government declined Prime Minister Vorster and Foreign Minister Muller an official state visit, but agreed to hold unofficial talks in Bonn. Although both Schmidt and Genscher would have preferred to hold talks outside of Germany, a meeting in Germany was again unavoidable as talks between the South African Prime Minister and US Secretary of State Henry Kissinger were scheduled to be held in Grafenau, a small Bavarian forest village. The Soweto uprisings in South Africa, a few days before Vorster's visit to West Germany, increased national and international pressure on the SPD-led government to confront Pretoria. Schmidt and Genscher were indeed outspoken, perhaps even confrontational, for the duo left Vorster with no doubt about Bonn's support for change in southern Africa.[96] In a private meeting with Muller, Genscher also stressed that it would be beneficial to include SWAPO in negotiations.[97] Overall, the talks were emo-

---

[92] It was not uncommon that Pretoria blackmailed countries with economic interests in South Africa by threatening retaliation in the case of severe measures against South Africa: A. Zacarias, *Security and the State in Southern Africa*, London, Tauris Academic Studies, 1999, 83.

[93] PAAA, Zwischenarchiv, Bd. 108220, 1975–1976, Zum Besuch des südfrikanischen Außenministers, 15.09.1975.

[94] Ibid.

[95] Ibid., Gespräch des Bundesministers mit dem südfrikanischen Außenminister Muller, 11.09.1975, 6.

[96] See Chapter Two, FDP.

[97] AAPD, 1976, Band I, Gespräch des Bundesministers Genscher mit dem südfrikanischen Außenminister Muller, 22.06.1976, 926. In late 1976, Genscher also motivated his counterpart in Washington, Henry Kissinger, to meet SWAPO representatives in New York. Kissinger responded positively to Genscher's initiative: Ibid., Band II, Gespräch Bundesministers mit Außenminister Kissinger, 08.10.1976, 1370.

tionally charged. Klaus Boelling, the cabinet spokesman and head of the public relations office, complained afterwards that Vorster and his entourage behaved like 'crew officers' and were 'boorish'.[98]

On 16 September 1976, Sole returned from South Africa to Bonn with a classified letter for Genscher from Muller. The letter expressed Muller's gratitude for the 'frank exchange of views' in Bonn, and confirmed that 'the constitutional committee of the constitutional future of South West Africa (Turnhalle Conference) announced on 18 August that it envisages 31 December 1978 as the date of independence for 'the territory as a whole'.[99] Pretoria's support for Namibian independence was, however, a calculated scheme to retain control over Namibia. There was no real willingness to give Namibia real independence, which becomes apparent in the fact that the Turnhalle Conference was held in protest of the 1972 UN decision to recognise SWAPO as the sole representative of the Namibian people.[100] Hardly surprising, therefore, the Turnhalle Conference received little international approval and was widely dismissed as a South African conspiracy to circumvent growing international pressure. In late 1976, at the 31st UN General Assembly, the Security Council voiced, in Resolution 31/146, its support for SWAPO's armed independence struggle, denounced the Turnhalle Conference as a continuation of South Africa's apartheid policy, and declared the situation in Namibia a threat to world peace.[101]

Nevertheless, Sole verbally affirmed to the Foreign Office in late 1976 that South Africa increasingly accepted that 'there is no way around SWAPO'.[102] Yet, although Pretoria acknowledged behind closed doors that the issue of nationhood for Namibia could not be solved without SWAPO, the prospect of 'a Nujoma-ruled Namibia was deemed entirely unbearable and hardly acceptable for South Africa', according to the Foreign Office.[103] Thus,

---

[98] 'Südafrika: Die Buren haben Angst', *Der Spiegel*, 27/1976, 28.06.1976.

[99] PAAA, Zwischenarchiv, Bd. 108220, Secret: Message from Dr. Hilgard Muller to His Excellency the Minister of Foreign Affairs Mr. Hans-Dietrich Genscher, 17.09.1976.

[100] For a detailed account of the role of the United Nations in the Namibian liberation struggle, see C. J. Tsokodayi, *Namibia's Independence Struggle: The Role of the United Nations*, Indiana, Xlibris Corporation, 2011.

[101] See Brenke, *Bundesrepublik*, 19. In a speech at 36th anniversary of the founding of the United Nations, Genscher came to similar conclusions. See PAAA, Zwischenarchiv, Bd. 178848, 1979–1981, Erklärung des Bundesministers des Auswärtigen Hans Dietrich Genscher zum 36. Jahrestag zur Gründung der Vereinten Nationen am 24. Oktober 1981, 23.10.1981.

[102] PAAA, Zwischenarchiv, Bd. 108220, 'Kritischer Dialog' mit der Republik Südfrika; hier: Botschaft des südfrikanischen Außenministers, Dr Hilgard Muller, an den Herrn Minister, 17.09.1976, 2. By 1978, the GDR's Ministry of State Security also came to believe that Pretoria increasingly accepted SWAPO's central role in Namibia's future. See BStU, MfS-Hauptverwaltung Aufklärung Nr. 69, Auskunft über Probleme des antiimperialistischen Befreiungskampfes in Zimbabwe und Namibia, 11.04.1978, 201.

[103] Ibid., Bd. 116802, 1977–1978, Politischer Halbjahresbericht Namibia/Südwestafrika, 24.08.1978, 3.

the Turnhalle Conference was a defining attempt by Pretoria to establish Namibia's independence without SWAPO.

When the SPD-led government tried to balance West Germany's economic and strategic interests in Namibia and South Africa by keeping its distance from the apartheid regime, the Vorster government forced the SPD-led government into two successive meetings on West German soil. These visits seemed to circumvent South Africa's increasing political isolation and created the impression that it still had reliable friends. Hence, West Germany's extensive economic relations with South Africa made Bonn vulnerable to Pretoria's manipulative tactics. That Muller informed Genscher in a personal letter of Pretoria's plans to support Namibia's independence was obviously a political step to propitiate Bonn. Although Pretoria did not appear to be overly concerned about international isolation, it needed Western support for its Namibian independence scheme, not least because African countries and the Soviet bloc were strongly opposed to any plan that received South Africa's backing.

However, international pressure was not the only factor that promoted Pretoria's push for such independence. In 1975, Angola achieved independence, bringing a Marxist, anti-South Africa party, the MPLA, to power. This not only strengthened SWAPO's political support in the region, it also improved its military position, for it became possible to plan and direct relatively unhindered military operations from neighbouring Angola.[104] The same year, Mozambique also achieved independence, bringing the Marxist liberation movement FRELIMO (Mozambique Liberation Front) to power, raising fears that the entire region would fall under the influence of communism.[105] These concerns were based on the Domino Theory, which was grounded in the belief that if one country in a region was to fall under the influence of communism; the surrounding states would follow in a domino effect. This theory was widely accepted in the West. In 1975 Pretoria used the domino theory to warn about the Soviet Union's involvement in Angola.[106]

Although Pretoria's plan for Namibia's independence might have surprised contemporary observers, in hindsight it seems reasonable to suggest that, in the mid-to-late 1970s, many signs pointed towards a changing regional status quo. First, domestic black opposition to white minority rule grew increasingly stronger in South Africa and Namibia. Second, Pretoria came under increasing pressure from some of South Africa's closest allies, including West Germany, to change course in both South Africa and Namibia. Third, the Marxist-led governments in newly independent Mozambique and Angola strengthened Moscow's

---

[104] Brenke, *Die Bundesrepublik*, 21.
[105] Independence: Mozambique, 25 June 1975 and Angola, 11 November 1975.
[106] PAAA, Zwischenarchiv, Bd. 108221, 1975–1976, Betreff: Angola, Pretoria, 04.12.1975.

influence in the region. Fourth, Cuba dispatched troops to Angola to strengthen the country against South African aggression. Fifth, the GDR advanced its already extensive collaboration with SWAPO and ANC.[107] Finally, West Germany dissolved its consulate in Windhoek and increased interactions with SWAPO.

In particular, the Soviet Union's advances in southern Africa became the source of widespread Western concern. In West Germany, however, the SPD-led government was not too worried about Moscow's ambitions in southern Africa, while the CDU/CSU opposition strongly echoed these concerns. Nonetheless, there was a pervasive consensus in Bonn that the Soviet Union followed an expansionist strategy in southern Africa. In this respect, the GDR's foreign-intelligence gathering department (HV A) of the Ministry of State Security reported in early 1977 that West Germany understood the GDR's involvement in Sub-Saharan Africa as part of the Soviet Union's expansionist foreign policy strategy:

> Within the framework of Soviet goals in Africa, the other socialist countries act, in the perception of West Germany, as a 'helper' or as 'deputy'. They become especially active where – Angola is listed as a classic example – liberation movements are preparing military engagement or even the seizing of power... The other socialist countries supporting activities become also visible where they can provide, for technological, economic and solidarity reasons, better assistance than the Soviet Union.[108]

Importantly, the GDR's solidarity with liberation struggles gave East Berlin opportunities to demonstrate its relative independence of action from the Kremlin. The regime of Erich Honecker attached great importance to exercising a foreign policy that was, at least to some degree, independent of that of the Kremlin. Although East Berlin strengthened its ties to Moscow in the mid-1970s, Honecker continued to emphasise the GDR's autonomy as a sovereign state, with regard to both West Germany and the Soviet Union.[109] Hence, it was probably frustrating for the SED to observe that West German political parties made little distinction between Soviet aims in Africa and the GDR's solidarity with liberation movements.[110]

---

[107] SWAPO opened a representative office in GDR in October 1978 and ANC in November 1978: BStU, MfS-HA II, Nr. 28977, Südafrikanische Volksorganisation (SWAPO) von Namibia, [no date], 171.

[108] BStU, MfS-Hauptverwaltung Aufklärung, Nr. 63, Information über das militärische Engagement der sozialistischen Länder in Afrika südlich der Sahara aus BRD-Sicht, 11.04.1977, 178–180.

[109] See K. Larres, 'Britain and the GDR: Political and Economic Relations 1949–1989', in K. Larres and E. Meehan (eds.), *Uneasy Allies, British-German Relations and European Integration since 1945*, Oxford, Oxford University Press, 2000, 93. See also A. J. McAdams, *Germany Divided: From the Wall to Reunification*, New Jersey, Princeton University Press, 104–105.

[110] See also Deutscher Bundestag, 8. Wahlperiode, Stenographischer Bericht, 197. Sitzung, 18.01.1980, 15692.

Both the SPD-led government and the CDU/CSU opposition harbored little doubt that the GDR played an active role in supporting Moscow in realising its power interests in the Third World. Indeed, West Germany firmly placed the GDR within the category of a Soviet satellite state, which often led to the reductive and derogatory portrayal of the GDR as a Soviet puppet, vassal, deputy or helper.[111] Hence, East Berlin's desire to enhance the GDR's regional and international standing, particularly as an independent state, led to concerted efforts to shed this image of being a Soviet satellite. In the late 1970s, the GDR gradually began to emancipate itself from its subordination to the Soviet Union in Africa, increasingly pursuing its own agenda, especially in southern Africa. The opportunity to develop initiatives and policies that were independent of the Soviet Union was especially important for the GDR. Moscow had no objection to allowing the GDR to strengthen its image as a sovereign and independent state, not least because it supported the Soviet Union's goal to further its power interests, particularly in Africa. Gradually, the Soviet Union appreciated the GDR as an equal and certainly valued partner, at least in Africa.[112] East Berlin, however, never fully succeeded in changing West Germany's image of the GDR as a 'Soviet puppet regime'.[113]

Bonn subordinated the GDR's solidarity with liberation struggles under the collective efforts of the communist bloc, even though East Germany occupied a unique position in Moscow's strategy to advance Soviet interests in southern Africa.[114] West Germany's political parties rarely acknowledged the GDR's growing influence in southern Africa, but rather expressed concerns about the communist bloc at large, although the GDR's involvement in southern Africa increased noticeably in the late 1970s.[115]

---

[111] See also Schleicher/Schleicher, *Special flights*, 3–4; Engel/Schleicher, *Die beiden deutschen Staaten*, 238; Winrow, *The Foreign Policy*, 6–14.

[112] See, e.g., van der Heyden, 'GDR Development Policy', 56; H.-G. Schleicher, 'Afrika in der Außenpolitik der DDR', in U. van der Heyden, I. Schleicher und H.-G. Schleicher (eds.), *Die DDR und Afrika*, 12–13.

[113] See C. Ross and J. Grix, 'Approaches to the German Democratic Republic', in J. Grix (ed.), *Approaches to the Study of Contemporary Germany: Research Mythologies in German Studies*, Birmingham, University of Birmingham Press, 2002, 50–51.

[114] Poland and CSSR officially started SWAPO cadre training after Nujoma's visit in December 1977. Yugoslavia's cooperation with SWAPO also became quite substantial after Nujoma's visits in 1977 and 1978. See BStU, MfS-HA II, Nr. 28977, Südafrikanische Volksorganisation (SWAPO) von Namibia, [no date], 169.

[115] PAAA, Zwischenarchiv, Bd. 116840, 1977–1978, Beziehungen DDR-Südafrika, 27.11.1978; Deutscher Bundestag, 8. Wahlperiode, Stenographischer Bericht, 197. Sitzung, 18.01.1980. Although the Bundestag discussed the GDR's involvement in Africa mainly within the wider context of Soviet expansionism in Africa, the GDR's involvement moved into the foreground of a *Bundestag* debate in 1978: Deutscher Bundestag, 8. Wahlperiode, Stenographischer Bericht, 100 Sitzung, 22.06.1978, 7966–7971.

Overall, southern Africa moved further into the focus of the East-West conflict in the late 1970s, emphasising to Moscow the importance of the GDR as a strategic partner in the region, particularly because of East Berlin's intimate relationships with national liberation movements.[116] However, Moscow's growing interest in southern Africa was ultimately also beneficial to the GDR. The Soviet Union's growing influence in southern Africa enhanced the GDR's potential to become a central player in one of the strategically most important regions of the Cold War. This boosted East Germany's influence within the communist bloc and had the potential to redefine the GDR's international standing. These developments moved the GDR further into West Germany's focus.[117] For, while intra-German enmity gradually decreased with the introduction of *Ostpolitik* in 1969, the movement towards decolonisation in the 1970s promoted intra-German rivalry for political influence in southern Africa, particularly in Namibia.[118] Though increasing tensions over Namibian issues did not visibly undermine the process of rapprochement between the two German states on German soil, the atmosphere between East and West Germany remained tense, hostile and volatile, at least until the early to mid-1980s. In 1979, for example, the GDR's defence Minister Heinz Hoffmann stated during a visit to Ethiopia that the GDR would not watch with 'crossed arms' West Germany's, and the other NATO powers, 'aggressive activities' in Africa. In a historical flashback, Hoffmann also claimed that, in 1956, West Germany had made preparations to 'militarily conquer' the GDR, leading to the establishment of the GDR's National Army (NVA).[119] The portrayal of West Germany as an aggressive power with colonial ambitions did not go unnoticed by the Foreign Office:

> Those remarks poison the good neighbourly relations between both states, which is so important for the elevation of tensions in Europe, as the GDR itself has continuously emphasised. The Federal Government can assess such statements only as a relapse into the jargon of the 'Cold War'.... Retrospectively, the Federal Government points out to the GDR that neither now nor in future will it accept such actions and will respond accordingly.[120]

---

[116] See also S. Lorenzi, 'East-South relations in the 1970s and the GDR involvement in Africa: Between bloc loyalty and self-interest', in M. Guderzo and B. Bagnato (eds.), *The Globalization of the Cold War and local confrontation, 1975–85*, New York, Routledge, 2010, 112.

[117] Deutscher Bundestag, 8. Wahlperiode, Stenographischer, Bericht, 197. Sitzung, 18.01.1980.

[118] See also BStU, MfS 6645, Informationsmitteilung Nr. 42/77, Information über charakteristische Merkmale der politischen, militärpolitischen und militärökonomischen Lageentwicklung in Afrika südlich der Sahara in der zweiten Hälfte der 70er Jahre, 11.08.1977.

[119] PAAA, B2, Mikrofilm, Band 222, 1974–1979, Addis Abeba, Afrikareise des DDR-Verteidigungsministers Heinz Hoffmann, 05.06.1979.

[120] Ibid., Äußerung des DDR-Verteidigungsministers Hoffmann anlässlich seines Besuchs in Äthiopien (27.05.1979–31.05.1979), 07.06.1979.

Not only did the Foreign Office take the GDR's propaganda campaign against West Germany in Africa seriously, it also emphasised that such tactics were counterproductive to German-German rapprochement.[121] Ultimately, neither Bonn nor East Berlin could deny that in the final analysis all intra-German frictions were intertwined with the division of Germany. This basic understanding opened up possibilities for moderating tensions on German soil while still competing for influence in Third World countries. Both German states understood that their involvement in local affairs in southern Africa, particularly Namibia, promised noteworthy international exposure. In some measure, both East and West Germany pragmatically exploited favourable opportunities for the increase in their influence, but also to further their international recognition and significance.[122]

In late 1977, the GDR's relationship with SWAPO 'reached a new quality'.[123] The SED and SWAPO established a 'co-operation agreement', which the Ministry of State Security recognised retrospectively as the 'zenith of SED-SWAPO co-operation'.[124] To this end, the Central Committee (ZK) of the SED invited Nujoma to visit the GDR in November and December 1977 and again in October to November 1978. In October 1978, SWAPO officially opened a representative bureau in East Germany.[125] However, SWAPO avoided entering into any firm ideological commitment in the late 1970s. According to a West German assessment, presented by the GDR's foreign intelligence gathering service, Nujoma took the view in 1977 that it was important to establish good relations with both the communist East and the capitalist West.[126] Considering that the UN General Assembly recognised SWAPO as the sole representative of the Namibian people in 1976, it is hardly surprising that Nujoma was careful not to alienate the West by committing SWAPO too deeply to the communist bloc.

Although West Germany's growing interactions with SWAPO in the late 1970s could be interpreted as an inevitable consequence of the liberation movement's improving status within the United Nations, the UN had little impact on the making of West German percep-

---

[121] PAAA, Zwischenarchiv, Bd. 116840, 1977–1978, Beziehungen DDR-Südfrika, 27.11.1978, 2. See also AAPD, 1979, Band II, Gegen uns gerichtete Aktivitäten der DDR in Afrika, 19.12.1979, 1945–1949.

[122] After becoming a full member in the United Nations, West Germany understood its improved international status as a mandate to become internationally more engaged, mainly to reduce conflict and tensions around the world: Deutscher Bundestag, 8. Wahlperiode, Stenographischer Bericht, 79. Sitzung, 10.03.1978, 6207.

[123] BStU, MfS-HA II, Nr. 28977, Südfrikanische Volksorganisation (SWAPO) von Namibia, [no date], 169.

[124] Ibid.

[125] Ibid., 171. See also PAAA, Zwischenarchiv, Bd. 116840, 1977–1978, Beziehungen DDR- Südfrika, 27.11.1978, 1–3.

[126] BStU, MfS-Hauptverwaltung Aufklärung, Nr. 62, Information über die Entwicklung in Südfrika aus der Sicht von BRD-Regierungskreisen, 16.02.1977, 111.

tion and policy toward SWAPO. The SPD-led government's growing solidarity with national liberation struggles in southern Africa was driven forward by the passionate campaign of various SPD heavyweights. SWAPO's international standing was not relevant from an inner-German perspective, for a conservative government would have adopted quite a different strategy to the one that was pursued by the SPD-led government.[127] In fact, the hardline faction within the CDU/CSU argued in late 1977 that 'the SPD-led government would be well advised to hinder SWAPO from gaining power'.[128] It is hardly surprising, therefore, that the GDR's Ministry of State Security reported in 1978 that the CDU/CSU 'deemed it necessary to prevent SWAPO from gaining power'.[129] Consequently, SWAPO's improving international standing was not directly relevant to positions within West Germany, for different interpretations and views of the liberation struggle determined attitudes and policies towards liberation movements.

The conservatives' approach to Namibia was driven largely by economic and commercial concerns and the perceived threat of communism in the region.[130] SWAPO's co-operation with communist-bloc countries was seen as a threat to the capitalist market system in Namibia. Of particular concern was the GDR's growing influence in Namibia.[131] However, economic interests, meaning good relations between West Germany and South Africa, stood above all else. It should perhaps not be surprising, therefore, that a number of leading CDU/CSU ministers accused the SPD-led government of acting irresponsibly.[132] This was mainly because the SPD-led government began to distance itself from Pretoria, as far as politically possible, while simultaneously moving closer to SWAPO. In the late 1970s, there was a growing consensus that Pretoria's policies in southern Africa promoted the spread of communism in the region.[133]

The CDU/CSU opposition felt uncomfortable with the active give-and-take strategy of the Federal Government. Based on the consideration that the communist bloc was beginning to gain ground in southern Africa, the CDU/CSU refused to support policies that might challenge the status quo in the region, not least because of West Germany's economic inter-

---

[127] Deutscher Bundestag, 8. Wahlperiode, Stenographischer Bericht, 197. Sitzung, 18.01.1980, 15691–15737.
[128] H. H. Klein, 'Uwe Holtz, die SPD und die SWAPO', *DUD*, Nr. 182, 22.09.1977, 6.
[129] BStU, MfS-Hauptverwaltung Aufklärung Nr. 69, Auskunft über Probleme des antiimperialistischen Befreiungskampfes in Zimbabwe und Namibia, 11.04.1978, 204.
[130] See, e.g., Deutscher Bundestag, 8. Wahlperiode, Stenographischer Bericht, 197. Sitzung, 18.01.1980, 15722; Ibid., Drucksache 8/2748, 11.04.1979.
[131] Ibid., Drucksache 8/2748, 11.04.1979.
[132] See Chapter Three, CDU/CSU.
[133] PAAA, Zwischenarchiv, Bd. 116840, 1977–1978, Wischnewski speech at the Socialist Internationale in Vancouver in 1978. Genscher also stated in his memoirs that he 'clearly distanced himself from Pretoria': Genscher, *Erinnerungen*, 467.

ests. In fact, the CDU/CSU policy-makers saw little reason to challenge the existing order in southern Africa. From the point of view of the conservative opposition, the communist bloc was the expansionist aggressor, pursuing a neo-colonial strategy in southern Africa. To this end, Hans Stercken (CDU), chairman of the *Bundestag* Foreign Relations Committee, made the following statement in 1980: 'In any case, I don't know any friendly and allied liberal power that continued to practice a colonial policy in Africa, apart from the Soviet Union and its helpers, especially the Africa-corps of Honecker'.[134]

From the GDR's perspective, however, the SPD-led government's growing interactions with SWAPO reflected the self-serving attitude of a neo-colonial power, following a policy of divide and rule, as the counter-intelligence department of the Ministry of State Security (HA II) reveals in a study of SWAPO completed between 1979 and 1981:

> The imperial states, especially USA, FRG, Great Britain, France and Canada, attempt to use their contacts to SWAPO (Nujoma visited the US in 1978, France in 1977) for dividing or infiltrating and weakening the organisation. The UN-Namibia-Institute (Lusaka, Zambia), which is predominantly financed by the FRG and USA, was established to take influence on SWAPO's cadres development. Especially the FRG tries, in connection with its 'special interests' in Namibia, to activate its relationship with SWAPO (among others, the talks with Genscher at the side-lines of the 33rd UN assembly).[135]

These concerns came to the fore in late 1978, when the SPD-led government and SWAPO met formally for the first time in Lusaka. Before the meeting, SWAPO was apprehensive that Bonn would attach certain conditions to the improvement of relations, in particular demanding that SWAPO reduce contact with the GDR. According to the post-meeting report, SWAPO was 'visibly relieved' when the SPD delegation acknowledged the liberation movement's autonomy, emphasising that 'relations with third party organisations or states fall exclusively within SWAPO's decision-making area'. Significantly, SWAPO indicated later that the GDR representatives in Lusaka had fuelled their concerns about Bonn's alleged opposition to SWAPO's close relations with East Berlin.[136] As East Berlin was convinced that the SPD-led government's objective was to drive a wedge between the GDR and SWAPO, intra-German rivalry on Namibia increased.

---

[134] Deutscher Bundestag, 8. Wahlperiode, Stenographischer Bericht, 197. Sitzung, 18.01.1980, 15693.
[135] BStU, MfS-HA II, Nr. 28977, Südwestafrikanische Volksorganisation (SWAPO) von Namibia, 169. For a similar assessment by Franz Bertele, Bonn's representative in East Berlin, see PAAA, Zwischenarchiv, Bd. 116840, 1977–1978, Beziehungen DDR – Südfrika, 27.11.1978.
[136] PAAA, Zwischenarchiv, Bd. 116802, 1977–1978, Afrika-Reise einer Delegation des SPD Parteivorstands, 20.11.1978.

The Foreign Office warned in 1978 that Namibia was in danger of becoming 'a bone of contention in East-West relations'.[137] In the late 1970s, Cold War competition over geopolitical influence in southern Africa promoted the rapid polarization of Namibia into Eastern and Western camps. This polarisation was further amplified by countries, political groups and private investors who attempted to influence the political status quo in Namibia through unilateral measures.[138] Given that East Berlin suspected in Bonn's move towards SWAPO a plot against the GDR, it is hardly surprising that the Ministry of State Security kept a close eye on West Germany's interactions with SWAPO in the late 1970s. Within this context, the MfS identified two key dates in West Germanys efforts to improve relations with the Namibian liberation movement: Brand's meeting with SWAPO during a southern Africa trip in January 1978, and the SPD's formal meeting with SWAPO in November 1978.[139] The GDR State Security's observation further underlines the central role Brandt played in West Germany's move towards SWAPO.

In late 1977, the closure of West Germany's consulate in Windhoek and the termination of the *Kulturabkommen* with Namibia was the SPD-led government's strongest indication of a change in approach to the Namibia question. Although many SPD and FDP party members exhibited considerable sympathy for SWAPO's cause in late 1977, the SPD-led government's attitude towards SWAPO did not begin to change noticeably until late 1978. As SWAPO gained increasing legitimacy within the SPD-FDP coalition government in the late 1970s, many in the government grew increasingly frustrated with Pretoria.[140] The lack of progress in southern Africa raised questions about the white minority's willingness to implement rapid change.[141] The Soweto Youth Uprising in June 1976 and the ensuing mass arrests on 19 October 1977 further exposed the shortcomings of West Germany's relationship with South Africa.[142] The apartheid regime's human rights violations pushed South Africa further into international isolation. This led to deep frustration, displayed most visibly

---

[137] Ibid., Politischer Halbjahresbericht Namibia/Südwestafrika, 24.08.1978, 4.
[138] Ibid.
[139] BStU, MfS-HA II, Nr. 28977, Südwestafrikanische Volksorganisation (SWAPO) von Namibia, 169.
[140] Deutscher Bundestag, 8. Wahlperiode, Stenographischer Bericht, 52. Sitzung, 27.09.1977; Ibid., 4001 and 4061.
[141] PAAA, Zwischenarchiv, Bd. 116840, 1977–1978, Gespräch StS van Well mit Vertretern des Parteivorstandes der SPD, 09.11.1978. See also Deutscher Bundestag, 8. Wahlperiode, Stenographischer Bericht, 52. Sitzung, 27.09.1977, 4061; Ibid., Drucksache 8/3462, 04.12.1979, 4.
[142] See, e.g., PAAA, AV Neues Amt, Bd. 7920, 1978, Sicherheitsrat, New York, 28.01.1978; Ibid., Sicherheitsrat, zweiter Tag der Südafrikadebatte, New York, 30.01.1978 Steve Biko's death in custody September 1977 led to the banning of the Black Consciousness Movement and mass arrests on 19 October 1977: S. M. Ndlovu, 'The Soweto Uprising', in *The Road to Democracy in South Africa, Vol. 2, 1970–1980*, Pretoria, Unisa Press, 2006, 317–350.

by Genscher's eagerness to point out that those arrested were mainly moderate representatives of the black majority, particularly those who were open to negotiation.[143] Genscher was particularly concerned about the potentially far-reaching negative consequences of the arrests: 'Isn't it possible to sense how this strengthens those amongst the black majority who argue not to seek talks but to fight. Indirectly, this supports the radicals'.[144] The Federal Government was, as Genscher emphasised, concerned that the arrests would 'lead to further radicalisation and inevitably play into the hands of communist powers'.[145]

Pretoria's uncompromising desire to retain control destabilised much of the region and complicated West Germany's close relationship with South Africa. By the late 1970s it became increasingly apparent that Pretoria was deliberately stalling and preventing any progress toward Namibia's independence.[146] In this light, in late 1977, Genscher indirectly blamed South Africa for SWAPO's armed resistance, arguing that if the non-white majority could express themselves through a 'policy of peaceful change', those who propagated violence would be deprived of their persuasiveness.[147] Consequently, Genscher strongly opposed Pretoria's attempt to muzzle the black majority.[148]

Moreover, a growing number of SPD and FDP parliamentarians questioned the wisdom of the CDU/CSU opposition's uncompromising support for close relations with Pretoria, while refusing to establish any meaningful contact with liberation movements. The problem with the CDU/CSU position was, as the FDP parliamentarian Helga Schuchardt pointed out, threefold. First, the legitimacy for closer relations with liberation movements derived from the fact that states built on a racist foundation, solely for the protection of minority rule, cannot represent the interests of the majority. Second, to refuse contact with SWAPO because it used violence ignored that Pretoria maintained its power through oppression and violence. Third, to avoid establishing relations with countries that were within the Eastern bloc's sphere of influence would only support the expansion of communism.[149] Along these

---

[143] See also Deutscher Bundestag, 8. Wahlperiode, Stenographischer Bericht, 52. Sitzung, 27.09.1977, 4069.
[144] Ibid., 4061.
[145] Ibid. See also PAAA, Zwischenarchiv, Bd. 116840, 1977–1978, Gespräch StS van Well mit Vertretern des Parteivorstandes der SPD, 09.11.1978.
[146] See also PAAA, AV Neues Amt, Bd. 7920, Sicherheitsrat; hier: Südfrika-Debatte am 26.01, 26.01.1978.
[147] Deutscher Bundestag, 8. Wahlperiode, Stenographischer Bericht, 52. Sitzung, 27.09.1977, 4061. See also PAAA, Zwischenarchiv, Bd. 116840, 1977–1978, Gespräch StS van Well mit Vertretern des Parteivorstandes der SPD, 09.11.1978.
[148] Deutscher Bundestag, 8. Wahlperiode, Stenographischer Bericht, 52. Sitzung, 27.09.1977, 4061.
[149] Ibid., 4005. The third point was based on the argument that West Germany should, as a measure of punishment, deny support to countries and liberation movements that had close ties to the Soviet bloc.

lines, the SPD-led government received strong support from within its own ranks for improving relations with SWAPO in late 1977.[150]

A further argument that encouraged the improvement of West Germany's relations with SWAPO was the establishment of the WCG. For West Germany, this promised to strengthen its diplomatic position within the international community and gave Bonn a proactive role in Western efforts to solve the crisis in southern Africa. Furthermore, the WCG promised to further improve West Germany's international image. West Germany was widely criticised, even condemned by name in General Assembly resolutions for its strong ties to South Africa.[151] Vergau points out that 'the GDR contributed, through its diligent one-sided involvement in the condemnation of West Germany in General Assembly resolutions, to our motivation to start the Namibia Initiative within the framework of the WCG in 1977'.[152] Thus, in the context of intensified Cold War rivalry between East and West Germany, the WCG gave Bonn a platform to counter GDR propaganda. Hence, West Germany's involvement with the WCG allowed Bonn to abandon its predominantly defensive response to criticism and instead emphasise its role in finding an internationally acceptable solution to the Namibian problem.[153] The SPD-led government's determination to soften political discrepancies between West Germany and SWAPO, combined with its efforts in the WCG, strengthened West Germany's international diplomatic standing and gradually improved its reputation in Africa.[154] For Genscher, on the other hand, the establishment of the WCG offered an opportunity to exercise leadership in foreign affairs. Genscher's enthusiasm for the WCG can thus be understood, in part, by his drive to establish his credentials in the realm of foreign affairs, as discussed previously.[155]

However, West Germany's change in attitude towards South Africa was not derived predominantly from international criticism. Bonn's loyalty towards Pretoria generated, as already discussed, increasingly strong disapproval within West Germany in the late 1970s. In the early and mid-1970s, *Bundestag* debates on the question of Namibian independ-

---

[150] For example, the parliamentarians Manfred Vohrer, (FDP), Uwe Holtz (SPD), Egon Bahr (SPD) and Lenelotte von Bothmer (SPD) expressed their support for improving relations with SWAPO and other liberation movements in 1977: Deutscher Bundestag, 8. Wahlperiode, Stenographischer Bericht, 52. Sitzung, 27.09.1977, 3984, 4003, 4056 and 4071.
[151] See, e.g., PAAA, AV Neues Amt, Bd. 15816, 1972–1979, Allgemeine Berichterstattung über die 33. GV; hier: Südliches Afrika, 23.01.1979, 9; Ibid., Allgemeine Berichterstattung über die 33. Generalversammlung der UN; hier: Fragen der Entkolonialisierung, New York, 23.01.1979, 9–11.
[152] E-mail interview with Hans-Joachim Vergau, 26.04. 2016.
[153] See also Vergau, *Negotiating the Freedom*, 4–5.
[154] AAPD, 1981, Band I, Arbeitsbesuch des französischen AM Cheysson in Bonn am 2. Juni 1981; hier: Namibia, 09.06.1981.
[155] For an assessment of the motives behind West Germany's participation in the WCG, see also Engel, *Die Afrikapolitik*, 158–159.

ence were still dominated by a focus on West Germany's traditionally close ties with South Africa. Hence, the continuation of minority rule in Namibia was still viewed as a viable possibility. In the late 1970s, however, the SPD-led government saw South Africa increasingly as part of the problem in Namibia. In the face of increasing South African aggression, it soon became apparent that the status quo was no longer sustainable. Hence, majority rule and SWAPO gradually became the central theme of discussion at *Bundestag* debates about Namibia.[156] In short, the political tide began to slowly turn against Pretoria in the late 1970s. The WCG's aim was to negotiate a 'peaceful solution' between SWAPO and South Africa. Hence, to avoid accusation of partisanship, West Germany's participation in the WCG meant it had to adopt a balanced approach towards both Pretoria and SWAPO. By late 1977, however, the SPD-led government's attitude swung steadily in SWAPO's favour, while its attitude vis-à-vis Pretoria became steadily more critical.[157]

East and West Germany's Intensification of Relations with SWAPO in the late 1970s

In the face of Pretoria's uncompromising approach to the Namibian question, the WCG demanded from West Germany full commitment to helping move the negotiation process forward.[158] Although international pressure pushed Pretoria to instigate elections, the Vorster government had no intention of losing control over Namibia. Pretoria announced, amidst growing international opposition to its Namibian policy, election plans for Namibia that were to lead to national independence by the end of 1978.[159] However, South Africa purposefully excluded SWAPO in its election strategy. In fact, Pretoria even arrested several SWAPO members, including Daniel Tjongarero, the deputy chairman of SWAPO, which caused Bonn great concern in late 1977. The Federal Government had little doubt that the arrests were an attempt 'to disrupt the WCG's efforts to find a negotiated solution and therefore undermining the chances of a peaceful transition to independence'.[160] Consequently,

---

[156] After the SPD moved closer toward SWAPO, the *Bundestag* debates became more diverse, addressing the Namibia question from both South Africa's and SWAPO's perspective. The first *Bundestag* debate that considered the liberation movements' position took place in late 1977: Deutscher Bundestag, 8. Wahlperiode, Stenographischer Bericht, 52. Sitzung, 27.09.1977.

[157] Despite these fundamental changes in late 1977, almost another year went by before the SPD-led government formally approached SWAPO in late 1978.

[158] See PAAA, AV Neues Amt, Bd. 7920, 1978, Sicherheitsrat-Sanktionen und sonstige westliche Druckmittel gegen Südfrika, 25.01.1978.

[159] See also Ibid., Namibia-Initiative; hier: Simultangespräche in New York, New York, 13.01.1978; Ibid., Namibia-Initiative; hier: Simultangespräche in New York, New York, 13.01.1977 (date seems to be wrong, should be 1978).

[160] PAAA, Zwischenarchiv, Bd. 116802, 1977–1978, Erklärung SWAPO's vom 6.12.1977 zur Ver-

the Federal Government had good reason to be sceptical about Pretoria's announcement to grant genuine independence to Namibia in 1978.[161]

In November 1977, the eleven groups of the Turnhalle Conference merged into a political party, the Democratic Turnhalle Alliance (DTA).[162] The DTA was established to become the transitional government in Pretoria's plan for Namibia's independence. The UN, SWAPO and the WCG declared the Pretoria-controlled proceedings unacceptable. Nonetheless, Pretoria pushed through the elections as scheduled, although the entire Turnhalle project was internationally rejected.[163] Ultimately, it had become apparent that there was little reason to be optimistic about the prospects for making real progress in Namibia. Genscher had almost, but not quite, given up hope for a breakthrough before the turn of the decade.[164]

Importantly, the WCG's aims in Namibia were essentially identical to the demands expressed by Schmidt and Genscher during Vorster's visit to Bonn in 1976. With this in mind, the Federal Government's changing attitude towards South Africa mirrored many of the concerns and attitudes expressed by Western powers in the late 1970s. Nonetheless, the Federal Government's move towards SWAPO was a self-determined adaptation to changing circumstances, pushed forward by political heavyweights such as Brandt and Wischnewski, and not a reflection of a more general trend in the West.[165] The GDR's intensification of relations with SWAPO and West Germany's deteriorating image in Africa played a central role in the revision of the Federal Government's attitude.[166] West Germany's participation in the WCG confirmed the validity of the revised approach. The autonomous motivation behind West Germany's changing attitude towards both Pretoria and SWAPO also becomes apparent in the Schmidt-Genscher government's outspoken opposition to Pretoria's domestic and regional polices in the mid-1970s. Thus, already before the establishment of the WCG, the Federal Government expressed concerns about Pretoria's domestic policy of apartheid and demanded Namibia's independence, but not without including SWAPO in the process.[167] The CDU/

---

haftung führender SWAPO-Mitglieder in Namibia, 09.12.1977.

[161] There were consistent doubts about Pretoria's willingness to carry out its promise to grant Namibia independence: PAAA, AV Neues Amt, Bd. 7920, 1978, Namibia-Initiative; hier: Simultangespräche in New York, New York, 11.01.1978.

[162] See, e.g., Udogu, *Liberating Namibia*, 55–85; Vergau, *Negotiating the Freedom*, 8–9.

[163] PAAA, Zwischenarchiv, Bd. 178773, 1978, Interne Wahlen in Namibia; hier: Interpretation dieser Wahlen durch die südafrikanische Regierung, 12.12.1978.

[164] Ibid., Brief: Genscher-Wilhelm Jung, Leiter des Amts für Mission und Evangelisation der Evangelischen Kirche von Kurhessen, 22.12.1978.

[165] Most Western countries had little or no contact with southern African liberation movements in the late 1970s.

[166] See Chapter Two, SPD.

[167] As discussed previously, the Federal Government made these demands already during Vorster's visit to Bonn in 1976.

CSU, however, did not go through such a revision of attitude and therefore remained firmly on Pretoria's side. Hence, the conservatives supported Pretoria's alternative to SWAPO, the DTA, and also the nationalist Namibian National Front (NNF).[168]

East Berlin assessed the SPD-led government's change in attitude towards SWAPO through the lens of Cold War rivalry. The GDR's Ministry of State Security even went so far as to predict future confrontations between the two German states in Namibia: 'In the GDR's relationship with an independent Namibia, particular confrontations are expected with FRG, which are determined by a relatively influential minority of approximately 30,000 Germans (many of them German citizens)'.[169] According to the MfS, German-German rivalry for influence in Namibia was bound to intensify as a consequence of the close relationship between the GDR and SWAPO on the one hand, and Bonn's support of 'pro-imperial powers' such as the DTA and NNF on the other hand.[170] The MfS anticipated strategic considerations behind the West's growing interest in SWAPO, namely to 'infiltrate and divide' the liberation movement, while at the same time strengthening and supporting the DTA and NNF.[171]

From the GDR's point of view the Western powers pursued in Namibia and South Africa, as Schleicher explains, three aims: to prevent the further isolation of South Africa, to protect Western influence in the region, and to halt any further advances of socialism in southern Africa.[172] The WCG's Namibia initiative was, in the eyes of the MfS, rooted in the desire to find a 'neo-colonial solution for Namibia'.[173] The overall foreign policy objective in southern Africa was grounded in the West's 'quest for world dominance' and thus to maintain the status quo or at least to retard revolutionary change in the region.[174] From this perspective, the continuation of white minority rule in southern Africa was strategically desirable. Furthermore, economic interests in Namibia undermined West Germany's willingness to increase pressure on Pretoria through sanctions and other means, as Peter Florin, the GDR's representative to the UN, correctly pointed out at the UN Namibia-Konferenz on 3 March 1981. Florin argued that Pretoria will only under significant pressure change course in Na-

---

[168] See 'Seid nett zu den armen Namibia-Deutschen', *Der Spiegel*, 35/1978, 28.08.1978. See also Chapter Two, CDU/CSU.
[169] BStU, MfS-HAII, Nr. 28977, Südfrikanische Volksorganisation (SWAPO) von Namibia, 163.
[170] Ibid.
[171] Ibid.
[172] Interview Hans-Georg Schleicher, Berlin, 20.02.2016. See also Schleicher, 'GDR Solidarity', 1069–1153.
[173] BStU, MfS-HAII, Nr. 28977, Südfrikanische Volksorganisation (SWAPO) von Namibia, 160–161.
[174] See Babing, *Gegen Rassismus*, 1977–1982, Rede Honecker auf der Wissenschaftlichen Internationalen Konferenz, 'Der gemeinsame Kampf der Arbeiterbewegung und der nationalen Befreiungsbewegung gegen Imperialismus, für sozialen Fortschritt', 20.10.1980, 425–432.

mibia and, therefore, the GDR demanded the implementation of coercive measures against South Africa.[175]

Interestingly, Julius Nyerere, the President of Tanzania, presumed that the Soviet Union was hoping the WCG's efforts would fail, for Moscow harboured doubts about SWAPO's allegiance to Marxism.[176] There was thus no guarantee that a SWAPO-led Namibia would benefit Moscow's power interests in the region. The MfS made a similar observation, pointing out that the 'political-ideological maturity level of the SWAPO leadership was still inadequate' in the late 1970s. Thus, the MfS was concerned that northern Europe's socialist democratic parties, such as the SPD, might gain increasing influence over SWAPO through extensive material assistance.[177] Hence, SWAPO's apparent weak sense of ideological affiliation to the communist-bloc was a further factor that motivated East Berlin to increase its commitment to SWAPO in the late 1970s. Understandably perhaps, both Moscow and East Berlin wanted to make sure that SWAPO's allegiance to the communist bloc would not crumble after Namibia achieved national independence. Neither Moscow nor East Berlin had reason to believe that SWAPO's affiliation to the communist bloc was indeed meaningful, which invited the assumption that SWAPO might turn towards the West should the WCG succeed in negotiating a settlement.

However, the WCG's efforts were marked by Pretoria's stubborn defence of the status quo in Namibia. The 'Western Five' tried to convince Pretoria that the failure to find a satisfactory solution for Namibia would have 'catastrophic consequences' at the UN, while simultaneously advising SWAPO to be moderate and realistic in its demands.[178] In fact, the Foreign Office motivated Genscher to warn Pretoria 'not to think that there could be an internationally acceptable negotiated solution that would give some sort of guarantee against a SWAPO election victory'. SWAPO, on the other hand, 'should not hope for a formula that guaranteed election victory in advance'.[179]

Although noteworthy advances were limited in 1977, the West German representative in the WCG, Hans-Joachim Vergau, pointed out that the acceptance of free and fair elections was a significant improvement, as it replaced the 'presumptuous claim to sole

---

[175] Ibid., Rede des Stellvertreters des Ministers für Auswärtige Angelegenheiten und Ständigen Vertreters der DDR bei den Vereinten Nationen, Peter Florin, auf der XXXV Tagung der UN-Vollversammlung zu Namibia, 03.03.1981, 462–463.
[176] Vergau, *Negotiating the Freedom*, 35–36.
[177] BStU, MfS-Hauptverwaltung Aufklärung, Nr. 69, Auskunft über Probleme des antiimperialistischen Befreiungskampfes in Zimbabwe und Namibia, 11.04.1978, 200.
[178] Vergau, *Negotiating the Freedom*, 24–27.
[179] PAAA, Zwischenarchiv, Bd. 116841, 1977–1978, Anregung für die Führung des Gesprächs mit dem südafrikanischen Botschafter, 2.

representation'.¹⁸⁰ Indeed, SWAPO's acceptance of democratic elections demonstrated the liberation movement's willingness to support the WCG's efforts. After all, the liberation movement could have insisted on the UN's recognition of SWAPO as the sole representative of the Namibian people. From this perspective, the election process would have been rendered unnecessary. Yet, despite SWAPO's willingness to make some concessions, the liberation movement was firm in its demand for South Africa to withdraw its troops from Namibia before the elections.¹⁸¹ This proved to be the biggest obstacle in late 1977, as Pretoria was not prepared to withdraw South African troops from Namibia while Cuban troops were stationed in Angola.¹⁸² Neither SWAPO nor Pretoria were willing to give in to any further demands. Despite ongoing negotiations with the WCG, Pretoria remained determined to lead the Turnhalle alliance to election victory. Without concealing its objective, Pretoria hoped that the Security Council would accept conditions that favoured the DTA's quest for power. Pretoria was prepared to achieve this objective through an 'internal solution', should the WCG and the Security Council fail to support South African interests in Namibia.¹⁸³ The threat of sanctions left South Africa unfazed, as Pretoria felt secure in the knowledge that most Western governments faced strong internal opposition against sanctions. For those who had hoped to end the election deadlock before the end of 1977, it became apparent in December that no imminent solution was in sight, due to uncompromising demands from both SWAPO and Pretoria.

In early 1978, the United Nations Council for Namibia, which represented Namibia in international conferences and maintained close cooperation with the Organization of African Unity (OAU), submitted a draft declaration and action programme for the joint declaration at the end of the UN General Assembly Special Session on Namibia. Perhaps inevitably, some points were considered unacceptable by the Foreign Office. First, the UN Council for Namibia called on all states to acknowledge SWAPO as the sole representative of the Na-

---

[180] Vergau, *Negotiating the Freedom*, 24. Hans-Joachim Vergau represented West Germany during the 1977 and 1978 negotiations in Cape Town. Known as the 'Gang of Five', Vergau was accompanied by Don McHenry (USA), James Murray (Great Britain), Albert Thabault (France) and Paul Lapointe (Canada).

[181] PAAA, AV Neues Amt, Bd. 7920, Namibia-Initiative; hier: Nujomas jüngste öffentliche Äußerungen in Dar-es-Salaam, Dar es Salaam, 01.02.1978.

[182] See also BStU, MfS-Hauptverwaltung Aufklärung, Nr. 69, Auskunft über Probleme des antiimperialistischen Befreiungskampfes in Zimbabwe und Namibia, 11.04.1978, 201.

[183] Vergau, *Negotiating the Freedom*, 43. Genscher's draft speech for the Special UN Session for Namibia contained the following statement: 'An internal solution would be no solution and thus unacceptable': PAAA, Zwischenarchiv, Bd. 178773, 1978, UN Sondergeneralversammlung über Namibia; hier: Entwurf des Namibia-Rats für Schlussdokument, New York, 22.04.1978; Anhang: Erklärung der Bundesrepublik Deutschland in der Sonder-Generalversammlung über Namibia. See also Rotberg, *Ending Autocracy*, 135–137.

mibian people. Second, South Africa's illegal occupation of Namibia presented a threat to world peace. Third, the Council for Namibia proposed assistance in the armed struggle by all means.[184]

On 2 February 1978, the WCG had already finalised a settlement plan based on Security Council Resolution 385.[185] On 10 February 1978, the WCG, represented in part by the five countries' ambassadors, held further talks with Nujoma and Pik Botha, South Africa's foreign minister. However, the talks failed, as Pretoria sabotaged the negotiations. Initially, SWAPO demanded the withdrawal of all South African troops from Namibia, mainly out of concern that the military would be used to intimidate voters. After SWAPO accepted a contingent of 1,500 South African troops would remain in Namibia, the South African delegation, which had counted on SWAPO to stall the negotiations, left the conference for fear that SWAPO's concession might lead to a settlement.[186] Throughout the talks, Genscher was determined not to let the negotiations break down. When it seemed that he might have contributed to the South African delegations' sudden and impulsive departure by stating that stationing South African troops in Walvis Bay did not fulfil Pretoria's commitment to withdraw troops from Namibia, and that Walvis Bay did not belong to South Africa, he made sure that he got Botha's affirmation that the door was still open for further talks.[187]

---

[184] PAAA, Zwischenarchiv, Bd. 178773, 1978, UN-Sondergeneralversammlung über Namibia; hier: Entwurf des Namibia-Rats für Schlussdokument, 21.04.1978.

[185] See, e.g., PAAA, AV Neues Amt, Bd. 7920, 1978, Initiative der fünf westlichen Sicherheitsratsmitglieder zur Lösung der Namibia-Frage, 06.02.1978; Ibid., Initiative der fünf westlichen Sr-mitglieder zur Lösung der Namibia-Frage, New York, 09.02.1978.

[186] Ibid., Namibia-Initiative; hier: Gespräche mit Vertretern der Front-linien-Staaten, New York, 13.02.1978; Vergau, *Negotiating the Freedom*, 50. For an assessment of Botha's early departure by Hans-Joachim Eick, the West German ambassador in New York, see PAAA, AV Neues Amt, Bd. 7920, 1978, Initiative der fünf westlichen Sicherheitsratsmitglieder zur Lösung der Namibia-Frage; hier: Simultangespräche in New York, 13.02.1978; Ibid., Simultangespräche Namibia in New York; hier: gemeinsame Pressekonferenz der Fünf, New York, 13.02.1978.

[187] See Vergau, *Negotiating the Freedom*, 48–51. That Pretoria might close the door during negotiations was indeed a concern in 1978: PAAA, AV Neues Amt, Bd. 7920, 1978, Namibia-Initiative; hier: Ministergespräche der Fünf mit Südfrika und SWAPO, New York, 12.02.1978. Genscher grew seriously concerned at the prospect that Pretoria might close its door to further talks, which becomes also apparent in the fact that, four weeks after the talks in New York, Genscher sent a personal message to Botha, stating, rather passionately, the following: 'Again, I appeal to you and the South African government not diminish the prospect of success of the proposed Western solution through unilateral impairment'. The main concern was that Pretoria might dismiss the Western solution because of a single issue: Ibid., Betr.: Initiative der Fünf zur Lösung der Namibia-Frage, 01.03.1978. Vorster stated that 'the whole question [of Walvis Bay] was of intense sensitivity and could even lead to the rejection of the whole package': Ibid., Initiative der fünf westlichen SR-Mitglieder zur Lösung der Namibia-Frage; hier: Sondierungen mit Sts. Furie, 17.02.1978.

SWAPO and Pretoria both used sabotaging tactics to thwart the WCG's Namibia initiative, but neither wanted to be responsible for the failure of negotiations.[188] Overall, Pretoria's confidence in the WCG was low, as a number of past General Assembly resolutions were favourable to SWAPO.[189] The WCG acknowledged the unbalanced focus on SWAPO's concerns, pledging a more balanced approach in future.[190] SWAPO found it difficult to trust the WCG, in part because of the Soviet bloc's critical attitude toward the West's Namibia initiative.[191] In late April, Nujoma accused the WCG of having made a secret deal with South Africa.[192] South African troops killed 18 SWAPO guerrillas in Angola in February 1978 and attacked SWAPO's refugee camp at Cassinga in May 1978. The SPD-led government saw the attack on Cassinga as a further attempt by Pretoria to sabotage the negotiations between the WCG and SWAPO.[193] Although South African troops claimed to have been attacked by SWAPO guerrillas on Namibian soil, it is suspicious that the apparent attacks on South African troops coincided with negotiations in New York. Hans-Joachim Eick, the West German Ambassador in New York, expressed his doubts about South Africa's account of events to the Foreign Office, for Pretoria had a strategic interest in underlining the necessity of South African troops in Namibia, particularly during a time of heated settlement negotiations at the UN.[194] The attack on the SWAPO refugee camp, which killed more than 500 men, women and children, clearly served the purpose of sabotaging further negotiations with SWAPO.[195] Sabotage became an integral part of Pretoria's tactic in Namibia in the late 1970s.[196] As expected, Nujoma cancelled further talks with the WCG.

---

[188] In late 1978 the Federal Government expressed its disappointment with Pretoria's decision to hold elections in Namibia without UN supervision, thus undermining the Western Namibia plan, which was almost ready for implementation. See PAAA, AV Neues Amt, Bd. 15817, 1977–1983, Namibia; hier: Reaktion der Bundesregierung auf die südfrikanische Entscheidung vom 19.09.1978 Wahlen in Namibia abzuhalten.

[189] Ibid.

[190] Vergau, *Negotiating the Freedom*, 52. See also BStU, MfS-Hauptverwaltung Aufklärung Nr. 21, 12.04.1982, Aktuelle Informationsübersicht Nr. 15/82, BRD-Regierungskreise zur Namibia-Problematik, 338; AAPD, 1979, Band I, Gespräch des Bundesministers Genscher mit dem britischen Außenminister Lord Carrington in London, 11.05.1979, 594.

[191] PAAA, Zwischenarchiv, Bd. 115779, 1977–1979, Namibia-Debatte im Plenum der XXXII Generalversammlung; hier: Erklärung u.a. von Mosambik und UDSSR, 24.10.1977.

[192] In the following years, SWAPO, the Soviet Union and the GDR continued to accuse the WCG of having made a pact with Pretoria. See, e.g., PAAA, Zwischenarchiv, Bd. 138100, 1982–1984, Namibia-Konferenz in Paris vom 25.–19.04.1983, Paris, 28.04.1983; PAAA, AV Neues Amt, Bd. 16414, 1983, SR-Debatte über Namibia; hier: Nachmittagssitzung, 31.05.1983.

[193] Deutscher Bundestag, 8. Wahlperiode, Stenographischer Bericht, 100. Sitzung, 22.06.1978, 7968.

[194] PAAA, AV Neues Amt, Bd. 7920, 1978, Initiative der 5 westl. SR-Mitglieder; hier: SA Nachteile-Aktion über Grenze nach Angola, 11.02.1978.

[195] See also Vergau, *Negotiating the Freedom*, 55; Dobell, *Swapo's Struggle*, 70.

[196] See also, H. Melber, 'Namibia-Politik'; W. Martin James III, *A Political History of the Civil War in Angola, 1974–1990*, New Jersey, Transaction Publishers, 1992, 147–149.

By early June, however, there were signs that Nujoma would return to the negotiation table.[197] The WCG gave the West German chancellor Helmut Schmidt, who was scheduled to visit Lagos and Lusaka at the end of June, a mandate to seek out further support from President Obasanjo and, on Schmidt's own initiative, from President Kaunda. Schmidt expressed his understanding of SWAPO's concerns about South African troops in Namibia, from the perspective that it was a legitimate concern to assume that Pretoria's troops might be used to intimidate voters, and he endorsed the re-integration of Walvis Bay into Namibia, leaving little doubt as to where his sympathies lay.[198] The Walvis Bay Resolution 432 of 27 July 1978 emphasised the UN's support for the reintegration of Walvis Bay into Namibia, leaving the fundamental issues of the crisis between SWAPO and Pretoria unchanged.[199] Yet, Resolution 432 represented, as Vergau points out, a small success for the WCG. All African Security Council members agreed to support the WCG's plan, even though the UN had repeatedly condemned the West, and especially Germany, for its cooperation with the apartheid government in Pretoria.[200]

South Africa continued to throw obstacles in the way of the WCG's plan for a transition to independence in Namibia. The UN Secretary General's (SG) plan to provide 7,500 plus 1,560 personnel for the elections came as a shock to Pretoria.[201] Aware of the organisational complexity to dispatch such a substantial contingent to Namibia, Pretoria announced its own election for 20–24 November 1978, later changed to 4–8 December 1978. Despite these unpromising developments, the Security Council approved the WCG's Namibia plan in Resolution 435 of 29 September 1978. Foreign Ministers Vance, Genscher and Owen emphasised to Pretoria that sabotaging the WCG's plan was only pushing SWAPO further into Moscow's arms.[202] Though Pretoria's attitude tested Genscher's patience to the limit, he was not easily intimidated, nor afraid to call attention to himself by grabbing his files and throwing them on the table, as PW Botha and his delegation soon found out.[203] Genscher's solution to the Namibia problem was deeply anchored in the conviction that the UN, and subsequently Resolution 435, was vital in leading Namibia to independence. Genscher con-

---

[197] Deutscher Bundestag, 8. Wahlperiode, Stenographischer Bericht, 100. Sitzung, 22.06.1978, 7968.
[198] Vergau, *Negotiating the Freedom*, 57.
[199] See also PAAA, MfAA, ZR 2765/84, Botschaft Dar es Salaam, Information über Gespräch mit Repräsentanten der SWAPO in Dar es Salaam, Katamila durch Gen. Weitz und Stark, 13.06.1978.
[200] See, e.g., BStU, MfS-ZAIG, Nr. 11475, Aktivitäten transnationale Monopole im Süden Afrikas, 02.05.1977.
[201] See also PAAA, AV Neues Amt, Bd. 7920, 1978, Namibia-Initiative; hier: zweites Vorgespräch mit SWAPO am 10.02.1978 in New York, New York, 11.02.1978; Ibid., Namibia-Initiative; hier: Gespräche mit Vertretern der Front-linien-staaten, New York, 13.02.1978.
[202] Vergau, *Negotiating the Freedom*, 66.
[203] Ibid., 71.

sistently emphasised the need to adhere to Resolution 435, and was uncompromising in his demand for all parties to observe the following main demands of the resolution. First, South Africa must withdraw its illegal administration of Namibia and transfer power to the Namibian people with the assistance of the UN. A UN Transitional Assistance Group (UNTAG) would ensure the early independence of Namibia through free and fair elections. SWAPO should sign and observe ceasefire provisions. South Africa should co-operate with the Secretary-General in the implementation of this resolution. All unilateral measures taken by the illegal administration in Namibia in relation to the electoral process, including unilateral registration of voters, or transfer of power, in contravention of Security Council Resolution 385 and 431 and this resolution were null and void.[204]

As it intended, Pretoria held an election between 4 and 8 December, which the DTA won with 82.2% of the votes.[205] Genscher wasted no time in declaring the election null and void.[206] In November 1978, the UN condemned, in Resolution 439, South Africa's single-handed attempt to force its 'internal solution' on Namibia. After the election Pretoria declared its willingness to participate in further negotiations but at the same time tried to advance its own agenda in Namibia. This time, its plan included bringing the DTA into the negotiation process, hoping 'to manoeuvre the internal solution somehow into an international one', as Vergau points out.[207] The 1970s ended without a solution to the crisis in Namibia. As critics of the WCG initiative have pointed out: 'The WCG in fact managed by means of diluted and inconsequent diplomatic 'tug-of-war' to offer South Africa the time bargained for to implement her own policy without any serious sanctions imposed'.[208]

---

[204] For Resolution 435 see un.org/documents – Security Council Resolutions.
[205] Udogu, *Liberating Namibia*, 58.
[206] See also Chapter Two, FDP.
[207] Vergau, *Negotiating the Freedom*, 72.
[208] H. Melber, 'Federal Republic'.

6 East and West German rivalry: the early to mid-1980s

In the early 1980s Pretoria continued to present South Africa as a bulwark against communism, while West Germany, including other Western countries, continued to warn Pretoria that its racial policies and the defence of the status quo promoted communism in southern Africa.[1] Genscher continued to complain that 'Pretoria does not understand that a peaceful solution to the Namibia problem will reduce the Soviet influence in southern Africa'.[2] The problem was, however, not that Pretoria was reluctant to recognise the dynamics of the Cold War, but rather that it used the East-West conflict to justify policies that supported the continuation of minority rule. In this context, Pretoria made it clear that South Africa was 'unwilling to accept a pro-Soviet government in a future autonomous Namibia'.[3] That a SWAPO government would turn Namibia into a de facto pro-Soviet state was used as a justification for Pretoria's reluctance to support majority rule in Namibia.[4]

Thus, the 1980s started with no sign of a breakthrough in the deadlock over the Namibia question. The election in Rhodesia/Zimbabwe in April 1980 only confirmed to Pretoria the dangers of free elections, as Robert Mugabe emerged triumphant, while the Pretoria-backed UANC party and its leader, Bishop Muzorewa, won only three out of 100 seats.[5] Furthermore, the DTA was rapidly losing support in Namibia, which raised questions about the DTA's significance in shaping Namibia's future.[6] There was no political party in Namibia in the early 1980s that received unquestionable support from Pretoria, or represented a challenge to SWAPO.[7] The deadlock over Namibia's independence triggered a growing demand for sanctions against South Africa, which West Germany declined to support. SWAPO and the GDR accused West Germany of supporting South Africa's neocolonial solution for Namibia. This led to an intensification of the SED's political and diplomatic support for SWAPO in the early

---

[1] See PAAA, Zwischenarchiv, Bd. 138104, 1984–1985, Namibia Regionalpolitik im südlichen Afrika; hier: Offizielle Darstellungen der amerikanischen Regionalpolitik im letzten Quartal 1984, 17.01.1985. See also Vergau, *Negotiating the Freedom*, 65–66.

[2] AAPA, 1983, Band II, Ministerialdirigent Schauer, z. Z. Helsinki an das Auswärtige Amt; Betr.: BM-Besuch in Helsinki, 03.11.1983, 1616–1620.

[3] 'Namibias Unabhängigkeit in weiter Ferne', *Frankfurter Allgemeine Zeitung*, 24.07.1981.

[4] Although the DTA claimed to represent the majority of the Namibian population, there was no proof to bear out such an assertion, particularly after the turn of the decade. See PAAA, Zwischenarchiv, Bd. 127477, 1981, Politische Halbjahresberichte; hier: Namibia, 12.03.1981.

[5] See R. von Lucius, 'Sam Nujoma (SWAPO) in Bonn', *Africa Journal*, No. 2, Jan/Feb 1981, 6.

[6] See AAPD, 1979, Band I, Gespräch des Bundesministers Genscher mit dem britischen Außenminister Lord Carrington in London, 11.05.1979, 594.

[7] 'Namibias Unabhängigkeit in weiter Ferne', *Frankfurter Allgemeine Zeitung*, 24.07.1981. See also Vergau, *Negotiating the Freedom*, 77–78.

1980s. On the diplomatic front, the objective was to underline the GDR's support of UN plans for Namibia. There was, however, a strong conviction that only coercive diplomacy could force Pretoria to comply with UN demands.[8]

The ever-increasing involvement in southern African affairs of the Soviet Union and its 'helper states' became a growing cause for tension between the SPD-led government and the CDU/CSU opposition. Although the government acknowledged the CDU/CSU concerns about the GDR's presence in Africa, and the Soviet Union's growing influence in southern Africa, the SPD approached the issue from a fundamentally different angle. While the CDU and, even more so, the CSU demanded pressure be exerted on the frontiers of Soviet influence in southern Africa, the SPD-led government concentrated its efforts on patiently trying to sway independent African states and liberation movements away from the Soviet bloc.[9] The SPD's objective was not, however, to convince African countries and liberation movements to align with the West, but to help them achieve independence without aligning with, or against, any of the major ideological blocs. In this respect, the Federal Government's move towards SWAPO in the late 1970s can also be understood within the wider context of the non-alignment principles. The goal was to improve African countries' and liberation movements' means to reduce their dependency on the Soviet bloc. This freedom from dependency could only be achieved by means of increasing Western solidarity with the liberation struggles in southern Africa. One main hindrance to such freedom was the high degree of polarisation in Africa due to the complex Cold War alliance systems. Once a major power bloc established an alliance with a liberation movement, political party or independent African state, ideological allegiance became an unspoken expectation, leaving little room for a middle ground. Nonetheless, Genscher by and large supported the non-aligned principles in the early 1980s, advising liberation movements to move towards the middle ground.[10]

In any case, South Africa was in no rush to end the deadlock in the early 1980s. Pretoria anticipated that the upcoming West German election would bring the conservative CDU/CSU to power, which also offered the prospect of Genscher's departure from his post as

---

[8] See PAAA, MfAA, ZR 1634/83, 1979–1981, Ministerrat der Deutschen Demokratischen Republik, der Minister für Auswärtige Angelegenheiten an Erich Honecker, Hermann Axen und Joachim Herrmann, 10.05.1981; Ibid., Vorsitzenden des Koordinierungsbüro der nichtpaktgebundenen Staaten, 14.04.1981. See also *Neues Deutschland*, SWAPO verurteilt westliche Manöver, 30.04.1981; Ibid., Afrika fest entschlossen zur Befreiung Namibias, Lothar Killmer, 05.05.1981; Ibid., Bonn stützt Pretorias Okkupationspolitik, 15.10.1980; Ibid., Sanktionen gegen Südafrika wurden durch Veto verhindert, 02.05.1981.
[9] See Chapter Three, The *Bundestag*.
[10] See PAAA, Zwischenarchiv, Bd. 138100, 1982–1984, Besuch von SWAPO-Präsident Sam Nujoma in Bonn am 01. und 02. Juni 1982, 03.06.1982.

foreign minister.¹¹ Pretoria perceived Genscher as not necessarily a friend of South Africa, mainly because of his good relations with Nujoma and his continued insistence on the implementation of UN Resolution 435. Moreover, Pretoria had reservations about the SPD-led government, for it was feared that radical left-wing elements within the SPD might take over the government. There were also concerns that *Ostpolitik* might lead to closer ties between West Germany and the Soviet bloc. After all, Pretoria's domestic and regional policies were deeply rooted in anti-communism.¹² The CDU/CSU, on the other hand, was supportive of Pretoria's tough stance on southern African issues. Furthermore, the British electorate had already voted in a conservative government under the leadership of Margaret Thatcher in 1979, while the US election in late 1980 promised to bring the conservative Ronald Reagan to power. Thus, Pretoria had reason to believe that such fundamental political changes within three of the five WCG countries would alter the WCG's approach. Lord Carrington, the British foreign minister, told Genscher that Pretoria believed that South Africa could 'expect more sympathy' from the conservative government in Britain than it had received from the previous labour government. In the same context, Genscher saw Pretoria's 'hope for advantageous change in Western countries', including in West Germany, as a hindrance to the WCG's efforts to find a negotiated solution.¹³ Hence, with US and West German elections not far off, Pretoria saw little reason to implement any drastic changes to the status quo in Namibia. As Pretoria had hoped, the Reagan administration was prepared to introduce changes to Resolution 435, not least because the US viewed the Soviet Union as part of the problem.¹⁴

On 12 July 1982, the WCG attached to Resolution 435, under Annex C, the following constitutional principles: firstly, the Constitutional Assembly must be elected according to democratic rules; secondly, the electoral system will satisfy its duty of fair representation in the Constitutional Assembly; thirdly, basic rights and principles, as listed in Annex C, for government and administration.¹⁵ The aim was to protect the rule of law and the fair representation of all parties in parliament.¹⁶ Although the SPD-led government, especially Genscher, emphasised the need for a democratic electoral process in Namibia, particularly by giving

---

11   See Vergau, *Negotiating the Freedom*, 77–78.
12   Dedering, 'Ostpolitik', 14–17.
13   AAPD, 1979, Band I, Gespräch des Bundesministers Genscher mit dem britischen Außenminister Lord Carrington in London, 11.05.1979, 595. See also Ibid., Band II, 1979, Gespräch des Bundesministers Genscher mit dem jugoslawischen Außenminister Vrhovec in Zagreb, 16.08.1979, 1124.
14   Ibid., 1981, Band I, Arbeitsbesuch des französischen AM Cheysson in Bonn am 2. Juni 1981; hier: Namibia, 09.06.1981, 884. See also PAAA, Zwischenarchiv, Bd. 127477, 1981, Politischer Halbjahresberichte; hier: Namibia: 08.09.1981; Ibid., Bd. 125282, 1981, Deutsche Namibiapolitik nach den Gesprächen von Washington 21./22. Mai 1981, 26.05.1981.
15   Vergau, *Negotiating the Freedom*, 87. See also 'West-Vorschlag zu Namibia', *Frankfurter Rundschau*, 28.1.1981; 'Neue Gespräche über Namibia', *Frankfurter Allgemeine Zeitung*, 27.10.1981.
16   Those principles were fully incorporated into the Namibian Constitution in 1990.

all candidates and parties equal rights to participate in elections, this did not imply that the Schmidt-Genscher government treated all political parties equally. In late 1981, a delegation of the DTA, under the leadership of its president Peter Kalangula, met Genscher, Strauß and various members of parliament in Bonn.[17] Although the DTA had no reason to anticipate a receptive audience within the SPD-led government, it received prominent support within the CDU/CSU.[18] In that regard, the 'ostentatious closeness' between CDU/CSU and DTA might have undermined a rapid approximation between Genscher and the DTA, as Engel suggests.[19] Genscher harboured reservations about the DTA's close ties with Pretoria, but considered all political parties important in shaping Namibia's future.[20] Overall, Genscher's attitude reflected the SPD's approach towards the DTA, which had openly expressed its reluctance to meet Kalangula, but without rejecting the DTA's role in Namibia.[21] Generally, there appeared to be little common ground between the Schmidt-Genscher government and the DTA, which was also reflected in a statement by the DTA president Kuaima Riruako: 'The Federal Government is the only power amongst the five [WCG] to step out of line, standing unconditionally behind SWAPO. This is Genscher's policy. If we, the elected representatives of the people, go to Bonn, he will not meet us'.[22]

Interactions with Pretoria's protégé became increasingly complicated after the SPD-led government moved closer to SWAPO.[23] The DTA and Pretoria argued along similar lines that

---

[17] See PAAA, Zwischenarchiv, Bd. 127477, 1981, Namibia-Initiative der westlichen Fünf; hier: Gesprächstermin für den DTA-Präsidenten Kalangula beim Bundesminister, 15.07.1981.

[18] By 1983, support for the DTA remained particularly strong within the CSU but decreased within the CDU: PAAA, Zwischenarchiv, Bd. 138099, 1982–1983, 'Demokratische Turnhallen Allianz' (DTA); hier: Gespräch BM-Dirk Mudge zwischen 14. und 17.06.1983, 24.05.1983.

[19] Engel, *Die Afrikapolitik*, 173.

[20] See PAAA, Zwischenarchiv, Bd. 138099, 1982–1984, 'Demokratische Turnhallen Allianz' (DTA); hier: Gespräch BM-Dirk Mudge zwischen 14. und 17.06.1983, 24.05. 1983. In retrospect, Genscher stated that he 'clearly distanced himself' from Pretoria: Genscher, *Erinnerungen*, 467.

[21] *Allgemeine Zeitung*, DTA-Delegation setzt sich durch, 30.11.1981.

[22] M. Germ, 'Zorn in Windhoek über Bonns Politik', *Die Rheinpfalz*, 24.10.1980. The accusation was not entirely justified, for representatives of the Foreign Office met DTA representatives in 1979 and 1980, while Genscher met DTA representatives twice in 1978: PAAA, Zwischenarchiv, Bd. 127747, 1981, Namibia-Initiative der westlichen Fünf; hier: Gesprächstermin für den DTA-Präsidenten Kalangula beim Bundesminister, 15.07.1981; Ibid., Besuch einer DTA-Delegation in Bonn, 24.07.1981. Genscher's tied schedule did not allow a meeting in 1980. However, the DTA's public relations agency, the Namibia Information Office, wanted to create the impression that Genscher was eager to meet the DTA in West Germany and thus arranged for a DTA delegation to travel to Bonn. The Foreign Office later stated that it was the DTA's clumsiness with regard to arranging a suitable date that stood in the way of meeting the Foreign Minister during the DTA's Bonn visit in late 1980. Finally, Genscher met a DTA delegation in late 1981: Ibid., Besuch DTA-Präsident Kalangula in Bonn, 26.11.1981. See also Engel, *Die Afrikapolitik*, 173–174.

[23] However, SWAPO found it difficult to believe that there were no contacts between the SPD-led government and the DTA, for members of the DTA frequently met with members of the government and the *Bundestag* in Bonn: AAPD, 1982, Band I, Gespräch des Bundesministers Genscher

a SWAPO government would lead to dependence on the GDR or Cuba, once Namibia became detached from South African rule. The DTA substantiated its assertion by claiming that the GDR was committed to establishing, through the education of 'SWAPO-cadres and SWAPO-majors', an infrastructure that would lead to a 'people's republic in Namibia'.[24] Similarly, Kalangula stated that 'SWAPO wants one-party rule and can only rule with the support of the Soviet Union, Cuba and the GDR'.[25] Yet, the DTA's alarmist verbiage did not lead to any improvement in relations with Bonn. To the contrary, the SPD parliamentarian, Wolfgang Roth, declared in late 1981 that SWAPO can 'rest assured' of the SPD's support, which was clearly not intended to improve relations with the DTA.[26] Nonetheless, the DTA celebrated its Bonn visit as further proof of its recognition on the international stage.[27]

Yet, the SPD's change in approach to SWAPO did not produce immediate results, as the liberation movement found it difficult to trust the West.[28] This also becomes evident in the fact that Nujoma visiting Bonn for the first time in late 1980, although Genscher had invited Nujoma numerous times between the late 1970s and early 1980.[29] However, the *Frankfurter Allgemeine* newspaper suggested that the GDR played no small part in SWAPO's reluctance to increase direct contact with Bonn.[30] During Nujoma's first Bonn visit, the news magazine *Der Spiegel* used this opportunity to ask the SWAPO leader personally whether he declined earlier invitations 'out of fear to anger his friends in East Berlin'. Nujoma avoided the question by stating that there simply had been too many differences with the Federal Government in the past.[31] Although Nujoma was probably not entirely truthful, relations between SWAPO and the SPD-led government had indeed improved by the time of his first Bonn visit.[32] The Foreign Office also observed that Nujoma displayed 'spontaneous reactions of

---

mit dem französischen Außenminister Cheysson, 18.02.1982, 887.

[24] 'Turnhallen-Allianz erinnert in Bonn an Macht der SWAPO', *Die Welt*, 09.09.1981.

[25] 'Turnhallen-Allianz siegessicher', *Saarbrücker Zeitung*, 10.09.1981.

[26] 'DTA-Delegation setzt sich durch', *Allgemeine Zeitung*, 30.11.1981.

[27] Ibid.

[28] See AAPD, 1981, Band I, Arbeitsbesuch des französischen AM Cheysson in Bonn am 2. Juni 1981; hier: Namibia, 09.06.1981, 884.

[29] PAAA, Zwischenarchiv, Bd. 127477, 1981, Besuch des SWAPO-Präsidenten Sam Nujoma vom 23. bis 27. Oktober 1980 in der Bundesrepublik; hier: Ablauf und Wertung, 27.10.1980; Ibid., Afrikapolitik der Bundesregierung; hier: Zusammenarbeit mit Befreiungsbewegungen, 02.01.1982. See also Ibid., Besuch des SWAPO-Präsidenten Sam Nujoma vom 23. bis 27. Oktober 1980 in der Bundesrepublik; hier: Ablauf und Wertung, 27.10.1981; Ibid., Namibia-Initiative der westlichen Fünf; hier: Gesprächstermin für den DTA-Präsidenten Kalangula beim Bundesminister, 15.07.1981.

[30] See R. von Lucius, 'Terroristen oder Freiheitskämpfer?', *Frankfurter Allgemeine Zeitung*, 22.10.1980.

[31] 'Bonn war nicht freundlich zu uns', *Der Spiegel*, 45/1980, 03.11.1980.

[32] PAAA, Zwischenarchiv, Bd. 127477, 1981, Besuch des SWAPO-Präsidenten Sam Nujoma vom 23. bis 27. Oktober 1980 in der Bundesrepublik; hier: Ablauf und Wertung, 27.10.1980. At the

sympathy' towards Genscher during his Bonn visit.[33] Nonetheless, evidence indicates that SWAPO was also concerned about a potentially negative impact on its relations with the Soviet bloc, and the GDR in particular.[34]

It was with growing concern that East Berlin watched the SPD-led government's carefully coordinated rapprochement with SWAPO. Overall, there was little doubt in the Foreign Office that the GDR was actively engaged in advising SWAPO against trusting West Germany.[35] East Berlin harboured two major concerns. There was unease that West Germany's improving relations with SWAPO might weaken GDR-SWAPO relations. And it was feared that Bonn's attempt to improve relations with SWAPO was part of an overall strategy to divide and weaken the liberation movement.[36] Ultimately, these concerns also derived from West Germany's strong economic position, for East Berlin seemed to believe that SWAPO was willing to lean sharply towards West Germany in return for extensive economic assistance.[37]

By mid-1981, however, the reverse was the case, mainly because SWAPO questioned Schmidt and Genscher's commitment to Resolution 435, for the SPD-led government was tied to Reagan's foreign policy due to Schmidt's 'double track decision' to deploy US middle-range missiles in Germany.[38] SWAPO believed that Schmidt's double track strategy had moved the SPD-led government closer to Washington. The liberation movement found it difficult to trust any government that had co-operative agreements with the Reagan administration for it was widely believed that Reagan was seeking ways 'to circumvent Resolution 435 and enforce constitutional guarantees for the white minority'.[39] SWAPO was particularly

---

   invitation of Genscher, Nujoma visited Bonn in October 1980 and June 1982.
[33] Ibid., Bd. 178820, 1977–1980, Talks between SWAPO-President Nujoma and Foreign Minister Genscher in Bonn, 23.10.1980, 8. See also AAPD, 1978, Band I, Begegnung Bundesminister-Sam Nujoma, Präsident der SWAPO, in New York am 12.02.1978, 20.02.1978, 276; H. J. Vergau, 'Die Verhandlungen um die Freiheit Namibias (1977–1990) als Vorstufe zur friedlichen Überwindung der Apartheid in Südafrika', in K. Brauckhoff and I. Schwaetzer (eds.), *Hans Dietrich Genscher Außenpolitik*, Wiesbaden, Springer Fachmedien, 2015, 119–122.
[34] PAAA, Zwischenarchiv, Bd. 116802, 1977–1978, Gespräch mit SWAPO-Vertreter, Lusaka, 15.06.1978; Ibid., Afrika-Reise einer Delegation des SPD Parteivorstands, 20.11.1978.
[35] AAPD, 1978, Band I, Begegnung Bundesminister-Sam Nujoma, Präsident der SWAPO, in New York am 12.02.1978, 20.02.1978, 276.
[36] PAAA, MfAA, ZR 1133/87, 1976–1985, Zur Entwicklung im südlichen Afrika unter besonderer Berücksichtigung des Namibia-Problems, Luanda, 21.08.1981.
[37] Such concerns would not have been unwarranted, for Nujoma declared in mid-1981 that SWAPO does not 'fight for Soviet interests' and will after independence establish, similar to Angola, extensive trade relations with the West: AAPA, 1981, Band 1, SWAPO; hier: Nujoma-Besuch in Bonn vom 25. bis 27.05.1981, 29.05.1981, 873.
[38] PAAA, MfAA, ZR 2765/84, Botschaft Luanda an ZK der SED, IV, Genossen Sieber treffen mit Genossen Sam Nujoma, 15.05.1981.
[39] Ibid. See also Ibid., Bd. 125282, 1981, Gespräch BM-Nujoma vom 26.05.1981; hier: BM-Brief an AM Haig, 26.05.1981.

peeved at the Reagan administration for 'lumping SWAPO into a group of international terrorist movements' and 'perceiving it as proxy of a foreign power'.[40] Importantly, Genscher actively tried to improve relations between Washington and SWAPO, emphasising that a form of bilateral trust was required between the West and SWAPO.[41] Thus, despite visible improvements in relations with SWAPO under the Schmidt-Genscher government, political realities dampened co-operation between West Germany and SWAPO in the early 1980s.[42]

In the early 1980s, it seemed that there was little reason to expect real progress in Namibia, not least because the newly elected Reagan administration was determined to confront the Soviet Union.[43] Thus, Reagan's foreign policy immediately assumed a more confrontational posture toward the Soviet bloc in southern Africa.[44] Yet, Reagan's aggressive approach had little effect on the GDR's close relations with SWAPO. The GDR's solidarity with liberation movements was not easily shaken by Western interference, partly because the GDR viewed it as prestige projects, and partly because it promised potential rewards.[45] Yet, despite the GDR's tight relations with SWAPO, the SED viewed the SPD-led government's move towards SWAPO a threat to both the GDR's tangible and intangible interests. Hence, East Germany focused its attention on gaining greater influence over the liberation movement. Andreas

---

[40] PAAA, Zwischenarchiv, Bd. 125282, 1981, SWAPO-Presseerklärung vom 13.05.1981, Luanda, 15.05.1981.

[41] See, e.g., Ibid., BM-Brief an AM Mc Guigan, 26.05.1981; Ibid., Gespräch BM-Nujoma vom 26.05.1981; hier: Brief BM an Lord Carrington, 26.05.1881; Ibid., Gespräch BM-Nujoma vom 26.05.1981; hier: BM-Brief an AM Haig, 26.05.1981. Chester Crocker stated the following: 'Before the WCG suspended its active group diplomacy, Genscher made efforts to strengthen our US contacts and communication with SWAPO leaders'. E-mail interview with Chester Crocker, 25.08.2016.

[42] See also PAAA, Zwischenarchiv, Bd. 125293, 1983, Namibia-Initiative der westlichen Fünf; hier: Gesprächsunterlagen für Treffen Bundesminister mit AM Schultz am 08.05.1983 in Paris, 04.05.1983. Nujoma's first Bonn visit further improved relations between West Germany and SWAPO. A second visit in 1981 continued this trend, but did not dispel SWAPO's distrust of West Germany. See, e.g., PAAA, Zwischenarchiv, Bd. 127477, 1981, Besuch des SWAPO-Präsidenten Sam Nujoma vom 23. bis 27. Oktober 1980 in der Bundesrepublik; hier: Ablauf und Wertung, 27.10.1980; Ibid., Bd. 127477, 1981, Namibia-Initiative; hier: Neues Gespräch des Bundesministers mit SWAPO-Präsident Nujoma, 05.05.1981; Ibid., SWAPO-Politik nach Europareise Nujomas im Mai 1981, 10.06.1981; PAAA, MfAA, ZR 2765/84, Botschaft Luanda an ZK der SED, IV, Genossen Sieber, Treffen mit Genossen Sam Nujoma, 15.05.1981.

[43] M. Turner, 'Foreign Policy and the Reagan administration', in J. D. Lees and M. Turner (eds.), *Reagan's First Four Years: A new Beginning?*, Manchester, Manchester University Press, 1988, 125–152.

[44] In 1981, Nujoma accused Reagan of 'integrating Namibia into his East-West strategy'. Nujoma's accusation was based on Reagan's doctrine of rolling back communism, which subsequently led to a strong focus on the presence of Cuban troops in Angola: PAAA, Zwischenarchiv, Bd. 125282, 1981, Gespräch BM-Nujoma vom 26.05.1981; hier: BM-Brief an AM Haig, 26.05.1981, 872.

[45] For more information about the GDR's deeper motives behind its solidarity with liberation movements, see Chapter Two, SED.

Shipanga, the leader of SWAPO-D, a breakaway faction of SWAPO, went so far as to label SWAPO 'a puppet of the East Germans'.[46]

Furthermore, the rivalry between the communist East and capitalist West over influence in Namibia made SWAPO, as the potential future Government of Namibia, a strategically significant ally. Although the SPD-led government might not have based its revision of West Germany's approach towards SWAPO on strategic calculations in the late 1970s, East Berlin interpreted Bonn's change in course as an attempt to gain influence over SWAPO, and subsequently, post-independence Namibia.[47]

One month prior to the DTA's Bonn visit, during Pik Botha's first meeting with the Reagan administration in Washington, both Reagan and Botha expressed the view that SWAPO was a firm ally of Moscow, East Berlin and Havana.[48] After the meeting, Botha emphasised that Washington and Pretoria had articulated common foreign policy objectives, namely to roll back the Soviet advance in southern Africa.[49] Reagan's understanding of the conflicts in southern Africa was based on the notion that Moscow aggressively tried to gain influence over one of the strategically vital regions in Africa. Given that Reagan was determined to push back the influence of the Soviet Union in the region, there was no reason to challenge Pretoria's claim of fighting Soviet aggression in southern Africa. Thus, the DTA had reason to feel increasingly confident, not least because opposition to SWAPO seemed to be growing under the Reagan administration. In 1983, the DTA argued that it was the only party that could unite all Namibians, claiming that Resolution 435 was finally 'dead'.[50] Yet, the DTA and Pretoria's hope of a friendly government in Bonn after the general elections were disappointed. Although Kohl won the 1983 election, the new conservative-liberal government gave Pretoria little reason for celebration, although the CDU/CSU had largely supported the Namibian election of 1978 and, therefore, promised to bring a new approach to the Namibia question. Kohl's election-pact with the FDP underlined continuity in foreign policy, which was a depressing realisation for those who had hoped for a change of direction after the general elections.[51] That Kohl did not appoint Strauß, a passionate DTA supporter, into his

---

[46] 'Bonn war nicht freundlich zu uns', *Der Spiegel,* 45/1980, 03.11.1980.
[47] See, e.g., PAAA, MfAA, ZR 2763/84, 1981–1984, Bericht über die Konsultation der Abteilung Ost und Zentralafrika mit dem sowjetischen Außenministerium, 21.06.1984, 9; Ibid., ZR 1133/87, 1976–1985, Zur Entwicklung im südlichen Afrika unter besonderer Berücksichtigung des Namibia-Problems, Luanda, 21.08.1981.
[48] See PAAA, Zwischenarchiv, Bd. 125282, 1981, SWAPO-Presseerklärung vom 13.05.1981, Luanda, 15.05.1981.
[49] Ibid., Namibia-Initiative der Fünf; hier: Pressekonferenz AM Bothas vom 17.05.1981 bei Rückkehr von seinem US-Besuch, Pretoria, 18.05.1981.
[50] PAAA, AV Neues Amt, Bd. 16413, 1983, Namibia-Initiative; hier: BM-Gespräch mit DTA-Delegation, Bonn AA, 15.06.1983.
[51] Jürgen Todenhöfer (CDU) saw the elections as the most democratic elections in Africa so far,

cabinet was another blow against change, though this did not prevent Strauß from acting as though he was foreign minister. Foreign policy disputes between Genscher and Strauß littered West German newspapers throughout the greater part of the 1980s.[52]

After the Namibian election of 1978, the CDU/CSU had declared that the DTA's election win confirmed its position as the actual representative of the Namibian people. Thus, SWAPO's claim to rightfully occupy this position was, for the CDU/CSU, no longer sustainable.[53] Genscher's continuation as foreign minister made it, however, impossible for Kohl to ignore SWAPO's role in Namibia's future. This presented a problem for Kohl, for the previous SPD-led government's move towards SWAPO had received little approval within the CDU/CSU.[54] The conservative coalition perceived the DTA as a democratic-orientated political party, worthy of receiving Bonn's undivided support. The difficulty of achieving some degree of cooperation with Genscher's policy towards Namibia was further emphasised by the fact that CDU/CSU delegates met DTA representatives six times in West Germany between 1980 and 1983.[55]

In mid-1983, the DTA met the newly elected chancellor in Bonn.[56] The meeting raised doubts about Kohl's preparedness to continue his predecessor's Namibia policy.[57] After all, Kohl was the first German chancellor and Western head of state willing to receive the DTA.[58] DTA President Kuaime Riruako was full of praise for the new chancellor, whom he saw bet-

---

while the CDU/CSU election observers Hans Hugo Klein (CDU), Hans Klein (CSU) and Paul Hugo Hammans (CDU) found only small and insignificant mistakes in an otherwise impeccable election process. See Brenke, *Die Bundesrepublik*, 181.

[52] See, e.g., R. von Lucius, 'Die künftige Politik Bonns gegenüber dem südlichen Afrika gewinnt Konturen', *Frankfurter Allgemeine Zeitung*, 25.04.1983; 'Strauß passt Afrika-Kurs nicht', *Frankfurter Rundschau*, 07.03.1984; 'Strauß kritisiert erneut Genschers Südafrika-Politik', *dpa*, 06.03.1984; 'Einigung auf neue Namibia-Politik in Bonn', *Frankfurter Allgemeine Zeitung*, 27.03.1987; W. Ebert, 'Der neue Außenminister', *Die Zeit*, 05.02.1988.

[53] Brenke, *Die Bundesrepublik*, 181.

[54] See, e.g., 'DTA-Delegation setzt sich durch', *Allgemeine Zeitung*, 30.11.1981; DUD, Nr. 12, 34. Jahrgang, 17.01.1980. See also Chapter Two, CDU/CSU.

[55] Brenke, *Die Bundesrepublik*, 182. DTA representatives met CDU/CSU delegates in December 1980. Kalangula met representatives of several West German parties twice in 1980. Katuutire Kaura, the DTA's spokesman for foreign affairs, visited Bonn in 1982 and Kohl met the DTA in June 1983.

[56] PAAA, AV Neues Amt, Bd. 16413, 1983, Namibia-Initiative, Gespräch BK mit DTA-Vorsitzendem Mudge, Bonn AA, 15.06.1983.

[57] To make matters worse, the CSU claimed two months before the DTA-Kohl meeting in Bonn that the Kohl government was about to introduce 'deep reaching changes' to its Africa, South Africa and Namibia policy: PAAA, Zwischenarchiv, Bd. 138099, 1982–1984, Südafrika/Namibia-Politik der Bundesregierung; hier: CSU-Äußerung über tiefgreifende Veränderungen, 15.04.1983. Strauß claimed in early 1983 that Kohl was supporting his approach towards Namibia and therefore will terminate Bonn's support for SWAPO: ibid., Deutsche Namibia Politik, 31.03.1983.

[58] See, e.g., K. Jonas, 'Wende in Bonns Namibia-Politik?', *Die Welt*, 18.06.1983; G. Schröder, 'Im Burenstaat kommt der Reformzug in Bewegung', *Die Welt*, 13.07.1983.

ter suited than his predecessor, mainly because 'Kohl knows how to listen and wants to do something for Namibia', as he explained.[59] The unexpected reappointment of the old foreign minister generated little enthusiasm within the DTA. With Genscher's influence not waning in the foreseeable future, it is hardly surprising that Riruako carefully worded his criticism against Genscher. In stark contrast to past statements, the DTA President assumed rather diplomatically that the foreign minister was, with regard to Namibia, 'too preoccupied with his own ideas'.[60] Dirk Mudge, the founder of the DTA, was equally careful with his words, expressing concerns about Genscher's close relations with SWAPO and the 'too simplistic' emphasis on Resolution 435.[61]

Both Mudge and Riruako rejected elections under UN supervision due to the UN General Assembly recognition of SWAPO as the sole representative of the Namibian people: 'You cannot expect from us that we accept a referee, who is already the trainer of one of the teams [SWAPO]'.[62] Obviously, the DTA had little reason to be overly optimistic about the newly elected Kohl government. The CSU remained the DTA's most reliable advocate in Bonn, with Strauß at the forefront of its campaign against the continuation of the Genscherian Namibia policy.[63] In this context, in 1983, Strauß voiced the following demands. First, to terminate all support for SWAPO. Second, to renounce Resolution 435. Third, to reopen the consulate in Windhoek. Fourth, to support the parties of the transitional government.[64]

Though the Kohl government confirmed the continuation of its predecessor's Namibia policy in early May 1983, Genscher left no doubt about his intention to neither reopen the consulate in Windhoek nor terminate relations with SWAPO.[65] Genscher underlined his position by meeting Nujoma in Bonn in September 1983. Accordingly, in a letter to Kohl, delegates of the CDU/CSU strongly opposed Nujoma's visit to Bonn.[66] Although the CDU/CSU

---

[59] K. Jonas, 'Wende in Bonns Namibia-Politik?', *Die Welt*, 18.06.1983.
[60] Ibid.
[61] PAAA, Neues Amt, Bd. 16414, Gespräche Bk mit DTA-Vorsitzendem Mudge, Bonn, 15.06.1983. For an account of Namibia's path to independence from the perspective of the founder of the DTA, see D. Mudge, *All the way to an independent Namibia*, Pretoria, Protea Book House, 2016.
[62] K. Jonas, 'Wende in Bonns Namibia-Politik?', *Die Welt*, 18.06.1983. The DTA also complained that the UN gave SWAPO favourable treatment over the DTA. See PAAA, Neues Amt, Bd. 16414, 1983, Namibia Information Office Bonn, 16.06.1983; Ibid., Namibia-Initiative der westlichen Fünf; hier: BM-Gespräch mit DTA-Delegation, 15.06.1983.
[63] See PAAA, Neues Amt, Bd. 16414, Gespräche Bk mit DTA-Vorsitzendem Mudge, Bonn, 15.06.1983.
[64] K. Jonas, 'Wende in Bonns Namibia-Politik?', *Die Welt*, 18.06.1983. See also 'Namibia: Bonn hält an Namibia-Politik und SWAPO-Kontakten fest', *dpa*, 12.05.1983.
[65] See, e.g., 'Namibia-Demokratische Allianz: Bonner Namibia-Politik unverändert', *dpa*, 17.06.1983; R. von Lucius, 'Die künftige Politik Bonns gegenüber dem südlichen Afrika gewinnt Konturen', *Frankfurter Allgemeine Zeitung*, 25.04.1983.
[66] See, e.g., 'SWAPO-Führer bei Union unerwünscht', *dpa*, 08.12.1983; 'Unions Abgeordnete gegen Bonn-Besuch von SWAPO-Führer Nujoma', *dpa*, 07.12.1983.

acknowledged already in 1981 that SWAPO had a good chance of winning the election, it was widely believed that victory was only possible with 'massive communist support' and 'by putting people under a state of fear and terror so that everyone believes that only a SWAPO election victory could end the constant threat of a guerrilla war', as Hans Stercken, CDU member of the *Bundestag*, claimed.[67] On the whole, the rejectionist stance towards SWAPO remained prevalent within the CDU/CSU after election victory in 1983. Hence, some CDU/CSU delegates remained defiant in their opposition to direct talks with SWAPO.[68] While the CDU/CSU had, in the role of the opposition party, strongly opposed the SPD-led government's policy towards Namibia, after gaining power, most delegates shifted towards more moderate positions on most Namibian issues. Kohl, for example, who had argued vehemently against the closure of the consulate in 1977, was after his election victory, quick to repel CSU demands to reverse the previous government's decision. The new chancellor made it clear that the Federal Government had no intention to reopen the consulate in Windhoek before establishing diplomatic relations with a government in an independent Namibia.[69] Nonetheless, there remained a strong support for pre-1983 positions within the CDU/CSU. Thus, the Reagan administration's desire to roll back communist influence in southern Africa received wide understanding in the CDU, and even more so in the CSU. It is therefore perhaps not unexpected that in his evaluation of the situation in southern Africa, Genscher came to a dramatically different conclusion to that of the Reagan administration. While Genscher believed that the Eastern bloc had lost ground in southern Africa, the Reagan administration was convinced that the Soviet Union posed an ever-growing threat in the region.

Those who supported the policy of rapprochement with the Eastern bloc accentuated areas that indicated signs of improvement in Cold War relations. Hence, Genscher's assessment focussed on the retreating influence of the Soviet Union in southern Africa as a whole and Mozambique in particular, but also in Angola, where 'the situation was not as bad as was generally believed'.[70] Although the Reagan administration acknowledged 'positive' changes in Mozambique, the strong influence of the communist bloc in Angola was the administration's most pressing concern, for it was feared that the Soviet Union would extend its activities into neighbouring countries, particularly Namibia.[71] The Reagan administration's confrontational

---

[67] H. Stercken, 'Unabhängigkeit, Menschenrechte und Demokratie für Namibia', DUD, Nr. 19, 28.01.1981.
[68] See Deutscher Bundestag, 10. Wahlperiode, Stenographischer Bericht, 243. Sitzung, 06.11.1986, 18852.
[69] 'Wandel nach der Wende, die Namibia-Politik der CDU', *Namibia Information Office,* Januar 1984, 13.
[70] PAAA, Zwischenarchiv, Bd. 125293, 1983, Deutsch-französischer Gipfel; hier: Gespräch des Bundesministers mit AM Cheysson am 16. Mai 1983, Paris, 17.05.1983, 4.
[71] Ibid., 2; G. Schröder, 'Im Burenstaat kommt der Reformzug in Bewegung', *Die Welt,* 13.07.1983.

stance towards the Soviet Union led to an increased accent on regional conflict, while Genscher's concentration on détente led to an increased accent on areas of co-operation. Reagan's strategic plan envisioned tying down the Soviet Union in long and costly conflicts.[72]

The Kohl government by and large followed in its predecessors' footsteps by pursuing an Africa policy that intended to further the independence of African states from foreign powers.[73] It is within this context that Genscher advised Nujoma to pursue 'a non-alignment policy and follow the corresponding developments' in 1984.[74] The CDU/CSU hardliners became increasingly isolated in their uncompromising stance against SWAPO. This position was based on the conviction that SWAPO was not necessarily needed for the formation of a government, as, for example, Hans Klein, a Strauß confidant in the BMZ, stated in 1985.[75]

In March 1983, the CDU-related Konrad Adenauer Foundation (KAS) came to the conclusion that SWAPO would win free elections in Namibia.[76] Given that the newly elected Kohl government was carefully considering its approach to SWAPO at the time, it seems plausible to suggest that the outcome of the KAS study had some influence on Kohl's decision-making process. If nothing else, the study confirmed that the time was ripe for a new approach towards SWAPO. Nonetheless, support for the DTA remained strong within both CDU and CSU. In late 1985, 114 CDU/CSU members of parliament and 25 delegates of the European Parliament signed a letter to the Kohl government, asking Bonn to support the parties of the transitional government in their national reconciliation efforts by increasing economic co-operation and development aid. UN Resolution 435 also became a focus of criticism within the CDU/CSU in 1985 and 1986, but, without a sound alternative plan, the majority of CDU/CSU delegates were reluctant to openly challenge the government to abandon a resolution that received widespread international support.[77]

Furthermore, the CSU was sceptical about West Germany's involvement in the WCG's Namibia-initiative, claiming that it had a negative influence on Bonn's foreign policy.[78] The fact that Genscher's central position in the WCG increased his international influence and standing, and subsequently also Bonn's policy towards Namibia, was unsettling for the CSU,

---

[72] See B. Zanchetta, *The Transformation of International American Power in the 1970s*, Cambridge, Cambridge University Press, 2014, 295.
[73] Deutscher Bundestag, 10. Wahlperiode, Drucksache 10/833, 21.12.1983, 2.
[74] BStU, MfS-Hauptverwaltung Aufklärung, Nr. 30, Information über die gegenwärtigen Kampfbedingungen der namibischen Befreiungsbewegung SWAPO, Nr. 172, 84, 5.
[75] Deutscher Bundestag, 10. Wahlperiode, Drucksache 10/5321, 14.04.1986, 4.
[76] Brenke, *Die Bundesrepublik*, 178. In 1983, the GDR also concluded that SWAPO would win elections under UN supervision: PAAA, MfAA, ZR 2765/84, Aktenvermerk über ein Gespräch des Generalsekretärs des Solidaritätskomitees der DDR, Genossen Achim Reichardt, mit dem Mitglied des ZK und Exekutivkomitees (PB) der SWAPO, Lucas Pohamba, am 14.02.1983, 25.02.1983.
[77] Brenke, *Die Bundesrepublik*, 189–190.
[78] Ibid., 184–185.

particularly Strauß. Differences on important policy issues within the coalition government made it increasingly difficult for Genscher to protect his Namibia policy against encroachment by supporters of the apartheid regime.[79]

Although the SPD's engagement with SWAPO lost momentum after the general elections, as Brenke points out, the SPD continued to seek out opportunities to build a bilateral trust relationship with SWAPO. True, the SPD's engagement in the Namibia question waned slowly after the general elections, for the SPD lost a number of *Bundestag* seats, promoting a concentration of political efforts on regional interests.[80] Yet, the assistant parliamentary party leader, Wolfgang Roth, was replaced by Günther Verheugen, who continued to concentrate on the relevant demands of the former SPD-led government: termination of racism, implementation of UN Resolution 435 and support of SWAPO. Furthermore, the SPD continued to play an active role in trying to bring about a change in Namibia and South Africa. In mid-1983, for example, a SPD delegation met Nico Bessinger, SWAPO's internal secretary for foreign affairs, in Windhoek. The delegation's Namibia visit was organised by the Interstate Department, responsible for overseeing the visits of foreign diplomatic representatives. This explains why the meeting with Bessinger was not part of the official programme and, therefore, only mentioned in a handwritten side note.[81] As a rule, Pretoria made sure that political visitors came solely in contact with proponents of the South African approach in Namibia.[82] It is hardly surprising, therefore, that meetings between SWAPO and Western politicians in Namibia have not been mentioned in past studies. Yet, the SPD delegates' meeting with Bessinger indicates that such secret meetings took place. Furthermore, Brandt continued to use his political influence to support SWAPO's cause throughout the 1980s.[83] For example, in the

---

[79] See Melber, 'Federal Republic', 8.
[80] R. von Lucius, 'Die künftige Politik Bonns gegenüber dem südlichen Afrika gewinnt Konturen', *Frankfurter Allgemeine Zeitung*, 25.04.1983.
[81] NAN, GAS 1/5/2, File 13/3/1/83 PS 2, Department of Governmental Affairs, Interstate Relations, Programme Members of Parliament (SPD), 8–16 April 1983, 7. Werner Hillebrecht, the former head of the National Archives of Namibia who was involved in the international anti-apartheid movement, also stated that meetings between West German politicians and SWAPO usually took place in neighbouring countries or Europe, but not in Namibia. Private discussion with Werner Hillebrecht, Windhoek, 29.07.2015. The former South African Permanent Representative at the UN in Geneva, Dieter Petzsch, who was involved in the Namibian independence process in 1989/90, also stated that there had been no official meetings between West German politicians and SWAPO in Namibia. Interview with Dieter Petzsch, Berlin, 22.03.2016.
[82] See, e.g., NAN, GAS 1/5/5, File: 13/3/2/81.V, Department of Governmental Affairs, Interstate Relations, Programme for Dr. and Mrs. Manfred Vohrer and Dr. and Mrs. Wolfgang Rumpf, 20.02.1981–01.03.1981; Ibid., 1/2/10, File 13/3/1/83 PS 2, Department of Governmental Affairs, Interstate Relations, Programme CDU Parliamentarians, 17–26 September 1983.
[83] See, e.g., B. Loff, 'Wer den falschen Eingang benutzt, wird barsch zurechtgewiesen', *Frankfurter Rundschau*, 24.03.1986; W. Brandt, 'Die Apartheid muss überwunden werden', *SPD-Fraktion im Deutschen Bundestag*, 13.06.1988; H. Schreitter-Schwarzenfeld, 'Brandt: Mit Zureden ist in Süd-

face of Pretoria's stalling tactics both Brandt and Genscher changed their position in the late 1980s in favour of using coercive economic measures to force Pretoria to change policies and both repeatedly stressed that apartheid can never be reformed.[84] In mid-1988, the SPD also organised a hearing on South Africa and Namibia.[85] However, the newly elected Green Party made both the Namibia question and the Kohl government's policy towards South Africa its prime foreign policy concern, which overshadowed the SPD's efforts on those matters.

Genscher's reappointment as foreign minister was one of the main factors that prevented a fundamental change in West Germany's policy towards Namibia after the 1983 general election. Also, Reagan's obsession with anti-communism soon indicated a drastic slow-down in progress towards Namibian independence. By 1983, both SWAPO and the DTA argued that Resolution 435 was no longer relevant.[86] Ironically perhaps, the GDR had stopped opposing Resolution 435 in the early 1980s. The Reagan administration's position was, therefore, met with incomprehension among GDR diplomats.[87] Furthermore, SWAPO's close relations with Moscow, Havana and East Berlin provided for those who had reservations about SWAPO, including Washington, Pretoria, the DTA and hardliners within the Federal Government, the context for their argument against a SWAPO-led Namibia.

The mid-1980s: the Kohl government and the Namibia question

From 1981, Chester Crocker, the Assistant Secretary of State for African Affairs, linked Namibia's independence to the withdrawal of Cuban troops from Angola.[88] For Pretoria, Washington's stance presented a welcome opportunity to further delay Namibia's independence with an additional demand. As a result, Pretoria's insistence on the simultaneous withdrawal

---

afrika nichts zu erreichen', *Frankfurter Rundschau*, 14.06.1988.

[84] W. Brandt, 'Die Apartheid muss überwunden werden', *SPD-Fraktion im Deutschen Bundestag*, 13.06.1988. See also H. Schreitter-Schwarzenfeld, 'Brandt: Mit Zureden ist in Südafrika nichts zu erreichen', *Frankfurter Rundschau*, 14.06.1988; 'Brandt: 'Ruf nach Sanktionen nicht unüberhörbar', *Unsere Zeit*, 14.06.1988; 'Die treffen, die es treffen soll', *Frankfurter Rundschau*, 28.05.1988. See, e.g., C. G., 'Genscher: Apartheid ist Rassenwahn', *Frankfurter Allgemeine Zeitung*, 26.05.1988; W. Brandt, 'Die Apartheid muss überwunden werden', *SPD-Fraktion im Deutschen Bundestag, 13.06.1988*

[85] See 'SPD-Fraktion beendet Hearing zu Südafrika und Namibia', *Die SPD-Fraktion im Deutschen Bundestag*, 14.06.1988.

[86] PAAA, AV Neues Amt, Bd. 16413, 1983, Namibia-Initiative; hier: BM-Gespräch mit DTA-Delegation, Bonn AA, 15.06.1983; Ibid., Presseerklärung der SWAPO gegen die vorgeschlagene Entwicklungshilfe für Namibia vor der Unabhängigkeit, 15.06.1983.

[87] Interview with Hans-Georg Schleicher, Berlin, 20.02.2016. In fact, the Soviet Union started to change its attitude towards Resolution 435 in the early 1980s: PAAA, Zwischenarchiv, Bd. 125282, 1981, Namibia-Initiative; hier: Positive sowjetische Haltung zu SR 435, 24.07.1981.

[88] For Chester Crocker's account of Namibia's path to independence, see C. Crocker, *High Noon in Southern Africa; making Peace in a Rough Neighbourhood*, New York, Norton, 1992.

of Cuban and South African troops complicated the situation further.[89] Thus, Washington supported Pretoria's stalling tactics by adding a further demand that hindered rapid progress at the negotiating table.[90] Moreover, the demand for complete withdrawal of the Soviet-backed Cuban troops from Angola buttressed Pretoria's claim of a communist threat in the region and firmly indicate that Reagan's 'roll-back strategy' suited Pretoria's strategic considerations.[91] Thus, it was not without calculation that South Africa increased its campaign against SWAPO. Of course, Pretoria claimed that the campaign was directed against the Soviet expansionist threat in southern Africa. Hence, Western powers, including West Germany, were concerned that Pretoria's actions in Angola were based on the strategic aim to turn the Namibia-Angola conflict into an East-West conflict and thus gain further support from Washington against the looming 'communist threat'.[92]

Neither Moscow nor SWAPO wanted the conflict to turn into an East-West conflict, which would, in the eyes of SWAPO, push the struggle to a 'higher level' and turn the liberation of Namibia into a 'war of attrition'.[93] In retrospect, Genscher identified the Reagan administration as one of the main obstacles on Namibia's path to independence:

> However, things became very difficult during Ronald Reagan's term of government. The Reagan Administration suddenly made a link between progress in the Namibia issue and civil war in Angola where, in addition to Angolans themselves, also Cuban military units and camouflaged military units of the Republic of South Africa were opposed

---

[89] For a detailed account of Pretoria's demands, see PAAA, MfAA, ZR 2434/89, 1981–1988, Telegramm, Brief RSA-AM Botha an UN-GS 27.11. als UN-Dokument veröffentlicht, 30.11.1984.

[90] It remains open to debate whether the Reagan administration took into consideration that demanding the withdrawal of Cuban troops might support Pretoria's delaying tactics. Reagan was at times slow in understanding the other side's point of view. For example, Reagan initially did not understand why the Soviet Union should feel threatened by his government's foreign policy: B. Farnham, 'Perceiving the End of Threat: Ronald Reagan and the Gorbachev Revolution', in S. A. Renshon and D. W. Larson (eds.), *Good Judgment in Foreign Policy: Theory and Application*, Maryland, Rowman & Littlefield Publishers, Inc., 159. Botha repeatedly threatened to abandon Resolution 435 entirely, should the US, Angola and South Africa not come to an agreement. The 'genuine withdrawal' of Cuban troops from Angola stood at the centre of any agreement that would be acceptable for Pretoria. See, e.g., PAAA, Zwischenarchiv, Bd. 138105, 1985, Namibia; hier: Reaktion der südafrikanischen Regierung auf die Vorschläge der 'Viel-Parteien-Konferenz', 19.04.1985; Ibid., Namibia-Politik, Kapstadt, 25.04.1985.

[91] The Reagan administration viewed Pretoria's 'simplistic ideas of the total onslaught by communists' with scepticism. Washington hoped that the policy of constructive engagement would alter Pretoria's view of South African interests. The objective was, of course, to influence Pretoria in such a way that its policies would be closer to US interests: PAAA, AV Neues Amt, 16413, 1982–1983, Namibia-Initiative; hier: südafrikanisch-amerikanische Verhandlungen in Washington, Kapstadt, 15.03.1983.

[92] PAAA, Zwischenarchiv, Bd. 138101, 1984, SWAPO-Brief an UN-GS wegen Feuereinstellung mit SA; hier: Sorgen über Zuspitzung Regionalkonflikts in Ost-West-Konflikt, 09.01.1984.

[93] Ibid., Angola und Namibia, Pretoria, 09.01.1984; Ibid., Bd. 125282, 1981, Informationsreise Namibia-Referentin nach Windhuk, Pretoria, 17.07.1981, 2.

to one another. The Reagan Administration said that only Cuba's withdrawal from Angola could free the way for Namibia's independence .... Looking back, today one can say that eight precious years were lost that way for Namibia's independence... as regards to Namibia, the United States' involvement was inhibitive.[94]

Overall, the Reagan administration's aggressive policies towards the Soviet Union in southern Africa became increasingly the focus of criticism among Third World countries.[95]

In the early 1980s, frustration over the slow progress towards national independence increased significantly in Namibia. In an attempt to overcome the deadlock in the negotiating process, Namibia's political parties organised the so-called Multi-Party Conference (MPC). In November 1983, the conference brought together seventeen political parties, aiming to negotiate a solution that was independent of foreign interests and influences. Although the DTA presented the numerical majority, political parties such as the South West Africa National Union (SWANU), Namibia's oldest political party, the SWAPO Democrats (SWAPO-D), the Namibia Christian Democratic Party (NCDP) and the National Party (NP) constituted an important contingent.[96] The formation of the MPC presented an opportunity to dissociate from Pretoria. Over the years, it had become apparent that Pretoria actively tried to disrupt independent political initiatives by encouraging friction between Namibia's political parties.[97] The MPC conveyed the unambiguous message that Namibia's political parties no

---

[94] Genscher, 'Germany's role in Namibia's', 56. SWAPO made similar assessments in the 1980s. See, e.g., BArch, DZ 9/2575, 1984–1988, Message of SWAPO President Sam Nujoma, World Peace Council, Helsinki, 21.07.1984; BArch, DZ 9/2557, 1984–1988, Circular Letter, SWAPO Youth League, New Year Message, 06.01.1988. Overall, the policies of the Reagan administration had a negative effect on relations between SWAPO and the WCG. See, e.g., PAAA, Zwischenarchiv, Bd. 127477, 1981, SWAPO; hier: Nujoma-Besuch in Bonn vom 25. bis 27.05.1981, 29.05.1981; Ibid., Bd. 125293, 1983, Statement by Dr Sam Nujoma, President of SWAPO, Security Council Debate on Namibia, 12 May 1983.

[95] See PAAA, Zwischenarchiv, Bd. 138105, 1985, BF-Konferenz in New Delhi, New Delhi, 19.04.1985. There was widespread acceptance of the notion that the Reagan administration's 'linkage' strategy blocked any progress in the Namibia question. There was, however, no real alternative but to accept Washington's dominant role in the negotiations, and thus there was no alternative to the Reagan administration's 'linkage' strategy. See, e.g., AAPD, 1985, Band 1, Vermerk über das Gespräch mit dem Bundeskanzler und dem Präsidenten der Vereinigten Republik Tansania, Dr. Julius Nyerere, am 22. Mai 1985 im Bundeskanzleramt, 22.05.1985, 681; PAAA, Zwischenarchiv, Bd. 138104, 1984–1985, Lösung der Namibiafrage; hier: Wie können wir wieder eine stärkere Rolle spielen?, 05.12.1984. In 1984, Nujoma also stated that the 'US-SA-Linkage blocked the Federal Republics' work in the Contact Group': Ibid., Bd. 138098, 1984, Gespräch mit SWAPO-President Sam Nujoma; hier: Unvermindertes Interesse an Besuch in Bonn zur Verstärkung der Zusammenarbeit, Luanda, 12.01.1984.

[96] Namibia Information Office, Nr. 26, März 1984, Die Namibische Vielparteienkonferenz– Eine Zwischenbilanz, Rehabeam Katjaimune, 6.

[97] *Namibia Information Bulletin*, Nr. 26, 1984, 3. The SPD-led government came to a similar conclusion in late 1981: PAAA, Zwischenarchiv, Bd. 127747, 1981, Besuch DTA-Präsident Kalangula in Bonn, 26.11.1981, 7.

longer accepted external control over Namibia's internal affairs. In 1981 already, the DTA believed that Pretoria had written off their chances to win elections and thus no longer considered the DTA a valuable political power.[98] No wonder, therefore, that the DTA tried to shake off its reputation as Pretoria's 'Anti-SWAPO-Front'.[99] The MPC presented an opportunity for the DTA to prove and consolidate its independence from Pretoria.[100] Appropriately, Mudge referred to the MPC as the 'Namibians Only-Konferenz'.[101] Unlike the Turnhalle Conference in 1978, SWAPO was invited to participate, but declined to take part.[102] SWAPO's most essential claim was to be the sole representative of the Namibian people and it was suspicious of initiatives that received South African support.[103]

The MPC expressed concern about Resolution 435, stating that some obstacles seemed insurmountable and, therefore, proposed immediate talks with all parties involved in finding a solution to the crisis in Namibia.[104] For Kohl and Genscher, both strongly committed to the UN Resolution, this was a major headache.[105] In the early 1980s, Namibia's transition to independence remained a distant dream, undermined by opposing interests and ideas between a complex composition of political parties and interest groups in Namibia on the one hand and foreign powers on the other hand.[106]

---

[98] PAAA, Zwischenarchiv, Bd. 125282, 1981, Informationsreise Namibia-Referentin nach Windhuk, Pretoria, 17.07.1981, 3. See also Ibid., Presse-Vorberichte zum Pariser Treffen der Namibia-Kontaktgruppe, 30.07.1981. In 1983, the Foreign Office reported that Pretoria had abandoned the DTA-experiment: Ibid., Bd. 138096, 1982–1984, Politischer Halbjahresbericht Namibia, 01.09.1082 – 01.03.1983, 2–3.

[99] *Namibia Information Bulletin*, Nr. 26, März 1984, 3.

[100] For further information about Namibia's path to independence from the DTA's perspective, see D. Mudge, *All the way to an independent Namibia*, Pretoria, Protea Book House, 2016.

[101] *Namibia Information Bulletin*, Nr. 26, März 1984, 4.

[102] PAAA, Zwischenarchiv, Bd. 138105, 1985, Unabhängigkeit Namibias; hier: Standpunkt der Bundesregierung; Stellungnahme von Legationsrat Dr. Seidt vom Auswärtigen Amt, 19.04.1985.

[103] See, e.g., Namibia Information Office, Nr. 26, März 1984, 5; PAAA, Zwischenarchiv, Bd. 138105, 1985, Unabhängigkeit Namibias; hier: Standpunkt der Bundesregierung; Stellungnahme von Legationsrat Dr. Seidt vom Auswärtigen Amt, 19.04.1985.

[104] 'Namibia soll über sich selbst bestimmen', *Süddeutsche Zeitung*, 14.12.1983.

[105] In 1985, the Kohl government became increasingly concerned about the growing consensus in Africa that West Germany 'silently accepted' Pretoria's 'circumvention or postponement' of Resolution 435. Hence, the Foreign Office ordered its relevant ambassadors in Africa to emphasise West Germany's unrestricted support for Resolution 435 and that it 'will regard any unilateral measures to be null and void': PAAA, Zwischenarchiv, Bd. 138105, 1985, Namibia; hier: Neue südafrikanische Versuche zur Umgehung bzw. Verzögerung von SR 435 und bevorstehenden Blockfreienkonferenz in New Delhi vom 18.–21.04., 17.04.1985.

[106] In 1985, the Western countries approach to the Namibia question came under increasing criticism, mainly because they declared support for Resolution 435 while simultaneously cooperating with South Africa on a political, economic and military level: PAAA, Zwischenarchiv, Bd. 138105, 1985, BF-Konferenz in New Delhi; hier: PM Gandhi und SWAPO-Präsident Nujoma in Eröffnungssitzung, 19.04.1985.

Despite all this, Pretoria tried to involve SWAPO, through both promises and pressure, in a transitional government.[107] The MPC was, however, more eager to convince the outside world that it was not Pretoria's puppet, while SWAPO suspected a 'trap' behind Pretoria's initiative.[108] SWAPO suspected that Pretoria pursued a threefold strategy: firstly, to involve SWAPO in an interim government; secondly, to agree on a transitional period of about three to four years, which will diminish the outlook for elections in the near future; thirdly, to use the transitional period and SWAPO's role in the interim government to weaken the liberation movement.[109] Yet, the MPC received support from within the Kohl government, which amplified the political division within the conservative-liberal coalition government.[110] Although, Genscher's influence became increasingly apparent, for the CDU/CSU moved away from its overemphasised support of the DTA, the continuation of the previous SPD-led government's policy towards Namibia was in no way guaranteed. Still, the continuation of Genscher's Namibia policy was the Kohl government's official policy line after 1983.

South Africa's extensive military operation in Angola between late 1983 and early 1984 undermined any potential progress towards Namibia's independence.[111] The Security Council condemned in two resolutions, on 20 December 1983 and 6 January 1984, South Africa's attacks on SWAPO in Angola, and declared that South Africa's occupation of Angola threatened world peace and international security.[112] The Reagan administration abstained from

---

[107] See PAAA, Zwischenarchiv, Bd. 138105, 1985, Namibia; hier: Reaktion der südafrikanischen Regierung auf die Vorschläge der 'Viel-Parteien-Konferenz', 19.04.1985, 3.

[108] See also C. Saunders, 'Namibian diplomacy before Independence', in A. Bösl, A. du Pisani and D. Zaire's (eds.), *Namibia's Foreign Relations*, Windhoek, Macmillan Education Namibia, 2014, 32.

[109] See PAAA, Zwischenarchiv, Bd. 138105, 1985, Unabhängigkeit Namibias; hier: Standpunkt der Bundesregierung; Stellungnahme von Legationsrat Dr. Seidt vom Auswärtigen Amt, 19.04.1985.

[110] For example, Graf Huyn (CDU) complemented the Multi-Party initiative, not least because Namibian Germans supported the conference. Karl-Heinz Hornhues, the CDU Namibia expert, was equally positive, emphasising that many Namibians felt represented by neither SWAPO nor South Africa and, therefore, needed alternative options. The CDU/CSU government was, as Hornhues stated, prepared to support the negotiations of the MPC: Namibia Information Office, Nr. 26, März 1984, 20.

[111] In late 1981 Pretoria started to destroy SWAPO camps near the Angolan border: PAAA, Zwischenarchiv, Bd. 125282, 1981, Informationsreise Namibia-Referentin nach Windhuk, Pretoria, 17.07.1981. For an assessment of Pretoria's military operation in Angola between late 1983 and early 1984, see, e.g., Ibid., Bd. 138101, 1984, Fortsetzung der SR-Debatte über Lage in Angola, New York, 06.01.1984. For a detailed assessment of Pretoria's campaign against SWAPO in Angola in the early 1980s, see S. L. Weigert, *Angola: A Modern military History*, New York, Palgrave Macmillan, 2011, 69–105. For an in-depth analysis of South Africa's military operations in southern Africa, see P. Johnson and D. Martin (eds.), *Frontline Southern Africa: Destructive Engagement*, New York, Four Walls Eight Windows, 1988.

[112] Resolution 54 (1983) and Resolution 546 (1984), in Brenke, *Die Bundesrepublik*, 101. Both South Africa and Angola issued extensive written statements to the Security Council concerning the military campaign against SWAPO in Angola, which can be found in the following Foreign Office file: PAAA, Zwischenarchiv, Bd. 138101, 1984.

voting and demanded the withdrawal of Cuban troops before commencing formal negotiations over Namibia's independence.[113] In 1984, the GDR's Institute for International Politics and Economy (IPE) voiced its concerns about Washington's 'confrontational course' and proposed greater co-operation between East and West in southern Africa.[114] This was a serious deviation from traditional foreign policy thinking. The IPE based its proposed change in approach on the understanding that Eastern European models of socialism had failed to provide deep-reaching solutions to Africa's complex problems. Thus, it was believed that co-operation between the two major blocs could bring about such change. The GDR's political elite showed, however, little interest in such 'new thinking'.[115] Still, the GDR approached southern Africa in the early 1980s from a more sober perspective, for it had become increasingly apparent that the further advancement of socialism in Africa was not feasible, due to the deteriorating economic power of virtually all socialist countries.[116]

In response to the IPE's analysis, the Foreign Ministry submitted its own paper, stressing that the GDR will not abandon the principles of international class struggle. Despite this, the ministry agreed that the ultimate objective was to establish peace and stability in southern Africa.[117] Thus, the ideologically emphasised objective of changing the balance of power in southern Africa in favour of socialism, as envisioned in the 1970s, moved into the background. Instead, a stronger emphasis was placed on preventing the further escalation of conflict and on defending the gains already made in the region.[118] East Germany became less willing to engage in a 'confrontational dispute' with the West in southern Africa. Perhaps even more significant, at least from an intra-German perspective, the IPE viewed West Germany's relative independence in foreign policy as an opportunity to return to détente

---

[113] See PAAA, Zwischenarchiv, Bd. 125282, 1981, US-Haltung zu Südafrika und zur Namibia-Frage; hier: an die Öffentlichkeit gelangte vertrauliche Papiere des State Departments, 02.07.1981.

[114] BArch-SAPMO, DY 30/ IV 2/2.115/25, Institut für Internationale Politik und Wirtschaft der DDR, Vorlage für die Außenpolitische Kommission des Zentralkomitees der SED. Betreff: Analyse zu den zwischenimperialistischen Widersprüchen, 08.10.1984, 40.

[115] See also Schleicher, 'GDR Solidarity', 1146–1148. The term 'new thinking' emerged in the Soviet Union in the early 1980s and progressed into Gorbachev's glasnost and perestroika policy in the late 1980s. For an analysis of the Soviet Union's changing foreign policy towards Africa under Gorbachev, see A. A. Nwankwo, *Perestroika and Glasnost: Their Implication for Africa*, Enugu, Fourth Dimension Publishing Company, 1990.

[116] See also BArch-SAPMO, DY 30/ IV 2/2.115/25, Abteilung Internationale Verbindung, Vorlage für die Außenpolitische Kommission beim Politbüro des ZK. Betreff: Potenzen und Perspektiven der Länder Asiens, Afrikas und Lateinamerikas in der internationalen Klassenauseinandersetzung, 15.10.1984, 27.

[117] Ibid., Minister für Auswärtige Angelegenheiten, Vorlage für die Außenpolitische Kommission beim Politbüro des Zentralkomitees der SED. Betreff: Zur gegenwärtigen Entwicklung in der Region des südlichen Afrikas und Schlussfolgerung für die Außenpolitik der DDR, 30.11.1984.

[118] Schleicher, 'GDR Solidarity', 1148.

between East and West.[119] The institute argued that West Germany's geopolitical situation in Europe did not allow Bonn to follow Washington's confrontational policies, for West Germany's geographical position required friendly relations with its socialist neighbours.[120] For this reason, West Germany actively tried to 'influence and complement' Washington's confrontational approach through 'increased dialog, contact and negotiations' with socialist states, as the IPE explained.[121] Hence, the shared concern for peace and stability motivated the IPE to propose the re-categorization of the relations between the two German states from a rivalry to a potential partnership in southern Africa.[122]

In sum, towards mid-1980s there emerged a growing consensus that it was desirable for the GDR to actively avoid confrontations with Western powers in southern Africa, with some influential thinkers even perceiving the GDR's relations with West Germany as a vehicle to further such objectives. Although the GDR's ruling elite was not yet prepared to pursue new ideas, this attitude slowly began to loosen. This raises the question of whether the conservative-liberal government in Bonn pursued a policy towards southern Africa that was indeed agreeable with the GDR's position and thus distinctly different from its conservative counterpart in Washington. Hence, it is useful to look briefly at the Kohl government's relations with both Pretoria and Washington, before examining further the emergence of 'new thinking' within the GDR.

Given that the CDU/CSU was firmly on Pretoria's side in the late 1970s, supported anti-communist policies in southern Africa and raised strong objections against a move towards SWAPO, it could be expected that a conservative-led government would firmly agree with Washington's policy towards southern Africa. This was, however, not the case. Bonn's relationship with Pretoria reached a new low point under the Kohl government.

In June 1984, after terminating military operations in Angola, South Africa's Premier, PW Botha, visited Kohl in Bonn and Thatcher in London. With the conservative US President firmly on Pretoria's side in Angola and in the struggle against Soviet expansionism in southern Africa, Botha felt compelled to test the waters with Europe's conservatives.[123] Kohl's

---

[119] BArch-SAPMO, DY 30/ IV 2/2.115/25, Institut für Internationale Politik und Wirtschaft der DDR, Vorlage für die Außenpolitische Kommission des Zentralkomitees der SED. Betreff: Analyse zu den zwischenimperialistischen Widersprüchen, 08.10.1984, 40.

[120] Ibid.

[121] BArch-SAPMO, DY30/ IV 2/2.115/25, Institut für Internationale Politik und Wirtschaft der DDR, Vorlage für die Außenpolitische Kommission des Zentralkomitees der SED. Betreff: Analyse zu den zwischenimperialistischen Widersprüchen, 08.10.1984, 37. Reagan's military armament programme, for example, contained the underlying purpose of beginning an arms race with the Soviet Union, intensified through increased US activity in the Third World. The ultimate aim was to bankrupt the economically weak communist state.

[122] Ibid.

[123] PAAA, Zwischenarchiv, Bd. 125282, 1981, Namibia-Initiative der Fünf; hier: Pressekonferenz

reappointment of Genscher raised questions about Strauß' position in the coalition government, and Genscher's influence over Kohl. While the CDU/CSU approached issues concerning southern Africa in the 1970s from a perspective that favoured and considered predominantly Pretoria's position, the reappointment of Genscher made the Kohl government somewhat unpredictable for Pretoria.

Efforts by the Foreign Office to improve relations between SWAPO and the IG were viewed with particular concern. After a meeting between SWAPO and the IG at the German embassy in Harare, Pik Botha directed his frustration against the Kohl government by denouncing Nujoma as an 'agent of Moscow' and described the IG-SWAPO meeting as an 'outrageous event'. Much to his frustration, the Federal Government gave, under strict secrecy, the consulate general in Cape Town the permission to pay the IG 50,000 deutsche mark, emphasising that the payment should be used to help advance efforts to implement Resolution 435. This also included establishing 'trust-generating contacts' with SWAPO. Later in the same year a second payment was made. Pretoria did not hold back from expressing its outrage, arguing that 'something like this would not have happened under Helmut Schmidt'.[124]

Kohl was under pressure to take a hard line against PW Botha. The opposition parties, the church and West Germany's anti-apartheid movement made their discontent heard nationally before his visit, while about 1,200 apartheid opponents protested in Bonn at the time of the meeting.[125] So his visit took place in a frosty atmosphere, which Bonn denied by claiming that the two heads of state were simply frank.[126] The meeting focused on the

---

AM Bothas vom 17.05.1981 bei Rückkehr von seinem US Besuch, Pretoria, 18.05.1981. During the meeting, Botha explicitly emphasised to Kohl that Pretoria and Washington were on the same page in Namibia and Angola. Hence, Botha expressed his hope to Kohl that the Western allies would support Washington's approach: AAPD, Band 1, 1984, Vermerk über das Gespräch des Herrn Bundeskanzler mit dem Ministerpräsidenten der Republik Südafrika, Peter William Botha, am 5. Juni 1984 im Bundeskanzleramt, 05.06.1984, 782. Although Washington was anxious to negotiate the departure of Cuban troops from Angola, the Reagan administration did not insist on Cuban troop withdrawal before initiating the Namibian independence process, as Pretoria demanded: Brenke, *Die Bundesrepublik*, 102.

[124] AAPD, 1983, Band I, Mein [Botschafter Lahusen] Antrittsbesuch bei AM Botha am 18.05.1983, Pretoria, 18.05.1983, 768–770. Dirk Mudge believed that the majority of the CDU/CSU-led government would not have supported an official IG-SWAPO meeting: PAAA, Neues Amt, Bd. 16414, Gespräche Bk mit DTA-Vorsitzendem Mudge, Bonn, 15.06.1983.

[125] See, e.g., AGG, Signatur 3, Bestand: B.II.1, 1983–1990, Pressemitteilung Nr. 237/84, Bundesregierung soll Südafrikas Ministerpräsident Botha wieder ausladen, 17.05.1984; *General-Anzeiger*, Anti-Apartheid-Demonstrationen begleiten den Bonner Botha-Besuch, June 1984. For a detailed assessment of the anti-apartheid movement in Germany, see H. Brendel, *"Freiheit für Nelson Mandela!" Wie der Kampf gegen die Apartheid nach Deutschland kam*, Hamburg, Diplomica Verlag GmbH, 2014.

[126] The meeting aroused suspicion that Kohl disapproved of Botha, as the two men did not follow the

importance of implementing Resolution 435, but also on the policy of apartheid.[127] Kohl voiced criticism about human rights violations in South Africa, stressing the importance of moving towards 'positive developments' and away from the 'main cause' of conflict in southern Africa.[128] This approach reflected the previous Schmidt-Genscher government's assertion that it was not Soviet arms that were responsible for the conflicts in southern Africa but the inheritance of colonialism, and South Africa's apartheid and hegemonial policies. The Kohl-Genscher government continued to state that Pretoria's draconian policies allowed Moscow to extent its influence rapidly in the region without draining the Soviet Union's financial and economic resources.[129] Not unexpectedly, therefore, both Pik and PW Botha expressed their disappointment at the Kohl government for failing their expectation of changing course in South Africa and Namibia.[130]

Pretoria's disappointment derived also from Bonn's lack of enthusiasm for PW Botha's declaration that South Africa was prepared to hand over Namibia to the governments of the WCG within two months. The handover was, however, attached to the withdrawal of Cuban troops from Angola and security guarantees by the WCG. The proposal was motivated by the high financial costs involved in managing Namibia.[131] Kohl made it clear that Bonn was, for many reasons, determined to support Washington's policies in southern Africa and thus agreed with Botha on the withdrawal of Cuban troops. Genscher was slightly more critical, stating that the demand for a withdrawal of Cuban troops 'has to be seen independently from the Namibia problem'.[132] The Foreign Office was even more criti-

---

custom of shaking hands in front of the press. See, e.g., A. Nacken, '"Mal ist das Sofa drinnen und mal draußen", Botha zeigt sich in Bonn unbeirrbar', *Frankfurter Allgemeine Zeitung,* June 1984; O. Steinbicker, 'Südafrikas Rassistenchef besucht Bonn, Bundeskanzler blieb in der Sofafrage knallhart', *Unsere Zeit,* June 1984.

[127] For a detailed account of the meeting between Kohl and Botha, see AAPD, Band 1, 1984, Vermerk über das Gespräch des Herrn Bundeskanzler mit dem Ministerpräsidenten der Republik Südafrika, Peter William Botha, am 5. Juni 1984 im Bundeskanzleramt, 05.06.1984, 781–793.

[128] AAPD, Band 1, 1984, Vermerk über das Gespräch des Herrn Bundeskanzler mit dem Ministerpräsidenten der Republik Südafrika, Peter William Botha, am 5. Juni 1984 im Bundeskanzleramt, 05.06.1984, 782–787. See also PAAA, Zwischenarchiv, Bd. 138104, 1984–1985, Namibia Regionalpolitik im südlichen Afrika; hier: Offizielle Darstellungen der amerikanischen Regionalpolitik im letzten Quartal 1984, 17.01.1985.

[129] PAAA, Zwischenarchiv, Bd. 138104, 1984–1985, Namibia Regionalpolitik im südlichen Afrika; hier: Offizielle Darstellungen der amerikanischen Regionalpolitik im letzten Quartal 1984, 17.01.1985.

[130] AAPD, Band I, 1985, Regionalpolitische Initiative Sambias; hier: Gespräch zwischen Präsident Kaunda und MD Haas, 09.05.1985, 590.

[131] Ibid., 1984, Vermerk über das Gespräch des Herrn Bundeskanzler mit dem Ministerpräsidenten der Republik Südafrika, Peter William Botha, am 5. Juni 1984 im Bundeskanzleramt, 05.06.1984, 782. See also PAAA, Zwischenarchiv, Bd. 138105, 1985, südafrikanische Namibia-Politik; hier: Erklärung Staatspräsident PW Botha im Parlament am 18.04.1985, Kapstadt, 19.04.1985.

[132] Ibid., 787.

cal, considering PW Botha's announcement to be 'propaganda', based on the notion that the West would reject the proposal, only to later claim that Western states were not fully committed to Namibia.[133] Pretoria could then claim that South Africa was the only power able to protect Namibia against Cuban troops in Angola, as the West German newspaper *Die Zeit* concluded.[134] As could be expected, Pretoria's claim to handover Namibia did not materialize.

The day after Botha's visit, the government's South Africa policy came to dominate the attention of the *Bundestag*. The Green Party voiced criticism about the government's approval of arms exports in 1983 and its intention to expand economic relations with South Africa.[135] The SPD demanded that Pretoria give up the 'constructed' interdependence of the departure of Cuban troops from Angola and Namibia's independence.[136] Moreover, the government was criticised for giving Botha an official reception, for it represented a basic support to enable Pretoria to break out of its international isolation.[137] A *Bundestag* application for sanctions against South Africa by the SPD and Greens was rejected.

Nonetheless, the Kohl government was still more critical towards Pretoria and less confrontational towards Moscow than the Reagan administration. During talks with Isidoro Malmierca, the foreign minister of Cuba, Genscher emphasised that the Federal Government was determined to improve relations with the GDR, the Soviet Union and other Eastern bloc countries.[138] Consequently, the proposal to approach West Germany as a potential partner in southern Africa by the Institute for International Politics and Economy was not at all unrealistic.

---

[133] H. J. Ginsburg, 'Namibia: Bothas unerwarteter Vorschlag', *Die Zeit*, 15.06.1984.
[134] Pretoria saw itself as the protector of the Namibian people, or at least that was the image Pretoria tried to convey: PAAA, Zwischenarchiv, Bd. 138105, 1985, Namibia; hier: Wortlaut der Erklärung STP PW Botha zu SWAPO-Namibia, Pretoria, 18.04.1985.
[135] 'Anti-Apartheid-Demonstrationen begleiten den Bonner Botha-Besuch', *General-Anzeiger*, June 1984. During the meeting, Botha and Kohl discussed further cooperation in the exchange of know-how for a U-boat production in a South African dockyard. See AAPD, Band I, 1984, Vermerk über das Gespräch des Herrn Bundeskanzler mit dem Ministerpräsidenten der Republic Südafrika, Peter William Botha, am 5. Juni 1984 im Bundeskanzleramt, 05.06.1984, 782.
[136] A. Nacken, '"Mal ist das Sofa drinnen und mal draußen", Botha zeigt sich in Bonn unbeirrbar', *Frankfurter Allgemeine Zeitung*, June 1984.
[137] 'Anti-Apartheid-Demonstrationen begleiten den Bonner Botha-Besuch', *General-Anzeiger*, June 1984. Moscow also interpreted Botha's Bonn visit as a victory for Pretoria, which was expressed by the Foreign Ministry during talks in East Berlin: PAAA, MfAA, ZA 1634/83, Vermerk über die Konsultation der Abteilung Ost- und Zentralafrika mit den sowjetischen Außenministerium, 21.06.1984, 9–10.
[138] AAPD, 1983, Band 1, Gespräch BM mit dem kubanischem Außenminister Malmierca am 02. 05.1983 im Auswärtigen Amt, 02.05.1983, 650.

That the Reagan administration's policy of confrontation increased disagreements with European countries did not go unnoticed in the GDR.[139] Although there could be little doubt about West Germany's close relations with the US, there was a recognition that the Kohl government's policy towards southern Africa diverged from that of the Reagan administration. The IPE viewed the Kohl government's emphasis on a close partnership with the Reagan administration as an attempt to heal the rift that had developed on political, economic and military matters between Washington and the previous Schmidt-Genscher government. The stationing of US medium-range missiles in West Germany was seen as 'a clear move towards the US course'.[140] This, however, was hardly surprising, for Kohl 'praised the close cooperation between Bonn and Washington on security issues after the *Bundestag* approved the stationing of US missiles in late 1983.[141] However, there was also a recognition that the Federal government's emphasis on good relations with Washington was based on factors such as security needs in Europe, closely linked economic interest overseas, the reliance on US military power to protect capitalist markets overseas and the joint objective to fight the spread of socialism, particularly in southern Africa. Crucially, however, there was also an understanding of Bonn's predicament. On the one hand, West Germany needed US military protection. On the other, Washington's confrontational approach towards the Soviet Union increased the threat of a major East-West conflict that would ultimately hit Europe harder than the United States. Thus, the IPE trusted that Bonn had a sincere interest in de-escalating the East-West conflict and, therefore, sought close relations with Washington to increase its influence over the Reagan administration.[142]

In 1985, the GDR's Foreign Ministry and ruling elite focused, however, mainly on the perceived threat emanating from Washington and thus on the Reagan administrations confrontational attitude. This made it, of course, difficult to trust the Kohl government, a government that emphasised its close relations with the Reagan administration.[143] Specifically, although

---

[139] See, e.g., BArch-SAPMO, DY 30/ IV 2/2.115/25, Institut für Internationale Politik und Wirtschaft der DDR, Vorlage für die Außenpolitische Kommission des Zentralkomitees der SED. Betreff: Analyse zu den zwischenimperialistischen Widersprüchen, 08.10.1984, 38–39; Ibid., Institut für Internationale Politik und Wirtschaft der DDR, Aspekte der Entwicklung ökonomischer und politischer Widersprüche im heutigen Imperialismus, Januar 1985.

[140] Ibid., Institut für Internationale Politik und Wirtschaft der DDR, Aspekte der Entwicklung ökonomischer und politischer Widersprüche im heutigen Imperialismus, Januar 1985, 41.

[141] J. M. Markham, 'Kohl against halt in missile plans', *New York Times*, 02.12.1983.

[142] BArch-SAPMO, DY 30/ IV 2/2.115/25, Institut für Internationale Politik und Wirtschaft der DDR, Aspekte der Entwicklung ökonomischer und politischer Widersprüche im heutigen Imperialismus, Januar 1985, 41.

[143] Ibid., Minister für Auswärtige Angelegenheiten, Vorlage für die Außenpolitische Kommission beim Politbüro des Zentralkomitees der SED. Betreff: Zur gegenwärtigen Entwicklung in der Region des südlichen Afrikas und Schlussfolgerung für die Außenpolitik der DDR, 30.11.1984, 2–3.

East Berlin's relations with Bonn improved in the early 1980s, not least because of the GDR's economic problems, the idea that both Germanys could work together to end the deadlock over Namibia was not yet imaginable. There was still an overly strong focus on the economic importance of southern Africa for both East and West, and the ideological struggle between the two major blocs in the region.[144]

However, although the Kohl government did not follow the Reagan administration's confrontational course towards the Soviet Union in southern Africa, both Kohl and Genscher found it necessary to take measures against Soviet influence in the region. The aim, however, remained to achieve this objective through political solutions and economic development, and not by turning southern Africa into an ideological battleground between East and West.[145] Differences in policy approach towards southern Africa became also visible between the US and the other members of the WCG. In this respect, Genscher stated during talks with Cheysson, the French representative on the WCG, that the break-up of the WCG would only create further problems with the US: 'There are already enough differences of opinion between us, the Europeans, and Washington'.[146] Yet, Reagan's support of anti-communist movements continued to increase East-West tensions in southern Africa.[147]

Pretoria was after its campaign against SWAPO in Angola in a position of strength.[148] This opened the door for negotiations between Angola and South Africa, which led to the Lusaka Accords of 1984, providing for a ceasefire between the two countries, the withdrawal of South African troops from Angola and the establishment of the Joint Monitoring Commission (JMC) to oversee the treaty's implementation.[149] The JMC consisted of South African Defence Force (SADF) and People's Armed Forces for the Liberation of Angola (FAPLA) personnel and infantry. Important from Pretoria's perspective, the agreemen also stated that Angola must not allow SWAPO or Cuban forces to enter Angola's southern Cunene province after South Africa's

---

[144] Ibid.
[145] See also BArch-SAPMO, DY 30/IV 2/2.115/25, Institut für Internationale Politik und Wirtschaft der DDR, Vorlage für die Außenpolitische Kommission des Zentralkomitees der SED. Betreff: Analyse zu den zwischenimperialistischen Widersprüchen, 08.10.1984, 38–39; PAAA, AV Neues Amt, Bd. 16413, 1983, UN-Rat für Namibia; hier: Bericht an die 37. GV, 11.12.1982.
[146] PAAA, Zwischenarchiv, Bd. 125293, 1983, Deutsch-französischer Gipfel; hier: Gespräch des Bundesministers mit AM Cheysson am 16. Mai 1983, Paris, 17.05.1983.
[147] For a detailed assessment of the increasing East-West tension in southern Africa during the Reagan presidency, see W. Minter, 'Destructive Engagement: The United States and South Africa in the Reagan Era', in Johnson, P. and Martin, D. (eds.), *Frontline Southern Africa: Destructive Engagement*, New York, Four Walls Eight Windows, 1988.
[148] Brenke, *Die Bundesrepublik*, 102.
[149] Nujoma interpreted South Africa's withdrawal from Angola as a façade to make the world believe that Pretoria's policies have changed for the better: PAAA, Zwischenarchiv, Bd. 138105, 1985, Namibia-Angola; hier: SA-Rückzug aus Südangola, Lusaka, 17.04.1985.

withdrawal.[150] As a consequence of the treaty, the SADF and FAPLA held joint operations in southern Angola.[151]

After Pretoria's Angola campaign in 1983, the West faced almost insurmountable obstacles in negotiating a peaceful solution between Pretoria and SWAPO. The WCG received strong criticism from both SWAPO and the GDR for not denouncing the Reagan administration's 'linkage' strategy.[152] To make matters worse, France abandoned its efforts within the WCG in late 1983, partly because the MPLA government in Angola argued that it would be fruitless for the group to continue.[153] The linkage strategy further contributed to the French position.[154]

Although the Lusaka Accord improved relations between South Africa and Angola, it had little significant effect on SWAPO's ability to infiltrate Namibia from Angola, and fell away in 1985, while the violence that increased in South Africa in the mid-1980s pushed Namibia's independence into the background for both Pretoria and the Reagan

---

[150] H.-R. Heitman and W. A. Dorning, 'The Joint Monitoring Commission', *Scientia Militaria, South African Journal of Military Studies*, Vol. 18, No. 1, 1988. Accessed online November 2014, available from: http://scientiamilitaria.journals.ac.za/pub/article/view/410

[151] Ibid., 10–17. See also PAAA, Zwischenarchiv, Bd. 138105, 1983, Namibia-Angola; hier: SA. Rückzug aus Südangola, Kapstadt, 18.04.1985.

[152] PAAA, AV Neues Amt, Bd. 16414, 1983, SR-Debatte über Namibia; hier: Nachmittagssitzung am 31.05, 31.05.1983. In 1983, Nujoma strongly criticised the members of the WCG for failing to disassociate themselves from the linkage between Namibian independence and the withdrawal of Cuban troops. Nujoma came to the conclusion that the WCG should be terminated, for it had no 'right to exist' anymore. The Foreign Office explained, however, that SWAPO showed no real interest in ending or restricting the WCG's mandate. The aim was to put pressure on the West, mobilize the WCG and drive forward the implementation of Resolution 435: PAAA, Zwischenarchiv, Bd. 13800, 1982-1984, Namibia-Konferenz in Paris vom 25.–19. April 1983, 28.04.1983. In early 1984, Nujoma repeated his criticism of the WCG. This time he argued that 'West Germany, as a UN member, should follow the example of France and support only the United Nations General Secretary'. In his view, the US used the WCG to 'prevent 435' and it was therefore necessary to 'send a political signal'. The aim was to 'isolate the US and its linkage demands': PAAA, Zwischenarchiv, Bd. 138098, 1984, Gespräch mit SWAPO-Präsident Sam Nujoma; hier: Unvermindertes Interesse an Besuch in Bonn zur Verstärkung der Zusammenarbeit, Luanda, 12.01.1984.

[153] Brenke, *Die Bundesrepublik*, 101. See also PAAA, Zwischenarchiv, Bd. 138098, 1984, Gespräch mit SWAPO-Präsident Sam Nujoma; hier: Unvermindertes Interesse an Besuch in Bonn zur Verstärkung der Zusammenarbeit, Luanda, 12.01.1984; Ibid., Bd. 138108, 1986–1987, Vermerk ber die Besprechung von Dg 32 mit SWAPO-Vertretern, 16.07.1986.

[154] Cheysson felt especially disheartened by the Cuban issue, stating in 1983 that it was 'impossible to act as if the WCG was still doing useful work': PAAA, Zwischenarchiv, Bd. 125293, 1983, Gespräch des Bundesministers mit AM Cheysson, 17.05.1983, 4. After a WCG meeting in Bonn in November 1984, the Foreign Office came to the following conclusion: 'In any case, France will still suspend its open participation in the Contact Group. At present, the Contact Group can be ruled out as a framework for our own role': Ibid., Bd. 138104, 1984–1985, Lösung der Namibiafrage; hier: Wie können wir wieder eine stärkere Rolle spielen?, 05.12.1984, Anlage 2, 04.12.1984.

administration.¹⁵⁵ Yet, Genscher was still determined not to let the WCG 'disintegrate', for the West had gained, in his opinion, considerable trust in recent years.¹⁵⁶ The termination of the WCG would only play into the hands of the Soviet Union, Genscher argued during the German-French Summit in mid-1983. During talks with the French Foreign Minister Claude Cheysson, Genscher evaluated the WCG's performance positively, stating that the group has helped to improve the West's image in Africa, and had an encouraging influence on SWAPO. The Soviet Union, on the other hand, has lost 'terrain' in Africa, while the West had 'gained a lot of ground without the deployment of troops, as a result of the establishment of the WCG'. Genscher warned, however, that 'the long period of forced passivity was threatening the WCG's credibility'.¹⁵⁷ Aware of this weakness, the Soviet Union was actively 'conducting, with the support of some radicals within UN-states, Security Council meetings for the purpose of putting the West in the hot seat'. Hence, it was of political and strategic importance to continue the mediating role of the WCG.¹⁵⁸

In January 1984, Moscow authorised a substantial increase in military support for FAPLA, while the US supported the National Union for the Total Independence of Angola (UNITA). The Soviet bloc viewed the military build-up as a strategic success, for it restored a military equilibrium between the opposing factions in Angola and, therefore, improved the chances of finding a political solution.¹⁵⁹ Obviously, the GDR's role in An-

---

[155] K. M. Campbell, 'Southern Africa in Soviet Foreign Policy', *The International Institute for Strategic Studies* (IISS), Adelphi Papers, 227, Winter 1987/8, 162.

[156] PAAA, Zwischenarchiv, Bd. 125293, 1983, Deutsch-französischer Gipfel; hier: Gespräch des Bundesministers mit AM Cheysson am 16. Mai 1983, Paris, 17.05.1983. See also AAPD, 1981, Band I, Arbeitsbesuch des französischen AM Cheysson in Bonn am 2. Juni 1981; hier: Namibia, 09.06.1981; PAAA, Zwischenarchiv, Bd. 178848, 1978–1981, Charta UN, Namibia-Initiative, June 1981.

[157] Between 1983 and 1988, the Western powers retreated into a wait-and-see attitude, which, however, was also an expression of resignation in the face of the Reagan administration's dominant role in the negotiations. In 1983, the Foreign Office reported the following: 'Unfortunately, the US efforts are leaving the Contact Group in a waiting state, which we can hardly present as active Namibia-engagement': PAAA, Zwischenarchiv, Bd. 125293, 1983, Namibia-Initiative der westlichen Fünf; hier: Treffen der fünf Außenminister am 28./29. Mai 1983 in Williamsburg, 27.05.1983; See also Ibid., Bd. 138108, 1986–1987, Vermerk über die Besprechung von Dg 32 mit SWAPO-Vertretern, 16.07.1986, 6.

[158] PAAA, Zwischenarchiv, Bd. 125293, 1983, Deutsch-französischer Gipfel; hier: Gespräch des Bundesministers mit AM Cheysson am 16. Mai 1983, Paris, 17.05.1983. See also Ibid., Namibia-Initiative der westlichen Fünf; hier: BM-Schreiben an AM Schulz, 18.05.1983. In Crocker's view, however, the WCG's agenda was finished in 1983, after all the details and issues of Resolution 435 were drawn up. With regard to the Angolan-Cuba agenda, the WCG chose not to address the issue as a group, as Crocker points out. E-mail interview with Chester Crocker, 25.08.2016. From West Germany's perspective, the negotiations between the US and Angola concerning Cuban troops were not part of the WCG's mandate: PAAA, Zwischenarchiv, Bd. 125293, 1983, Betr.: Namibia-Initiative der westlichen Fünf; hier: SR-Debatte, 25.05.1983, 5; Ibid., Namibia-Initiative der westlichen Fünf; hier: Treffen der fünf Außenminister am 28./29. Mai 1983 in Williamsburg, 27.05.1983.

[159] See PAAA, MfAA, ZR 2434/89, 1981–1988, Vermerk über Aussagen von Elisas Augusto, amtie-

gola was also thrust into the spotlight. In 1978 already, the West German newspaper *Die Zeit* reported that 2,500 troops and officers of the NVA were stationed in Angola, while the news magazine, *Der Spiegel*, reported in 1980 that the GDR had 1,000 NVA advisors in Angola.[160] Strauß claimed to know in late 1978 that '5,000 soldiers of the GDR army, particularly Special Forces such as paratroopers', were stationed in Angola.[161] Consequently, Pretoria not only demanded the withdrawal of Cuban troops, but also that other foreign powers, such as the GDR, refrain from increasing their military activities in the region.[162] But the GDR had no interest in seeing the NVA getting entangled in military conflict, which could have had wide-reaching political consequences.[163] The international community would not have tolerated the involvement of a German army in a non-defensive military conflict. Furthermore, the two German states anxiously tried to gain international trust and recognition. For them to have got entangled in military conflicts overseas would have undermined such efforts; perhaps even led to the threat of suspension and expulsion from the UN and possibly even sanctions.

In June 1985, Pretoria agreed with the MPC on the instalment of the Transitional Government of National Unity (TGNU), which was still dominated by the DTA. This was condemned by the UN, the WCG and Washington, as well as the Non-Alignment Movement and the OAU.[164] Although the Federal Government did not recognize Namibia's new government, the CSU welcomed the instalment of the TGNU.[165] Some support came also from within the

---

render Leiter der Abteilung sozialistischer Länder im Ministerium für Auswärtige Angelegenheiten der Volksrepublik Angola und US-Unterstaatssekretär Chester Crocker in Brazzaville am 06 April 1987, Luanda, Mai 1987. It was also believed that FAPLA's improved military strength would allow Cuban troops to withdraw from Angola. The military build-up gave Angola the power to negotiate from a position of strength and make it undesirable for both Pretoria and the Reagan-backed UNITA to opt for a military solution: PAAA, MfAA, ZR 2434/89, 1981–1988, Telegramm, Arbeitsbesuch angolanischen Präsidenten in Kuba, 10.08.1987.

[160] J. Nawrocki, 'Hoffmans "Afrikakorps"', *Die Zeit*, 26.05.1978, 4; K. Storkmann, 'Helping Decolonisation or Fighting the Cold War in Southern Africa? East German military support for FRELIMO of Mozambique', Militärgeschichtliches Forschungsamt. Accessed online January 2014, available from: www.mgfa-potsdam.de.

[161] F. Streletz, 'Der Nationale Verteidigungsrat der DDR und das Vereinte Oberkommando des Warschauer Vertrages', *Der Tagesspiegel*, 02.12.1978, in K. Storkmann, *Geheime Solidarität: Militärbeziehungen und Militärhilfen der DDR in die "Dritte Welt"*, Berlin, Christoph Links Verlag, 2012, 39.

[162] See PAAA, MfAA, ZR 2434/89, 1981–1988, Telegramm, Brief RSA-AM Botha an UN-GS 27.11. als UN-Dokument veröffentlicht, 30.11.1984; *Scientia Militaria*, Vol. 18, Nr. 1, 1988, 22–25.

[163] K. Storkmann, 'Helping Decolonisation'.

[164] Brenke, *Die Bundesrepublik*, 104. See also PAAA, Zwischenarchiv, Bd. 138105, 1985, Namibia; hier: Fortsetzung der Namibia-Debatte des UN-SR am 13.06.1985, New York, 13.06.1985; Ibid., Namibia-Frage, Reaktion des UN-GS und der USA auf die südafrikanische MPC-Vorschläge, Statement by spokesman of the Secretary General, New York, 19.04.1985.

[165] Ibid., Namibia: Haltung der Bundesregierung, 26.06.1985. This document indicates that the CDU parliamentarians Jürgen Hedrich und Werner Marx also supported the TGNU. It is, however,

CDU, FDP and SPD. The parliamentarians, Klein (CSU), Hedrich (CDU) and Rumpf (FDP) even participated in the inauguration ceremony in Windhoek, which the Kohl government shrugged off as meaningless, for the ministers acted on their own initiative.[166] Rumpf was accompanied by former FDP Minister Josef Ertl and FDP Bundestag member Olaf Feldman. That their first class tickets were paid for by the Namibia Information Office stirred up further controversy.[167] The Kohl government and Genscher declared the interim government as 'null and void', which Feldman ridiculed by stating that 'something that actually exists can hardly be null and void'.[168] Genscher, however, questioned Feldman's credibility, telling people close to him that the gratis trip has made them 'susceptible to blackmail', as *Der Spiegel* reported.[169] There is ample evidence that the Namibia Information Office made generous travel arrangements on behalf of Pretoria for numerous CDU, CSU and FDP ministers.[170] Pretoria rewarded loyal West German politicians with luxurious holidays in southern Africa.[171]

---

not surprising, for the CSU and the CSU affiliated Hanns Seidel Foundation supported the DTA already during the election of 1978. See, e.g., Ibid., Bd. 116841, 1977–1978, Pressegespräch über Südafrika am 02.11.1978; hier: Aktivitäten der Hanns-Seidel Stiftung in Namibia, 31.10.1978; 'Spiegelbild der Entwicklungspolitik', *Namibia Nachrichten,* 7. Juni 1989, 7.

[166] *Deutscher Bundestag,* 10. Wahlperiode, Drucksache 10/5312, 14.04.1986. Wolfgang Zeitler, SPD member and President of the Federal Constitutional Court, also announced his participation in the inauguration ceremony, which was strongly condemned by the SPD. Zeitler stated that he would participate as a scientist and, therefore, on his own initiative: 'SPD verurteilt Windhoek-Reise', *IPS-Nachrichtendienst,* 14.06.1985.

[167] 'Tiefe Sorge', *Der Spiegel,* 31/1985, 29.07.1985.

[168] Ibid. See also PAAA, Zwischenarchiv, Bd. 138105, 1985, Namibia: Haltung der Bundesregierung, 26.06.1985.

[169] 'Tiefe Sorge', *Der Spiegel,* 31/1985, 29.07.1985. The extent to which Pretoria tried to politically influence West German delegates becomes evident in a letter by Volker Stoltz, Pretoria's West German middleman and head of the Namibia Information Office: 'I am expecting from the visit that Mr Hornhues can be turned to an active promoter of the internal set up [Pretoria's plan for Namibia] and a more negative view of SWAPO than before': NAN, GAS, 1/2/1, File 13/3/1/84 R 1, Carl von Bach/Volker Stoltz, Visit of Parliamentarians, 22.07.1983.

[170] There are numerous documents in the National Archives of Namibia that give detailed information about the luxurious Namibia holidays of West German politicians and influential thinkers, who were often accompanied by their wives. The South African Interstate Relations in Windhoek worked closely with Stoltz, who was responsible, inter alia, for recommending suitable politicians for South Africa funded holidays in Namibia. Obviously, politicians who displayed a critical attitude towards South Africa did not qualify for such holidays. The aim was to gain greater support for South Africa's policies in the *Bundestag.* Ultimately, it was an attempt to influence West Germany's policy towards both South Africa and Namibia. The documents can be found in the NAN under the following signatures: GAS 1/5/5; GAS 1/6/19; GAS 1/6/21; GAS 1/5/6; GAS 1/1/138; GAS 1/1/2; GAS 1/2/11.

[171] *Deutscher Bundestag,* 8. Wahlperiode, Stenographischer Bericht, 197. Sitzung, 18.01.1980, 15725. See also 'Ausflug nach Windhuk', *Der Spiegel,* 25/1985, 17.06.1985; Dedering, 'Ostpolitik', 13. Pretoria's efforts to reward loyal West German politicians seemed to have continued throughout the 1980s. See e.g., PAAA, Zwischenarchiv, Bd. 155883, 1987–1989, Gespräch Dg 32 mit Dr Nicky Lyambo, Sekretär für Erziehung und Kultur des SWAP-Politbüros im Auswärtigen Amt, 06.09.1988; R. Gevers, 'BRD-Abgeordnete auf Politsafari', *Neues Deutschland,* 25.07.1990;

In 1985, Crocker pointed out that Washington has adopted a 'concept of contentment [*Befriedungskonzept*]' for Namibia.[172] The probability that SWAPO would eventually gain power was no longer seen as a major predicament, provided it would calm the overall situation. Crocker saw no discrepancy between the 'linkage' strategy and the implementation of Resolution 435.[173] In any event, the Foreign Office had little option but to hope that the Crocker initiative would lead to the implementation of the UN Resolution, for it conceded in late 1984 that the WCG was incapable of acting.[174] The Foreign Office also stated that it would carry 'considerable political risks' for West Germany to interfere with the US-led efforts.[175] It is not surprising, therefore, that support for the TGNU within the Kohl government was viewed with growing concern. In 1985, the FDP spokesman for Foreign Affairs warned right-wing elements of the CDU/CSU not to oppose Washington or risk Bonn's isolation.[176] The Foreign Office also made it clear that it was strictly against taking sides in the Namibian independence process.[177]

For Strauß, this position was unacceptable, claiming that the Foreign Office represented 'by no means' the position of the majority in the CDU/CSU, while Genscher's policies benefited only the Cubans and subsequently Moscow.[178] Kohl, however, carefully refuted all such claims during talks with Julius Nyerere, the President of Tanzania, emphasising Bonn's 'obligations to the UN's resolution plan'.[179] Nonetheless, given that the CDU/CSU

'Protest gegen Besuch von Abgeordneten in Bophuthatswana', *epd*, Nr. 138, 20.07.1990.

[172] 'Tiefe Sorge', *Der Spiegel*, 31/1985, 29.07.1985.

[173] PAAA, Zwischenarchiv, Bd. 138104, 1984–1985, Vertrauliche Konsultation über die Namibia/Angola-Entwicklung mit Crocker, Johnson (GB) Bergbusch (KAN) und begleitenden Experten, 26.11.1984. It is important to note that Crocker initially wanted to abandon Resolution 435. E-mail interview with Hans-Joachim Vergau, 26.04.1016.

[174] Thus, without the possibility to 'mobilize' [bewegungsfähig machen] the WCG, the Foreign Office saw no alternative to the US-led initiative, hoping that it would lead to the implementation of Resolution 435. Given the limited options the Foreign Office had available, it argued that West Germany should focus on promoting better relations between all political forces in Namibia, particularly between the IG and SWAPO: PAAA, Zwischenarchiv, Bd. 138104, 1984–1985, Lösung der Namibiafrage; hier: Wie können wir wieder eine stärkere Rolle spielen?, 05.12.1984. See also PAAA, Zwischenarchiv, Bd. 125282, 1981, Deutsche Namibia-Politik ohne Kontaktgruppe, 25.05.1984 [wrong date; should be 25.05.1981].

[175] The Foreign Office acknowledged that any West German initiative at a ministerial level had to be closely coordinated with Washington: PAAA, Zwischenarchiv, Bd. 138104, 1984–1985, Lösung der Namibiafrage; hier: Wie können wir wieder eine stärkere Rolle spielen?, 05.12.1984, Anlage 2, 04.12.1984, 3.

[176] 'Tiefe Sorge', *Der Spiegel*, 31/1985, 29.07.1985.

[177] PAAA, Zwischenarchiv, Bd. 138105, 1985, Namibia; hier: Einsetzungsfeierlichkeiten der 'VPK-Interimsregierung, 04.06.1985.

[178] 'Tiefe Sorge', *Der Spiegel*, 31/1985, 29.07.1985.

[179] PAAA, Zwischenarchiv, Bd. 138105, 1985, Der Bundesminister des Auswärtigen, an den Präsidenten der South West Africa People's Organisation, Herr Sam Nujoma-Luanda, 30.06.1985.

supported Pretoria and the DTA in the 1970s, it seems not surprising that there was growing concern about the Kohl government's position towards the TGNU. In May 1985, Nujoma accused the Kohl government of being involved in 'a very dangerous complot' with the 'racist South African regime against decolonisation and the achievement of real Namibian independence'.[180] Although Genscher found Nujoma's statement 'incomprehensible and unwarranted, considering the government's clear and unambiguous Namibia policy', as he explained in 1986, the fact that the CDU/CSU showed little sympathy for SWAPO in the 1970s warranted such scepticism. Importantly, however, Genscher took these accusations seriously, which was reflected in his personal letter to Nujoma in 1985.[181] The characteristically polemic rhetoric of Strauß, and the open support for the TGNU by members of the government, was not helpful in promoting an atmosphere of trust with African states, let alone SWAPO. The Kohl government had yet to prove that it was not secretly supporting Pretoria's agenda in Namibia.

SWAPO believed it was seeing a change in West Germany's Namibia policy, based on the fact that influential members of the government took part in the TGNU's inauguration ceremony and demanded Bonn's support for the Interim Government, that in 1985, the CDU affiliated Konrad Adenauer Foundation held a constitutional seminar for the TGNU in Bonn, which raised the suspicion that the conference had already articulated a future constitution for Namibia, and that the KAS seminar was related to development objectives of private foundations before independence.[182]

Genscher's emphasis on foreign policy continuity appeared increasingly meaningless in the mid-1980s. He not only faced considerable opposition from many quarters within

---

[180] Ibid., Entwicklung unserer Beziehungen zur SWAPO; hier: Kritik der SWAPO an der Namibiapolitik der Bundesrepublik Deutschland, 12.06.1985. See also deutscher Bundestag, 10. Wahlperiode, Drucksache 10/5312, 14.04.1986, 3. In 1981 already, Nujoma made similar accusations against the SPD-led government. Nujoma even stated that 'if the conflict continues to escalate, Namibian Germans will die'. He emphasised, however, that West Germany would be responsible for the death of Namibian Germans, for Bonn continued to sell arms to Pretoria: 'Namibia', CDU/CSU Pressedienst, Nr. 01073, Namibia, 27.05.1981.

[181] Deutscher Bundestag, 10. Wahlperiode, Drucksache 10/5312, 14.04.1986, 3. Genscher underlined the government's continuing support for Resolution 435 and that it would not recognize the interim government. Furthermore, Genscher emphasised the 'great value' of past meetings between him and Nujoma, proposing personal talks at the next UN General Assembly: PAAA, Zwischenarchiv, Bd. 138105, 1985, Der Bundesminister des Auswärtigen, an den Präsidenten der South West Africa People's Organisation, Herr Sam Nujoma, Luanda, 30.06.1985.

[182] PAAA, Zwischenarchiv, Bd. 138105, 1985, Entwicklung unserer Beziehungen zur SWAPO; hier: Kritik der SWAPO an der Namibiapolitik der Bundesrepublik Deutschland, 12.06.1985. See also Deutscher Bundestag, 10. Wahlperiode, Drucksache 10/5312, 14.04.1986, 3. The seminar participation of Hans Hugo Klein, a judge of federal constitutional court and representative of the CDU, and Karl-Heinz Hornhues, CDU Africa-expert, was justified on the grounds that the delegates acted independently of the government: Deutscher Bundestag, Drucksache 10/5312, 14.04.1986, 3.

the government, including the FDP.[183] The WCG, a platform that had played a vital role in increasing his importance and influence in the Namibian independence process, gradually drifted towards insignificance in the mid-1980s.[184] Furthermore, the Foreign Office found itself increasingly in opposition to the Federal Ministry for Economic Cooperation and Development (BMZ) in Namibia.[185] Under Kohl, the BMZ received greater leeway, which was one of the strongest indications that Bonn's policy towards Namibia gradually changed under the conservative government.[186] There were even indications that a return to the anticommunist attitude of the 1970s was simmering underneath the government's emphasis on foreign policy continuity. In 1987, Hans Klein (CSU) became the head of the BMZ. Klein

---

[183] In late 1982 already, Wolfgang Rumpf (FDP) organised a petition in favour of development assistance for pre-independence Namibia. 53 delegates, from all parties, signed the petition (20 SPD, 15 FDP and 18 CDU). See, e.g., B. Conrad, 'Abgeordnete fordern Namibia-Hilfe', *Die Welt*, 21.09.1982; 'Interfraktioneller Gesprächskreis für sofortige Hilfe an Namibia', fdk-freie demokratische korrespondenz, Nr. 680, 20.09.1982. The statement that accompanied the petition can be found in the National Archives of Namibia in the following file: GAS 1/5/2, File 13/3/1/83 PS 2, Müller-Emmert, Rumpf, Hornhues an Genscher, 16.09.1982.

[184] Although Vergau argues that the WCG continued to function as a group after 1983, evidence paints a more complex picture. E-mail interview with Hans-Joachim Vergau, 26.04.2016. High-ranking members of the five UN missions came together at various occasions throughout the 1980s; the momentum was, however, lost after 1983, for the Reagan administration linked Namibia's independence to the withdrawal of Cuban troops from Angola. In April 1983, the Angolan ambassador to France, Alfredo Salvaterra, stated that the WCG was 'practically not active anymore'. Salvaterra explained that the Reagan administration had 'paralyzed' the group: PAAA, MfAA, ZR, 2434/89, 1981–1988, Vermerk: Gespräch mit dem 1. Sekretär der Botschaft der VR Angola in Frankreich, Genossen Salvaterra, in der angolanischen Botschaft, 07.04.1983, 5. France did not take part in two WCG meetings in Bonn in 1984: PAAA, Zwischenarchiv, Bd. 138104, 1984–1985, Betr.: Hintergrundgespräch DG 32 zur deutschen Namibiapolitik und zur Politik im südlichen Afrika; hier: Leitfaden für das Hintergrundgespräch, 07.03.1985. West Germany remained optimistic about the future of the group, despite the fact that the WCG was not a coherent unit anymore, as stated by the Foreign Office in 1985: 'Contrary to France, we stand by the Contact Group [halten an der Kontaktgruppe fest]; it [the Contact Group] is for our Namibia policy an important instrument and can, at any time, be fully reactivated for political initiatives in Namibia, especially also with regard to Resolution 435, which is binding for us': PAAA, Zwischenarchiv, Bd. 138114, 1986–1987, Betr.: Namibia-Konferenz in West-Europa; hier: Vorschlag des Namibia-Rates, die Konferenz in der Bundesrepublik Deutschland abzuhalten, 06.01.1985. Chester Crocker also stated that the 'WCG suspended its active group diplomacy' after 1983. E-mail interview with Chester Crocker, 25.08.2016. Yet, evidence shows that in 1984 the WCG was still acting in co-operative ways internally, that is, at the level of high-ranking members of the five UN missions: PAAA, Zwischenarchiv, Bd. 138104, 1984–1985, Namibia-Regionalpolitik im südlichen Afrika; hier: Offizielle Darstellung der amerikanischen Regionalpolitik im letzten Quartal 1984, 07.01.1985; See also Ibid. Bd. 138114, 1986–1987, 'Mögliches Abrücken' der südafrikanischen Regierung von Resolution 435, 10.04.1987.

[185] See PAAA, Zwischenarchiv, Bd. 138105, 1985, Namibia; hier: Einsetzungsfeierlichkeiten der 'VPK-Interimsregierung', 04.06.1985.

[186] H. Melber, 'Namibia-Politik: Umgang mit einer "historischen Hypothek"', *Frankfurter Rundschau*, 22.06.1987.

left little doubt about the BMZ's position, arguing that the West had no reason to subordinate itself to the Marxist opinions represented in the UN.[187]

Considering the escalation of the Cold War under Reagan's presidency and the Kohl government's ambiguous policy towards southern Africa, it should hardly come as a surprise that Brandt stressed during a meeting with Gorbachev in Moscow that a 'a new phase' in detente and 'East-West dialogue' was urgently needed. Brandt also voiced his regret that the Kohl government did not see the value of dialogue with Moscow and stated his doubts about any breakthroughs during Reagan's tenure.[188] Importantly, both Genscher and the Foreign Office also lobbied for the reactivation of détente.[189]

Despite the Kohl government's emphasis on foreign policy continuity, underlying efforts to influence Namibia's future in Pretoria's favour became apparent in the mid-1980s. Although Genscher tried reviving the WCG, he entered a period of limited influence, marked by the breakdown or stagnation of negotiations between the relevant actors in the Namibian independence process. Overall, SWAPO and the Namibia question moved into the background, for the growing violence in South Africa became one of the most pressing concerns of the international community in the mid-to-late 1980s. Yet, behind the scenes, the Namibia question continued to play a central role in West German politics.

---

[187] Ibid.
[188] 'Brandt bei Gorbachev', *Namibia Nachrichten*, 02.06.1985.
[189] 'Reagan droht Westeuropa, "primitiver Amerika-Hass der Sozis"', *Allgemeine Zeitung*, 11.06.1985.

7 The mid-to-late 1980s

Non-governmental organisations and West Germany's policy towards Namibia

In 1982, the CSU hardliner Jürgen Warnke became the head of the Ministry of Economic Co-operation (BMZ), further increasing Strauß' influence within the Ministry. Warnke harboured considerable resentment against SWAPO, mainly out of concern that a SWAPO-led Namibia would play into the hands of Moscow's geostrategic aspirations in the region. From the BMZ's perspective, it therefore made perfect sense to support Pretoria's 'internal solution' for Namibia through non-governmental organisations.[1] However, the implementation of any such measures risked confrontation with the Foreign Office.

In mid-1983, Genscher expressed, during a meeting with Warnke, the Foreign Office's interest in 'especially close co-operation' with the BMZ. Considering that Genscher and Strauß competed over the direction of the Kohl government's Namibia policy at the time, it is plausible to suggest that the foreign minister tried to gain greater influence within the BMZ. Not unexpectedly, therefore, Warnke underlined the BMZ's determination to increase development co-operation with pre-independence Namibia. Genscher, however, did not support such endeavours unless the executing agencies were politically neutral.[2] In fact, Genscher made it clear that the new Kohl government 'will not throw a spanner into the implementation of private initiatives', although it contradicted the non-partisan attitude represented by the Foreign Office.[3] Obviously, Genscher had to make compromises in a CDU/CSU-led government.

---

[1] See H. Melber, 'Bundesdeutsche Entwicklungspolitik als Intervention: Hilfsmaßnahmen für ein neokoloniales Namibia', *Peripherie: Zeitschrift für Politik und Ökonomie in der Dritten Welt*, Nr. 25/26, 1987, 52–53.

[2] AAPD, 1983, Band II, Vermerk über das Gespräch des Bundesministers mit BM Dr. Warnke am 12. Juli 1983 im Gästehaus Venusberg, 13.07.1983, 1102–1105. Genscher viewed the work of the Otto Benecke Foundation in a positive light.

[3] PAAA, Zwischenarchiv, Bd. 138099, 1982–1984, Frage entwicklungspolitischer Zusammenarbeit mit Namibia; hier: Rehoboth (Hans Diergaardt, Rehoboth Liberation Front), 16.12.1982. At an earlier occasion, Genscher stated that financial co-operation was not possible as long as Namibia was not independent. However, he admitted that the Kohl government might consider the implementation of such measures at some stage: PAAA, Zwischenarchiv, Bd. 138099, 1982–1984, Namibia; hier: Frage von Entwicklungshilfe vor Unabhängigkeit, 28.10.1982. See, e.g., B. Conrad, 'Abgeordnete fordern Namibia-Hilfe', *Die Welt,* 21.09.1982; PAAA, Zwischenarchiv, Bd. 138099, 1982–1984, Frage entwicklungspolitischer Zusammenarbeit mit Namibia; hier: Rehoboth (Hans Diergaardt, Rehoboth Liberation Front), 16.12.1982.

Hence, Genscher's opinion concerning non-governmental involvement in Namibia softened under the Kohl government. When the DTA approached Genscher regarding development assistance in late 1981, the foreign minister made it clear that the Schmidt government would not 'support any actions that might call into question the government's neutrality'. With the understanding that Namibia could not expect development assistance from Bonn before independence, the DTA insinuated that the government might want to consider providing financial support via non-governmental channels. To avoid political controversy, financial assistance could be declared humanitarian aid. Genscher, however, 'expressed unequivocal opposition to such considerations', indirectly also indicating that neither the BMZ constituted a viable option for such endeavours.[4] Instead, Genscher stated that Bonn's position should motivate the DTA to work seriously towards the implementation of resolution 435.[5] Similarly, Genscher also rejected in early 1982 a proposal for an education project by the Konrad Adenauer Foundation on the grounds that it would jeopardize West Germany's 'impartiality' in future negotiations over Namibian independence.[6]

In 1983, however, Genscher's position changed, confirming in the *Bundestag* that the Kohl government intended to support NGOs in Namibia, particularly in the area of education. Although Genscher stressed that NGO projects could not be implemented without first consulting both SWAPO and the DTA, the deviation from the previously held position was unmistakable.[7] This new approach translated into a greater openness by the Foreign Office towards non-governmental projects in Namibia. Obviously, this may have been a tactical consideration, based on the notion that co-operation might help to increase the Foreign Office's influence within the BMZ. After all, Genscher's principal concern at the time was how to deal with the BMZ.[8] Yet, although the change in approach seemed to indicate a reasonable

---

[4] Genscher also emphasised that foundations that financed their projects with taxpayer money followed a policy of neutrality in Namibia: PAAA, Zwischenarchiv, Bd. 127747, 1981, Besuch DTA-Präsident Kalangula in Bonn, 26.11.1981, 4.

[5] The DTA's financial woes derived mainly from two factors. First, Pretoria lost confidence in the DTA's ability to win elections. Second, the DTA increasingly tried to gain independence from Pretoria and thus sought financial assistance from alternative sources.

[6] PAAA, Zwischenarchiv, Bd. 138107, 1982–1984, Ausbildungsprojekt der Konrad-Adenauer-Stiftung in Namibia; Bezug: Schreiben des KAS-Vorsitzenden Dr. Heck an BM vom 21.07.1982.

[7] Deutscher Bundestag, 10. Wahlperiode, Drucksache 10/833, 21.12.1983, 14. However, in the 1980s, the Foreign Office blocked a number of BMZ proposed non-governmental projects by arguing that SWAPO would oppose such endeavours. Hence, the Foreign Office used the argument that it needed the approval of both SWAPO and the DTA as an excuse to block BMZ proposed projects in Namibia: 'Einigung auf neue Namibia-Politik in Bonn', *Frankfurter Allgemeine Zeitung*, 27.03.1987.

[8] See, e.g., AAPD, 1983, Band I, Beziehungen zu Simbabwe, hier: Termin für Regierungsverhandlungen über Entwicklungshilfe, 13.05.1983, 707–712; H. Melber, 'Namibia-Politik, Umgang mit einer "historischen Hypothek"', *Frankfurter Rundschau*, 22.06.1987; 'Einigung auf neue Namibia-Politik in Bonn', *Frankfurter Allgemeine Zeitung*, 27.03.1987; H. Melber, 'Federal Republic'.

degree of agreement between the Foreign Office and the BMZ, the Foreign Office continued to stress that there would be no development assistance 'from government to government' before independence.[9] In the mid-1980s, there was a growing demand within the Kohl government for a change of course in Namibia, particularly with regard to development assistance and educational programmes. Supporters of the interim government (TGNU) were particularly forceful in demanding greater assistance before independence.

In 1985, the instalment of the TGNU mobilised widespread opposition to Pretoria's Namibia policy, which eventually also raised questions about how Bonn viewed the status of Namibia's new government. Although the TGNU failed to secure recognition by the United Nations, the Greens observed with concern that leading delegates of the Kohl government advocated supporting the interim government 'under certain circumstances'.[10] Some CDU/CSU delegates argued in favour of providing aid to the TGNU. This, of course, raised questions about the Kohl government's de facto position.[11] That the BMZ, which holds responsibility for development co-operation, drove forward non-governmental involvement in Namibia under the Kohl government raised further questions.

Overall, the Kohl government denied that development projects supported the interim government.[12] The government underlined its non-partisan standpoint, while at the same time emphasising that it considered 'preparing the Namibian people for independence' was especially important. In this respect the government was, under the condition of neutrality, not against the promotion of non-governmental projects, particularly in the area of vocational education.[13] However, contemporary observers criticised the government's position, particularly its attempt to increase majority support for the interim government by improv-

---

[9] See, e.g., PAAA, Zwischenarchiv, Bd. 138099, 1982–1984, Frage entwicklungspolitischer Zusammenarbeit mit Namibia; hier: Rehoboth (Hans Diergaardt, Rehoboth Liberation Front), 16.12.1982; 'Der Bundesminister des Auswärtigen Informiert', Mitteilung für die Presse, Nr. 1290/86, 06.11.1986.

[10] AGG, Akte 1473, Petra Kelly, 1983–1986, Pressemitteilung Nr. 109/85, Politische Solidarität mit der SWAPO, 01.03.1985.

[11] Ibid., Pressemitteilung Nr. 471/85, Grüne protestieren gegen CDU-Forderung einer Hilfe für die Zwischenregierung in Namibia, 06.08.1985. Further support for the Interim Government came from Dr. Marx (CDU), and Klein (CSU) stated that the Federal Government could also recognize a government without SWAPO: Deutscher Bundestag, 10. Wahlperiode, Drucksache 10/3568, 06.08.1985, Namibia-Politik der Bundesregierung, 4. See also H. Melber, 'Namibia-Politik, Umgang mit einer "historischen Hypothek"', *Frankfurter Rundschau*, 22.06.1987.

[12] The newsmagazine *Der Spiegel* reported in late 1986 that the DTA and the Zulu leader Gatsha Buthelezi received funding from the Foreign Office via secret funds administered by Andreas Meyer-Landrut, the undersecretary of the Foreign Office. The funds came apparently out of Genscher's slush funds: 'Genschers Reptilienfonds', *Der Spiegel*, 39/1986, 22.09.1986. Vergau, however, stated that such accusations were baseless, for Genscher did not politically support the DTA. E-mail interview with Hans-Joachim Vergau, 26.04.2016.

[13] Deutscher Bundestag, Drucksache 10/833, 21.12.1983, 15.

ing the poor economic conditions of the black majority through non-governmental development assistance and educational programmes. The interim government's aim was to 'create a skilled black workforce with opportunities for advancement into 'white collar jobs', as the West German SWAPO activist Henning Melber points out.[14] Thus, the creation of a small black middle class was supposed to fulfil the purpose of establishing a loyal internal power base. Ultimately, the support of a cross section of the non-white majority would also serve to demonstrate the legitimacy of the interim government. Overall, development assistance before independence would predominantly aid the interim government and thus Pretoria's internal solution, as critics pointed out.[15]

SWAPO held similar views and thus was strictly against development assistance as long as Namibia was illegally occupied by South Africa.[16] After the change of government in Bonn, SWAPO grew particularly frustrated with Genscher for a number of failures and broken promises. In this regard, SWAPO observed with concern that Genscher had promised continuity in foreign policy, but then failed to carry out his pledge by announcing that Bonn intended to support non-governmental projects in Namibia. Hence, the growing debate among Bonn's advocates of the interim government over development assistance raised alarm bells within SWAPO. That members of all political parties, including Genscher, were seemingly prepared to include the DTA in such talks was for SWAPO the ultimate betrayal, for it contradicted Bonn's support of Resolution 435 and Genscher's role in the WCG.[17]

Importantly, however, the concept of using development aid to further political objectives in Namibia was not a new phenomenon.[18] Yet, never before had the BMZ intervened to such an extent in the southern African country. By the mid-1980s, the BMZ showed a higher level of involvement in Namibia than the Foreign Office.[19] The momentum remained with the BMZ throughout most of the 1980s.[20] To make matter worse, the capacity of the Foreign Office to have an impact in Namibia appeared increasingly limited, which led to

---

[14] Melber, 'Bundesdeutsche Entwicklungspolitik', 58.
[15] Ibid., 53–60.
[16] PAAA, Neues Amt, Bd. 16414, 1983, South West Africa People's Organisation: Presseerklärung der SWAPO gegen die vorgeschlagene Entwicklungshilfe für Namibia vor der Unabhängigkeit, 15.06.1983; S. Nujoma, 'SWAPO tritt kompromsslos für freie Wahlen ein', in: ISSA wissenschaftliche Reihe 21(ed.), *Im Brennpunkt*, 49.
[17] Ibid.
[18] See Chapter Four, The decision-making processes toward Namibia.
[19] Melber, 'Federal Republic', 3. While Genscher and the Foreign Office did not recognize the interim government and were strictly against any departure from Resolution 435, the BMZ sought increasing co-operation with the TGNU.
[20] U. Engel, 'Germany: Between value-based solidarity and bureaucratic interests', in U. Engel and G. R. Olsen (eds.), *Africa and the North: Between Globalization and Marginalization*, London, Routledge, 2005, 87.

the understanding that Genscher should concentrate on the one strategy that will have the greatest potential impact, namely, helping to improve relations between SWAPO and the IG.[21] Thus, given Genscher's limited options, the increasing focus on SWAPO and the IG was a measure to counteract the growing support from within the Kohl government for the interim government.[22] The DTA was strongly against IG-SWAPO meetings, for there were concerns that 'the Foreign Office was working towards a special arrangement between the Namibians of German descent and SWAPO'.[23]

Furthermore, the Reagan administration's initial lack of commitment to Resolution 435 motivated the Foreign Office to pursue a policy towards Namibia that would significantly deviate from Washington's approach.[24] As a counter measure to Reagan's support of Pretoria's interest in Namibia, the Foreign Office proposed to 'drastically increase the support of SWAPO, particularly in the area of scholarships and in non-military areas via the FES and the church'.[25] SWAPO initially declined to accept scholarships for SWAPO students through the Otto-Benecke Foundation (OBS). In 1980, however, Nujoma perceived the proposal in a much more positive light.[26] By 1982 he openly considered the Otto-Benecke, Friedrich Ebert and Friedrich Naumann Foundation as 'friends'.[27] The BMZ and Strauß voiced their

---

[21] E-mail interview with Hans Joachim-Vergau, 26.04.2016. See also PAAA, Zwischenarchiv, Bd. 125282, 1981, Deutsche Namibia-Politik nach den Gesprächen von Washington vom 21/22 Mai 1981, 26.05.1981; Ibid., Bd. 138104, 1984–1985, Lösung der Namibiafrage; hier: Wie können wir wieder eine stärkere Rolle spielen?, 05.12.1984.

[22] The correctness of the assertion that Genscher's increasing focus on SWAPO and the IG was a measure to counteract the growing support for the interim government has been confirmed by Hans-Joachim Vergau: E-mail interview with Hans Joachim-Vergau, 26.04.2016.

[23] See PAAA, Neues Amt, Bd. 16414, Bonn Namibia Information, 20.06.1983.

[24] In late 1984, the Reagan administration stressed again that doubts about US commitment to Resolution 435 were not justified. Nevertheless, doubts remained over the depth of Washington's commitment to the UN Resolution: PAAA, Zwischenarchiv, Bd. 138104, 1984–1985, Lösung der Namibiafrage; hier: Wie können wir wieder eine stärkere Rolle spielen?, 05.12.1984 und Vorlage, 15.11.1984.

[25] The Foreign Office further stated that the Reagan administration showed little appreciation of the achievements of the WCG. The 'Crocker-Team' gave the impression that Washington will follow Crocker's line of approach 'no matter what the other four [members of the WCG] think'. Hence, the Foreign Office stressed the importance of Resolution 435 and the need to strengthen cooperation with its partners in the WCG in order to prevent the disintegration of the group. The aim was to exert their combined influence on the Reagan administration: PAAA, Zwischenarchiv, Bd. 125282, 1981, Deutsche Namibia-Politik nach den Gesprächen von Washington vom 21/22 Mai 1981, 26.05.1981. Vergau also stated that Crocker 'initially wanted to dismiss both the WCG and Resolution 435. In the end, he gave in to the demands of the WCG [hat sich alsbald doch in die KG eingegliedert]': E-mail interview with Hans-Joachim Vergau, 26.04.2016.

[26] PAAA, Zwischenarchiv, Bd. 127477, 1981, Besuch des SWAPO-Präsidenten Sam Nujoma vom 23. bis 27. Oktober 1980 in der Bundesrepublik; hier: Ablauf und Wertung, 27.10.1980.

[27] PAAA, Zwischenarchiv, Bd. 138100, 1982–1984, Namibia-Initiative; hier: Nujoma-Besuch in Bonn, 27.05.1982. For more information about the Friedrich-Ebert Foundation's co-operation with political parties and liberation movements in Africa, see V. Vinnai, *Demokratieförderung in*

strict opposition to such support as long as Namibia was not independent. Obviously, the BMZ showed no such concerns when projects were directed towards supporting the DTA. Genscher had little understanding for such a position, not least because the funds were designated for the education of non-white Namibians.[28] In 1984 alone, the education of non-white Namibians was supported with four million deutsche marks.[29]

Importantly, however, both the Schmidt and the Kohl government rejected supporting SWAPO directly, largely because both governments repudiated the armed struggle.[30] The main concern was that financial assistance, even for civilian purposes, might end up supporting armed conflict.[31] Reagan's seeming willingness to support Pretoria's 'internal solution' in Namibia, the deteriorating influence of the WCG and the failure of both the Foreign Office and Genscher to carry out aggressively the promise of foreign policy continuity contributed to the BMZ's increasing involvement in Namibian affairs.[32] Melber came to the

---

Afrika, die Zusammenarbeit der Friedrich Ebert Stiftung mit politischen Parteien und Befreiungsbewegungen in Afrika, Berlin, LIT, 2007.

[28] PAAA, Zwischenarchiv, Bd. 138099, 1982–1984, Lage Namibia; hier: Presseinterview des Bayrischen Ministerpräsidenten, 08.03.1984. See also '"Bonner versprechen" nur kosmetische Korrektur, Exklusiv-Interview mit Franz Josef Strauß', *Allgemeine Zeitung*, 06.03.1984. In the early 1980s, the Foreign Office did not endorse talks between the BMZ and Dirk Mudge in Bonn, not least because the talks were bound to focus on development aid: AAPD, 1983, Band I, Beziehungen zu Simbabwe; hier: Termin für Regierungsverhandlungen über Entwicklungshilfe, 13.05.1983, 709.

[29] Between 1976 and 1984, West Germany made available over 58 million deutsche marks for educational projects in Namibia and 12 million deutsche marks for projects of the OBS: Ibid, 138106, 1982–1984, Entwicklungshilfe-Leistungen an Namibia aus Mitteln der Bundesregierung (Stand: 01.02.1984), 18.09.1984.

[30] Nonetheless, SWAPO also received direct support from the SPD-led government in the mid-to-late 1970s, albeit not indiscriminately. During this period, the government provided the following support: (a) Humanitarian aid in 1975: glasses frames worth 2,500 deutsche marks directly to SWAPO; dried fish worth 1,600 deutsche marks, which SWAPO declined. (b) Contributions to organisations that directly benefit SWAPO: 200,000 U.S. dollars to the UN Namibia trust for the Namibia-Institute in Lusaka, between 1976 and 1978; 120,000 U.S. dollars to the United Nations International Children's Emergency Found (UNICEF) for Namibian refugees living in Angola in 1977. (c) Contributions to international organisations, foundations and churches that benefited SWAPO: 24 million US dollars donation to the UN World Food Programme (WFP); 267,000 deutsche marks donation to the Evangelical Centre for Development Aid (EZE) for the establishment of the Institute for Social Advancement in Windhoek in 1975. The institute was strongly influenced by SWAPO. Since 1969, the government also contributed the total amount of 375,000 US dollars to the United Nations Relief and Works Agency for southern Africa: PAAA, Zwischenarchiv, Bd. 116802, 1977–1978, Hilfeleistungen der Bundesregierung an SWAPO, 31.05.1978.

[31] See, e.g., PAAA, Zwischenarchiv, Bd. 138099, 1982–1984, Namibia; hier: Frage von Entwicklungshilfe vor Unabhängigkeit, 28.10.1982; Ibid., Bd. 138104, 1984–1985, Namibia; hier: Förderung von TZ-Projekten zugunsten von namibischen Flüchtlingen, 20.12.1984.

[32] Engel made a similar assessment, stating that 'during phases of high-level political initiatives, the BMZ came second to the Foreign Office, but once these phases ceased and the Africa policy routine ruled again, the centre of gravity shifted to the BMZ (this was the case throughout the 1980s

conclusion that Genscher's failure to map out his own course in Namibia and thus passively accepted Reagan's lead, helped the BMZ to establish itself as the 'spearhead of the conservatives' policy towards Namibia'.[33] In this respect, the focus on improving relations between SWAPO and the IG, as well as increasing the support of SWAPO in the area of scholarships and in non-military areas, can be at least partly understood as an attempt by the Foreign Office to move out of the shadow of US policy towards Namibia and effectively distance Genscher from Reagan's policies in southern Africa.[34]

In the light of these developments, the Green Party in mid-1985 posed a major interpellation in the *Bundestag* concerning the government's Namibian policy and organized in co-operation with the Information Centre southern Africa (ISSA) a 'Namibia Hearing' in Bonn.[35] Ultimately, the Kohl government declined to participate in the hearing and rejected the platform.[36] The active and high level participation of a wide range of representatives included, among others, SWAPO president Sam Nujoma and GDR ambassador and permanent representative Wolfgang Bergold.[37] Delegates and ministers of the government and the Foreign Office, as well as political foundations, decisively shunned the Hearing.[38]

---

and 1990s)': Engel, 'Germany: Between', 87. Melber also came to a similar conclusion: Melber, 'Bundesdeutsche Entwicklungspolitik', 53.

[33] Ibid.

[34] See also PAAA, Zwischenarchiv, Bd. 125282, 1981, Deutsche Namibia-Politik nach den Gesprächen von Washington vom 21/22 Mai 1981, 26.05.1981; Ibid., Bd. 138104, 1984–1985, Lösung der Namibiafrage; hier: Wie können wir wieder eine stärkere Rolle spielen?, 05.12.1984.

[35] Deutscher Bundestag, 10. Wahlperiode, Drucksache 10/3568, 26.06.1985. See also AGG, Akte 1473, Petra Kelly, 1983–1986, Pressemitteilung Nr. 357/85, Stillschweigende Anerkennung aus Bonn. The Kohl government answered the Greens major interpellation in April 1986, nine months after the questions were issued, in the *Bundestag*: Deutscher Bundestag, 10. Wahlperiode, Drucksache 10/5312, 14.04.1986, 11. The Bundestag debated the interpellation in late 1986: Deutscher Bundestag, 10. Wahlperiode, Stenographischer Bericht, 243. Sitzung, 06.11.1986, 18850.The contributions to the Namibia Hearing have been published in the form of a book: ISSA wissenschaftliche Reihe 21(ed.), *Im Brennpunkt: Namibia und die Bundesrepublik Deutschland*, Köln, MVR, 1987.

[36] The government also declined to elaborate the issue of non-governmental projects in the *Bundestag*, pointing out that it had already addressed the issue shortly after gaining power: Deutscher Bundestag, Drucksache 10/5312, 14.04.1986, 11.

[37] Representatives of West Germany's Anti-Apartheid Movement, the German Development Institute, the Evangelic and Catholic Church, the United Nations, the South African Non-Racial Olympic Committee and several African ambassadors also participated in the Hearing. For the full list of participants in the Namibia Hearing, see 'Anhang', in ISSA wissenschaftliche Reihe 21(ed.), *Im Brennpunkt*, 1–3.

[38] The BMZ, the Konrad Adenauer and Friedrich Naumann Foundation also decline to participate in the hearing. Only the Otto Benecke Foundation, which was not related to any political party, followed the invitation. Nevertheless, the OBS was also accused of funding the Interim Government. Hence, the foundations' reluctance to participate in the Hearing was a reflection of their policy of secrecy.

The Greens argued that the Kohl government actively undermined the implementation of Resolution 435 by promoting non-governmental financial involvement in Namibia.[39] Significantly, this view, widely represented at the Namibia Hearing, reflected also SWAPO's concerns, and was effectively summed up by Christa Brandt, editor of ISSA, in the Hearing's closing statement:

> The Federal Government contributes through substantial financial appropriation to the political enforcement of the so called Interim Government. Development aid funded on public expense and channelled through private organizations and foundations as a cover, is pumped to an ever greater extent into Namibia for the development of a political alternative to SWAPO.[40]

In this regard, Vesper accused the HSS, KAS and the FNS of conducting, under the banner of 'social structural aid' and 'socio-political education', multiple projects in Namibia.[41] However, the government did not acknowledge any violations, stating that foundations and NGOs acted on their own initiative. Indeed, foundations were non-governmental and independent private non-profit organizations, although loosely linked to political parties and supported by the federal state budged. The foundations' affiliation with established political parties and their reliance on the federal state budged was viewed as problematic in the 1980s, despite their emphasis on formal autonomy. In this regard, their independence from political parties seemed questionable. That even the foundations private initiatives were largely funded by the BMZ was conveniently ignored, as Vesper pointed out.[42]

Thus, the Greens accused the Kohl government of secretly supporting Pretoria's plans for Namibia.[43] This accusation was based on the notion that the MPC would be politically irrelevant without Pretoria's endorsement and West German financial support, 'disguised as development aid'. 'Why else would they fear free elections as the devil fears the holy water,' a press statement concluded.[44]

---

[39] M. Vesper, 'Die Namibia-Politik der Bundesrepublik Deutschland', in ISSA wissenschaftliche Reihe 21 (ed.), *Im Brennpunkt*, 66–67.

[40] S. Nujoma, *SWAPO tritt kompromisslos für freie Wahlen ein*, in ISSA wissenschaftliche Reihe 21(ed.), *Im Brennpunkt*, 49. See also PAAA, Neues Amt, Bd. 16414, 1983, South West Africa People's Organisation: Presseerklärung der SWAPO gegen die vorgeschlagene Entwicklungshilfe für Namibia vor der Unabhängigkeit, 15.06.1983. Brandt, C., 'Abschlusserklärung', in ISSA wissenschaftliche Reihe 21 (ed.), *Im Brennpunkt*, 247.

[41] Vesper stated that the Hanns Seidel Foundation planned to establish a management consulting institute for the education of managers, and the Konrad Adenauer Foundation worked in collaboration with the Democratic Turnhalle Alliance and the University Centre for Studies in Namibia (TUCSIN) on the promotion of projects in Namibia: Vesper, 'Die Namibia-Politik', 66.

[42] Vesper, 'Die Namibia-Politik', 66–67.

[43] See Deutscher Bundestag, 10. Wahlperiode, Stenographischer Bericht, 243. Sitzung, 06.11.1986, 18850.

[44] AGG, Akte 1473, Petra Kelly, 1983–1986, Pressemitteilung Nr. 109/85, Politische Solidarität mit

In 1984, the BMZ allocated 30 Million deutsche marks for projects in Namibia. The BMZ acknowledged its support of private initiatives in Namibia, while simultaneously underlining that the government currently provided no development assistance to Namibia.[45] Here, however, lay the problem, for non-governmental projects had opened up a serious loophole through which financial aid could be channelled into directions that favoured one side over the other. Evidence seems to suggest that aid was channelled into projects that reinforced the status quo. It is, however, impossible to determine, under the current restrictions on archival access, the extent to which non-governmental projects directly benefitted the interim government.[46] Yet, there can be little doubt that the BMZ firmly favoured the interim government, particularly in the 1980s.[47] This also becomes evident in that the BMZ denied support to a school project for SWAPO children in the People's Republic of the Congo in late 1984. The BMZ provided, next to financial reasons, the explanation that 'location and SWAPO, as the responsible body, stood in the way'.[48] At some point, Strauß even personally attempted to cut off funds from two foundations that supported SWAPO.[49]

---

    der SWAPO, 01.03.1985. For an overview of the Green Party's position towards Namibia, see ISSA wissenschaftliche Reihe 21(ed.), *Im Brennpunkt: Namibia und die Bundesrepublik Deutschland*, Köln, MVR, 1987.

[45] Vesper, 'Die Namibia-Politik', in ISSA wissenschaftliche Reihe 21(ed.), *Im Brennpunkt*, 67. For a more detailed account of development assistance between 1978 and 1986, see Melber, 'Bundesdeutsche Entwicklungspolitik', 61–66.

[46] Unfortunately, primary sources that might have offered conclusive insights into the foundations financial involvement in Namibia are sealed under the foundations' secrecy policy. However, the Kohl government disclosed non-governmental projects in the *Bundestag*, which offer a glimpse into non-governmental initiatives. See, e.g., Deutscher Bundestag, Drucksache 10/5312, 14.04.1986, 8–11; Deutscher Bundestag, 10. Wahlperiode, Drucksache 10/5840, 11.07.1986. For information on budget funds for Namibia from the European Community (EC), see, e.g., Deutscher Bundestag, 10. Wahlperiode, Drucksache 10/6746, 12.12.1986, 5; Ibid., Drucksache 10/6564, 25.11.1986, Bericht der Bundesregierung über die deutsche Humanitäre Hilfe im Ausland 1982 bis 1985. Furthermore, Foreign Office files also provide a valuable glimpse into Bonn's financial involvement in Namibia, see, e.g., PAAA, Zwischenarchiv, Bd. 116802, 1977–1978, Hilfeleistungen der Bundesregierung an SWAPO, 31.05.1978; Ibid., Bd. 138106, 1982–1984, Konzept eines Hilfsprogramms für Namibia, 18.09.1984.

[47] See, e.g., Ibid., Bd. 138105,1985, Namibia; hier: Einsetzungsfeierlichkeiten der 'VPK-Interimregierung, 04.06.1985; H. Melber, 'Namibia-Politik, Umgang mit einer "historischen Hypothek"', *Frankfurter Rundschau*, 22.06.1987. See also AAPD, 1983, Band I, Beziehungen zu Simbabwe; hier: Termin für Regierungsverhandlungen über Entwicklungshilfe, 13.05.1983, 709; 'Kleine Hebel', *Der Spiegel*, 11/1988, 14.03.1988; H. Melber, 'Bundesdeutsche Entwicklungspolitik'.

[48] PAAA, Zwischenarchiv, Bd. 138104, 1984–1985, Namibia; hier: Förderung von TZ-Projekten zugunsten von namibischen Flüchtlingen, 06.12.1984. See also Ibid., Schulprojekt SWAPO in VR Kongo für namibische Flüchtlinge, 11.10.1984; Ibid., Der Bundesminister für Wirtschaftliche Zusammenarbeit: UN-Bildungsstätte in der VR Kongo für Fachkräfte aus Namibia, 31.10.1984.

[49] One programme was funded by the FES since 1983, largely for the education of thirteen SWAPO leaders. A further programme was established by the OBS, allocating scholarships, worth 80 million deutsche marks, to SWAPO refugees. See 'Warnkes Streichaktion', *Der Spiegel, 19/1986*,

Similarly, in 1984, there was growing support for educational projects for Namibian refugees, but the BMZ refused to lend its support. That the East-West conflict continued to be the dominant underlying issue becomes apparent in Vergau's argument in favour of such projects: 'The education of Namibian refugees would promote a less one-sided support (particularly the critics of our Namibia policy complain constantly about the communist enemy's strong influence on SWAPO's education)'.[50]

Despite controversy, support for non-governmental projects in Namibia remained strong in the late 1980s. In 1986, Rumpf (FDP) proposed in the *Bundestag* that financial support through NGOs should be increased to advance Namibia's economic independence from South Africa.[51] Supported by factions within the FDP and CDU/CSU, he argued that Namibia could not achieve independence as long as its economy was heavily dependent on South Africa.[52] Although direct development assistance remained inconceivable, his proposal received significant support within the coalition-government.[53] But the involvement of non-governmental projects in Namibia, under the condition of neutrality, left room for various interpretations. To abide by a strict policy of neutrality would have required that Bonn neither supported nor challenged any of the main political forces in Namibia. Although West German development assistance and educational programmes were generally geared towards benefitting Namibia's black majority, it is clear that this was not always achieved in practise and instead might have benefitted Pretoria's objectives in Namibia.[54] Studies on development assistance have argued that financial aid may perpetuate an unjust status quo,

---

05.05.1986.

[50] PAAA, Zwischenarchiv, Bd. 138104, 1984–1985, Namibia; hier: Förderung von TZ-Projekten zugunsten von namibischen Flüchtlingen, 20.12.1984.

[51] Rumpf mentioned the OBS as a successful non-governmental organisation, particularly with regard to educational projects in Namibia. See Deutscher Bundestag, 10. Wahlperiode, Stenographischer Bericht, 243. Sitzung, 06.11.1986, 18853.

[52] Deutscher Bundestag, 10. Wahlperiode, Stenographischer Bericht, 243. Sitzung, 6.11.1986, 18853. See also Vesper, 'Die Namibia-Politik', 66.

[53] See also 'Interfraktioneller Gesprächskreis für sofortige Hilfe an Namibia', fdk-freie demokratische Korrespondenz, Nr. 680, 20.09.1982. Rumpf proposed to increase non-governmental investment in rural development, apprenticeship and advanced education, and development in the social field. In 1981 already, Rumpf established the Interfraktionelle Gesprächskreis für Namibia. The intention was to bring together ministers from all political parties who supported, among other things, development assistance for Namibia before independence. Rumpf's frequent Namibia visits are documented in the National Archives of Namibia under the following signature: GAS, 1/2/11.

[54] See PAAA, Zwischenarchiv, Bd. 138106, 1982–1984, Konzept eines Hilfsprogramms für Namibia, 18.09.1984. Vergau explained that 'NGOs were geared towards providing development assistance. The DTA was perhaps interested in some of the programmes, which might have received the authorisation of Genscher. However, the assumption that Genscher wanted to politically support the DTA is false'. E-mail interview with Hans-Joachim Vergau, 26.04. 2016.

as it can contribute to a strengthening of the established political and economic structures, obstructing progressive social change.[55]

After the re-election of the conservative-liberal government in 1987, the reshuffle of both the Foreign Office and the BMZ placed the two ministries into opposing camps, for the Foreign Office came firmly into the hands of the FDP and the BMZ into the hands of the CSU. In an attempt to overcome differences, the Foreign Office and the BMZ, including two members of each coalition party, established a working group on Namibia in early 1987.[56] Nonetheless, demands for developing assistance became louder after Hans Klein (CSU) became head of the BMZ in 1987.[57] Siegfried Lengl, state secretary in the BMZ and a close friend of Strauß, was, however, steering the course of the BMZ in Africa, which ensured that 'the partners of Strauß' received 'plentiful' development assistance, as *Der Spiegel* reported in early 1988.[58] A few weeks earlier, Lengl had bragged about his accomplishments in Namibia through the channels of the HSS: 'The things that I have constructed in this country (Namibia) using all sorts of tricks and bypassing Genscher'.[59] Perhaps not unexpectedly, therefore, SWAPO became increasingly frustrated with the BMZ's efforts to influence events in Namibia, even to the point of threatening in 1987 to 'blow up' development projects proposed by Klein.[60]

Contemporary observers concluded that Strauß tried to circumvent Genscher's foreign policy by pursuing some kind of 'Bavarian foreign policy' through the BMZ.[61] In any

---

[55] For a detailed examination concerning issues surrounding development aid, see N. Islam, *Exploration in Development Issues: Selected Articles of Nurul Islam*, New Delhi, Academic Foundation, 2005.

[56] Melber, 'Federal Republic', 7.

[57] See, e.g., 'Klein will Hilfe für Namibia', *Frankfurter Rundschau*, 23.06.1978; 'Mehr Hilfe für Namibia?', *Frankfurter Rundschau*, 05.11.1988. See also Melber, 'Federal Republic', 5–6.

[58] 'Kleine Hebel', *Der Spiegel*, 11/1988, 14.03.1988. From 1973 to 1982, Lengl was the directing manager of the Hanns-Seidel- Foundation and thus also in charge of the foundation's interactions with the DTA. In 1983 already, the Foreign Office voiced its concerns about the DTA's close contacts to the BMZ and a planned Namibia visit of Lengl. See, e.g., PAAA, Zwischenarchiv, Bd. 138099, 1982–1983, Südafrika-/Namibia-Politik der Bundesregierung; hier: CSU-Äußerung über tiefgreifende Veränderungen, 15.04.1983; ibid., 'Demokratische Turnhallen-Allianz' (DTA); hier: Gespräch BM-Dirk Mudge zwischen 14. und 17.06.1983, 24.05.1983; ibid., Bonn-Besuch des DTA-Vorsitzenden Dirk Mudge Ende März 1983, 06.04.1983. That Lengl intended to congratulate Dirk Mudge on the instalment of the interim government caused further outrage in the Foreign Office in 1985. The Foreign Office made the following comment in a side note: 'This is not possible': ibid., Bd. 138105, 1985, Namibia; hier: Einsetzungsfeierlichkeiten der 'VPK-Interimregierung, 04.06.1985.

[59] ISSA, Akte: Namibia 1986–1990, Franz Josef Strauß: "Ich bin ein Südwester!", *taz*, 30.01.1988.

[60] See, e.g., AAG, Akte 1608, Dringliche Fragen für die Fragestunde der Sitzung des Deutschen Bundestages am Mittwoch, dem 6. Mai 1987, 05.05.1987; D. Cornelsen, 'SWAPO lehnt Hilfe vor der Unabhängigkeit Namibias ab', *Frankfurter Rundschau*, 04.04.1987; A. Remde, 'Klein: Kluft zum Auswärtigen Amt', *Die Welt*, 14.05.1987.

[61] 'Kleine Hebel', *Der Spiegel*, 11/1988, 14.03.1988. See also R. Tetzlaff, 'Die entwicklungspolitische

event, Strauß continued to demand, up until his sudden death in 1988, greater economic support for Namibia on the basis that 'politics of sanctions cannot prepare the country for transition'.[62]

This raises the question of how the GDR interpreted West Germany's development assistance to Third World countries. Generally, the GDR saw development assistance as a 'tool of Western imperialism' and thus as a means to further the foreign policy objectives of capitalist states. Although East Berlin also used aid to further political interests overseas, the GDR pursued its foreign policy objectives more openly than West Germany and therefore was also less secretive about its aid programmes.[63] Furthermore, the centralised structures of the GDR gave East Berlin greater control over the flow of aid into Third World countries. With regard to non-governmental projects, East Berlin considered West German foundations as agents of the government, pursuing the following objectives. First, their task was to establish platforms for 'propagating West German policies and anti-communism'. Second, foundations played a role in countering GDR influence abroad. Third, the aim was to further enhance West Germany's political influence in developing countries through educational programmes. And fourth, the objective was to promote change in social structures 'without creating the impression of intervening politically in the affairs of recipient countries'.[64] East Berlin had little doubt that non-governmental organizations acted as an extension of Bonn's foreign policy. Thus, it seems hardly surprising that the OBS assumed that the GDR was stirring up unrest among Namibian refugees enrolled in educational programmes organized by the OBS.[65]

All this was significant with regard to the increasing tensions between the two blocs in southern Africa in the 1980s. Hardliners in the CDU, CSU and FDP displayed a tendency to think of events in Namibia in Cold War terms rather than to acknowledge that the country was undergoing a decolonization process in which white minority rule was no longer sustainable. Obviously, however, those with hardline views exploited the dynamics of the Cold War as a pretext for demanding the reinforcement of the status quo. Hence, the BMZ was,

---

Bilanz der Ära Kohl', in G. Wewer (ed.), *Bilanz der Ära Kohl*, Opladen, Leske & Budrich, 1998, 318; H. Fedderson, 'Raketen verdrängen Namibia, *Allgemeine Zeitung*, 11.10.1983; H. Melber, 'Bundesdeutsche Entwicklungspolitik', 53.

[62] ISSA, Akte: Namibia, 1983–1990, Monitor-Dienst (DW), Strauß sichert Namibia mehr Wirtschaftshilfe zu, 29.01.1988.

[63] Schulz, B. H., *Development Policy in the Cold War Era: The two Germanies and Sub-Saharan Africa, 1960–1985*, Münster, LIT, 1995,121 and 180–181.

[64] See BStU, MfS-AG XVII, Nr. 1137, Auskunft über die Rolle der Friedrich Ebert Stiftung und ihre außenpolitische Aktivität gegenüber den Ländern Lateinamerikas, Afrikas und Asiens sowie den sozialistischen Staaten, 30.07.1971, 14–17.

[65] PAAA, Zwischenarchiv, Bd. 138107, 1982–1984, Ausbildungsprogramme der OBS im südlichen Afrika, 26.06.1984.

under the CSU, firmly on the side of Pretoria and the interim government in Namibia, that is, those forces that claimed to defend southern Africa against Soviet-led communist aggression. Thus, it comes as no surprise that the Greens accused the Kohl government of trying to transfer the East-West confrontation onto southern Africa.[66]

Contemporaries, such as Henning Melber, saw in the significant expansion of development assistance, under the Kohl government, a 'substitution of foreign policy'.[67] Critics argued that Bonn concealed its support for the interim government by coordinating financial aid through non-governmental projects in Namibia, aiming to strengthen the interim government and subsequently weaken SWAPO.[68] That government delegates participated in the 'enthronement ceremony' of the MPC provided critics with further evidence about Bonn's questionable commitment towards Resolution 435.[69] The government's standard excuse became that delegates and non-governmental organisations were acting on their own initiative.[70] Thus, it seems understandable why SWAPO believed in 1985 that the Kohl government had changed course in Namibia.[71] Yet, although the Federal Government received considerable criticism for its apparent support of the status quo in Namibia and South Africa, Pretoria would have disagreed with such assertions.[72] In a sense SWAPO's allegations were not necessarily unjustified, given the efforts of government delegates and the BMZ to bring about a change in Bonn's policy towards Namibia.

In sum, the BMZ's growing involvement in Namibia was, to some degree, the consequence of the Kohl government's unchallenged acceptance of the Reagan administration's leadership. The failure of Genscher and the Foreign Office to aggressively map out an alternative course to the Reagan administration's policy towards Namibia became the central point of criticism. Thus, the reluctance of both the Federal Government and the Foreign

---

[66] Deutscher Bundestag, 10. Wahlperiode, Stenographischer Bericht, 54. Sitzung, 10.02.1984, 3873.
[67] Melber, 'Federal Republic', 3.
[68] AGG, Akte 1473, Petra Kelly, 1983–1986, Pressemitteilung Nr. 357/85, Stillschweigende Anerkennung aus Bonn.
[69] Deutscher Bundestag, 10. Wahlperiode, Stenographischer Bericht, 243. Sitzung, 06.11.1986, 18850. At the Namibia Hearing, Vesper made a similar statement, accusing the government of treating Resolution 435 as one of many possible solutions for Namibia: Vesper, 'Die Namibia-Politik', 65.
[70] The government did not recognise any controversy, mainly because the delegates Klein (CSU), Hedrich (CDU) and Rumpf (FDP) had financed the trip independently of their party and the government. The government conveniently overlooked that the trips were paid for by the Namibian Information Office, which received funding from South Africa: Deutscher Bundestag, Drucksache 10/5312, 14.04.1986, 3.
[71] PAAA, Zwischenarchiv, Bd. 138105, 1985, Entwicklung unserer Beziehungen zur SWAPO; hier: Kritik der SWAPO an der Namibiapolitik der Bundesrepublik Deutschland, 12.06.1985.
[72] See AAPD, 1985, Band I, Regionalpolitische Initiative Sambias; hier: Gespräch zwischen Präsident Kaunda und MD Haas, 09.05.1985, 590.

Office to show greater initiative in Namibia gave the BMZ room for independent policy manoeuvres. Although Klein underlined in late 1987 that there existed no rivalry between the Foreign Office and the BMZ, his statement was designed to refute publicly the notion that there was a dispute within the re-elected CDU/CSU-FDP government over Namibia, as a close associate of Klein later explained in the Foreign Office.[73] In early 1987, the differences within the Kohl government over its policy towards Namibia led to the proposed establishment of a Namibia-Committee, which included delegates from all three parties of the coalition government.[74] Yet, by late 1987, it had become apparent that it was impossible to bridge fundamental differences between the Foreign Office and the BMZ. Still, the Foreign Office continued to defend successfully the position that development assistance can be provided only to a legitimate government of an independent Namibia.[75]

Genscher was not in position of strength, because of the BMZ's success in bypassing the Foreign Office in Namibia, the strong opposition towards his Namibia policy from within the FDP and SWAPO's growing criticism of him.[76] In the mid-to-late 1980s, SWAPO increasingly vented its frustration about the lack of tangible progress in achieving the objectives of Resolution 435, accusing West Germany of waging a 'hostile campaign' against SWAPO. The liberation movement complained particularly about an increasing number of West German politicians that came to Namibia at the invitation of Pretoria. SWAPO also repeated its concern about the growing support in West Germany for providing development assistance to Namibia before the achievement of independence, which was seen as mainly benefiting the interim government. Yet SWAPO remained hopeful about Genscher's Namibia policy and West Germany's influence in the Security Council. The Foreign Office made it clear, however, that West Germany's 'options are very limited, especially in the face of the virtual omission of the Contact Group'.[77] It is perhaps not surprising therefore that, in early 1987, Genscher expressed his disappointment that the WCG was 'practically dead today'.[78] Throughout most of 1987 and 1988, Genscher channelled his frustration into

---

[73] PAAA, Zwischenarchiv, Bd. 155883, 1987–1989, Betr.: Namibiapolitik der Bundesregierung; hier: Vortrag von BMZ Hans Klein 'Namibia Modell für das südliche Afrika?' am 3. November 1978, 05.11.1987.
[74] See 'Einigung auf neue Namibia-Politik in Bonn', *Frankfurter Allgemeine Zeitung*, 27.03.1987.
[75] See also '"Hilfe bedarf gewisser Voraussetzung"', *Der Spiegel*, 1/1988, 04.01.1988.
[76] See also, R. Hofmeier, 'Deutsch-afrikanische Beziehungen', in R. Hofmeier (ed.), *Afrika Jahrbuch 1987: Politik, Wirtschaft und Gesellschaft in Afrika südlich der Sahara*, Opladen, Leske Verlag & Budrich GmbH, 1988, 36–38.
[77] PAAA, Zwischenarchiv, Bd. 1381009, 1987, Betr.: Unsere Beziehungen zu SWAPO, 24.02.1987.
[78] Howe took the view that 'there was no chance that, in this confused situation, the WCG could be of any help': AAPD, Band I, 1987, Gespräch des Bundesministers Genscher mit dem britischen Außenminister Howe, 25.02.1987, 257.

efforts to revive the WCG, which can be partly understood as an attempt by the foreign minister to regain greater influence, both domestically and internationally.[79]

However, all this further underlines the difficulty of determining the true extent to which the BMZ successfully pursued a policy towards Namibia that was independent of the government. It also raises questions about Kohl's commitment to the continuation of his predecessor's course in Namibia. It is nonetheless possible to conclude that, although the BMZ's involvement in Namibia cannot be underestimated, the wider impact on both West Germany's policy towards Namibia and the political reality in Namibia was marginal.[80]

This also raises questions about the Federal Government's position on sanctions against South Africa. On 2 October 1986, the US Congress approved sanctions against South Africa. Both houses of Congress overruled Reagan, who had vetoed the bill. The SPD and the Green party urged the Kohl government to implement the same measures against South Africa.[81] The US sanctions prohibited, amongst other things, the import of uranium, coal, steel, iron and textiles from South Africa, as well as prohibiting new investments. Obviously, the implementation of US sanctions would have harmed West Germany's economy, for its industry depended on South African natural resources, while German industry in South Africa needed free and unhindered exchange with industry at home. In short, trade relations with South Africa stopped the government from implementing sanctions.

In 1986 already, the SPD challenged the Kohl government in the *Bundestag* to follow Washington's example in South Africa, to 'give up resistance against sanctions in the European Community (EG), and demand that sanctions should at least reach the level of US sanctions'.[82] Furthermore, the SPD challenged the government to 'demand a worldwide prohibition of capital transfer [*Kapitalausfuhren*] to South Africa, technology transfer with South Africa and natural resource import from South Africa'.[83]

Among West German political parties, resistance to sanctions was most dominant in the CSU. Hans Graf Huyn (CSU), former foreign policy adviser to Strauß, argued that sanctions 'only help the wrong people' and harm the poor black majority.[84] Instead, it was argued that

---

[79] PAAA, Zwischenarchiv, Bd. 156671, 1985–1990, Betr.: Deutsch-französiche Außenminister-Konsultation anlässlich des 25. Jahrestages der Unterzeichnung des Elysee-Vertrags am 22. Januar 1988 in Paris; hier: Auszug für Referat 320, 26.01.1988. See also BStU, MfS-Hauptverwaltung Aufklärung, Nr. 53, BRD-Einschätzungen zur Namibia-Problematik, 25.09.1988; Hofmeier, 'Deutsch-afrikanische', 36–38.
[80] Vergau came to a similar conclusion. E-mail interview with Hans-Joachim Vergau, 26.04.2016.
[81] Deutscher Bundestag, 10. Wahlperiode, Drucksache 10/6165, 15.10.1986.
[82] Ibid., 11. Wahlperiode, Drucksache 11/1753, 03.02.1988.
[83] Ibid.
[84] 'Tiefe Sorge', *Der Spiegel*, 31/1985, 29.07.1985.

German companies can help the poor black majority through education.[85] The Greens, on the other hand, argued that, although sanctions would be felt most severely by Namibia and South Africa's black population, using that as an argument against sanctions was deeply cynical. The black population's situation was characterised by poverty, unemployment, segregation, persecution and the constant threat of imprisonment and torture. Sanctions contained the potential to force the apartheid regime into implementing progressive policies for both South Africa and Namibia, which, in return, would justify, in the Greens' view, a temporary deterioration of the overall situation. The Green Party's rationale for sanctions received support from leading South African anti-apartheid campaigners such as Winnie Mandela and Desmond Tutu.[86]

The late 1980s: The two Germanys and Namibia

In December 1987, Genscher consulted his 'ministerial colleagues in the USA, Canada, Great Britain and France in order to find out their views on reactivating the WCG for the settlement of the Namibian problem'. France's ongoing 'reservations' remained the main stumbling block to this Genscher-led effort to revive the WCG. France argued that the political framework conditions had changed, which implied that the 'work' of the WCG had also 'considerably changed'.[87] In early 1988, Genscher reminded Jean-Bernard Raymond, the French Foreign Minister, of 'his initiative to revive the Namibia-Contact Group'. Genscher underlined that 'the U.S., Canada, and Great Britain had confirmed their interest in his initiative'. Paris, however, took the view that 'the WCG has fulfilled its task', as Raymond pointed out. The Reagan administration's linkage strategy further contributed to the French position.[88]

In late 1988, Nujoma, as well as the presidents of Angola and Zambia, voiced their opposition to Genscher's initiative, not least because the negotiations between Angola, Cuba, South Africa and the U.S. had already entered a 'more intense stage', although there was no good solution yet in sight.[89] However, the fact that all sides accepted Resolution 435 as the

---

[85] Deutscher Bundestag, 8. Wahlperiode, Stenographischer Bericht, 52. Sitzung, 27.10.1977, 4071–4072.
[86] AGG, Petra Kelly, Akte 1473, 1983–1986, Pressemitteilung Nr. 537/85.
[87] BStU, MfS-Hauptverwaltung Aufklärung, Nr. 53, BRD-Einschätzungen zur Namibia-Problematik, 25.09.1988. See also PAAA, Zwischenarchiv, Bd. 138114, 1986–1987, "Mögliches Abrücken" der südafrikanischen Regierung von Resolution 435, 10.04.1987.
[88] PAAA, Zwischenarchiv, Bd. 156671, 1985–1990, Betr.: Deutsch-französische Außenminister-Konsultation anläßlich des 25. Jahrestages der Unterzeichnung des Elysee-Vertrags am 22. Januar 1988 in Paris; hier: Auszug für Referat 320, 26.01.1988.
[89] Alexandre Rodrigues 'Kito', the Angolan minister of interior, stated in 1986 that the 'revival of the WCG' was not a 'realistic' option: PAAA, Zwischenarchiv, Bd. 138114, 1986–1987, Betr. Friedensbemühungen für Angola/Namibia, 04.03.1986. Efforts to revive the WCG, on the basis that

basis for the settlement of the Namibia question was seen as a breakthrough.[90] Evidently, Genscher strongly believed that the WCG should once again assume a central and visible role in Namibia's path to independence, probably also for the personal reason of regaining an influential position in the ongoing negotiation process. Though the WCG faded into the background after 1983, Genscher continued to play an active intermediary role in the mid-to-late 1980s, though often behind the scenes.[91] For example, when the Reagan administration clashed with Nujoma in 1984, Washington and the frontline states asked the Foreign Office to talk to SWAPO, for 'Nujoma doesn't trust anyone more than the foreign minister'.[92] In late 1987, Genscher reassured the president of Angola that Washington 'was very serious about the implementation of Resolution 435', which was based on a request brought forward by George P. Schultz, Secretary of State in the Reagan administration.[93] On another occasion, in mid-1989, the South African foreign minister asked Genscher to contact Nujoma, for he had information that some elements of SWAPO were preparing to cross the Angolan border into Namibia because South Africa had reduced its troop strength in Namibia. Pik Botha believed that SWAPO was trying to achieve a propaganda coup,

---

the group could take up vital tasks during the implementation phase of Resolution 435, continued throughout 1988: Ibid., Bd. 155883, 1987–1989, Termine und Sachthemen die im Zusammenhang mit dem sich konkretisierenden Unabhängigkeitsprozess von Bedeutung sind, 07.12.1988. Already in late 1986, during a meeting with a SWAPO delegation (Bessinger, Lubowsky and Shoombe) in Bonn, the Foreign Office proposed trying to 'revive' the WCG. However, the delegation was sceptical about the proposal, underlining that 'four Contact Group countries saw the mandate as finished' and that 'Namibia's independence could come unexpectedly, by other means and virtually overnight'. The Foreign Office also reported that Pretoria was equally sceptical about the 'revival of the WCG'. The growing opposition within the US Congress, and the question of whether it would be possible to encourage France's cooperation were named as the main obstacles: PAAA, Zwischenarchiv, Bd. 138108, 1986–1987, Vermerk über die Besprechung von Dg 32 mit SWAPO-Vertretern, 16.07.1986, 5–6.

[90] BStU, MfS-Hauptverwaltung Aufklärung, Nr. 53, BRD-Einschätzungen zur Namibia-Problematik, 25.09.1988.
[91] Chester Crocker also stated that 'before the WCG suspended its active group diplomacy, Genscher made efforts to strengthen US contacts and communication with SWAPO leaders': E-mail interview with Chester Crocker, 25.08.2016. See also AAPD, 1981, Band I, SWAPO; hier: Nujoma-Besuch in Bonn vom 25. bis 27.05.1981, 29.05.1981.
[92] PAAA, Zwischenarchiv, Bd. 138098, 1984, Nächste Begegnung des BM mit SWAPO-Präsident Nujoma, 08.02.1984. Furthermore, in early 1984, SWAPO agreed to respect the Angolan-South African disengagement agreement, for it had the potential to lead to the implementation of Resolution 435. Genscher and Nujoma agreed that the Foreign Minister should convince the European community to show a united front and use his connections in Washington to promote the implementation of Resolution 435: PAAA, Zwischenarchiv, Bd. 138098, 1984, Namibia-Initiative der westlichen Fünf; hier: Begegnung BM mit Nujoma am 18. Februar 1984 in Paris, 18.02.1984
[93] Ibid., Bd. 155883, 1987–1989, Namibia-Frage; hier: Gespräch des BM mit dem Präsidenten von Angola, 30.10.1987. During Genscher's visit to Angola, he also discussed, 'in close consultation' with Washington, the withdrawal of Cuban troops: Deutscher Bundestag, 11. Wahlperiode, Stenographischer Bericht, 58. Sitzung, 04.02.1988, 3976.

which would have made it difficult for him to justify in South Africa the continuation of the peace process.[94]

Nevertheless, in the late 1980s, Genscher remained in a relatively weak position, for he experienced further disappointments in Bonn. In 1988, Strauß once again made headlines by assuming the role of the foreign minister, visiting both the Soviet Union and South Africa in quick succession.[95] Even though his first diplomatic foray into South Africa received Kohl's blessing, the de facto Foreign Minister was once again not consulted.[96] To make matter worse, Strauß underlined his contempt for Genscher's policy towards Namibia with a private excursion to Namibia and a meeting with Jonas Savimbi, the UNITA leader.[97] The whole episode reignited the question of whether Kohl and Strauß were pursuing their own unofficial policy towards southern Africa.[98] Kohl's decision to dispatch Strauß, an ardent supporter of white minority rule and opponent of Resolution 435, on a diplomatic journey to southern Africa seemed to confirm that the chancellor was secretly pursuing a two-pronged foreign policy.[99]

The FDP demanded from Kohl an acknowledgment that foreign policy was the sole responsibility of the foreign minister, while the SPD stressed that foreign policy responsibilities do not exist outside the cabinet and Strauß was not a member of Kohl's cabinet.[100] Furthermore, the SPD acknowledged Genscher's commitment to the continuation of the foreign policy initiated by the former SPD/FDP coalition government. The SPD pointed out, however, that Genscher was unable to set the tone and direction of the government's policy

---

[94] Ibid., Bd. 155890, 1989, Gespräch BM Genscher/ AM Pik Both in Bonn, 02.06.1989.
[95] C. G., 'Der neue Außenminister', *Die Zeit*, 03.02.1988. See also, J. Leinemann, 'Das macht ihm keiner nach', *Der Spiegel*, 5/1988, 01.02.1988; C. G., 'Kein Alleinvertretungsanspruch der FDP in der Außenpolitik', *Frankfurter Allgemeine Zeitung*, 03.02.1988; Deutscher Bundestag, 11. Wahlperiode, Stenographischer Bericht, 58. Sitzung, 04.02.1988, 3983.
[96] For additional information on Strauß' visit to southern Africa in early 1988, see Wenzel, *Südafrika-Politik*, 68–73.
[97] The Kohl government did not recognize UNITA, mainly because it was widely viewed as a puppet of Pretoria.
[98] See, e.g., Deutscher Bundestag, 11. Wahlperiode, Stenographischer Bericht, 58. Sitzung, 04.02.1988, 3968; C. G., 'Kein Alleinvertretungsanspruch der FDP in der Außenpolitik', *Frankfurter Allgemeine Zeitung*, 03.02.1988.
[99] See also A. Brugger, 'Gespaltene Zunge', *Lingener Tagespost*, 01.02.1988. Ursula Eid stated in a rather passionate *Bundestag* speech that Kohl's 'South Africa policy was fork-tongued': Deutscher Bundestag, 11. Wahlperiode, Stenographischer Bericht, 58. Sitzung, 04.02.1988, 3968.
[100] 'FDP verlangt Klarstellung von Kohl zu Strauß-Reise', *Lingener Tagespost*, 01.02.1988. See also 'Baum-Interview zu Südafrika', fdk-freie demokratische korrespondenz, Ausgabe 69, 28.03.1988; M. Gräfin Dönhoff, 'Zweierlei Wege', *Die Zeit*, 05.02.1988. The press was equally critical of the wider implications of the Strauß visit to southern Africa, questioning his role as an ancillary foreign minister [Neben-Außenminister] and whether Strauß pursued an ancillary foreign policy [Neben-Außenpolitik]. See, e.g., J. Leinemann, 'Das macht ihm keiner nach', *Der Spiegel*, 5/1988, 01.02.1988; M. Gräfin Dönhoff, 'Zweierlei Wege', *Die Zeit*, 05.02.1988.

towards southern Africa because the CSU, particularly Strauß, and to lesser degree the CDU, consistently 'fought to undermine' the foreign minister's efforts.[101] Obviously, the continuation in foreign policy gave the SPD reason to support Genscher's Namibia policy. SWAPO also voiced its disapproval of Strauß' endeavour, which, however, did not stop the Bavarian leader from repeating his demand for immediate economic aid for Namibia and an end to sanctions against South Africa.[102]

Genscher refrained from criticising Strauß, preferring instead to emphasise the government's continuing commitment to Resolution 435. Genscher was the main beneficiary of this situation, for he received strong approval in the *Bundestag*.[103] Ultimately, Kohl also emphasised that there were no foreign policy departures, leaving the CSU in an increasingly isolated position.[104] Nonetheless, in what can only be described as a counter-push against the private Namibia initiative of Strauß, Genscher voiced increasingly strong criticism of Pretoria. On one occasion, Genscher invited the scorn of Pik Botha by voicing his support for the boycott of South African goods.[105] On another occasion, Genscher left no doubt about his opinion of apartheid, stating inter alia that it was 'racial fanaticism'.[106] Pik Botha did not doubt that the Federal Government's abstention in the Security Council vote on sanctions against South Africa was Genscher's 'revenge' on Strauß.[107]

Contemporary observers were, however, more critical of Genscher, pointing out that the foreign minister's apparent lack of political self-assertion undermined his authority in the Kohl government. One observer, for example, argued that it would require a much stronger

---

[101] 'Pressekonferenz: Hans-Jochen Vogel', Service der SPD für Presse, Funk, TV., Ausgabe 83/88, 26.01.1988.

[102] 'Franz Josef Strauß im südlichen Africa', SWAPO of Namibia, Luanda, 29.01.1988; ISSA, Akte: Namibia, 1983–1990, Monitor-Dienst (DW), Strauß sichert Namibia mehr Wirtschaftshilfe zu, 29.01.1988. It was in this context that Nghidimondjila Shoombe, SWAPO representative in West Germany, complained to Genscher that 'SWAPO and therefore the majority of Namibians were convinced that they have only few friends in Germany, perhaps some individuals'. Genscher stated that he did not share these views and pointed out that West Germany was a democracy. Genscher, of course, intended to underline the importance of political freedom and diversity in West Germany: PAAA, Zwischenarchiv, Bd. 155883, 1987–1989, Gespräch Dg 32 mit SWAPO-Vertreter im Auswärtigen Amt, 06.07.1988.

[103] Deutscher Bundestag, 11. Wahlperiode, Stenographischer Bericht, 58. Sitzung, 04.02.1988, 3968–3983. Gerhardt Baum (FDP) concluded: 'With regard to South Africa, we have more consensus now than ever before. And we have to thank Strauß for it': 'Zwischen den Ohren', *Der Spiegel*, 6/1988, 08.02.1988.

[104] Ibid., 3968–3983; 'Die CSU isoliert sich', *Süddeutsche Zeitung*, 05.04.1988. See also 'Zu den heutigen Vorwürfen gegen die CSU im Zusammenhang mit der aktuellen Diskussion über die Südafrika-Politik', CSU Presse-Mitteilungen, Nr 84/1988, 17.03.1988.

[105] 'Südafrika rüffelt Genscher', *Frankfurter Rundschau*, 24.03.1988; 'Südafrikas Außenminister greift Genscher an', *Süddeutsche Zeitung*, 24.03.1988.

[106] C. G., 'Genscher: Apartheid ist Rassenwahn', *Frankfurter Allgemeine Zeitung*, 26.05.1988

[107] 'Wie bei Hitler', *Der Spiegel*, 22/1988, 30.05.1988.

engagement if Genscher wanted to avoid being 'temporarily overridden'.¹⁰⁸ The notion that Genscher had been overridden in his role as foreign minister was, of course, further amplified by the fact that Genscher and Strauß represented opposing approaches towards both South Africa and Namibia. Thus, for some observers it seemed reasonable to conclude that the Kohl-Strauß initiative represented a clear break with Genscher's strategic approach towards southern Africa.¹⁰⁹ This raises the question of whether the continuation of foreign policy had finally come to an end.

Although there had been deliberate attempts, particularly by hardliners, to interfere in Genscher's diplomatic efforts on Namibia, in the overall scheme of things 'these elements had only a marginally disruptive effect', as Vergau points out.¹¹⁰ Furthermore, Kohl had inner-political reasons for dispatching Strauß on foreign policy missions, for he had interest in keeping the peace with the Bavarian hardliner. An assistant within the chancellery even conceded that there was a desire to 'restrain' Strauß, as *Der Spiegel* reported.¹¹¹ Persistent intra-coalition quarrels, largely between Kohl, Strauß and Genscher, led Kohl to take recourse to appeasement tactics. To some degree, Kohl's strategy seemed to bear fruit, for Strauß refrained from attacking Bonn's policy towards southern Africa at the CSU party conference in late 1987.¹¹² Hence, Kohl was not trying to undermine Genscher per se, or 'put a damper on Genscher', as some have argued.¹¹³ Kohl was mainly concerned about defusing tensions within the coalition government. Although the inclusion of Strauß in foreign policy increased tensions with Genscher, it fulfilled the desired purpose of rendering Strauß' opposition to the government's foreign policy mild and forbearing.¹¹⁴

Despite mounting criticism, Strauß had reason to congratulate himself upon the diplomatic success of his visit to South Africa. During a visit to Moscow, which directly preceded Strauß' trip to South Africa, he established, despite his known disdain of communism, cordial relations with both Mikhail Gorbachev, the new Soviet leader, and Eduard Shevardnadze, the foreign minister.¹¹⁵ Shevardnadze gave Strauß an unmistakable message for

---

[108] A. Brugger, 'Gespaltene Zunge', *Lingener Tagespost*, 01.02.1988.

[109] See also, R. Apel, 'Strauß: Gorbachev's envoy in Africa', *Executive Intelligence Review (EIR) News Service*, Vol. 15, No. 7, 12.02.1988.

[110] E-mail interview with Hans-Joachim Vergau, 04.05. 2016.

[111] The newsmagazine *Der Spiegel* used the German term 'ruhigstellen', which also means sedate. However, restrain seems to be more suitable within this context: 'Erster Erfolg', *Der Spiegel*, 49/1987, 30.11.1987.

[112] Ibid.

[113] 'Zwischen den Ohren', *Der Spiegel*, 6/1988, 08.02.1988.

[114] Von der Ropp offered a similar assessment, stating that 'Kohl wanted to keep Strauß happy'. Phone interview with Klaus Freiherr von der Ropp, 12.04.2016. The Strauß-GDR deal in 1983 took place under similar circumstances and thus can be viewed in the same light.

[115] Importantly, Genscher developed equally good relations with Gorbachev. In 1987, Genscher ap-

Pretoria regarding Angola and Namibia: 'The Soviet Union supports any settlement that is supported by all parties'.[116] This change in attitude was prompted by two factors: Gorbachev's influence on Soviet foreign policy and the developments in Angola.

From late 1987 to early 1988, the continued military conflict in Angola grew into what became known as the Battle of Cuito Cuanavale, which turned into the largest battle in Africa since the Second World War. Moscow recognized in early 1988 that the ongoing military conflict between South African and Cuban troops had the potential to lead to a full-blown confrontation between Cuba and South Africa, and risked drawing the two superpowers into direct conflict on African soil. Furthermore, few doubted that Pretoria was ready to use nuclear weapons should it come under serious threat from Cuban troops. Thus, the effects on détente between the superpowers, let alone the preservation of world peace, were undeniable and serious concerns of all the parties involved.[117] It was in this sense of urgency that Shevardnadze's message for Pretoria gained its importance. Strauß was, without doubt, the most appropriate messenger, for he maintained a relationship of mutual trust and respect with both Pik and PW Botha.[118] Quite reasonably, therefore, Moscow hoped 'that the positive reputation Strauß so far had in Pretoria may help to get the South Africans 'in line'', as German intelligence sources reported.[119] Strauß stated in Pretoria that he had observed 'significant changes in the Soviet approach on African issues' and that there was reason to be optimistic that 'Moscow wants to pull out from Africa, though not completely'.[120] Given the fact that it was widely known that Strauß harboured little sympathy for both Moscow and communism, his upbeat evaluation carried significant weight. Had Genscher delivered such an analysis, the full significance would not have been communicated. After all, Pretoria did not regard Genscher to be a friend of South Africa. In fact, Pretoria praised Strauß for raising South African concerns in Moscow, which led Pretoria to believe that Strauß was

---

pealed to take Gorbachev by his word on 'new thinking', which was criticised in Washington as 'appeasement' and 'Genscherism': M. Zimmer, 'The German Political Parties and the USA', in D. Junker (ed.), *The United States and Germany in the Era of the Cold War, 1945–1990, Volume 2, 1968–1990*, Cambridge, Cambridge University Press, 2004, 94.

[116] F. J., Strauß, *Die Erinnerungen*, Berlin, Siedler Verlag, 1989, 526–527. Strauß met Shevardnadze again in Bonn before departure to South Africa, where he received the message for Pretoria.

[117] See also C. Saunders, 'The Angola/Namibia crisis of 1988 and its resolution', in S. Onslow (ed.), *Cold War in Southern Africa: White Power, Black Liberation*, London, Routledge, 2009. Détente between the two superpowers had only emerged in the mid-1980s, after Gorbachev introduced 'new thinking'.

[118] Dieter Petzsch also stated that Strauß, Pik and P.W. Botha had similar personality traits, which probably gave Strauß an advantage in his dealings with Pretoria. Interview with Dieter Petzsch, Berlin, 22.03.2016.

[119] R. Apel, 'Strauß: Gorbachev's envoy in Africa', *Executive Intelligence Review (EIR) News Service*, Vol. 15, No 7, 12.02.1988.

[120] Ibid.

capable of driving forward a peace plan for the region.[121] The 'Gorbachev effect' was strong among West German hardliners.[122] Even Strauß could not fail to recognize that there were undeniable changes taking place under Gorbachev's leadership.[123]

Despite the heated political atmosphere in Bonn, Liselotte Berger, the CDU undersecretary in the chancellery, and a number of CDU/CSU delegates went, not long after the Strauß controversy, to Namibia on a private visit. It was later claimed that the visit was commissioned by Kohl under the pretence of gathering information about the interim government and the situation in Namibia.[124] Although it would seem plausible to suggest that Kohl wanted to re-evaluate the situation in Namibia after Moscow indicated a drastic overhaul of its policy towards southern Africa, the government denied these claims.[125] The opposition parties, the FDP and apartheid opponents became increasingly concerned that these visits would harm West Germany's image in Africa. In fact, Strauß' foray into southern Africa had already generated much criticism, particularly among South Africa's black majority. Winnie Mandela, the wife of Nelson Mandela, left little doubt about her disapproval of Strauß: 'The arrogance of his appearance with the oppressors is unbearable and an affront to the people. The Federal Government is responsible for his behaviour and the political consequences, but the responsibility lies most of all with the chancellor'.[126] There was also concern that the black majority might believe 'the Federal Government was in South Africa's racial conflict on the side of the white power holders'.[127]

---

[121] G. Shaw, 'Nach dem Strauß-Besuch in Südafrika: Nur die Weißen sind zufrieden', *Die Zeit*, 12.02.1988.

[122] See also 'Wir werden niemals das Schwert erheben', *Der Spiegel, 1/1988,* 04.01.1988.

[123] However, Kohl only slowly realised that Gorbachev was a new kind of Soviet leader, which undermined relations between the two heads of state in the mid-1980s. Kohl's most regrettable faux pas came in late 1986, when he compared Gorbachev to Goebbels. For a far-reaching analysis of relations between West Germany and the Soviet Union from Khrushchev to Gorbachev: M. J., Sodaro, *Moscow, Germany, and the West from Khrushchev to Gorbachev*, London, Cornell University Press, 1990.

[124] 'Namibia: BRD-Delegation bei "illegaler Regierung"', Politische Berichte, Nr. 7, 01.04.1988.

[125] *Deutscher Bundestag*, 11. Wahlperiode, Stenographischer Bericht, 61. Sitzung, 25.02.1988, 4195–4197.

[126] J. Leineman, 'Das macht ihm keiner nach', *Der Spiegel*, 5/1988, 01.02.1988.

[127] SPD-Fraktion im deutschen Bundestag, Verheugen: Die Südafrika-Reise von Frau Berger ist ein politischer Skandal, 03.03.1988. See also epd, Evangelischer Pressedienst, Bischof protestiert bei Kohl gegen Reise von Berger und Burr, 19.02.1988. Strauß' visit generated similar concerns, for it was also seen as an official state visit, despite the emphasis on its private character: PAAA, Zwischenarchiv, Bd. 155883, 1978–89, Aufzeichnung des Gesprächs Dg 32/Frau Abrahams (Namibia-Nationhood Programme Coordinating Committee (NNPCC), Windhuk, 02.05.1988. The main issue was that the media in South Africa and Namibia presented the West German politicians as official state visitors. Consequently, even private trips carried the potential to generate political scandals.

Although Kohl might not have adopted a two-pronged strategy towards Namibia, the Kohl-Strauß initiative placed the government in an advantageous position, for it allowed Bonn to establish good relations with whomever was in power. This, however, was not the case because Kohl had cleverly devised an open-door strategy. The government's favourable position was a by-product of the political discrepancies within the coalition government.[128] Therefore, Kohl benefitted from both Strauß' good relations with Pik Botha and P.W. Botha and Genscher's close relations with Nujoma.[129] This gave Kohl some political flexibility with regard to both Namibia and South Africa. Precisely for this reason, some sided with Kohl's decision to send Strauß and not Genscher to southern Africa, as it was believed that Strauß was the only West German politician who had a chance of achieving some kind of breakthrough in Pretoria.[130]

Whatever the case, it had become impossible to ignore the fact that attitudes in Moscow began to change markedly in 1988. Gorbachev's impact was felt in most countries that came under the Soviet sphere of influence, including southern African. Although Moscow struggled over two decades to realize its power interests in southern Africa, when the Soviet Union's influence in the region steadily declined in the mid-to-late1980s, Moscow felt little pressure to set out new measures for countering the Soviet Union's deteriorating influence. This was a clear departure from policies adopted by Moscow in the past. When African nations opened themselves to the West in the late 1980s, Moscow showed little interest in trying to bind them to the Soviet Union.[131] Moscow was still interested in exercising influence over African states, but not with the same determination as in the pre-Gorbachev era. Moscow saw debt, for example, as an 'important instrument to secure the political and economic influence of the socialist states', for debt enforced the depend-

---

[128] Importantly, Kohl relied on the support of both Strauß and Genscher for inner-political purposes. Kohl needed Genscher in order to have a majority, for he could not have won the elections without the FDP. Strauß, on the other hand, was vital for keeping the CDU/CSU hardliners and the Right from joining up with the far right nationalist parties: H. Bering, *Helmut Kohl*, Washington, Regnery Publishing, 1999, 70–73. See also J. M. Markham, 'Visits to East by Strauß Startles Bonn', *New York Times*, 27.07.1983.

[129] However, the evidence suggests that all parties developed a more flexible and pragmatic attitude in the late 1980s. For example, Pretoria's decision to ask Genscher to get in contact with Nujoma, as discussed above, demonstrated a growing openness on the part of reaching across political divides.

[130] M. Gräfin Dönhoff, 'Zweierlei Wege', *Die Zeit*, 05.02.1988. Nonetheless, it was still viewed as regrettable that neither the Foreign Office nor Genscher were consulted by Kohl.

[131] The following assessment was made during a meeting of the socialist countries ambassadors' in Mozambique in June 1988: 'The influence of socialist countries in the People's Republic of Mozambique and southern Africa continues to decline. This tendency is acknowledged, but can only to a small extent be influenced': BStU, MfS HA I, Nr. 13933, Haltung der UDSSR zu einigen Problemen der Lageentwicklung im südlichen Afrika, August 1988, 4.

ency of the debtor.¹³² In this respect, Moscow determined that socialist countries should not demand the immediate repayment of debt but rather adapt an interest payment policy, as practiced by the West.¹³³

East Berlin's views also began to undergo a gradual transformation. Although the GDR's ruling elite resisted Gorbachev's 'new thinking' policy of 'openness and restructuring', new modes of thought undeniably had become part of the Zeitgeist. While Honecker stubbornly resisted Gorbachev's push for internal reforms, a change in foreign policy became increasingly discernible. Behind closed doors, East Berlin acknowledged that its approach towards southern Africa required modification, resulting in a new and more pragmatic form of thinking. Not only had it become increasingly apparent that the West would continue to attempt to increase its economic influence in Africa; the GDR had no illusions about its inability to compete with West Germany economically. East Berlin banked instead on its 'political influence and authority' in Africa. After all, there was little reason to doubt that the GDR had earned its positive image in Africa via its 'political, moral and material support of the African liberation struggles, social support in strengthening national independence and protection against imperial encroachment'.¹³⁴ Although economic cooperation between the GDR and African countries remained limited, East Berlin emphasised the need to 'strengthen the national economic potential and economic independence' of African states. However, what can only be described as a drastic policy overhaul, the GDR began to motivate African countries to 'develop and stabilize capitalist relations of production'.¹³⁵ In fact, evidence suggests that GDR diplomats and advisors in Africa received Foreign Office level instructions not to advise newly independent states to focus on building up socialism because there were other more pressing problems.¹³⁶

Already in 1983, Günter Sieber, director of the International Relations Department, instructed Schleicher not to advise Zimbabwe, which had achieved independence only three years earlier, to focus on establishing socialism, but concentrate on achieving political and economic stability and normality. Angola and Mozambique served as an example of countries that after independence had focused too much on building socialist societies, leading to economically weak and politically unstable states. Thus, in the mid-to-late 1980s, the GDR

---

¹³² BStU, MfS HA I, Nr. 13933, Haltung der UDSSR zu einigen Problemen der Lageentwicklung im südlichen Afrika, August 1988, 3.
¹³³ Ibid.
¹³⁴ BArch-SAPMO, DY30/ IV 2/2.115/30, Minister für Auswärtige Angelegenheiten, Vorlage für die Außenpolitische Kommission beim Politbüro des Zentralkomitees der SED, Betreff: die Bedeutung Afrikas in den internationalen Beziehungen am Ende des 20. Jahrhunderts. Tendenzen der politischen, ökonomischen und sozialen Entwicklung. Schlußfolgerungen, 16.03.1989.
¹³⁵ Ibid., 8–9.
¹³⁶ Interview with Hans-Georg Schleicher, Berlin, 20.02.2016.

increasingly advised African states to also seek economic relations with the West. In this respect, GDR advisors in Namibia received, in the late 1980s, the instruction to recommend SWAPO not to 'undertake any economic experiments nor orient itself entirely towards the GDR'. Instead, the GDR should advise African states also to seek close co-operation with West Germany.[137]

As discussed previously, in the mid-1980s there emerged a growing awareness among progressive thinkers in the GDR of the potential benefits of seeking cooperation with West Germany in Africa. However, it was only in the late 1980s that high-level political officials commissioned a change in approach, which translated into clear instructions for its execution by diplomats and advisors involved in Africa.[138] Considering that in the GDR orders always came from the top, it seems reasonable to conclude that these changes in the GDR's approach towards Africa came from the very top of the political hierarchy.[139]

Overall, there was an understanding that 'multilateral activities for the improvement of the international conditions in favour of African states, including the cooperation with political and economic circles of the West, was becoming more important'.[140] This however, did not imply that the GDR no longer had any economic interests in the continent.[141] On the contrary, East Berlin simply acknowledged that 'a rapid extension of bilateral economic relations was not feasible in the near future'. There was also acknowledgment that the GDR had little to offer economically. However, on the level of cultural exchange, that is, the education of cadres, and cultural and scientific cooperation, East Berlin had little doubt that the GDR was well placed to compete with West Germany. More importantly, although the GDR emphasised the need to support existing socialist states in Africa against capitalist pressure, the objective of establishing ideological hegemony moved into the background. In

---

[137] Ibid.
[138] In the case of Namibia, Professor Pilz, the GDR's advisor to SWAPO, received the clear instruction to advice SWAPO not to undertake any economic experiments after independence was achieved, but try to sort out the economic problems, as well as work closely with West Germany. Interview with Hans-Georg Schleicher, Berlin, 20.02.2016.
[139] Schleicher also suggested that ultimately the instructions came from the top, considering that he received his directives for Zimbabwe from Siebert in 1983: Interview with Hans-Georg Schleicher, Berlin, 20.02.2016.
[140] BArch-SAPMO, DY 30/IV 2/2.115/30, Minister für Auswärtige Angelegenheiten, Vorlage für die Außenpolitische Kommission beim Politbüro des Zentralkomitees der SED, Betreff: die Bedeutung Afrikas in den internationalen Beziehungen am Ende des 20. Jahrhunderts. Tendenzen der politischen, ökonomischen und sozialen Entwicklung. Schlußfolgerungen, 16.03.1989, 8.
[141] In fact, Schleicher noted in late 1989 that Namibia's economic partners felt insecure about the political future of Namibia. However, Schleicher argued that the situation was quite different for the GDR, given its long history of supporting SWAPO. Unquestionable, the GDR expected favourable relations with an independent Namibia: PAAA, MfAA, ZR 5405/90, 1989, Hans-Georg Schleicher, Beobachtermission Windhoek, an Ministerium für Auswärtige Angelegenheiten, Stellvertreter des Ministers Gen. Dr. Heinz-Dieter Winter, 27.10.1989, 3.

fact, East Berlin had every intention of avoiding excessive ideological competition with the West.[142]

Overall, Moscow and East Berlin's foreign policy changes and Pretoria's increasing willingness to solve the crisis in Angola and Namibia within the framework of a negotiated solution once more raised hopes for a possible breakthrough.[143] However, the prospect of reaching a lasting settlement seemed to deteriorate again after Pretoria blamed SWAPO for a bomb attack in northern Namibia, leading to the bombardment of SWAPO camps in Angola in February 1988. But Pretoria became increasingly aware that the political reality in Washington required making strategic adjustments. The prospect of George Bush or Michael Dukakis occupying the presidency after the upcoming elections pressed South Africa to work towards a negotiated settlement under the Reagan administration, for Reagan was sympathetic towards Pretoria's position.[144] Moscow expressed the desire to settle regional conflicts, including the conflict over Namibia, through negotiation. Pretoria was concerned about 'the lengthening casualty lists from a distant war', as well as the heavy financial burden caused by the conflict in Angola.[145] There were indeed many, including SWAPO, who argued that Pretoria's change of heart was heavily influenced by the Battle of Cuito Cuanavale.[146] In the face of military stalemate, South Africa for the first time conceded that military defeat was possible, which left Pretoria little choice but to seek a negotiated settlement.[147]

---

[142] BArch-SAPMO, DY 30/ IV 2/2.115/30, Minister für Auswärtige Angelegenheiten, Vorlage für die Außenpolitische Kommission beim Politbüro des Zentralkomitees der SED, Betreff: die Bedeutung Afrikas in den internationalen Beziehungen am Ende des 20. Jahrhunderts. Tendenzen der politischen, ökonomischen und sozialen Entwicklung. Schlußfolgerungen,16.03.1989.

[143] Moscow was determined to push Pretoria towards negotiated solutions. However, the Kremlin was not prepared to remove South Africa's international isolation as long as apartheid existed: PAAA, MfAA, ZR 5393/90, 1989–1990, Bericht über die Konsultation des Leiters der Abteilung Ost- und Zentralafrika im MfAA, Genossen Huettner, mit dem Leiter der Hauptverwaltung Afrika im MID, Genossen Jukalow, 27.02.1989.

[144] See also Brenke, *Die Bundesrepublik*, 106–107.

[145] Africa Institute of South Africa (AISA), Bulletin, Volume 28, No. 10, 1988, Regional Implications of the Negotiation on Angola and Namibia. The report listed two further points, which aren't omitted above for the sake of brevity: 'The South African Air Force's loss of air superiority over Angola and the indication that the interim government would probably not win the political fight against SWAPO'.

[146] PAAA, Zwischenarchiv, Bd. 155883, 1987–1989, Gespräch Dg 32 mit Dr Nicky Lyambo, Sekretär für Erziehung und Kultur des SWAP-Politbüros im Auswärtigen Amt, 06.09.1988.

[147] The military achievement of Cuban troops in Angola at the Battle of Cuito Cuanavale and subsequently South Africa's agreement to Namibian independence has been well documented. See, e.g., G., Edward, *The Cuban Intervention in Angola: 1965–1991: From Che Guevara to Cuito Cuanavale*, New York, Franc Cass, 2005; Documentary Film, 'Cuba: An African Odyssey', directed by Jihan el Tahri (documentary film) 2007. Accessed online July 2015, available from: www.youtube.com/watch?v=3jAJhvJOxzM

In May 1988, Angola, Cuba and South Africa came together under the watchful eyes of Chester Crocker, in the hope of achieving a negotiated settlement for the problems in Angola and subsequently Namibia. In July, the group achieved a major breakthrough, agreeing on the implementation of Resolution 435 under the condition of Cuban troop withdrawal from Angola. It has been claimed that SWAPO was not included in the negotiation process because the Reagan administration made a 'tactical concession to Pretoria's desire to minimize the role played by SWAPO in bringing about Namibia's independence'.[148] However, Nicky Lyambo, SWAPO secretary for Education and culture, insisted during a meeting at the Foreign Office in Bonn that Pretoria wanted SWAPO to participate.[149] In fact, SWAPO made the deliberate decision not to participate in the negotiation process, as Lyambo explained. SWAPO believed that a settlement should be twofold: a de facto cessation of hostilities between South Africa and Angola and a de facto cessation of hostilities between South Africa and SWAPO. However, SWAPO was concerned that its stance might lead to the attachment of new terms to Resolution 435 and therefore additionally complicate its implementation. Instead, it was expected that the Security Council would consult SWAPO after achieving a negotiated settlement to the Angola conflict to launch negotiations towards reaching an agreement on the implementation of Resolution 435.[150]

It remains questionable, however, whether Pretoria's intentions to include SWAPO were genuine, for the aim might have been to construct a scapegoat should the negotiations fail. A bomb attack on 2 September 1988 in Windhoek raised such suspicion. SWAPO claimed that South Africa was behind the bombing, intent on creating the impression that SWAPO was 'not interested in peace'.[151] In any event, the withdrawal of Cuban troops remained a cause for friction.[152] Pretoria demanded full withdrawal by June 1989, while Cuba proposed withdrawing its troops within four years, but finally agreed on two years.[153] On 15 November 1988, the US, the Soviet Union, Cuba and South Africa agreed on Cuban withdrawal from Angola and on Namibian independence. It later emerged that 'all parties agreed that the first and most crucial ingredient [for the breakthrough] was the change in

---

[148] L. Dobell, *Swapo's Struggle for Namibia, 1960–1991: War by Other Means*, Basel, P. Schlettwein Publishing, 2000, 72.
[149] PAAA, Zwischenarchiv, Bd. 155883, 1987–1989, Gespräch Dg 32 mit Dr. Nicky Lyambo, Sekretär für Erziehung und Kultur des SWAP-Politbüros im Auswärtigen Amt, 06.09.1988.
[150] Ibid.
[151] Ibid.
[152] See PAAA, MfAA, ZR 3100/93, 1989, Notiz über Aussagen von Sackey Namugongo, Chefredakteur der Luanda-Filiale des Senders 'Voice of Namibia' zum Verhandlungsprozess VRA/Kuba-USA, Luanda, 20.03.1988.
[153] Brenke, *Die Bundesrepublik*, 107.

Soviet foreign policy brought about by Gorbachev'.[154] The WCG played no part in the negotiations between the US, Soviet Union, Cuba and Angola that led to the Geneva Protocol in August 1988.[155] The Protocol determined the implementation of Resolution 435, designating the 1 April 1989 as the date for starting the independence process.[156] Subsequently, SWAPO agreed on a cessation of hostilities. For the supervision of the peace process, a Joint Military Monitoring Commission (JMMC) was established, with the two superpowers taking part in the observer mission.[157]

After the breakthrough in mid-1988, the Foreign Office increased efforts to 'revive the WCG', mainly for the purpose of involving the group in Namibia's first free elections as observers of both the election process and the implementation of Resolution 435.[158] However, the Foreign Office expected resistance from the US and Great Britain, and to some degree also from France.[159] Also, there were some indications in late September 1989 that Canada had no interest in reviving the WCG.[160] Nevertheless, in October 1989, Pik

---

[154] 'Regional Implications of the Negotiation on Angola and Namibia', *AISA*, Bulletin, Vol. 28, No. 10, 1988. Vergau came to the same conclusion, stating that 'what was then finally initiated in 1988 (on the basis of the New York Agreement of 22 December between Angola and Cuba as well as between South Africa, Angola and Cuba) would also have occurred without 'linkage' due to the change in Soviet UN and security policy prepared by Mikhail Gorbachev from 1985 and openly propagated and vigorously practised world-wide from 1988': Vergau, *Negotiating the Freedom*, 95.

[155] West Germany was not involved in the final negotiation process that led to Namibia's independence, as Crocker confirmed: 'I am not aware of West German 'participation' in any of these talks, but of course we periodically met with and consulted our close allies throughout': E-mail interview with Chester Crocker, 25.08.2016.

[156] In early 1989, both East Berlin and Moscow expressed optimism with regard to the Namibian independence process. Yet, although both sides believed that SWAPO had a 50% chance of winning the election, neither side was certain about SWAPO's role in an independent Namibia. There was concern that SWAPO was not ready to lead independent Namibia: PAAA, MfAA, ZR 5393/90, 1989–1990, Vermerk über ein Gespräch des Stellvertreters des Ministers für Auswärtige Angelegenheiten, Genossen Dr. Heinz-Dieter Winter, mit dem Leiter der Afrikaverwaltung des MID der UDSSR, Genossen J. A. Jukalow, am 24.03.1989 im MfAA, 27.02.1989, 4. See also Ibid., ZR 5392/90, 1984–1990, Informationen zur Politik der Bush-administration gegenüber dem südlichen Afrika, 17.04.1989, 7.

[157] For a detailed account of the events that led to the implementation of Resolution 435, see C. J., Tsokodayi, *Namibia's Independence Struggle: The Role of the United Nations*, Indiana, Xlibris Corporation, 2011.

[158] In 1978, the five foreign ministers of the WCG declared that the WCG would take up an observer role with regard to the implementation of Resolution 435 and Namibia's first free elections, which was reconfirmed in 1982: PAAA, Zwischenarchiv, Bd. 155883, 1987–1989, Namibia; hier: Termine und Sachthemen, die im Zusammenhang mit dem sich konkretisierenden Unabhängigkeitsprozeß von Bedeutung sind, 07.12.1988.

[159] Ibid.

[160] Ibid., Seminar der 'Foundation for Democracy in Namibia' zum Thema 'Principles for a Constitution for an Independent Namibia', 28.09.1989.

Botha asked the five foreign ministers of the Contact Group countries to 'make a joint public statement'. Against substantial inner-political opposition, the South African government had accepted the 435 process on the ground that it 'would get rid of the Cubans' and lead to a democratic Namibia.[161] However, misinterpretations of the binding principles of Resolution 435 raised for Pretoria the troubling question as to whether independence might actually propel Namibia towards a 'non-democratic political system. Pik Botha explained that concerns were raised when 'some fool of SWAPO' argued that in the case of a SWAPO election victory by a majority of over 50 percent, the two-third majority rule and the principles concerning the constitution for an independent Namibia, as outlined in the 1982 declaration of the WCG, were no longer binding. Obviously, the two-third majority rule was of utmost importance in terms of guaranteeing that changes to the constitution followed a democratic process.[162] Overall, Namibia's transition to independence was still on shaky grounds, for attacks on the entire 435 process and thus on the constitutional principles came from many different directions.

On 31 October 1989, a few days before Namibia's first free elections, the West German UN mission in New York stressed with great urgency that the WCG needed to present a united front against the efforts of conflicting parties, including non-aligned states, to circumvent the binding agreements of Resolution 435 after the election. With this end in mind, the UN mission argued that the French government's self-imposed 'suspension' from the WCG could no longer be justified simply on the ground that it opposed the Reagan administration's linkage strategy. Hence, France should take not only full credit for its role in authoring Resolution 435 but also 'play an active role in defending it'.[163] As in recent years, the issue was ultimately addressed on a local level by representatives to the UN Security Council's Western Contact Group.[164] The five foreign ministers of the WCG remained unable to come together and present a united front against attacks on the 435 process.[165]

Yet, although the WCG played no role in the final events that led to Namibia's first free elections, Resolution 435 provided, a decade after it was drafted by the WCG, the founda-

---

[161] PAAA, Zwischenarchiv, Bd. 155885, 1987–1989, Namibia-Regelung, 28.10.1989.
[162] The WCG authored in mid-1982 a letter that outlined the 'Principles concerning the Constituent Assembly, and the Constitution for an Independent Namibia'.
[163] PAAA, Zwischenarchiv, Bd. 155885, 1987–1989, Ausführung von SR 435 (Namibia); hier: Dringende Notwendigkeit französischer Mitwirkung bei den westlichen Fünf (Kontaktgruppe), 31.10.1989.
[164] Vergau, *Negotiating the Freedom*, 104–105.
[165] Throughout most of 1988, efforts were made to revive the WCG, predominantly on the grounds that the group could take up vital tasks during the implementation phase of Resolution 435: PAAA, Zwischenarchiv, Bd. 155883, 1987–1989, Termine und Sachthemen die im Zusammenhang mit dem sich konkretisierenden Unabhängigkeitsprozess von Bedeutung sind, 07.12.1988.

tion for Namibia's independence. Understandably, the FDP used the successful implementation of Resolution 435 to emphasis the role of its party leader in paving the way for Namibia's first free elections.[166] Nujoma also showered Genscher with praise, acknowledging Genscher's unwavering commitment to the implementation of Resolution 435, and his 'important role within the framework' of this resolution.[167] Nujoma's statements clearly amplified the importance of Genscher's determination to prevent any deviation from Resolution 435, especially when considered that the Reagan administration never displayed much attachment towards Resolution 435.[168] Although Genscher's importance was, apart from his intermediary efforts, to a large degree symbolic, the value of his persistence cannot be denied, for it was impossible to brush aside Resolution 435 as long as Genscher occupied the post of foreign minister. By the early 1980s, four out of the five foreign ministers who had been responsible for drafting Resolution 435 were no longer in office. Genscher was the only foreign minister of the original WCG who witnessed the implementation of Resolution 435 while still in office.

However, Nujoma's greatest concerns were related to the economic relations between West Germany and post-independent Namibia.[169] Finally, developments in Namibia opened the door for unrestricted economic interactions with West Germany. In late 1988, the Foreign Office outlined the potential focus areas for pre-independence support.[170] Yet, although Namibia was about to elect its first government in free and fair elections, there were still some concerns regarding economic relations and development aid in Bonn. In early 1989, Genscher invited Nujoma to Bonn, where he promised extensive development aid under the condition that a SWAPO-led Namibia would emulate 'Western democracy'.[171] Evidently, two major concerns still existed at a subliminal level. First, the possibility remained that a SWAPO-led government might introduce radical reforms that would negatively affect the white minority. Second, there was still the long-held fear that an independent Namibia might emulate the

---

[166] See 'Namibia muss Modellfall werden', die FDP Bundestagsfraktion informiert, 24.02.1989.
[167] 'SWAPO-Chef spricht mit der Bundesregierung', *dpa*, 03.03.1989; PAAA, Zwischenarchiv, Bd. 155894, 1989–1990, Besuch BM Warnke in Namibia, 05.07.1990.
[168] Importantly, Kohl also indicated in 1987 that he would not indiscriminately hold on to Resolution 435, which was widely seen as a success of Strauß' influence over Kohl. See, e.g., Hofmeier, *Afrika Jahrbuch 1987*, 36; ISSA, Akte: Namibia 1972–1986, Interview mit Ministerpräsident Dr. h.c. Franz Josef Strauß, April 1987.
[169] ISSA, Akte: Namibia, 1986–1990, Nujoma verspricht demokratisches Namibia, dpa 753.
[170] PAAA, Zwischenarchiv, Bd. 155883, 1987–1989, Namibia; hier: Unsere Hilfe für ein unabhängiges Namibia, 22.09.1988. The Foreign Office's initiative was based on the government's declaration to support the economic and social development of an independent and internationally recognized Namibia.
[171] BArch-SAPMO, DY 30/11568, Information für das Politbüro des ZK, Betreff: Zur Politik der SWAPO am Beginn des Unabhängigkeitsprozesses von Namibia, 21.03.1989. See also, ISSA, Akte: Namibia, 1986–1990, *dpa*, Nujoma verspricht demokratisches Namibia, dpa 753.

Soviet political and economic system. Despite these concerns, all major parties confirmed, in early 1989, the Federal Republic's special historic and moral responsibility towards Namibia and its obligation to support Namibia's peaceful transition to independence.[172] The *Bundestag* agreed on the expansion of West Germany's economic ties with Namibia after independence, including the provision of immediate economic aid.

Thus, by the time independence became tangible, Bonn's focus was once again directed towards economic relations with Namibia. The GDR was equally fixated on the pre-independence era. Thus, competition between the two German states over economic access to Namibia increased once again in the late 1980s. In early 1989, the MfS reported in a 'top-secret' paper that West Germany 'wants to prevent the GDR from realizing its extensive economic and political interests in Namibia'.[173] However, it should have been expected that the two Germanys would continue to compete over economic interests and influence. Competition between states over national interests, particularly in the sphere of economic access, is a natural occurrence even between friendly states.

Perhaps surprisingly, BMZ minister Warnke led the preparatory negotiations with SWAPO over potential development projects in Namibia.[174] Although the BMZ and SWAPO did not see eye to eye in the past, economic considerations quickly eradicated past differences after Namibia achieved independence, particularly between Warnke and Nujoma.[175] SWAPO obviously did not want Namibia to become another failed state and thus had an interest in establishing strong economic relations with one of the most powerful economies in the world, while independent Namibia represented for West Germany a potentially lucrative new market.

The two German states' involvement in the UNTAG mission in Namibia between 1989 and 1990

Daniel Lange's book *Auf deutsch-deutscher UN-Patrouille: Die polizeiliche Beobachtereinheit der DDR in Namibia 1989/90* investigates both German states' involvement in the United Nations Transition Assistance Group (UNTAG) in Namibia in 1989 and 1990.[176] His book should be consulted for an in-depth investigation of both German states' involvement in the

---

[172] Interpellation's in the *Bundestag*: SPD (11/3996), FDP, CDU/CSU (11/3924) and the Green Party (11/4039).
[173] BStU, MfS-HA XVIII, Nr. 9062, Hinweise zu Aktivitäten und Standpunkten in BRD Regierungskreisen zur Namibiafrage, Streng Geheim, 28.02.1989.
[174] See, e.g., H. Feddersen, 'Der Warnke-Besuch', *Allgemeine Zeitung*, 26.06.1990.
[175] PAAA, Zwischenarchiv, Bd. 155904, 1989–1990, Reise BM Dr. Warnke nach Namibia; hier: Dankschreiben, 24.01.1990.
[176] D. Lange, *Auf deutsch deutscher UN Patrouille. Die polizeiliche Beobachtereinheit der DDR in Namibia, 1989/90*, Schkeuditz: Schkeuditzer Buchverlag, 2011.

UN supervised elections in late 1989.[177] The start of the UNTAG mission on 1 April 1989 was overshadowed by heavy fighting between SWAPO guerrillas and South African troops. The intimidating behaviour of the South-West African Police (SWAPOL), a police force that had been established by Pretoria to provide law enforcement and counter-insurgency policing in occupied Namibia, raised particular concerns.[178] In direct response, Martti Ahtisaari, the UN special envoy and UN supervisor of UNTAG, decided to increase the civilian UNTAG police from 500 to 1494 men in late 1989.[179] The UN asked both German states to provide peacekeepers for the UNTAG mission.[180] In May 1989, the GDR had already expressed a strong interest in getting actively involved in UNTAG.[181] The UN proposed to include West Germany only as a 'compromise' that would restore 'balance', for Pretoria had voiced strong opposition to a GDR contingent.[182] Thus, East Germany's insistence on participating in the UNTAG mission promoted the push for West German involvement, although the Federal Government had not shown much interest in participating.

In mid-1989, Pretoria voiced its concerns about East Germany's desire to participate in peacekeeping operations in Namibia. South Africa opposed the GDR's participation due to its close relations with SWAPO.[183] On 20 June 1989, the negotiations collapsed in the face

---

[177] However, Lange's work offers only limited insights into West Germany's participation in the UNTAG mission, for he had no access to Foreign Office files that fall within the 30-year rule. Although the relevant files have been available for this book, for reasons of space the author cannot here provide an in-depth analysis of West Germany's role in the UNTAG mission.

[178] In fact, the Foreign Office demanded from the South African ambassador in West Germany an explanation concerning the continuing intimidation of the civil population: PAAA, Zwischenarchiv, Bd. 155885, 1987–1989, Durchführung von SR 435, Pretoria, 01.09.1989; Ibid., Ausführung von SR 435 (Namibia); hier: Bericht des GS vor dem SR, 03.08.1989.

[179] A steady growth in the number of complaints from the Namibian population against SWAPOL contributed to the decision to increase the number of foreign police in Namibia. See, e.g., PAAA, Zwischenarchiv, Bd. 155885, 1987–1989, Ausführung von SR-RES. 435 (Namibia); hier: Drittes UNTANG-Polizeikontingent, New York, 29.09.1989; Ibid., Ausführung von SR 435; hier: Zunehmende Beschwerden über Einschüchterungen durch ehemalige Koevoet-Angehörige, 02.08.1989.

[180] For more information regarding the BGS mission in Namibia, see PAAA, Zwischenarchiv, Bd. 155883, 1987–1989, Beteiligung von PVB des Bundesgrenzschutzes an der UN Friedensmission 'UNTAG' in Namibia, 10.08.1989. It is worth noting that West Germany did not expect to be asked to participate in the UNTAG mission. Until mid-1989, there were no indications that the UN was considering West Germany's participation in UNTAG: PAAA, Zwichenarchiv, Bd. 155890, 1989, Namibia; hier: Polizeikräfte aus der Bundesrepublik Deutschland für UNTAG, New York, 16.06.1989.

[181] In May 1989 already, the GDR offered its participation in peacekeeping operations in Namibia. See also PAAA, MfAA, ZR 3100/93, 1989, His Excellency Mr. Martti Ahtisaari, Special Representative of the Secretary-General of the United Nations Organization for Namibia, Berlin, 20.04.1989; Ibid., His Excellency Mr. Louis Pienaar Administrator-General, Berlin, 20.04.1989.

[182] BStU, MfS-HA XXII, Nr. 750/3, Blitz, Kutschan an Winter, Neugebauer und die Leiter der Abt. UNO, Rose und OZA, Hauke, New York, 17.05.1989. It was further stated that the GDR's participation was only realistic if both West Germany and the Netherlands would also participate.

[183] BArch, DO 1/11762, Teilnahme der DDR an der UN-Polizeibeobachtereinheit im Rahmen der

of Pretoria's opposition. For the sake of balance, the UN regarded West Germany's appointment also as inappropriate.[184] Nonetheless, East Berlin left no doubt about its expectation to occupy at least an active role in the civilian election observation mission. In July 1989, the GDR's application to send election observers to Namibia seemed also to fail due to Pretoria's objections. Numerous meetings between the UN Secretary General Javier Perez de Cuellar, South Africa's UN Ambassador Jeremey Shearar and Pik Botha finally eliminated Pretoria's concerns.[185] The trio sanctioned the deployment of 20 to 25 GDR election observers. Nonetheless, the GDR's participation was not yet clearly determined, for the Federal Government still had to approve West Germany's involvement in UNTAG.[186]

The possible participation of West Germany in the UN peacekeeping mission did not receive unanimous support in Bonn. On 14 September 1989, one day before the dispatch of 50 men of the Federal Border Police (BGS), the Greens unsuccessfully tried to stop the mission in the law and home affairs select committee *[Rechts-und Innenauschuss]* of the *Bundestag*.[187] The Green Party strongly opposed the involvement of the BGS, raising concerns that young and unprepared police personnel might get dragged into fighting, which seemed a reasonable possibility as UNTAG troops had come under fire in the past, as the Greens pointed out. Furthermore, the Greens argued that the employment of West German troops needed to be debated in the *Bundestag* and cannot simply be decided by the Kohl cabinet. The deployment of troops overseas presented for the Green Party also constitutional questions, for the Foreign Office and the Federal Security Council determined in 1982 that it was unconstitutional for the Federal Defence Force to undertake military operations outside NATO.[188] To this end, Genscher was prepared to support changes in the constitution, if necessary.

---

zivilen Komponente der Gruppe der Vereinten Nationen zur Unterstützung des Übergangs Namibias in die Unabhängigkeit (UNTAG), 11.09.1989.

[184] BStU, MfS, Abt. X, Nr. 921, Blitzt, Kutschan an Winter, Neugebauer und die Leiter der Abt. UNO, Rose und OZA, Hauke, New York, 30.05.1989, 213. See also Lange, *Auf deutsch-deutscher*, 56.

[185] Ibd., Blitzt, K. Kutschan an H.-D. Winter und B. Neugebauer sowie die Leiter der Abt. UNO, H. Rose und OZA, B. Hauke, New York, 14.07.1989, 222–223.

[186] Ibd., DDR-Beteiligung an ziviler Komponente UNTAG, New York, 28.07.1989, 224–225. See also Lange, *Auf deutsch-deutscher*, 61.

[187] For more information regarding the UN request for West German participation in the UNTAG mission and BGS's involvement in Namibia, see, e.g., PAAA, Zwischenarchiv, Bd. 155890, 1989, Anfrage des UN-GS Perez de Celluar an die Bundesregierung, Polizeikräfte aus der Bundesrepublik Deutschland zur Verstärkung von UNTAG bereitzustellen, 19.05.1989; Ibid., Bd. 155883, 1987–1989, Beteiligung von PVB des Bundesgrenzschutzes an der UN Friedensmission 'UNTAG' in Namibia, 10.08.1989; Ibid., Bd. 155890, 1989, Entsendung von 50 BGS-Beamten nach Namibia im Rahmen der Unterstützungsgruppe der Vereinten Nation (UNTAG) für Namibia, 28.06.1989.

[188] AGG, Akte 1475, Petra Kelly, Entschließungsantrag, 14.09.1989.

In 1989, this was, however, not an option, for the UNTAG mission required immediate support. For this reason, Genscher proposed the deployment of the BGS. To strengthen his position, Genscher emphasised West Germany's role as the co-author of Resolution 435, as well as the fact that the Federal Government fought, despite substantial obstacles, over the last 10 years for the implementation of Resolution 435. Genscher amplified his argument by pointing towards 'Germany's responsibility for Namibia and its people'.[189] The Greens, however, remained defiant in their position against uniformed personnel to be deployed outside of Germany. Wolfgang Schäuble, the Federal Minister for Special Relations, finally agreed on the grounds that it was an 'entirely civilian mission' and that 'the BGS personnel participated on a voluntarily basis'.[190]

The deployment of German troops in a former German colony was, of course, controversial in many respects, but seemed less contentious within the context of a peacekeeping mission under the umbrella of the UN. Nonetheless, German troops on foreign soil remained 45 years after the Second World War still debatable. Furthermore, the memory of German atrocities in its former colony made it impossible to approach the debate from an entirely non-emotional perspective.[191] Notably, East Germany was not visibly affected by Germany's past, mainly because it claimed to have cleansed the GDR society of the remnants of Nazi-Germany and the country's imperial past. The GDR's image as a fascist-free state was a fundamental aspect of GDR propaganda. In reality, however, the GDR sentenced far fewer Nazi criminals than West Germany between 1951 and 1989. Instead, the GDR integrated former Nazi members into its state apparatus and thus failed to emotionally engage with Germany's fascist past.[192] Furthermore, the GDR was in a position to approach Germany's colonial past from a detached perspective, as the state's Marxist-Leninist ideological foundation was embedded in anti-colonialism and anti-imperialist principles and thus firmly on the side of colonised people against neo-colonialism.

---

[189] PAAA, Zwischenarchiv, Bd. 155885, 1987–1989, Debattenbeitrag von BM im Deutschen Bundestag zu Namibia am 15. September 1989, 13.09.1989. Interestingly, the United Nations Council for Namibia argued in favour of West German participation in the UNTAG mission along the same lines as Genscher: PAAA, Zwischenarchiv, Bd. 155885, 1987–1989, Besuch des Präsidenten des Namibiarats und UN Botschafter Sambias, Zuze, in Bonn; hier: Gespräch am 15.09.1989 mit StS Lautenschlager und D3, 18.09.1989.

[190] 'Schäuble: Polizeilicher Auftrag in Namibia', *Frankfurter Allgemeine Zeitung*, 15.9.1989, in Lange, 'Deutsch-deutscher', 2.

[191] P. Kelly, 'MdB, Die Grünen, Namibia – the first genocide in the history of the Germans', in ISSA wissenschaftliche Reihe 21(ed.), *Im Brennpunkt*, 42–45. In 1907, German troops killed 65,000 members of the Herero tripe in German South-West Africa. For a detailed account of German colonial atrocities in Namibia, see D. Olusoga and C. W. Erichsen, *The Kaiser's Holocaust, Germany's Forgotten Genocide and the Colonial Roots of Nazism*, London, Faber and Faber Ltd, 2010.

[192] 'DDR – Mythos und Wirklichkeit: "Die DDR stand für Antifaschismus"', Konrad Adenauer Foundation (KAS). Accessed online December 2016, available from: www.kas.de/wf/de/71.6641/

However, even as late as 1989, the SED's strategic focus remained on the GDR's international standing and image. The MfS expected that the GDR's participation in UNTAG would 'strengthen its position within the United Nations', which 'complied with the GDR's overall foreign policy interests'.[193] However, decades of solidarity with SWAPO provided the most convincing argument for the GDR's participation in the UN Peacekeeping Operations (PKO).[194] Additionally, the GDR did not face a constitutional crisis over a possible participation of the National Defence Force (NVA) in UNTAG. In mid-1989, the constitutional legitimacy was determined by the Workgroup PKO, which included the cooperation of the Ministry for Foreign Affairs (MfAA), the Ministry of National Defence (MfNV) and Institute for International Relations (IIB). The workgroup approved the participation of NVA personnel in UNTAG on the grounds that the GDR constitution emphasised in Article 6 (4) the pursued of 'a stable blueprint for lasting peace in the World'.[195] Furthermore, Article 2 of the Warsaw Pact (May 1955) stated that the 'Contracting Parties declare their readiness to participate in a spirit of sincere cooperation in all international actions designed to safeguard international peace and security, and will fully devote their energies to the attainment of this end'.[196] The SED programme also emphasised that 'the GDR, as a member of the United Nations, contributes to the UN role in solving international problems, stabilise peace and increase the cooperation of nations and the defence of human rights'.[197] The GDR's participation in UN peace-keeping missions was, therefore, constitutionally legitimate.[198] In October 1989, the GDR despatched 30 peacekeepers to Namibia.

This was the first and last time East Germany participated in a UN mission, for the GDR collapsed in the first two months of 1990. The two Germanys were reunited in October 1990. Hence, when Namibia achieved national independence in November 1990, SWAPO's most loyal supporter, the GDR, had ceased to exist. Both the reunification of Germany and Namibia's independence were victories of freedom over oppression. The people of both the GDR and Namibia celebrated the realisation of a dream that decades of repression could not

---

[193] BStU, MfS-HA I, Nr. 13985, Studie: Friedenserhaltene Operationen der UNO (PKO) – Voraussetzung und Konsequenzen einer Teilnahme der DDR an der militärischen komponente von PKO, 30.06.1989, 84.
[194] D. Lange, 'Deutsch-deutscher Dienst in Namibia', United Nations, 6/2013, 3. Accessed online September 2014, available from: www.dgvn.de/fileadmin/publications/PDFs/Zeitschrift_VN/VN_2013/Heft_6_2013/06_Lange_VN_6-13_29-11-2013.pdf
[195] BStU, MfS-HA I, Nr. 13985, Studie Friedenserhaltende Operationen der UNO, Arbeitsgruppe PKO der UNO, 30.06.1989, 13.
[196] Ibid.
[197] Ibid.
[198] Ibid., 14.

destroy. More ironically still, the GDR presented for the Namibian majority over decades a loyal partner in the fight against tyranny and repression.

Understandably, therefore, Namibians who had direct contact with the GDR, such as the SWAPO leadership, could not comprehend at the time that the people in the GDR experienced on 3 October 1990 similar emotions as the people in Namibia on 21 March 1990. Hans-Georg Schleicher, the Head of the GDR's Diplomatic Observer Mission in Namibia, remembered that Nujoma expressed his incomprehension about the events in East Germany in November 1989, which were marked by mass protests and ultimately the fall of the Berlin Wall.[199]

For decades, the GDR provided SWAPO men, women and children with a sophisticated, progressive living and learning environment. East Berlin created for members of liberation movements a positive environment within the GDR, not comparable to the day-to-day life of ordinary GDR citizens. Hence, the high level of discontent among the GDR population was not revealed in the SWAPO cadres' experience of East Germany. That discontent ultimately led to the demand for democratic reform, the right to assemble, freedom to travel and free election under UN supervision. Consequently, Nujoma's and other SWAPO members experience of the GDR was not an accurate reflection of reality. The rapid spike in protests and social unrest in the late 1980s contained, therefore, an element of incomprehensibility for SWAPO cadres. After all, the GDR represented for liberation movements an 'intact world', a model state. In fact, in Nujoma's view, Gorbachev was responsible for the problems in the GDR in the late 1980s.[200]

However, the events of October 1989 had little effect on East Berlin's decision to participate in the UN peacekeeping mission, because the decision had been already made by the Secretariat of the SED-Central Committee in September 1988. Although thousands of Germans had fled the GDR via Hungary and Czechoslovakia by October 1989, SED hardliners were solely concerned about the continuation of the status quo. In denial of the changing political reality, the SED-state forced its Head of State to resign, only to continue oblivious to the impact of Gorbachev's 'new thinking' on the entire communist bloc.

The UN peacekeeping mission in Namibia generated great international interest, which presented for East Berlin the opportunity to underline the continuation of the GDR by ob-

---

[199] Schleicher, *Die Haltung der DDR zu Befreiungsbewegungen*, 94. Telephone interview with Hans-Georg Schleicher, 04.01.2019. Uwe Zeise, the GDR Ambassador to Zimbabwe (1988–1990), stated that Robert Mugabe, the President of Zimbabwe, was also surprised about the events in the GDR. In his view, it was the destruction of a state that had provided unrelenting support for the liberation struggles of the peoples of southern Africa. Thus, in the late 1980s, the growing and destabilizing social unrest in the GDR raised many questions and concerns. Still today, former liberation movement cadres want to talk about the GDR, as Uwe Zeise pointed out. Telephone interview with Uwe Zeise, Windhoek, 20.04.2016.

[200] Interview with Hans-Georg Schleicher, Berlin, 20.02.2016.

serving its commitment to the UNTAG mission, despite the rapidly deteriorating situation in the GDR. Mass protests and the prospect of imminent state bankruptcy presented serious challenges, but was at the time not a reliable indication of the GDR's imminent disintegration. Consequently, East Berlin treated the protests, up until the GDR's total collapse, as a challenge to the status quo and not a direct challenge to the existence of the GDR as a state. Consequently, there was an effort to convey an image of strength and control despite the growing upheavals within the GDR's sealed borders. By the end of 1989, contemporary observers regarded the growing mass unrest as an early indication for the GDR's transition towards democracy. Ironically, the GDR's peacekeepers in Namibia experienced the transition to democracy twice: first in Namibia and then in the GDR.[201]

In mid- and late 1989, the GDR still made plans for the education of relatively large numbers of Namibian children in the GDR.[202] The establishment of the GDR embassy in Windhoek in March 1990, at a time when the GDR was on the brink of total breakdown, indicates that the SED elite were not expecting the imminent collapse of the GDR. Obviously, it can be also interpreted as a last desperate attempt to accentuate the GDR's continuation.

Ironically, in the late 1980s, the GDR's international standing as a sovereign state was probably stronger than ever before. Kohl received Honecker, the first East German head of state to visit West Germany, with full state honours in 1987, and the GDR's participation in the UNTAG mission presented, apart from its admission into the United Nations in 1973, the hitherto most meaningful international acknowledgment of the GDR's sovereignty.

In the past, both German states opposed participating in 'blue helmet' missions, as both sides wanted to avoid a possible encounter between the GDR's People's Army and West Germany's Federal Defence Forces.[203] However, by the time the UN asked the two Germanys to participate in UNTAG, such concerns had disappeared, for the relations between the two states had improved significantly. It was even expected that the UNTANG mission would have a positive effect on intra-German relations.

---

[201] 'Den Übergang zur Demokratie erleben die Vopos zweimal', *Die Welt*, 28.12.1989.
[202] See, e.g., PAAA, MfAA, ZR 3112/93, 1990, Protokoll über die Gespräche des Ministers für Bildung, Kultur and Sport der Republik Namibia, Herr Nahas Angula, im Ministerium für Bildung und Wissenschaft der DDR im Zeitraum von 28.05.1990–31.05.1990; BArch, DR 2/13853, Information über die Ergebnisse der Verhandlungen mit Südwestafrikanischen Volksorganisation (SWAPO) von Namibia über Massnahmen zur Unterstützung auf dem Gebiet des Bildungswesens im Jahr 1989, 03.05.1989. See also BArch, DR 2/13854, Bilaterale Zusammenarbeit DDR-SWAPO/Namibia, Bd. 1, 1988–1990.
[203] Deutsche Gesellschaft für die Vereinten Nationen (DGVN), 2011, 40 Years of German membership in the United Nations. Accessed online November 2015, available from: www.dgvn.de/germany-in-the-united-nations/40-years-of-german-membership-in-the-united-nations/

However, considering that East Berlin has always attached great importance to the GDR's sovereignty, it is not surprising that *Neues Deutschland*, the SED's official party newspaper, left no doubt about the GDR peacekeepers' autonomy in Namibia.[204] East Berlin still felt compelled to underline the GDR's sovereignty, even though there could no longer be any doubt about the GDR's role as an internationally recognized state. Ultimately, however, international recognition could not compensate for the SED's failure to gain the active support of the majority of the GDR population.

Yet, the events in late 1989 also amplified further the significance behind the co-operation of the two German states in UNTAG. Considering that, in the broadest sense, a dived Germany united for a peacekeeping mission in a former German colony; contemporary observers' acknowledgment of the historical significance of the intra-German co-operation in Namibia was appropriate.[205] This was also strongly reflected in the national and international interest in the two German states' involvement in the UNTAG mission.[206] Obviously, the Namibian German newspaper *Die Allgemeine Zeitung* observed the arrival of East and West German peacekeepers with great enthusiasm. The CDU/CSU sponsored newspaper emphasised the historical importance of the two German states' cooperation in the UN peacekeeping mission: 'In SWA/Namibia happens what in Germany nobody dared to think'.[207] Still, West German policy force found itself at the centre of a controversy.

The ultra-conservative fringe of the Namibian Germans hijacked the arrival of West German men in uniform to reawaken memories of the German colonial past and the more recent Nazi past, mainly by publicly exhibiting symbols of these eras and by chanting '*Sieg Heil*'.[208] Obviously, it was in the interest of both Germanys, as well as the Namibian Germans, that the first free election in Namibia would not be overshadowed by Germany's dark past. Considering the emotionally charged historical reality behind symbols of the German Empire and Nazi-Germany, these incidents had the potential to make headlines around the world. In order to avoid any more controversy, the West German election observers were quickly dispatched to remote areas because there were no German speaking communities.[209]

---

[204] 'Das Khaki des Krieges wich dem Blau-Weiß der UNO. Unter harten Bedingungen erfüllen DDR-Polizeibeobachter Friedensdienst in Namibia', *Neues Deutschland*, 23.11.1989.

[205] Interview with Hans-Georg Schleicher, Berlin, 20.02.2015.

[206] See, e.g., 'Weihnachten am Kavango', *Der Spiegel*, 44/1989; 'Den Übergang zur Demokratie erleben die Vopos zweimal', *Die Welt*, 28.12.1989; 'Das Khaki des Krieges wich dem Blau-Weiß der UNO. Unter harten Bedingungen erfüllen DDR-Polizeibeobachter Friedensdienst in Namibia', *Neues Deutschland*, 23.11.1989. See also Lange, *Auf Deutsch-deutscher*, 101.

[207] 'Deutsch-deutschePatrouille, VOPOs und BGS gemeinsam im Einsatz', *Allgemeine Zeitung*, 30.10.1989, in Lange, 'Deutsch-deutscher', 118–119.

[208] See, e.g., 'Weihnachten am Kavango', *Der Spiegel*, 44/1989, 30.10.1989; 'Würstchen und Waffen', *Der Spiegel*, 41/1989, 09.10.1989. See also Lange, *Auf Deutsch-deutscher*, 118–119.

[209] 'Weihnachten am Kavango', *Der Spiegel*, 44/1989, 30.10.1989.

Between 7 and 11 November 1989, Namibia held its first free elections: SWAPO won 57 percent of the 670,000 votes cast and thereby giving SWAPO a 41 seats majority in the 72-member assembly. The DTA came in second with 28.5 percent of the votes and 21 seats. On 9 February 1990, the 72-member assembly adopted the Namibian Constitution. On 21 March 1990, Namibia's newly elected president Sam Nujoma declared that 'Namibia is forever free, sovereign and independent'.[210] By the time Namibia achieved independence the GDR's peacekeepers were no longer in Namibia.[211]

After the collapse of the GDR, West Germany showed no interest in East Germany's substantial knowledge about southern African liberation movements.[212] One might have expected that some sort of exchange between Bonn and the former GDR diplomats, who had significant experience dealing with SWAPO in the decades of the Namibian liberations struggle, took place after reunification.[213] The GDR simply ceased to exist for West Germany.

---

[210] C. S. Wren, 'Namibia achieves independence after 75 years of Pretoria's rule', *New York Times*, 21.03.1990.
[211] Lange, *Auf deutsch-deutscher*, 128.
[212] Interview with Hans-Georg Schleicher, Berlin, 20.02.2016.
[213] Telephone interview with Willi Sommerfeld, 25.04.2015. Sommerfeld was a member of the GDR Solidarity Committee.

8 Conclusion

This study has explored how the division of Germany into two separate and competing states shaped policy on the question of Namibian independence. While Namibia's history as a German colony influenced attitudes in both Germanys, as did many other factors, the two German states' foreign policy making was strongly shaped by the wider reality of East-West Cold War rivalry in southern Africa. Though intra-German relations improved after the Brandt government implemented *Ostpolitik* in 1969, Namibia's independence struggle was one of the most frequent causes for friction between East and West Germany in the mid-to-late 1970s and until at least the mid-1980s. East Germany increasingly saw West Germany as a rival in Namibia.

Both domestic and foreign policy issues played a key role in the GDR's attitude vis-a-vis West Germany in Namibia. Although the normalisation of intra-German relations benefitted both German states, the GDR continued to propagate the image of West Germany as a traditional class enemy. East Berlin sought to establish the GDR on the international stage as profoundly different from West Germany, and convince its disgruntled population that their state was the better Germany. Consequently, the GDR's propaganda machine directed its attention to foreign policy issues, portraying West Germany as being on the wrong side of history. West German relations with the apartheid regime in Pretoria provided the underlying context for the GDR's claim that West Germany was an exploitative neo-imperialistic power that harboured neo-colonial ambitions in southern Africa. As a countermeasure against West Germany's changing attitude towards the Namibian liberation struggle and the question of Namibian independence, East Germany placed increasing emphasis on countering West Germany's efforts to improve its image in southern Africa.

Western reluctance to support Namibia's liberation struggle proved advantageous to the GDR's quest to play a stronger role on the international stage. The Western world's evaluation of liberation movements as `communist' and `terrorist' organizations left liberation movements with no option but to seek help from the communist bloc. East Berlin's preparedness to provide substantial aid to liberation struggles, allowed the GDR to build strong relations outside of the Iron Curtain, in this case with SWAPO.

In West Germany, conservatives were particularly swayed by the emotional underpinnings of the Cold War. In the late 1970s, *Bundestag* debates on Namibia gradually became increasingly imbued with strong ideological undertones, reflecting broader Cold War dynamics. Liberation movements were largely seen as militantly Marxist-Leninist, willing to do Moscow's bidding in southern Africa after achieving independence. This narrow perspective led to an uncompromising attitude against those movements, especially by those who harboured deep anti-communist sentiments. In the 1980s, however, there was a clear move away from such hardened positions in West Germany. It became increasingly accepted that the 'heritage of colonialism', not the Soviet Union and its weaponry, was the main reason for southern Africa's many problems. Nevertheless, for those who had reservations about SWAPO, including Washington, Pretoria and hardliners within the Federal Government, the liberation movement's close relations with Moscow, Havana and East Berlin continued to provide the context for their argument against the idea of SWAPO coming to power in Namibia.

In general, the social-liberals kept the highly emotional nature of the Cold War out of the rational process of policy making, and the decision making-process was not held hostage by the ideological overload of the Cold War. Still, both sides of the political divide expressed concerns about the growing influence in southern Africa of the GDR and the Soviet Union. For the GDR, solidarity with liberation movements played a central role in its growing importance as Moscow's junior partner in southern Africa. East Germany's close relationship with liberation movements improved its standing in the Eastern bloc countries and the international community more broadly.

Though intra-German relations improved slowly, tensions still rose over the Namibia issue. Both German states attempted to influence the future political direction of Namibia. There was little risk of this triggering a confrontation between the two German states on African soil, however, not least because neither state was prepared to face up to the political costs of becoming involved in overseas military conflicts. Both were concerned with international standing and status and neither wanted to risk compromising their hard-won position at the UN in the late 1970s. Unlike Cuba, the GDR never deployed troops in southern Africa and West Germany's constitution forbade an 'out-of-area' deployment of its troops, so the rivalry of the two Germanys in their pursuit of national interests in southern Africa did not run the risk of a direct conflict between them.

The effects of intra-German rivalry in relation to Namibia were most strongly felt at the level of propaganda. On both sides of the Wall, the political leadership tried to present their state as the better Germany. The continued international attention on southern Africa provided opportunities for trying to instil such an image in the minds of the international community, and to discredit the other side, domestically and internationally. By the late 1970s, however, West Germany increasingly emphasised the need to keep the East-West conflict out of Africa. There was a move away from the notion that national liberation struggles were propelled by the Soviet Union's drive to establish ideological hegemony in Africa. Consequently, the focus was now less on the possible ideological dimension of the liberation struggle but its de facto objective: decolonisation. Still, South Africa's claim that a SWAPO-led Namibia would play into the hands of Moscow's geostrategic objectives in southern Africa did not fall on deaf ears, particularly in conservative circles. Yet, despite diverging opinions along political lines in West Germany, there was a general consensus that the Soviet Union played a central role in perpetuating conflict in southern Africa and wide agreement that the GDR was key in assisting Soviet geostrategic ambitions in the region.

While East Berlin supported Moscow's power ambitions in southern Africa, the GDR also pursued its own national interests in the region. Its economic interests moved into the foreground from the mid-1970s. The SED sought to counter the influence of the capitalist West in southern Africa by supporting liberation struggles, and the GDR pursued this objective aggressively, not least because it assisted the Soviet Union's great power interests and thus enhanced East Germany's standing within the Eastern bloc countries. Hence, an increase in tensions between the two Germanys was unavoidable, for West Germany's position towards Namibia posed a challenge to the GDR's objectives.

GDR propaganda played a central role in the Federal Government's motivation to increase its efforts to finding a negotiated solution to Namibian independence in the late 1970s. West Germany needed a platform to counteract East Berlin's efforts to discredit West Germany internationally. Overall, West Germany's image gradually improved in Africa, predominantly because of its stronger commitment in solving the Namibia question. Despite these efforts, scepticism about the seriousness and motives of West Germany's changing attitude remained. This was, in no small part, due to the GDR's persistent propaganda work.

West Germany's ability to play an influential role in Namibia's path to independence dramatically weakened in the 1980s. The Reagan administration's linkage of Namibia's independence to Cuban troop withdrawal from Angola took the momentum out of the Western Contact Group's Namibia plan. Reagan's obsession with both military solutions and communism steered the US policy in southern Africa into a direction that was in strong opposition to the Federal Government's trust in the benefit of seeking to improve relations with those on the other side of the ideological spectrum, including liberation movements. While the Reagan administration was prepared to risk confrontation with Moscow in southern Africa, Bonn left little doubt about its determination to continue the previous governments' policies of detente. Yet, between 1983 and 1988, the Western powers retreated into a wait-and-see attitude, an expression of resignation in the face of the Reagan administration's dominant role in the negotiations. Though there was widespread acceptance of the notion that the Reagan administrations 'linkage' strategy blocked any progress in the Namibia question, West Germany had to accept Washington's dominant role in the negotiations, and saw no alternative to the Reagan administration's 'linkage' strategy. Though West Germany's ability to drive the negotiation process forward came to a halt after 1983, the Federal Government remained confident that Namibia would not become a communist state after independence; and hence, unlike Pretoria, Bonn was not particularly concerned that independence might produce a non-democratic political system in Namibia. De-escalation of East-West tensions in southern Africa remained one of the central aspects of West Germany's foreign policy.

In the GDR, a subtle yet important realignment in thinking slowly took place in the mid-to-late 1980s. Although the ruling elite were not yet susceptible to such changes, a need for new approaches in southern Africa became slowly apparent. In the mid-1980s, the GDR began to advise socialist states to seek economic relations with the West, including West Germany. That the GDR acknowledged West Germany as a potential partner in southern Africa heralded a dramatic change in the GDR's strategic thinking. By the time the UN asked the two German states to participate in the UN peacekeeping mission in Namibia, the GDR's leadership had accepted that multilateral activities, such as co-operation with West Germany, was key to building a thriving economy and creating political stability in newly independent African states. Naturally, the two German states continued to compete with each other in the pursuit of their national interests, but their rivalry was no longer propelled by an intense ideological undertone. The two states' interest in Namibia was largely grounded in economic considerations. At the heart of this competition was uncertainty as to whether the other side would receive preferential or favourable treatment in an independent Namibia. Both the GDR's unwavering solidarity with the Namibian liberation struggle and West Germany's economic power seemed to justify such concerns. In economic terms, Western countries were in an overall stronger position to offer economic rewards for post-independence co-operation than the Eastern bloc countries. Thus, the attractiveness of the free market system, which the Eastern bloc countries were not linked to, gave West Germany an economic advantage over the GDR.

Gorbachev's reforms changed attitudes on both sides of the ideological divide and brought about the change that made Namibia's independence possible. The battle of Cuito Cuanavale helped South Africa accept that there was no military solution to the most pressing issues in southern Africa, and Gorbachev's policy of glasnost and perestroika opened the door to a negotiated settlement. After all possible options had been exhausted, including armed struggle and full-blown military confrontation, all sides came to understand that the improvement in East-West relations presented a window of opportunity to end the conflict over Namibian independence. Moscow's new openness towards closer co-operation with the West and its strong support for a negotiated settlement over Namibia played a key role here. Thus, the same political dynamics that improved relations between the two German states, as well as between West Germany and SWAPO, namely rapprochement, engagement, co-operation and dialogue, also ultimately helped lead to Namibia's independence. In his Nobel Lecture in 1971 Brandt had said:

> The solution of mutual problems implies establishing links through meaningful co-operation among states beyond inter-bloc frontiers. This means transforming the conflict; it means doing away with actual and supposed barriers with peaceful risks on both sides. It means building up confidence through practical arrangements. And this confidence may then become the new basis for the solution of long-standing problems...Peace, like freedom, is no original state, which existed from the start; we shall have to make it, in the truest sense of the word.[1]

For the young Namibians who were raised and educated in East Germany, the collapse of the GDR and Namibia's independence presented immediate challenges, for though the GDR Kids life in East Germany was geared towards a future in Namibia, they were ill-prepared for losing what they had called home for the greater part of their lives. Without adequate preparation, these young people had to embrace life in an unfamiliar country at the southern tip of Africa. While it is impossible to describe what wider impact such an experience had on the young children and teenagers, and though it provides only a glimpse into one person's unique experience of this particular moment in time, the following poem offers valuable insights. Selma Kamati, who wrote it as a young adult, emphasises that her poem was not meant to be a criticism of the GDR, but was a window into her feelings and state of mind during a time of tremendous change; when it became ever more apparent to her that fundamental decisions in her life had been made by others, determined by political dynamics and without regard for the individual. Her thought-inspiring poem provides a unique perspective on some of the issues discussed in this book:

I Think, Therefore I am

Be brave, they said to me –
and I fought off all those fears.

Work hard, they said to me –
and I got many As.

Behave yourself, they told me –
and I never forgot to say thank you.

They told me I belonged to the elite –
and I was very proud.

---

[1] T. Frängsmyr and I. Abrams (eds.), *Nobel Lectures: Peace, 1971–1980*, Singapore, World Scientific Publishing, 1997, 20–34.

They told me to remember the hungry children –
and I cleared my plate.

They told me to be a pioneer –
and I learned to march in line.

Now go home, they told me –
and I went to my unfamiliar homeland.

I think, therefore I am, I told myself –
and now I have my own dream.

The repatriation of Namibians in exile began in 1989 and about 40,000 men, women and children, who had lived under SWAPO's care in exile, returned to Namibia. The repatriation of exiles posed many challenges for the newly independent Namibia, which provided inadequate support during the immediate post-repatriation period. The lack of counselling and re-integration programmes was especially strongly felt by exile-children and combat veterans, placing them in a vulnerable situation.

After 1990, the new united Germany came to the aid of the new country, providing more development assistance than any other country in the decades that followed independence. This was partly because of Germany's sense of responsibility to its former colony, in which it had perpetrated genocide, even if the German government refused to use that term. Germany's relations with independent Namibia also flowed out of the role the two Germanys had played during the Namibian liberation struggle, the subject of this study.

List of Abbreviations

AA	Auswärtiges Amt (Foreign Office, FRG)
AAPD	Akten zur Auswärtigen Politik der Bundesrepublik Deutschland
AISA	Africa Institute of South Africa
ANC	African National Congress
AGG	Archiv Grünes Gedächtnis
BArch	Bundesarchiv, in Berlin-Lichterfelde
Bd	Volume
BDI	Federation of German Industry
BGS	Federal Border Police
BK	Federal Chancellor
BMF	Ministry of Finance
BMWi	Ministry for Economics and Technology
BMZ	Federal Ministry for Economic Cooperation and Development
BStU	Representative in Charge of the State Security Service Documents of the Former GDR
CCB	Civil Cooperation Bureau
CSCE	The Commission on Security and Cooperation in Europe
CDU	Cristian Democratic Party
DDR	German Democratic Republic
DGB	German Federation of Trade Union
DGVN	United Nations Association of Germany
DIHT	Association of German Chambers of Industry and Commerce
DTA	Democratic Turnhalle Alliance
DUD	Deutschland Union Dienst
EG	European Community
EIR	Executive Intelligence Review
EKD	Evangelical Church in Germany
FAPLA	The People's Armed Forces for the Liberation of Angola
FES	Friedrich Ebert Foundation
FNS	Friedrich Naumann Foundation
FRG	Federal Republic of Germany
fdk	Free Democratic Correspondence (FDP)
GDR	German Democratic Republic
HSS	Hanns Seidel Foundation
HV	Main/Central Department
HV A	Ministry of State Security Headquarter of Reconnaissance
HA I	Ministry of State Security Espionage in the Military Sphere
HA II	Ministry of State Security General Counter Intelligence
IG	Interest Group for German-speaking Southwest Africans
IIB	Institute for International Relations (at the academy of the Ministry of State Security)
IMF	International Monetary Fund

IPS	Inter Press Service
JMC	Joint Monitoring Commission
JMMC	Joint Military Monitoring Commission
KAS	Konrad Adenauer Foundation
MfAA	Ministry of Foreign Affairs
MfS	Ministry of State Security
MfNV	Ministry of National Defence
MPLA	People's Movement for the Liberation of Angola
NAM	Non-Aligned Movement
NAN	National Archives of Namibia
NATO	North Atlantic Treaty Organisation
NCDP	Namibia Christian Democratic Party
NFDG	National Front of Democratic Germany
NFF	Namibian National Front
NP	National Party
NVA	National Volksarmee
OAU	Organization of African Unity
OBS	Otto Benecke Foundation
PKO	UN Peacekeeping Operations
SADF	South African Defence Force
SED	Socialist Unity Party Germany
SI	Socialist International
SSG	Socialist Federal Community
SWANU	South West African National Union
SWAPO	South West African People's Organisation
SWAPO-D	South West Africa People's Organisation Democrats
TUCSIN	University Centre for Studies in Namibia
UN	United Nations
UNTAG	United Nations Transition Assistance Group
UNITA	National Union for the Total Independence of Angola
WFP	UN World Food Programme
ZK	Central Committee

Bibliography

Archival Sources

Political Archive of the Foreign Office in Berlin (PAAA)

AV Neues Amt, Bd. 7897, 7920, 7959, 7987, 16413, 16414

B1, Band 388; B2, Band 222

Zwischenarchiv, Bd. 108202, 108204, 108220, 115782, 116802, 116840, 116841, 116845, 125282, 125293, 127747, 138098, 138099, 138100, 138101, 138102, 138103, 138104, 138105, 138106, 138108, 155883, 155885, 155890, 155894, 156671, 178610, 178680, 178773, 178848

Political Archive of the Foreign Office in Berlin, GDR Ministry for Foreign Affairs (MfAA)

MfAA, C 3000, 1426/75, 1428/75

MfAA, ZR 439/86, 1133/87, 1634/83, 2434/89, 2495/86, 2763/84, 2765/84, 3100/93, 3112/93, 5392/90, 5393/90, 5405/90

Bundesarchiv, Berlin-Lichterfelde (BArch)

DZ 8/3a, 8/33, 8/37, 8/40, 8/52, 8/535, 9/2575, 2/11382, 2/13854, 2/13855, 2/11434

DO 1/11762

DQ 4/5433,

Stiftung Archiv der Parteien und Massenorganisationen der DDR im Bundesarchiv (SAPMO), Berlin-Lichterfelde

BArch-SAPMO, DY 30/ IV 2/2.115/25, DY30/ IV 2/2.115/30, DY 30/5918, DZ 8/39

The Agency for the Federal Commissioner for the Stasi records (BStU), Berlin

MfS 6645

MfS-AG XVII

MfS-ZAIG, Nr. 6147, Nr. 8357, Nr. 11115, Nr. 11475

MfS-HA I, Nr. 13985

MfS-HA II, Nr. 28977

MfS-HA II, Nr. 29532

MfS-HA XXII, Nr. 750/3

MfS-HA XVIII, Nr. 8379

MfS-HA XVIII, Nr. 9062

MfS, Abt. X, Nr.921/213

MfS-HVA, Nr. 84

MfS-Hauptverwaltung Aufklärung, Nr. 12, Nr. 30, Nr. 40, Nr. 62, Nr. 63, Nr. 65, Nr. 69

JHS Potsdam, Mikrofilmstelle, VVS JHS o001–110/82

Archive Grünes Gedächtnis (AGG)

Akte 342, Uschi Eid

Akte 1473, Petra Kelly

Akte 1608

Akte 2127

B.II.1, Die Grünen im Bundestag, Signatur 3

National Archives of Namibia (NAN)

GAS 1/1/2, 1/5/2, 1/5/5, 1/5/6, 1/6/19, 1/6/21, 1/1/138, 1/2/11

AACLRS.004AACLRS.304

Documents of the *Bundestag*

Bundestag debates, interpellations and declarations are available online at www.bundestag.de/dokumente/

Published Primary Sources, West Germany

(AAPD), *Akten zur Auswärtigen Politik der Bundesrepublik Deutschland, 1969–1985* (ed.), im Auftrag des Auswärtigen Amtes vom Institut für Zeitgeschichte, München, R. Oldenbourg Verlag.

Auswärtiges Amt (ed.), *Außenpolitik der Bundesrepublik Deutschland, Dokumente von 1949 bis 1994,* Coburg, Druckhaus Coburg GmbH, 1995.

Genscher, H.-D., *Deutsche Außenpolitik, Ausgewählte Reden und Aufsätze 1974–1985*, Bonn, Verlag Bonn Aktuell GmbH, 1985.

Published Primary Sources, GDR

Babing, A., *Gegen Rassismus, Apartheid und Kolonialismus, Dokumente der DDR, 1949–1977*, Berlin, Staatsverlag der Deutschen Demokratischen Republik, 1978.

Babing, A., *Gegen Rassismus, Apartheid und Kolonialismus, Dokumente der DDR, 1977–1982*, Berlin, Staatsverlag der Deutschen Demokratischen Republik, 1983.

Honecker, E., 'Party and Revolutionary Young Guard Firmly Allied', Honecker speech to the Free German Youth in 1984 and 1989, German Propaganda Archive, Calvin College. Accessed online November 2014, available from: http://research.calvin.edu/german-propaganda-archive/fdj.htm

Memoirs and publications by contemporary witnesses

Crocker, C., *High Noon in Southern Africa: Making Peace in a Rough Neighbourhood*, New York, Norton Publisher, 1992.

Genscher, H.-D., *Deutsche Außenpolitik*, Stuttgart, Verlag Bonn Aktuell GmbH, 1981.

Gorbatschow, M., *Über mein Land: Russlands Weg ins 21. Jahrhundert*, München, Ullstein, 2002.

Kohl, H., *Erinnerungen, 1930–1982*, München, Droemer Verlag, 2004.

Kohl, H., *Erinnerungen, 1982–1990*, München, Droemer Verlag, 2005.

Kohl, H., *Erinnerungen, 1990–1994*, München, Droemer Verlag, 2007.

Mudge, D., *All the way to an independent Namibia*, Pretoria, Protea Book House, 2016.

Nujoma, S., *Where Others Wavered: The Autobiography of Sam Nujoma*, London, Panaf Books, 2001.

Schleicher, H.-G. and I. Schleicher, *Special Flights: The GDR and Liberation Movements in Southern Africa,* Harare, SAPES Trust, 1998.

Schleicher, I., *Zwischen Herzenswunsch und politischem Kalkül: DDR Solidarität mit dem Befreiungskampf im südlichen Afrika. Annäherung an ein Erbe*, Berlin, Hefte zur DDR-Geschichte, 1999.

Schmidt, H., *Menschen und Mächte*, Berlin, Siedler Verlag, 1987.

Strauß, F. J., *Die Erinnerungen*, Berlin, Siedler Verlag, 1989.

Vergau, H. J., *Negotiating the Freedom of Namibia, The diplomatic achievement of the Western Contact Group*, Basel, Basler Africa Bibliographien, 2010.

Verheugen, G., *Apartheid: Südafrika und die deutschen Interessen am Kap*, Köln, Verlag Kiepenheuer und Witsch, 1986.

Wischnewski, H. J., *Mit Leidenschaft und Augenmaß*, München, Bertelsmann, 1989.

Ya-Otto, J., *Battlefront Namibia: An Autobiography*, Connecticut, Lawrence Hill & Co, 1981.

Newspapers

West German

Dpa, 1983–1989.

Frankfurter Allgemeine Zeitung, 1978–1988.

Frankfurter Rundschau, 1983–1998.

General Anzeiger, 1984.

Lingener Tagespost, 1988.

Münchner Merkur, 1978.

Das Parlament, 1988.

Die Rheinpfalz, 1980.

Saarbrücker Zeitung, 1981.

Der Spiegel, 1978–1989.

Süddeutsche Zeitung, 1980–1988.

Der Tagesspiegel, 1978.

Taz, 1988.

Die Welt, 1977–1983.

Die Zeit, 1970–1988.

Unsere Zeit, 1988.

BPA-Nachrichtenabteilung, Rundfunk-Auswahl Deutschland, 1978.

Deutsche Welle (DW) Monitor-Dienst, 1974–1988.

East German

DDR Panorama (foreign press agency), 1980.
Horizont, 1977.
Neues Deutschland, 1981–1989.

Namibian Newspapers

Allgemeine Zeitung, 1981–1984.
Namibia Nachrichten, 1985–1989.
Namibia Information Bulletin (journal), 1983–1984.
SWAPO of Namibia, Pressedienst, 1985–1988.

English Newspapers

Financial Mail, 1985.
The Times London, 1985.
New York Times, 1983–1990
Executive Intelligence Review (EIR) News Service, 1988.

Newspapers and Journals by Political Parties

CDU/CSU Fraktion im Deutschen Bundestag, Pressedienst
Deutschland Union Dienst (DUD), CDU/CSU
fdk tagesdienst, 1981–1988.
freie demokratische korrespondenz (fdk), FDP
Grünes Bulletin, Green Party
Service der SPD für Presse, Funk and TV, SPD
Die SPD-Fraktion im Deutschen Bundestag, SPD

The above-mentioned newspapers and journals may be consulted at the following institutions: the archive of the Konrad Adenauer Foundation, the archive of the Friedrich Naumann Foundation, Archive Grünes Gedächtnis, the National Library of Namibia, the *Informationsstelle Südliches Afrika* and the *Zeitgeschichtliches Archiv*.

Documentary Films

'Cuba: An African Odyssey', directed by Jihan el Tahri (documentary film), 2007. Accessed online July 2015, available from: www.youtube.com/watch?v=3jAJhvJOxzM

'Hans-Dietrich Genscher: Ein Politikerleben', Spiegel TV, 08.10.2014 (TV program). Accessed online August 2015, available from: www.youtube.com/watch?v=94xj_1BnK70

'Der Kanzlersturz – Die Wende von 1982', ZDF (TV documentary film). Accessed online March 2015, available from: www.youtube.com/watch?v=D4pfC48kr9o&spfreload=10

'Millardenkredit für den Feind, Der Aufsehen erregende Strauß-Deal mit der DDR', ARD (TV documentary film). Accessed online October 2014, available from: www.youtube.com/watch?v=KwtfD04qVZg

Books and Chapters in Books

Adams, C., *Ideologies in Conflict: A Cold War Docu-Story*, Lincoln, iUniverse, Inc., 2001

Albertini, R. v., *Dekolonisation: Die Diskussion über Verwaltung und Zukunft der Kolonien, 1919–1960,* Köln, Opladen, 1966.

Apor, B., 'Sovietisation, Imperial Rule and the Stalinist Leader Cult in Central and Eastern Europe', in R. Healy and E. Dal Lago (eds.), *The Shadow of Colonialism on Europe's Modern Past*, Hampshire, Palgrave Macmillan, 2014.

Barber, J. and J. Barratt, *South Africa's Foreign Policy: The Search for Status and Security 1945–1988*, Cambridge, Cambridge University Press, 1990.

Baron, U., *Kalter Krieg und heisser Frieden: Der Einfluss der SED und ihrer westdeutschen Verbündeten auf die Partei "Die Grünen"*, Münster, LIT, 2003.

Baruch, H., *Year of Fire, Year of Ash. The Soweto Revolt: Roots of a Revolution?*, London, Zed Press, 1979.

Bering, H., *Helmut Kohl*, Washington, D.C., Regnery Publishing, 1999.

Bley, H. and R. Tetzlaff (eds.), *Afrika und Bonn. Versäumnisse und Zwänge deutscher Afrika-Politik*, Hamburg, Rowohlt, 1978.

Bley, H. and H.-G. Schleicher, 'Deutsch-Deutsch-Namibische Beziehungen 1960–1990', in L. Förster, D. Henrichsen and M. Bollig (eds.), *Namibia–Deutschland: Eine geteilte Geschichte. Widerstand–Gewalt–Erinnerung* (Ethnologica New Series 24), Köln, Edition Minerva, 2004.

Blumenau, B., *The United Nations and Terrorism: Germany, Multilateralism & Antiterrorism Efforts in the 1970s*, Basingstoke, Palgrave Macmillan, 2014.

Bock, S., I. Muth and H. Schwiesau (eds.), *DDR-Außenpolitik im Rückspiegel, Diplomaten im Gespräch*, Münster, LIT, 2004.

Bock, S., I. Muth and H. Schwiesau (eds.), *Alternative deutsche Außenpolitik? DDR-Außenpolitik im Rückspiegel (II)*, Berlin, LIT, 2006.

Bortfeldt, H., 'In the Shadow of the Federal Republic, Cultural Relations Between the GDR and the United States', in D. Junker (ed.), *The United States and Germany in the Era of the Cold War, 1945–1990,* Volume 2: 1968–1990, Cambridge, Cambridge University Press, 2004.

Bracia, J. and D. Leidig, *"Kauft keine Früchte aus Südafrika!": Geschichte der Anti-Apartheid-Bewegung*, Frankfurt/M., Brandes & Apsel, 2008.

Brauckhoff, K. and I. Schwaetzer (eds.), *Hans-Dietrich Genschers Außenpolitik,* Wiesbaden, Springer Verlag, 2015.

Brendel, H., *"Freiheit für Nelson Mandela!"'Wie der Kampf gegen die Apartheid nach Deutschland kam*, Hamburg, Diplomica Verlag GmbH, 2014.

Brenke, G., *Die Bundesrepublik Deutschland und der Namibia-Konflikt*, München, R. Oldenbourg Verlag, 1989.

Brown, M. B., *Condi: The Life of a Steel Magnolia*, Nashville, Thomas Nelson Publisher, 2008.

Brüne, S., *Die französische Afrikapolitik, Hegemonialinteressen und Entwicklungsanspruch*, Baden-Baden, Nomos Verlagsgesellschaft, 1993.

Burns, R. (ed.), *German Cultural Studies: An Introduction*, New York, Oxford University Press, 1995.

Byg, B., 'Solidarity and Exile, Blonder Tango and the East German Fantasy of the Third World', in E. Rueschmann (ed.), *Moving Pictures, Migrating Identities*, Jackson, University Press of Mississippi, 2003.

Carter, A. F., 'Did Reagan "Win" the Cold War?', in R. Summy and M. E. Salla (eds.), *Why the Cold War Ended: A Range of Interpretations*, Connecticut, Greenwood Press, 1995

Cervenka, Z., and B. Rogers, *The Nuclear Axis: Secret Collaboration between West Germany and South Africa*, London, Julian Friedmann Ltd, 1978.

Childs, D., *The GDR: Moscow's German Ally*, London, George Allen & Unwin, 1983.

Childs, D., 'The SED faces the challenges of Ostpolitik and Glasnost', in T. A. Baylis, D. Childs, E. L. Collier and M. Rueschemeyer (eds.), *East Germany in Comparative Perspective*, London, Routledge, 1989.

Childs, D., T. A. Baylis and M. Rueschemeyer (eds.), *East Germany in Comparative Perspective*, London, Routledge, 1989.

Clapham, C., 'Peacekeeping and the Peacekept: Developing Mandates for Potential Intervenors', in R. I. Rotberg, (ed.), *Peacekeeping and Peace Enforcement in Africa: Methods of Conflict Prevention*, Washington, D.C., Brookings Institution Press, 2000.

Clemens, C., 'West Germany and New Superpower Détente', in M. Cox (ed.), *Beyond the Cold War: Superpowers at the Crossroads?*, Lanham, University Press of America, Inc., 1990.

Cosgrove, K., 'Erich Honecker', in D. Wilsford (ed.), *Political Leaders of Contemporary Western Europe: A Biographical Dictionary*, Connecticut, Greenwood Press, 1995.

Dagne, H. G., *Das entwicklungspolitische Engagement der DDR in Äthiopien*, Münster, LIT, 2004.

Daum, A. W., 'The Two German States in the International World', in Smith H. W. (ed.), *The Oxford Handbook of Modern German History*, Oxford, Oxford University Press, 2011.

Dobell, L., *Swapo's Struggle for Namibia, 1960–1991: War by Other Means,* Basel, P. Schlettwein Publishing, 2000.

Döring, H.-J., *"Es geht um unsere Existenz": Die Politik der DDR gegenüber der Dritten Welt am Beispiel von Mosambik und Äthiopien*, Berlin, Ch. Links Verlag, 1999.

Döring, H.-J. und U. Rüchel (eds.), *Freundschaftsbande und Beziehungskisten: Die Afrikapolitik der DDR und der BRD gegenüber Mosambik*, Frankfurt/M., Brandes & Apsel Verlag, 2005.

Duignan, P. and L. H. Gann, *The Cold War: End and Aftermath*, Stanford, Hoover Institution Press, 1996.

Eckhard, J. (ed.), *Bundesrepublik Deutschland und Deutsche Demokratische Republik: Die beiden deutschen Staaten im Vergleich*, Berlin, Colloquium Verlag, 1985.

Edward, G., *The Cuban Intervention in Angola: 1965–1991: From Che Guevara to Cuito Cuanavale*, New York, Franc Cass, 2005.

Edwards, O., *The USA and the Cold War*, London, Hodder & Stoughton, 1979.

Eichenberg, R. C., 'Dual Track and Double Trouble: The Two-Level Politics of INF', in P. B. Evans, H. K. Jacobson and R. D. Putnam (eds.), *Double-Edged Diplomacy: International Bargaining and Domestic Policies*, California, University of California Press, 1993

Engel, U., R. Hofmeier, D. Kohnert and A. Mehler (eds.), *Wahlbeobachter in Afrika, Erfahrungen Deutscher Wahlbeobachter, Analysen und Lehren für die Zukunft*, Hamburg, Institut für Afrika-Kunde, 1996.

Engel, U. and H.-G. Schleicher, *Die beiden deutschen Staaten in Afrika, Zwischen Konkurrenzkampf und Koexistenz 1949–1990*, Hamburg, Institut für Afrika-Kunde, 1998.

Engel, U., *Die Afrikapolitik der Bundesrepublik Deutschland 1949–1999: Rollen und Identitäten*, Hamburg, LIT, 2000.

Engel, U. and R. Kappel (eds.), *Germany's Africa Policy Revisited: Interests, Images and Incrementalism*, Münster, LIT, 2002.

Engel, U., 'Germany: Between value-based solidarity and bureaucratic interests', in U. Engel and G. R. Olsen (eds.), *Afrika and the North: Between Globalization and Marginalization*, London, Routledge, 2005.

Eriksen, T. L. (ed.), *Norway and National Liberation in Southern Africa*, Stockholm, Elanders Gotab, 2000.

Etges, A., 'Western Europe', in R. H. Immerman and P. Goedde (eds.), *The Oxford Handbook of the Cold War*, Oxford, Oxford University Press, 2013.

Eyinla, B. M., *The Foreign Policy of West Germany towards Africa*, Ibadan, Ibadan University Press, 1996.

Farnham, B., 'Perceiving the End of Threat: Ronald Reagan and the Gorbachev Revolution', in S. A. Renshon and D. W. Larson (eds.), *Good Judgment in Foreign Policy: Theory and Application*, Maryland, Rowman & Littlefield Publishers, Inc., 2003.

Frängsmyr, T. and I. Abrams (eds.), *Nobel Lectures: Peace, 1971–1980*, Singapore, World Scientific Publishing, 1997.

Fulbrook, M., *Anatomy of a Dictatorship: Inside the GDR, 1949-1989*, Oxford, Oxford University Press, 1995.

Fulbrook, M., 'Jenseits der Totalitarismustheorie? Vorläufige Bemerkungen aus sozialgeschichtlicher Perspektive', in P. Barker (ed.), *The GDR and Its History: Rückblick und Revision*, Amsterdam and Atlanta, Rodobi, 2000.

Garthoff, R. L., *A Journey through the Cold War: A Memoir of Containment and Coexistence*, Washington, D. C., The Brookings Institution, 2001.

Gasteyger, C. W., *Die beiden deutschen Staaten in der Weltpolitik*, München, R. Piper & Co. Verlag, 1976.

Glaeser, A., *Political Epistemics: The Secret Police, the Opposition and the End of East German Socialism*, Chicago, University of Chicago Press, 2011.

Gorodnov, V., *Soweto: Life and Struggles of a South African Township*, Moscow, Progress Publishers, 1988.

Gray, W.G., *Germany's Cold War: The Global Campaign to Isolate East Germany, 1949–1969*, Chapel Hill, NC, University of North Carolina Press, 2003.

Griese, O., *Auswärtige Kulturpolitik und Kalter Krieg, Die Konkurrenz von Bundesrepublik und DDR in Finnland 1949–1973*, Wiesbaden, Harrassowitz Verlag, 2006.

Griffith, W. E., *The Ostpolitik of the Federal Republic of Germany*, Massachusetts, MIT Press, 1978.

Haftendorn, H., *Coming of Age: German Foreign Policy since 1945*, Maryland, Rowman & Littlefield Publishers, 2006.

Hanlon, J., *Beggar your Neighbours: Apartheid Power in Southern Africa*, Indiana, Indiana University Press, 1987.

Hatzky, C., *Kubaner in Angola: Süd-Süd-Kooperation und Bildungstransfer 1976–1991*, München, Oldenbourg Verlag, 2012.

Helbig, H. und L. Helbig, *Mythos Deutsch-Südwest, Namibia und die Deutschen*, Weinheim und Basel, Beltz Verlag, 1985.

Hertle, H.-H., 'Germany in the Last decade of the Cold War, in O. Njolstad, *The Last Decade of the Cold War: From Conflict Escalation to Conflict Transformation*, New York, Routledge, 2004.

Heyden, U. van der, I. Schleicher and H.-G. Schleicher (eds.), *Die DDR und Afrika: Zwischen Klassenkampf und neuem Denken*, Münster, LIT, 1993.

Heyden, U. van der, I. Schleicher and H.-G. Schleicher (eds.), *Engagiert für Afrika: Die DDR und Afrika II*, Münster, LIT, 1994.

Heyden, U. van der, *Zwischen Solidarität und Wirtschaftsinteressen: Die "geheimen" Beziehungen der DDR zum südafrikanischen Apartheidregime*, Münster, LIT, 2005.

Heyden, U. van der and G.-R. Stephan (eds.), *Deutsch-südafrikanische Beziehungen: DDR, Bundesrepublik, vereintes Deutschland*, Potsdam, Rosa-Luxemburg-Stiftung Brandenburg, 2009.

Heyden, U. van der, *GDR International Development Policy Involvement, Doctrine and Strategies between Illusions and Reality 1960–1990. The example (South) Africa*, Berlin, LIT, 2013.

Hobson, E., *The Age of Extremes, 1914–1991*, London, Abacus, 1995.

Hobson, E., *Revolutionaries*, London, Abacus, 1999.

Hocking, B. and M. Smith, *World Politics: An Introduction to International Relations*, New York, Routledge, 2014.

Hofmeier, R., 'Deutsch-afrikanische Beziehungen', in R. Hofmeier (ed.), *Afrika Jahrbuch 1987: Politik, Wirtschaft und Gesellschaft in Afrika südlich der Sahara*, Opladen, Leske Verlag & Budrich GmbH, 1988.

Hofmeier, R., 'Five decades of German-African relations: limited interests, low political profile and substantial aid donor', in Engel U. and R. Kappel (eds.), *Germany's Africa Policy Revisited: Interests, Images and Incrementalism*, Münster, LIT, 2002.

Honecker, E., *Moabiter Notizen*, Berlin, edition ost, 1994.

Islam, N., *Exploration in Development Issues: Selected Articles of Nurul Islam*, New Delhi, Academic Foundation, 2005.

Jabri, V., *Mediating Conflict: Decision-Making and Western Intervention in Namibia*, Manchester and New York, Manchester University Press, 1990.

James III, W. Martin, *A Political History of the Civil War in Angola, 1974–1990*, New Jersey, Transaction Publishers, 1992.

Johnson, P. and D. Martin (eds.), *Frontline Southern Africa: Destructive Engagement*, New York, Four Walls Eight Windows, 1988.

Jordan, G. G. and C. Weedon, *Cultural Politics, Class, Gender, Race and the Postmodern World*, Oxford, Blackwell Publishers, 1995.

Kaela, Laurent C.W., *The Question of Namibia*, London, McMillan Press Ltd, 1996.

Katz, M. N. (ed.), *The USSR and Marxist Revolutions in the Third World*, Canada, Woodrow Wilson International Center for Scholars, 1990.

Kenna, C. (ed.), *Homecoming: The GDR Kids of Namibia*, Windhoek, New Namibia Books, 1999.

Kenna, C. (ed.), *Die "DDR-Kinder" von Namibia: Heimkehrer in ein fremdes Land*, Göttingen, Klaus Hess Verlag, 2010.

Kilian, W., *Die Hallstein-Doktrin. Der diplomatische Krieg zwischen der BRD und der DDR 1955–1973*, Berlin, Duncker & Humblot, 2001.

Krasno, J., 'Namibian Independence: A UN Success Story', in I. Shapiro and J. Lampert (eds.), *Charter of the United Nations*, London, Yale University Press, 2014.

Labrenz-Weiss, H. 'Stasi at Humboldt University: State Security's Organizational Structures and Control Mechanism in the University, in B. Becker-Cantarino, *Berlin in Focus: Cultural Transformations in Germany*, Connecticut, Greenwood Publishing Group, 1996.

Lange, D. *Auf deutsch-deutscher UN-Patrouille. Die polizeiliche Beobachtereinheit der DDR in Namibia, 1989/90*, Schkeuditz, Schkeuditzer Buchverlag, 2011.

Larres, K. 'Britain and the GDR: Political and Economic Relations 1949–1989', in K. Larres and E. Meehan (eds.), *Uneasy Allies, British-German Relations and European Integration since 1945*, Oxford, Oxford Press, 2000.

Lawrence, M. A., 'The Rise and Fall of Nonalignment', in R. J. McMahon (ed.), *The Cold War in the Third World*, Oxford, Oxford University Press, 2013.

Lenin, V. I., *Collected Works*, Vol. 23, London, Lawrence & Wishart, 1964.

Lenin, V. I., *Imperialism, the Highest Stage of Capitalism*, London, Penguin Books, 2011

Leys, C. and S. Brown (eds.), *Histories of Namibia: Living Through the Liberation Struggle*, London, Merlin Press, 2005.

Lindemann, H. and K. Müller, *Auswärtige Kulturpolitik der DDR*, Bonn-Bad Godesberg, Verlag Neue Gesellschaft GmbH, 1974.

Löwis of Menar, H. von, *Namibia im Ost-West-Konflikt*, Köln, Verlag Wissenschaft und Politik, 1983.

Lopes, R. *West Germany and the Portuguese Dictatorship, 1968–1974: Between Cold War and Colonialism*, Basingstoke, Palgrave Macmillan, 2014.

Lorenzini, S. 'East-South Relations in the 1970s and the GDR Involvement in Africa: Between Bloc Loyalty and Self-Interest', in M. Guderzo and B. Bagnato (eds.), *The Globalization of the Cold War: Diplomacy and Local Confrontation, 1975–85*, New York, Routledge, 2010.

Lüthi, L. 'The Non-Aligned: Apart from and still within the Cold War', in N. Miskovic, H. Fischer-Tine and N. Boskovska (eds.), *The Non-Aligned Movement and the Cold War*, New York, Routledge, 2014.

Macgregor, D. A., *The Soviet-East German Military Alliance*, Cambridge, Cambridge University Press, 1989.

McAdams, A. J., *Germany Divided: From the Wall to Reunification*, New Jersey, Princeton University Press, 1993.

Megas, A., *Soviet Foreign Policy Towards East Germany*, Heidelberg, Springer-Verlag, 2015.

Melber, H. and G. Wellmer, 'West German Relations with Namibia', in A. D. Cooper (ed.), *Allies in Apartheid: Western Capitalism in Occupied Namibia*, Houndmills, Basingstoke, Hampshire and London, The Macmillan Press LTD, 1988.

Meyns, P., *Cooperation without Change. The Foreign Policy of the Federal Republic of Germany in Southern Africa*, Bonn, Friedrich Ebert Stiftung, 1987.

Minter, W., 'Destructive Engagement: The United States and South Africa in the Reagan Era', in P. Johnson and D. Martin (eds.), *Frontline Southern Africa: Destructive Engagement*, New York, Four Walls Eight Windows, 1988.

Möller, H., *DDR und Äthiopien, Unterstützung für ein Militärregime (1977–1989)*, Berlin, Verlag Dr. Köster, 2003.

Morris, K. E., *Jimmy Carter, American Moralist*, Georgia, University of Georgia Press, 1969.

Mott, W. H., *The Economic Basis of Peace, Linkages between Economic Growth and International Conflict*, Connecticut and London, Greenwood Press, 1997.

Nation, R. C. and M. V. Kauppi, *The Soviet Impact in Africa*, Toronto, Lexington Books, 1984.

Ndlovu, S. M., 'The Soweto Uprising: Soweto', in *The Road to Democracy in South Africa, Vol 2, 1970–1980*, Pretoria, Unisa Press, 2006.

Ndlovu, S. M., 'Mandela's Presidential Years: An Africanist View', in R. Barnard (ed.), *The Cambridge Companion to Nelson Mandela*, New York, Cambridge University Press, 2014

Niedhart, G., 'The Federal Republik of Germany Between the American and Russian Superpowers: "Old Friend" and "New Partner"', in D. Junker (ed.), *The United States and Germany in the Era of the Cold War, 1945–1990: A Handbook*, Cambridge, Cambridge University Press, 2004.

Niven, B., 'The Sideways Gaze: The Cold War and Memory of the Nazi Past, 1949–1979', in T. Hochscherf, C. Laucht and A. Plowman (eds.), *Divided but not Disconnected: German Experiences of the Cold War*, New York, Berghahn Books, 2010.

Nwankwo, A.A., *Perestroika and Glasnost: Their Implication for Africa*, Enugu, Fourth Dimension Publishing Company, 1990.

Nye, Jr., J. S., *Bound to Lead: The Changing Nature of American Power*, New York, Basic Books, 1990.

Oldhaver, M., *Die deutschsprachige Bevölkerungsgruppe in Namibia: Ihre Bedeutung als Faktor in den deutsch-namibischen Beziehungen*, Hamburg, Verlag Dr. Kovak, 1997.

Olusoga, D. and C. W. Erichsen, *The Kaiser's Holocaust, Germany's Forgotten Genocide and the Colonial Roots of Nazism*, London, Faber and Faber Ltd, 2010.

Peires, J., *Ruling by Race: Nazi Germany and Apartheid South Africa*, eBook, 2008.

Petkovic, R., *Non-Alignment: An Independent Factor in the Democratization of International Relations*, Belgrade, STP, 1979.

Pipes, R., *Communism: A Brief History*, London, Weidenfeld & Nicolson, 2001.

Pittman, A., *From Ostpolitik to Reunification: West German-Soviet Political Relations since 1974*, Cambridge, Cambridge University Press, 1992.

Port, A. I., 'The Banalities of East German Historiography', in M. Fulbrook and A. I. Port (eds.), *Becoming East Germany: Socialist Structures and Sensibilities after Hitler*, New York, Berghahn Books, 2013.

Quirk, R. E., *Fidel Castro*, New York, W. W. Norton & Company, Inc., 1993

Rais, R. B., *The Indian Ocean and the Superpowers: Economic, Political and Strategic Perspectives*, New Jersey, Barnes & Nobel, 1987

Rhode, R., *Die Südafrikapolitik der Bundesrepublik Deutschland 1968–1972*, München, Chr. Kaiser Verlag, 1975.

Ross, C. and J. Grix, 'Approaches to the German Democratic Republic', in Grix, J. (ed.), *Approaches to the Study of Contemporary Germany: Research Mythologies in German Studies*, Birmingham, University of Birmingham Press, 2002.

Rotberg, R. I., *Ending Autocracy, Enabling Democracy: the Tribulations of Southern Africa, 1960–2000*, Washington, D.C., Brookings Institution Press, 2002.

Rubinstein, A. Z., *Moscow's Third World Strategy*, Princeton, Princeton University Press, 1988.

Rüchel, U., *"Wir hatten noch nie einen Schwarzen gesehen". Das Zusammenleben von Deutschen und Namibiern rund um das SWAPO-Kinderheim Bellin, 1979–1990*, Schwerin, Landesbeauftragter für Mecklenburg-Vorpommern fuer die Unterlagen des Staatssicherheitsdienstes der ehemaligen DDR, 2001.

Rüdiger, K. H., *Die Namibia-Deutschen: Geschichte einer Nationalität im Werden*, Stuttgart, Franz Steiner Verlag, 1993.

Saalfeld, T., 'Germany: Multiple Veto Points, Informal Coordination and Problems of Hidden Action', in K. Strom, W. C. Müller and T. Bergman (eds.), *Delegation and Accountability in Parliamentary Democracies*, Oxford, Oxford University Press, 2003.

Sarotte, M. E., *Dealing with the Devil: East Germany, Détente, and Ostpolitik, 1969–1973*, Chapel Hill, University of North Carolina Press, 2001.

Saunders, C., 'The Angola/Namibia Crisis of 1988 and its Resolution', in S. Onslow (ed.), *Cold War in Southern Africa: White Power, Black Liberation*, London, Routledge, 2009.

Saunders, C. and S. Onslow, 'The Cold War and southern Africa, 1976–1990', in M. P. Leffler and O. A. Westad (eds.), *The Cambridge History of the Cold War: Volume 3, Endings*, Cambridge, Cambridge University Press, 2010.

Saunders, C., 'Namibian diplomacy before Independence', A. Boesl, A. Du Pisani and D. U. Zaire (eds.), *Namibia's Foreign Relations*, Windhoek, Macmillan Education Namibia, 2014.

Schleicher, H.-G., 'Africa in der Außenpolitik der DDR', in U. van der Heyden, I. Schleicher and H.-G. Schleicher (eds.), *Die DDR und Afrika: Zwischen Klassenkampf und neuem Denken*, Münster, LIT, 1993.

Schleicher, H.-G. 'Waffen für den Süden Afrikas. Die DDR und der bewaffnete Befreiungskampf', in U. van der Heyden, I. Schleicher and H.-G. Schleicher (eds.), *Engagiert für Afrika: Die DDR und Afrika II*, Münster, LIT, 1994.

Schleicher, H.-G. and I. Schleicher, *Die DDR im südlichen Afrika: Solidarität und Kalter Krieg*, Hamburg, Institut für Afrika-Kunde, 1997.

Schleicher, H.-G., 'Interessenlage der Afrikapolitik der DDR', S. Bock, I. Muth and H. Schwiesau (eds.), *DDR-Außenpolitik im Rückspiegel, Diplomaten im Gespräch*, Münster, LIT, 2004.

Schleicher, H.-G., 'GDR Solidarity: The German Democratic Republic and the South African Liberation Struggle', in *The Road to Democracy in South Africa: International Solidarity*, Volume 3, Pretoria, Education Trust, 2008.

Schleicher, I., *DDR-Solidarität im südlichen Afrika. Auseinandersetzung mit einem ambivalenten Erbe*, Berlin, Solidaritätsdienst-international e.V., 1999.

Schmidt, E., 'Africa', in R. H. Immerman and P. Goedde (eds.), *The Oxford Handbook of the Cold War*, Oxford, Oxford University Press, 2013.

Scholz, M. F., 'Active Measures and Disinformation as Part of East Germany's Propaganda War, 1953-1972', in K. Macrakis, T.W. Friis and H. Mueller-Enbergs (eds.), *East German Foreign Intelligence: Myth, Reality and Controversy*, New York, Routledge, 2010.

Schulz, B. H., 'The German Democratic Republic and Sub-Saharan Africa: The Limits of East-South Economic Relations', in B. H. Schulz and W. W. Hansen (eds.), *The Soviet Bloc and the Third World*, London, Westview Press, 1989.

Schulz, B. H., 'The politics of East-South relations: The GDR and Southern Africa', in Baylis, T. A., Childs, D., Collier, E. L. and Rueschemeyer, M. (ed.), *East Germany in Comparative Perspective*, London, Routledge, 1989.

Schulz, B., *Development Policy in the Cold War Era: The two Germanies and Sub-Saharan Africa, 1960–1985*, Münster, LIT, 1995.

Sellström, T., *Sweden and National Liberation in Southern Africa: Solidarity and Assistance, 1970–1994*, Volume II, Stockholm, Uppsala, Nordiska Afrikainstitutet, 2002.

Silvester, J. (ed.), *Re-Viewing Resistance in Namibian History*, Windhoek, University of Namibia Press, 2015.

Slaveski, F., *The Soviet Occupation of Germany: Hunger, Mass Violence and the Struggle for Peace, 1945–1947*, Cambridge, Cambridge University Press, 2013

Smith, D., *Walls and Mirrors: Western Representation of Really Existing German Socialism, in the German Democratic Republic*, Lanham, New York and London, University Press of America, 1988.

Sodaro, M. J., *Moscow, Germany, and the West from Khrushchev to Gorbachev*, London, Cornell University Press, 1990.

Southall, R., *Liberation Movements in Power, Part and State in southern Africa*, Suffolk, James Currey, 2013.

Spanger, H.-J. and L. Brock, *Die beiden deutschen Staaten in der Dritten Welt. Die Entwicklungspolitik der DDR – eine Herausforderung für die Bundesrepublik Deutschland?*, Opladen, Westdeutscher Verlag, 1987.

Steel, J., *Soviet Power, The Kremlin's Foreign Policy – Brezhnev to Cherenkov*, New York, Simon & Schuster, Inc., 1983.

Stibbe, M., 'Fighting the First World War in the Cold War, East and West German Historiography on the Origins of the First World War, 1949–1959', in T. Hochscherf, C. Laucht and A. Plowman (eds.), *Divided but not Disconnected: German Experiences of the Cold War*, New York, Berghahn Books, 2010.

Stiers, W., *Perzeptionen der Entwicklung im südlichen Afrika in der Bundesrepublik Deutschland: 1960–1979*, Frankfurt/M., Peter Lang GmbH, 1983.

Storkmann, K., *Geheime Solidarität: Militärbeziehungen und Militärhilfen der DDR in die "Dritte Welt"*, Berlin, Christoph Links Verlag GmbH, 2012.

Swain, G. G. and N. Swain, *Eastern Europe since 1945*, New York, Palgrave Macmillan, 2009

Tetsuji, S., *Ein Irrweg zur deutschen Einheit? Egon Bahrs Konzeptionen, die Ostpolitik und die KSZE 1963–1975*, Frankfurt/M., Peter Lang GmbH, 2010.

Tetzlaff, R., 'Die entwicklungspolitische Bilanz der Ära Kohl', in Wewer, G. (ed.), *Bilanz der Ära Kohl – Christlich-liberale Politik in Deutschland 1982–1998*, Opladen, Leske & Budrich, 1998.

Thomson, A., *U.S. Foreign Policy towards Apartheid South Africa, 1948–1994*, London, Palgrave Macmillan, 2008.

Tsokodayi, C. J., *Namibia's Independence Struggle: The Role of the United Nations*, Indiana, Xlibris Corporation, 2011.

Turner, M., 'Foreign Policy and the Reagan Administration', in J. D. Lees and M. Turner (eds.),*Reagan's First Four Years: A new Beginning?*, Manchester, Manchester University Press, 1988.

Udogu, E. I., *Liberating Namibia: The Long Diplomatic Struggle Between the United Nations and South Africa*, Jefferson, NC, MacFarland, 2012.

Vanneman, P., *Soviet Strategy in Southern Africa, Gorbachev's Pragmatic Approach*, Stanford, Hoover Institution Press, 1990.

Vergau, H. J., 'Die Verhandlungen um die Freiheit Namibias (1977–1990) als Vorstufe zur friedlichen Überwindung der Apartheid in Südafrika', in K. Brauckhoff and I. Schwaetzer (eds.), Hans Dietrich Genscher Außenpolitik, Wiesbaden, Springer Verlag, 2015, 119–122.

Vinnai, V., *Demokratieförderung in Afrika: Die Zusammenarbeit der Friedrich Ebert Stiftung mit politischen Parteien und Befreiungsbewegungen in Afrika*, Berlin, LIT, 2007.

Voss, J. (ed.), *Development Policy in Africa*, Bonn-Bad Godesberg, Verlag Neue Gesellschaft GmbH, 1973.

Voss, M. (ed.), *Wir haben Spuren hinterlassen! Die DDR in Mosambik: Erlebnisse, Erfahrungen und Erkenntnisse aus drei Jahrzehnten*, Berlin, LIT Verlag, 2005.

Weigert, S. L., *Angola: A Modern Military History*, New York, Palgrave Macmillan, 2011.

Wenzel, C., *Die Südafrikapolitik der USA in der Ära Reagan, Konstruktives oder destruktives Engagement?*, Hamburg, Institut für Afrika-Kunde, 1990.

Wenzel, C., *Südafrika-Politik der Bundesrepublik Deutschland 1982–1992: Politik gegen Apartheid?*, Wiesbaden, Deutscher Universitäts-Verlag GmbH, 1994.

Whitaker, J. S. (ed.), *Afrika and the United States*, New York, New York University Press, 1978.

Wick, R., *Die Mauer muss weg – Die DDR soll bleiben: Die Deutschlandpolitik der Grünen von 1979 bis1990*, Stuttgart, Kohlhammer GmbH, 2012.

Winrow, G. M., *The Foreign Policy of the GDR in Africa*, Cambridge, Cambridge University Press, 1990.

Witkowski, G., 'Between Fighters and Beggars, Socialist Philanthropy and the Imagery of Solidarity in East Germany', in Q. Slobodian (ed.), *Comrades of Color: East Germany in the Cold War*, New York, Berghahn Books, 2015

Yahuda, M. B., 'The Significance of Tripolarity in China's Policy Toward the United States Since 1972', in R. S. Ross (ed.), *China, the United States, and the Soviet Union: Tripolarity and Policy Making in the Cold War*, New York, M. E. Sharpe, Inc., 1993

Zacarias, A., *Security and the State in Southern Africa*, London, Tauris Academic Studies, 1999.

Zanchetta, B., *The Transformation of International American Power in the 1970s*, Cambridge, Cambridge University Press, 2014.

Zimmer, M., 'The German Political Parties and the USA', in D. Junker (ed.), *The United States and Germany in the Era of the Cold War, 1945–1990, Volume 2: 1968–1990*, Cambridge, Cambridge University Press, 2004.

Online Articles

Bley, H. and H.-G. Schleicher, 'Deutsch-Deutsch-Namibische Beziehungen 1960–1990', inL. Förster, D. Henrichsen and B. Bollig (eds.), *Namibia-Deutschland. Eine geteilte Geschichte. Widerstand-Gewalt-Erinnerung*, Köln, Ethnologica, 2004. Accessed online April 2015, available from: www.vip-ev.de/text85.htm

Danielson, E. S., 'Privacy Rights and the Rights of Political Victims: Implications of the German Experience', *The American Archivist*, Vol. 67, 2004. Accessed online November 2015, available from: www.americanarchivist.org/doi/abs/10.17723/aarc.67.2.1w06730777226771

Dedering, T., 'Ostpolitik and the Relations between West Germany and South Africa'. academia.edu. Accessed online February 2015, available from: www.academia.edu/3843165/Ostpolitik_and_the_Relations_between_West_Germany_and_South_Africa

Forsberg, R., 'Toward a Nonaggressive World', *Bulletin of the Atomic Scientists*, Vol. 44, No.7, Chicago, Foundation for Nuclear Science, September 1988. Accessed online January 2015, available from: www.tandfonline.com/doi/abs/10.1080/00963402.1988.11456202?journalCode=rbul20

Genscher, H.-D., 'Germany's Role in Namibia's Independence', speech at the Humboldt University of Berlin, 13.04.2010. Accessed online December 2015, available from: www.kas.de/upload/Publikationen/2014/namibias_foreign_relations/Namibias_Foreign_Relations_genscher.pdf

Heitman, H.-R. and W. A. Dorning, 'The Joint Monitoring Commission', *Scientia Militaria, South African Journal of Military Studies*, Vol. 18, No. 1, 1988. Accessed online November 2014, available from: www.scientiamilitaria.journals.ac.za/pub/article/view/410

Jabulani, J. J., 'The Bonn-Pretoria Alliance', South African History Online (SAHO). Accessed December 2014, available from: www.sahistory.org.za/sites/default/files/DC/Acn3167.8/Acn3167.8.pdf

Lange, D., 'Deutsch-deutscher Dienst in Namibia', *Deutsche Gesellschaft für die Vereinten Nationen* (DGVN), 2013. Accessed online September 2014, available from: www.dgvn.de/fileadmin/publications/PDFs/Zeitschrift_VN/VN_2013/Heft_6_2013/06_Lange_VN_6-13_29–11–2013.pdf

Schäfer, B., H. Hoff and U. Mählert (eds.),'The GDR in German Archives, A Guide to Primary Sources and Research Institutions on the History of the Soviet Zone of Occupation and the German Democratic Republic, 1945-19190', German Historical Institute (Washington, DC), Reference Guide No. 14, available from: http://www.bundesstiftung-aufarbeitung.de/uploads/pdf/ghiguide.pdf (accessed November 2015).

Schuchardt, E. (ed.), 'Brückenbau – 15 Jahre Begegnungsschulen im Südlichen Afrika. Erfolgsmodell deutscher Auswärtiger Kulturpolitik', 2005. Accessed February 2015, available from: www.d-nb.info/977821978/34

Stevens, S., '"From the Viewpoint of a Southern Governor": The Carter Administration and Apartheid, 1977–1981'. *Diplomatic History* 36(5), November 2012. Accessed online February 2015, available from: www.researchgate.net/publication/259550725_From_the_Viewpoint_of_a_Southern_Governor_The_Carter_Administration_and_Apartheid_1977-81

Vergau, H.-J., 'Die Rolle Deutschlands bei der Lösung der Namibia-Frage im Rahmen der Vereinten Nationen', speech at the Potsdamer UNO-Konferenz, 28.06.2003. Accessed online April 2016, available from: www. publishup.uni-potsdam.de/opus4-ubp/frontdoor/index/index/year/2012/docId/5882

'The Bonn-Pretoria Alliance', Afro-Asian Solidarity Committee of the GDR. Accessed December 2014, available from: www.sahistory.org.za/sites/default/files/DC/Acn3167.8/Acn3167.8.pdf

'40 Years of German membership in the United Nations', *Deutsche Gesellschaft für die Vereinten Nationen* (DGVN), 2011. Accessed online November 2015, available from: www.dgvn.de/germany-in-the-united-nations/40-years-of-german-membership-in-the-united-nations/

Studies by Institutions

'Africa Volume II', *The International Institute for Strategic Studies (IISS)* Adelphi Papers, London/New York, Routledge, 2006.

Campbell, K. M., 'Southern Africa in Soviet Foreign Policy', *The International Institute for Strategic Studies* (IISS), Adelphi Papers, 227, Winter 1987/8

'Regional Implications of the Negotiation on Angola and Namibia', Bulletin of the Africa Institute of South Africa (AISA), Volume 28, No. 10, 1988,

'South Africa: Time Running Out', The Report of the Study Commission on U.S Policy toward Southern Africa, Los Angeles, University of California Press, Ltd, 1981.

'Symposium: The Conflict in South Africa, International Strategies and Internal Change', Friedrich Ebert Foundation, Bonn, 25 and 26 May, 1981.

Dissertations

Hagen, K. M., 'Internationalism in Cold War Germany', PhD Thesis, University of Washington, 2008.

Heyden, U. van der, 'GDR Development Policy with Special Reference to Africa, c. 1960–1990', PhD Thesis, Rhodes University, 2012.

N'Tani, S. F., 'The Image of African National Liberation Movements in the West German and Soviet Press', Focussing on the South West African People's Organization (SWAPO of Namibia) and the African National Congress (ANC of South Africa), PhD Thesis, Rheinische Friedrich-Wilhelms-Universitaet Bonn, 1987.

Weiss, T., 'Shaping the Discourse on Africa. The Concept of "Solidarity" in East German Relations with SWAPO', Master's Thesis, University of Oxford, 2008.

Williams, C. A., 'Exile History: An Ethnography of the SWAPO Camps and the Namibian Nations', PhD Thesis, University of Michigan, 2009.

Wisotzki, S., 'Die Unterstützung der SWAPO in Namibia durch die DDR in den Jahren 1975–1989', Magisterarbeit, Humboldt-Universität zu Berlin, 2002.

Papers, journals and booklets

Apel, R., 'Strauss: Gorbachev's Envoy in Africa', *Executive Intelligence Review (EIR) News Service*, Volume 15, Number 7, 12.02.1988.

Bevan, R. A., 'Petra Kelly: The Other Green', *New Political Science*, Vol. 23, No. 2, 2001.

Forsberg, R., 'Toward a Nonaggressive World', *Bulletin of the Atomic Scientists*, Vol. 44, No.7, Chicago, Foundation for Nuclear Science, September 1988.

Holdren, J. P., 'North-South Issues and East-West Confrontation', *Bulletin of the Atomic Scientists* Vol. 41, No 7, Chicago, Foundation for Nuclear Science, August 1985.

'Im Brennpunkt: Namibia und die Bundesrepublik Deutschland', *ISSA wissenschaftliche Reihe 21*, Köln, MVR, 1987.

Kühne, W. and B. von Plate, 'The two Germanys in Africa', in *Africa Report*, July/August, Vol. 25, No. 4, New York, 1980.

Löwis of Menar, H. von, 'Die Ausbildung von SWAPO-Kadern in der Deutschen Demokratischen Republik', *Forschungsinstitut für Politische Wissenschaft und Europäische Fragen der Universität zu Köln*, Oktober, 1983.

Löwis of Menar, H. von, *'Bonn und Namibia, Die Positionen der Bundestagsparteien in der Namibia-Frage', Deutsche Afrika Stiftung,* 1981.

Melber, H., 'Attempts within the Federal Republic of Germany for a Postponement of Genuine Namibian Independence', *Information Centre of Southern Africa* (ISSA), Bonn, 1985.

Melber, H., 'Bundesdeutsche Entwicklungspolitik als Intervention: Hilfsmaßnahmen für ein neokoloniales Namibia', *Peripherie: Zeitschrift für Politik und Ökonomie in der Dritten Welt*, Nr. 25/26, 1987.

Melber, H., 'Federal Republic of Germany and Namibia, West German support to continued Occupation – with special reference to the Ministry for Economic Cooperation', paper submitted on the behalf of the Anti-Apartheid-Movement in the Federal Republic of Germany on occasion of EC-summit, December 4th and 5th, *Anti-Apartheid-Movement* (AAM), 1987.

Ropp, K. Freiherr von der, Nord-Süd-Infos, NEIA. e.V – Nachhaltige Entwicklung in Afrika, in *Afrika Süd, Zeitschrift zum südlichen Afrika*, Mai/Juni 2007.

Schleicher, H.-G. and U. Engel, 'DDR-Geheimdienst und Afrika-Politik', *Außenpolitik, Zeitschrift fuer Internationale Fragen,* Jg. 47, 4. Quartal, Hamburg, Interpress Verlag GmbH, 1996

Weis, T., 'The Politics Machine: On the Concept of "Solidarity" in East German Support for SWAPO', *Journal of Southern African Studies*, Vol. 37, No 2, June 2011.

Wellmer, G., 'Background Paper on Relations between Federal Republic of Germany and Namibia', presented at the International Seminar on the Role of Transnational Corporations in Namibia, *Anti-Apartheid Movement* (AAM), Federal Republic of Germany, 1982.

Index

A

Adenauer, Konrad 6, 11, 26, 30, 56, 58, 151, 185, 204, 208, 213f.
Afghanistan 19, 70f., 74, 91, 93, 95, 118
Ahtisaari, Martti 238
Axen, Herman 78

B

Bahr, Egon 26f., 39f., 47, 85, 131f., 164
Bessinger, Nico 186, 223
Botha, Peter W. 'PW' 101, 124, 172, 193–196, 227
Botha, Roelof Frederik 'Pik' 170, 181, 194, 224, 226, 229, 235, 239
Brandt, Willy 13, 26f., 30–35, 39, 41–47, 59, 72f., 84f., 94, 97, 102, 162, 166, 186f., 206, 214, 246, 250
Brenke, Gabriele 3, 39, 41, 49, 53, 56f., 81, 102, 108, 130, 133, 138, 141–143, 150, 154f., 182, 185f., 191, 194, 198f., 201, 232, 234
Bundesnachrichtendienst (BND) 148

C

Cambodia 58, 91, 93
Canada 4, 37, 105, 108, 110, 161, 169, 222, 235
Cape Route 95f., 120
Carrington, Lord 171, 174, 176, 180
Carter, Jimmy 85, 91, 93, 110
Central Committee (ZK) 104, 159
Cheysson, Claude 164, 176, 178, 184, 198–200
Communist Party of Germany (KPD) 24f.
Corterier, Peter 71, 94
Crocker, Chester 180, 187, 200f., 203, 205, 211, 223, 233f.
Cuba 74, 83, 85, 88, 90, 99, 118–120, 156, 169, 178, 180, 187–189, 192, 194–196, 198–201, 205, 223, 227, 233f., 247f.
Cuito Cuanavale 227, 233, 249

D

Democratic Turnhalle Alliance (DTA) 53, 56, 60, 101, 112f., 133, 141, 166f., 169, 173f., 177f., 181–183, 185, 187–191, 194, 201f., 204, 208–212, 217, 245

E

Eggebrecht, Heinrich 25
Ehmke, Horst 47, 71
Engel, Ulf 1, 3, 27, 40, 49, 59, 68, 77, 130, 145, 157, 164, 177, 210, 213
European Community (EG) 115, 215, 222

F

Federal Border Police (BGS) 238–240, 244
Federal Defence Forces 244
Federal Ministry for Economic Cooperation and Development (BMZ) 59, 111f., 185, 205, 207–210, 212–221, 237
Fischer, Oscar 14, 78

Florin, Peter 24, 78, 109, 135, 167f.
France 1, 4, 36, 96, 103, 108, 150–152, 161, 169, 198–200, 205, 222f., 235
Free German Trade Unions Federation (FDGB) 23
Friedrich Ebert Foundation (FES) 39, 42, 45, 112, 211f., 216, 218
Friedrich Naumann Foundation (FNS) 6, 212–214

G

GDR Kids 79f., 250
Gorbachev, Mikhail 28, 188, 192, 206, 226–230, 234, 242f., 249
Great Britain 1, 96, 103, 108, 161, 169, 222, 235

H

Hallstein Doctrine 11, 13, 26, 28, 58, 67, 94, 126, 147
Hanns Seidel Foundation (HSS) 56, 112, 202, 214, 217
Heyden, Ulrich van der 1, 3, 5, 12, 14, 23, 28, 67, 70, 74, 108, 120f., 157
Honecker, Erich 14f., 17, 21, 26, 68, 70, 75, 78, 104, 118, 123, 129, 156, 161, 167, 175, 230, 243
Huyn, Hans Graf 57, 101, 191, 222

I

Information Centre southern Africa (ISSA) 7, 60, 64, 134, 139, 147, 210, 213–215, 217–219, 225, 236, 237, 240
Institute for International Politics and Economy (IPE) 192, 196f.
Institute for International Relations (IIB) 72f., 75–77, 241
Interest Group for German-speaking Southwest Africans (IG) 7, 133

J

Joint Military Monitoring Commission (JMMC) 234
Joint Monitoring Commission (JMC) 198f.

K

Kalangula, Peter 177f., 182, 189, 208
Katutura 66
Kaunda, Kenneth 44, 71, 172, 195, 220
Kelly, Petra 48, 62–66, 134, 209, 213, 215, 219, 222, 240
Kissinger, Henry 50, 153
Klein, Hans 57, 89, 160, 182, 185, 202, 204f., 209, 217–220
Köhler, Volkmar 86
Konrad Adenauer Foundation (KAS) 6, 56, 140, 185, 204, 208, 214, 241
Kulturabkommen 143–147, 149, 162

L

Lengl, Siegfried 217
Lenin, Vladimir 21f.
Lubowski, Anton 66, 138

M

Mandela, Nelson 70, 147, 194, 228
Mandela, Winnie 222, 228
Marxism-Leninism 11, 29, 46, 76f., 80f., 107
Melber, Henning 48, 57, 171, 173, 186, 205, 207–210, 213, 215, 217–219

Ministry for Foreign Affairs (MfAA) 5, 23, 35, 42, 72f., 77, 80, 98, 102, 123–125, 147f., 172, 175, 179–181, 185, 188, 196, 201, 205, 232, 234, 238, 241, 243
Ministry of State Security General Counter Intelligence (HA II) 41, 67, 97, 109, 122f., 156f., 159, 161f.
Ministry of State Security Headquarter of Reconnaissance (HV A) 95–98, 156
Ministry of State Security (MfS) 5, 26, 41–43, 67–69, 72, 76f., 95–97, 99, 108f., 119–124, 126, 128, 141, 154, 156–162, 167–169, 171f., 185, 218, 221–223, 230, 237, 239, 241
Mozambique 57, 63, 70, 77, 88, 91, 95, 105, 118,f., 127, 153f., 184, 201, 230f.
Mudge, Dirk 60, 177, 182f., 190, 194, 212, 217
Mugabe, Robert 52, 174, 242
Muller, Hilgard 50f., 144, 151–155
Multi-Party Conference (MPC) 189–191, 201, 214, 219

N

Namibian Germans 10, 33, 35, 43, 52, 59, 63, 105, 130–139, 141, 191, 204, 244
National Party (NP) 24, 150, 189
National People's Army (NVA) 26, 57
National Union for the Total Independence of Angola (UNITA) 94, 200f., 224
Neto, Angostinho 46
Non-Aligned Movement (NAM) 32
North Atlantic Treaty Organization (NATO 12, 95, 138, 158, 240
North Atlantic Treaty Organization (NATO) 74
Nyerere. Julius 168, 189, 203

O

Organisation of African Unity (OAU) 51, 102, 169, 201
Ostpolitik 13, 24, 26–29, 31f., 39, 46, 58f., 72, 76, 82, 84f., 94, 98, 102, 115, 121, 126, 150, 158, 176, 202, 246
Otto-Benecke Foundation (OBS) 211, 219

P

People's Armed Forces for the Liberation of Angola (FAPLA) 198, 200f.
Politburo of the Central Committee of the SED 68, 74f., 78
Portuguese 85, 91, 108, 145

R

Raymond, Jean-Bernard 222
Rhodesia 12, 29, 37, 85, 95, 152, 174
Riruako, Kuaima 177, 182f.
Roth, Wilhelm 45
Roth, Wolfgang 90, 92, 178, 186
Rumpf, Wolfgang 52f., 186, 202, 205, 216, 219

S

Schleicher, Hans-Georg 1f., 14, 16f., 24f., 40, 67–72, 74f., 77–80, 108, 129f., 157, 167, 187, 192, 231f., 242, 244f.
Schleicher, Ilona 1, 25
Schmidt, Helmut 39, 42, 46f., 49–51, 57, 64, 82–84, 87, 99, 118, 128, 130f., 153, 166, 172, 177, 179, 194f., 197, 208, 212
Schultz, George P. 224
Seibt, Kurt 14f., 20f., 79

Shevardnadze, Eduard 227
Shipanga, Andreas 39, 44, 97, 181
Socialist International (SI) 41f., 44f.
Solidarity Committee 12, 20f., 23–25, 67, 79, 103, 142, 245
South African Defence Force (SADF) 136, 198
South West Africa National Union (SWANU) 189
South-West African Police (SWAPOL) 238
South West Africa People's Organisation Democrats (SWAPO-D) 181, 189
Soweto 50, 153, 162
Stercken, Hans 88, 91, 96, 101, 161, 184

T

Tanzania 1, 80, 168, 203
Thatcher, Margret 176, 193
Todenhöfer, Jürgen 87, 92, 111
Transitional Government of National Unity (TGNU) 201–204, 209f.
Turnhalle Conference 154f., 166, 190
Tutu, Desmond 145f., 222

U

United Nations Transition Assistance Group (UNTAG) 173, 238–241, 243f.
United Nations (UN) 4, 15, 24, 27, 37f., 40, 51, 75, 98, 103, 108, 114, 121, 154, 159, 169, 199, 209, 212f., 234, 238, 240f., 243f.
UN Peacekeeping Operations (PKO) 241
UN Security Council 37, 51, 236

V

Vergau, Hans-Joachim 4, 37, 164, 166, 168–174, 176, 179, 203, 205, 209, 211, 216f., 221, 226, 234, 236
Verheugen, Günther 3, 101, 133, 186, 229
Vesper, Michael 63f., 66, 214–216, 219
Vohrer, Manfred 53, 84f., 164, 1876

W

Warnke, Juergen 207, 236f.
Warsaw Pact 78, 88, 241
Wechmar, Baron Rudiger von 106f., 111
Western Contact Group (WCG) 4, 37, 44, 47, 49, 117, 143f., 164–168, 170–173, 176, 180, 185, 189, 195, 198–201, 203, 205f., 210–212, 221–223, 234–236
Wischnewski, Hans-Juergen 40–43, 45–47, 117, 142, 160, 166

Z

Zambia 40, 44, 65, 71, 102, 119, 161, 223
Zimbabwe 12, 52f., 60, 70, 80, 95, 98, 141, 153f., 160, 168f., 174, 231f.
Zimbabwe African People's Union (ZAPU) 70

www.ingramcontent.com/pod-product-compliance
Lightning Source LLC
Chambersburg PA
CBHW060418300426
44111CB00018B/2899